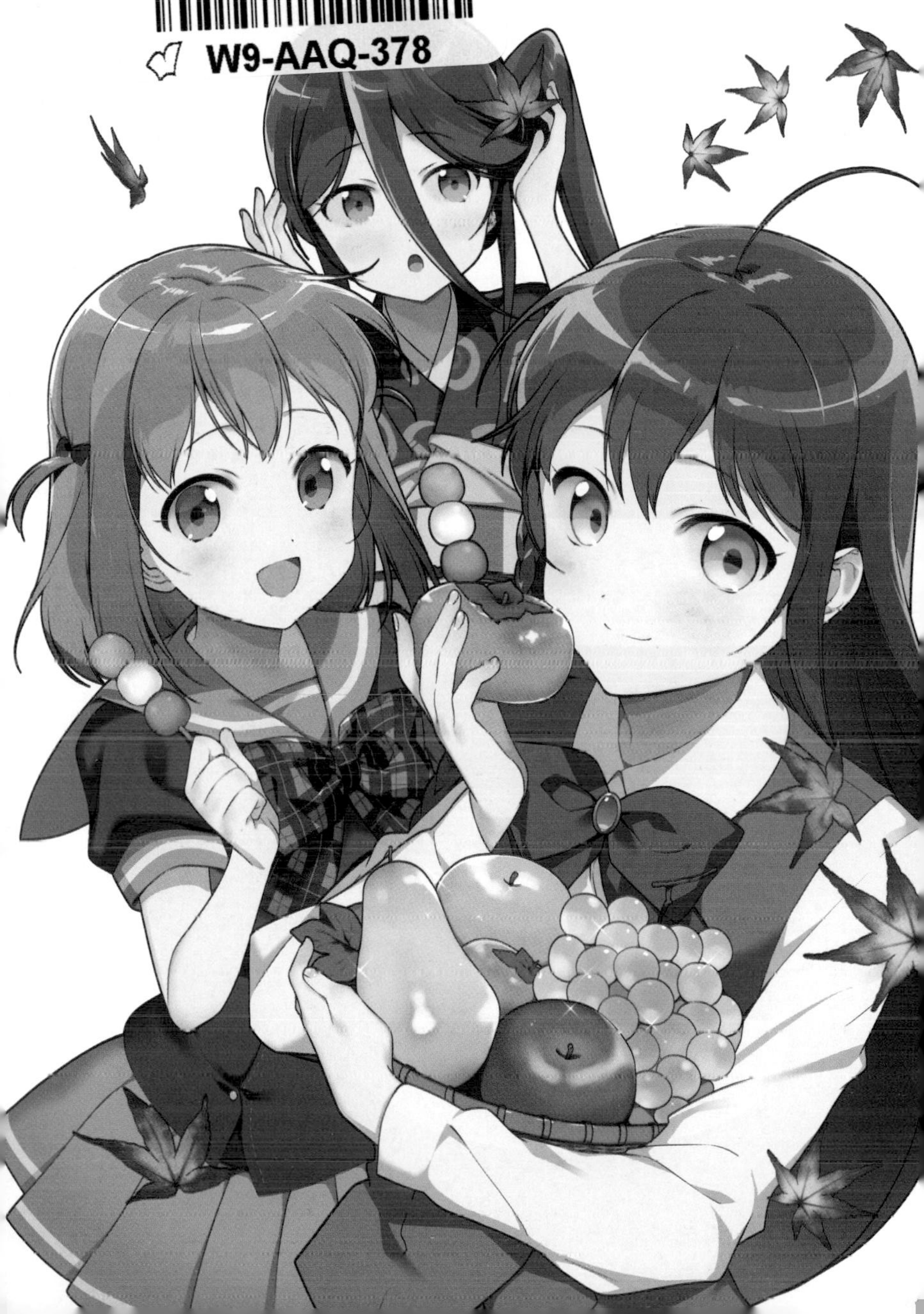

THE DEVIL IS A PART-TIMER! ⑬

Chapter 60: The Devil Grabs a Handful · p3
Chapter 61: The Hero Enters a Car Through the Roof · · · · · · · · · p35
Chapter 62: The Devil Gets Invited Back Next Summer · · · · · · · · p68
Chapter 63: The Devil Brings a Guest to the Castle · · · · · · · · · · · p95
Chapter 64: The Devil Wishes His Rescued Friend Good Health · p129
Chapter X: The Devil, Hero, and High Schooler · · · · · · · · · · · · · · · · p163
            Ring In the New Year

Afterword · p192

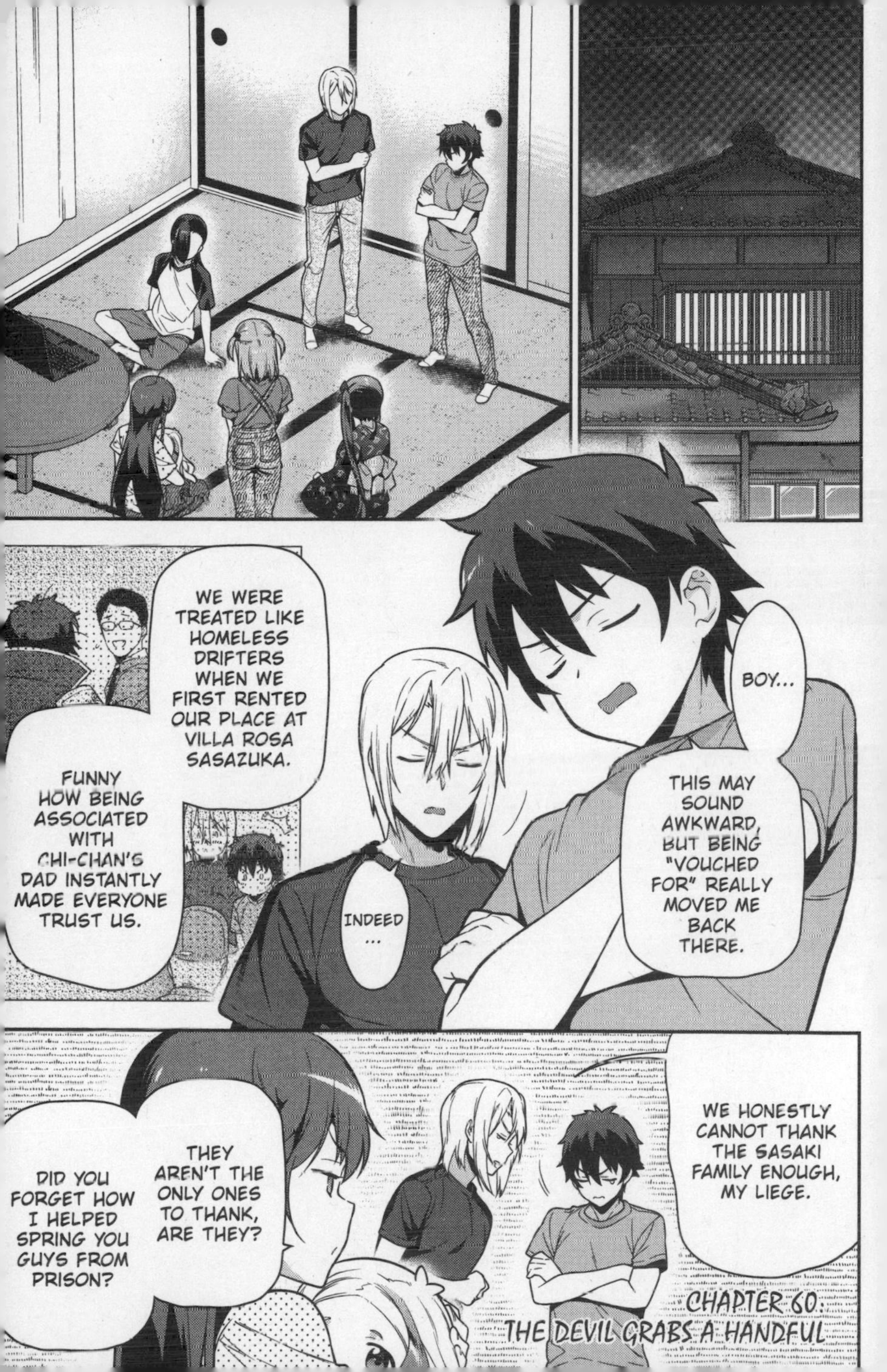
BOY...
THIS MAY SOUND AWKWARD, BUT BEING "VOUCHED FOR" REALLY MOVED ME BACK THERE.
INDEED...
WE WERE TREATED LIKE HOMELESS DRIFTERS WHEN WE FIRST RENTED OUR PLACE AT VILLA ROSA SASAZUKA.
FUNNY HOW BEING ASSOCIATED WITH CHI-CHAN'S DAD INSTANTLY MADE EVERYONE TRUST US.
WE HONESTLY CANNOT THANK THE SASAKI FAMILY ENOUGH, MY LIEGE.
THEY AREN'T THE ONLY ONES TO THANK, ARE THEY?
DID YOU FORGET HOW I HELPED SPRING YOU GUYS FROM PRISON?
CHAPTER 60: THE DEVIL GRABS A HANDFUL

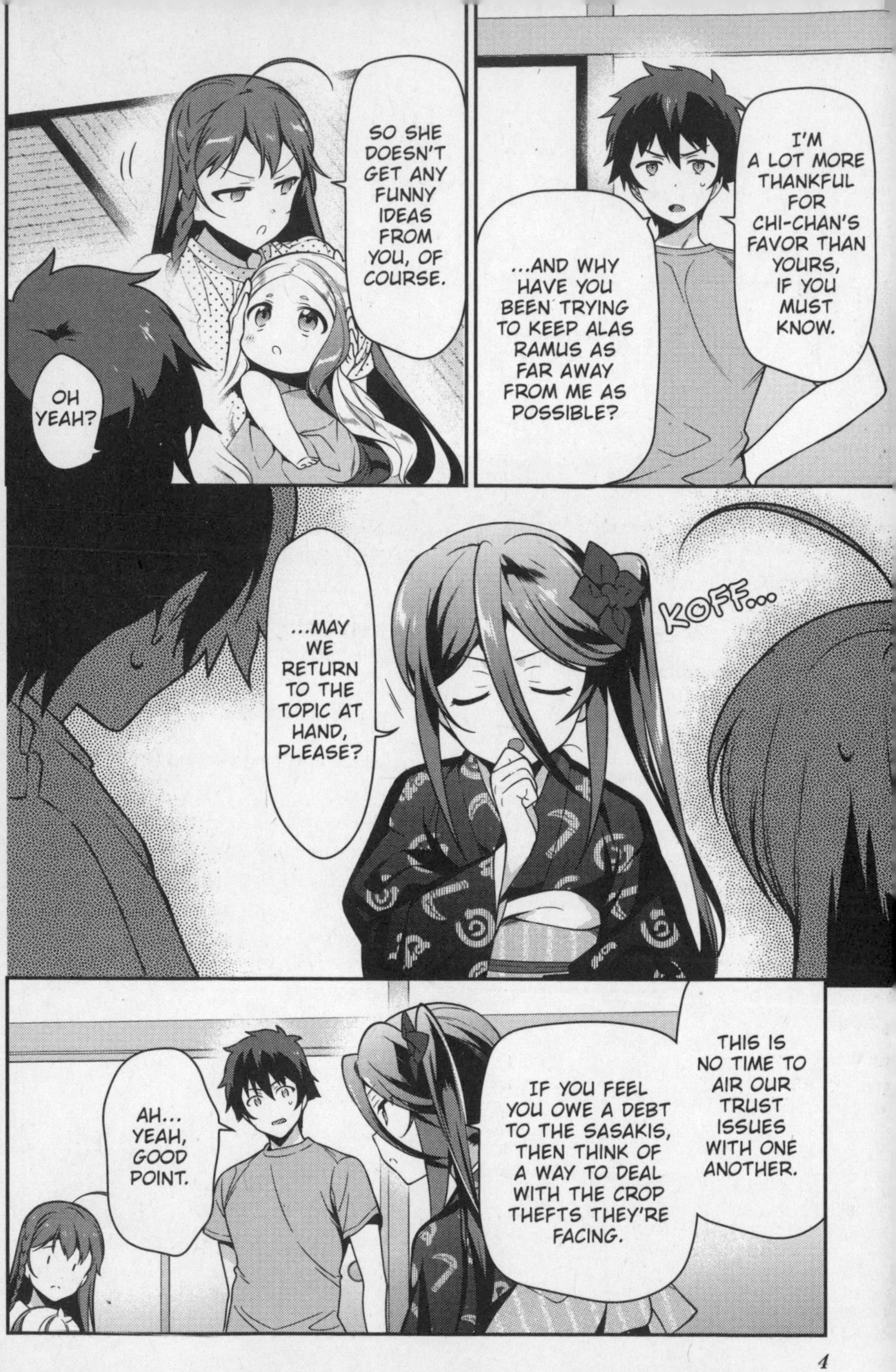
I'M A LOT MORE THANKFUL FOR CHI-CHAN'S FAVOR THAN YOURS, IF YOU MUST KNOW.
...AND WHY HAVE YOU BEEN TRYING TO KEEP ALAS RAMUS AS FAR AWAY FROM ME AS POSSIBLE?
SO SHE DOESN'T GET ANY FUNNY IDEAS FROM YOU, OF COURSE.
OH YEAH?
KOFF...
...MAY WE RETURN TO THE TOPIC AT HAND, PLEASE?
THIS IS NO TIME TO AIR OUR TRUST ISSUES WITH ONE ANOTHER.
IF YOU FEEL YOU OWE A DEBT TO THE SASAKIS, THEN THINK OF A WAY TO DEAL WITH THE CROP THEFTS THEY'RE FACING.
AH... YEAH, GOOD POINT.

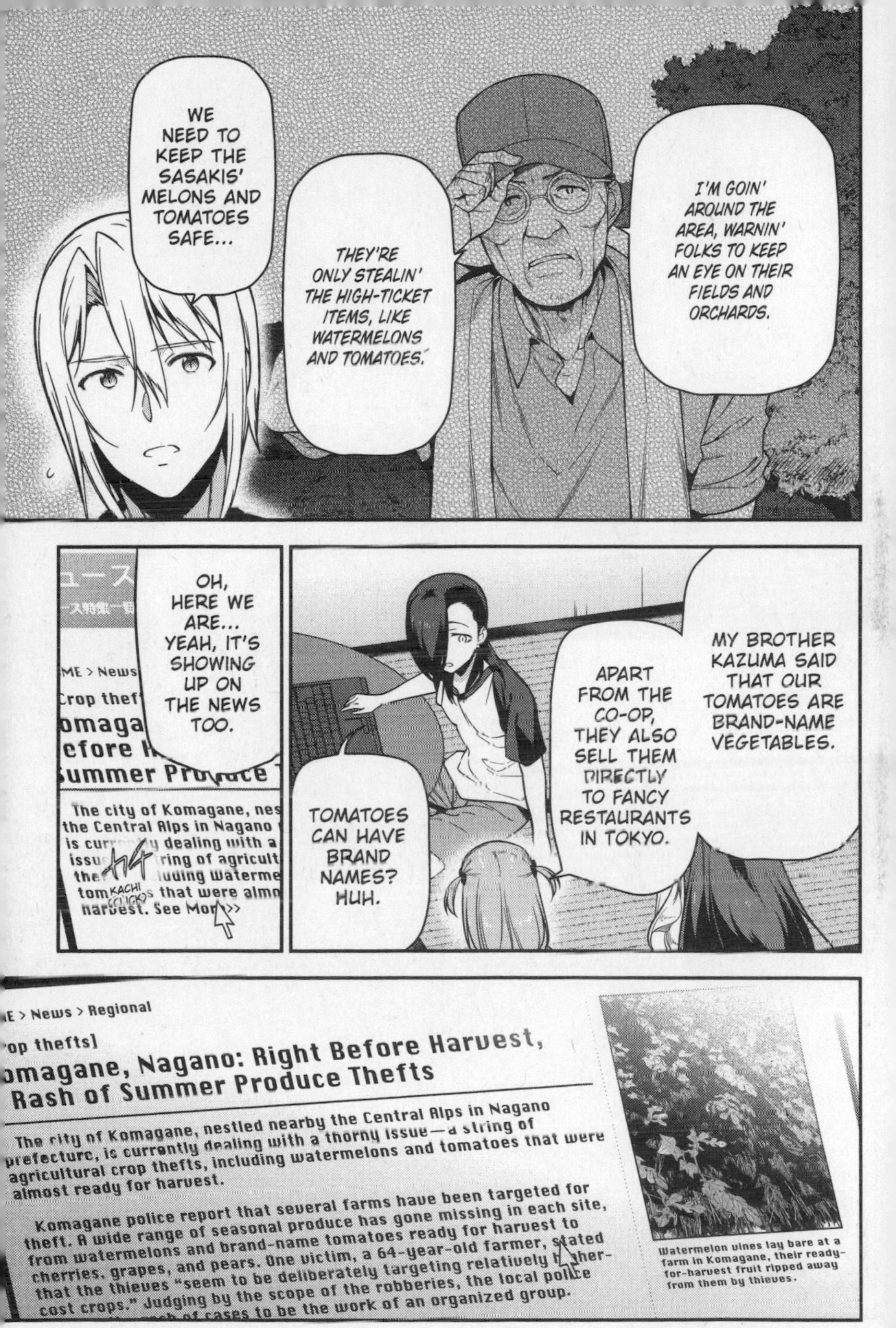
I'M GOIN' AROUND THE AREA, WARNIN' FOLKS TO KEEP AN EYE ON THEIR FIELDS AND ORCHARDS.
THEY'RE ONLY STEALIN' THE HIGH-TICKET ITEMS, LIKE WATERMELONS AND TOMATOES.
WE NEED TO KEEP THE SASAKIS' MELONS AND TOMATOES SAFE...
MY BROTHER KAZUMA SAID THAT OUR TOMATOES ARE BRAND-NAME VEGETABLES.
APART FROM THE CO-OP, THEY ALSO SELL THEM DIRECTLY TO FANCY RESTAURANTS IN TOKYO.
TOMATOES CAN HAVE BRAND NAMES? HUH.
OH, HERE WE ARE... YEAH, IT'S SHOWING UP ON THE NEWS TOO.
ME > News
Crop theft
omagan
efore H
Summer Produce T
The city of Komagane, nes
the Central Alps in Nagano
is currently dealing with a
issue string of agricult
the including waterme
tom s that were almo
harvest. See More>>
KACHI (CLICK)
E > News > Regional
rop thefts]
omagane, Nagano: Right Before Harvest,
Rash of Summer Produce Thefts
The city of Komagane, nestled nearby the Central Alps in Nagano
prefecture, is currently dealing with a thorny issue—a string of
agricultural crop thefts, including watermelons and tomatoes that were
almost ready for harvest.
Komagane police report that several farms have been targeted for
theft. A wide range of seasonal produce has gone missing in each site,
from watermelons and brand-name tomatoes ready for harvest to
cherries, grapes, and pears. One victim, a 64-year-old farmer, stated
that the thieves "seem to be deliberately targeting relatively higher-
cost crops." Judging by the scope of the robberies, the local police
of cases to be the work of an organized group.
Watermelon vines lay bare at a farm in Komagane, their ready-for-harvest fruit ripped away from them by thieves.

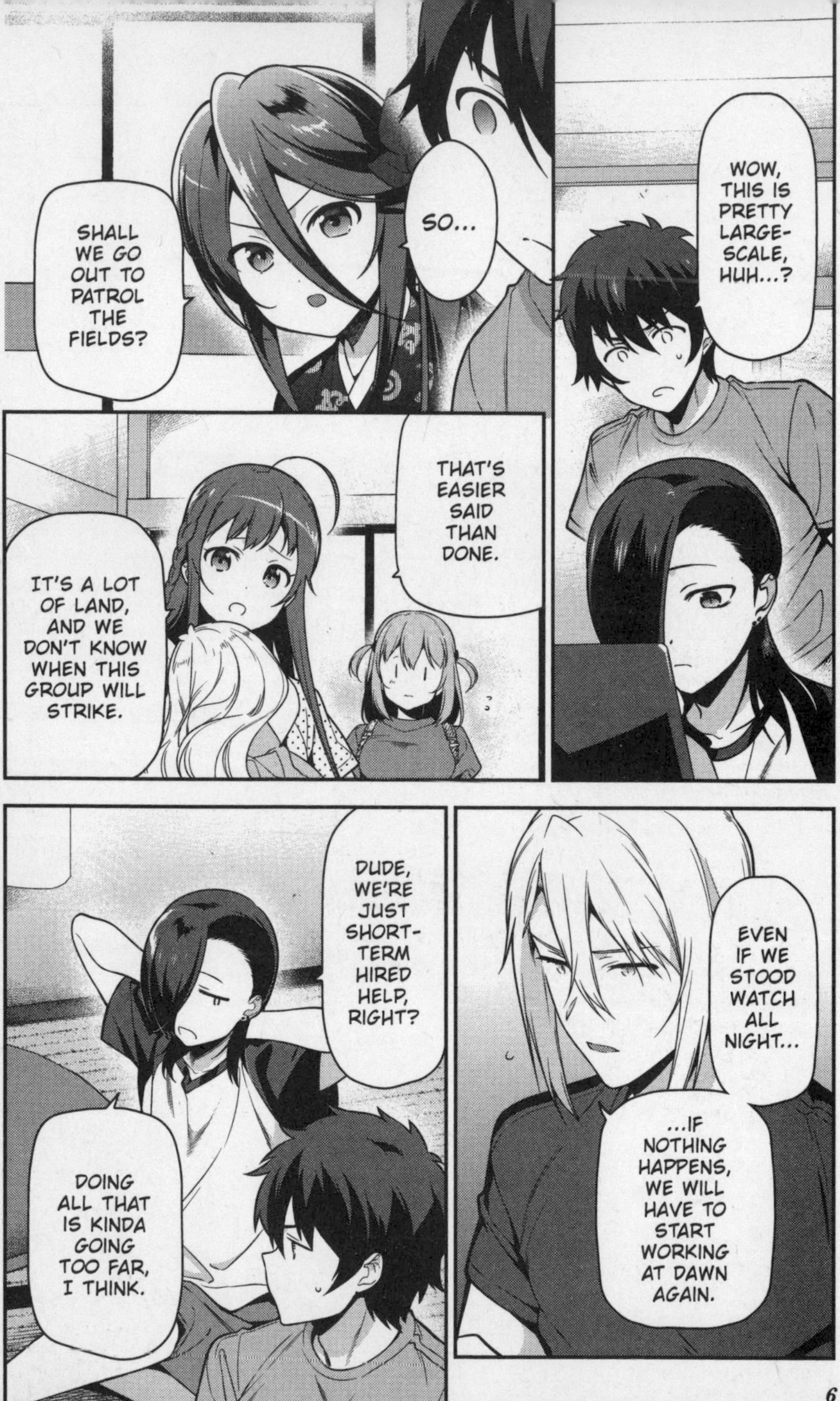
WOW, THIS IS PRETTY LARGE-SCALE, HUH...?
SO...
SHALL WE GO OUT TO PATROL THE FIELDS?
THAT'S EASIER SAID THAN DONE.
IT'S A LOT OF LAND, AND WE DON'T KNOW WHEN THIS GROUP WILL STRIKE.
EVEN IF WE STOOD WATCH ALL NIGHT...
...IF NOTHING HAPPENS, WE WILL HAVE TO START WORKING AT DAWN AGAIN.
DUDE, WE'RE JUST SHORT-TERM HIRED HELP, RIGHT?
DOING ALL THAT IS KINDA GOING TOO FAR, I THINK.

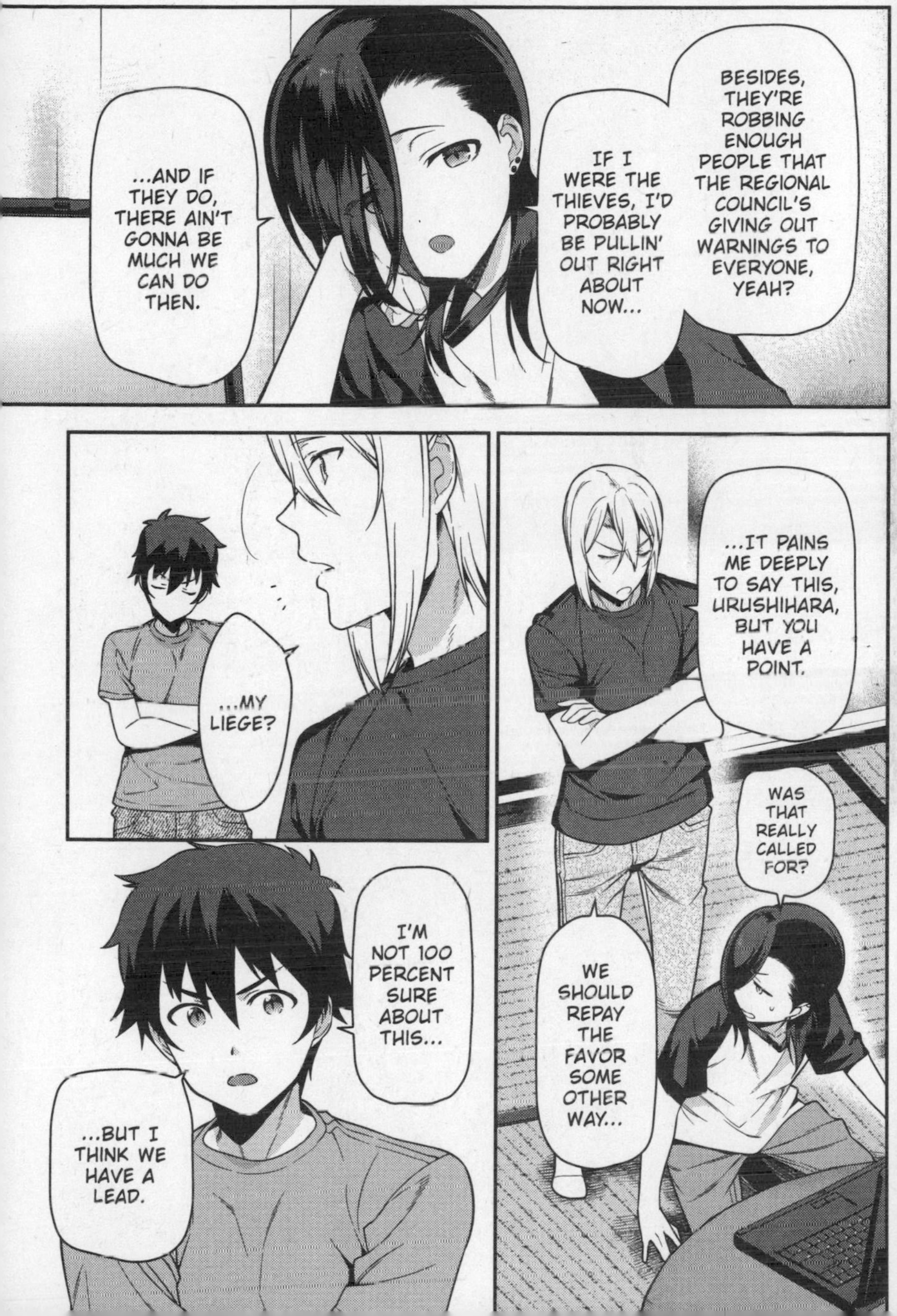
BESIDES, THEY'RE ROBBING ENOUGH PEOPLE THAT THE REGIONAL COUNCIL'S GIVING OUT WARNINGS TO EVERYONE, YEAH?
IF I WERE THE THIEVES, I'D PROBABLY BE PULLIN' OUT RIGHT ABOUT NOW...
...AND IF THEY DO, THERE AIN'T GONNA BE MUCH WE CAN DO THEN.
...IT PAINS ME DEEPLY TO SAY THIS, URUSHIHARA, BUT YOU HAVE A POINT.
WAS THAT REALLY CALLED FOR?
WE SHOULD REPAY THE FAVOR SOME OTHER WAY...
...MY LIEGE?
I'M NOT 100 PERCENT SURE ABOUT THIS...
...BUT I THINK WE HAVE A LEAD.

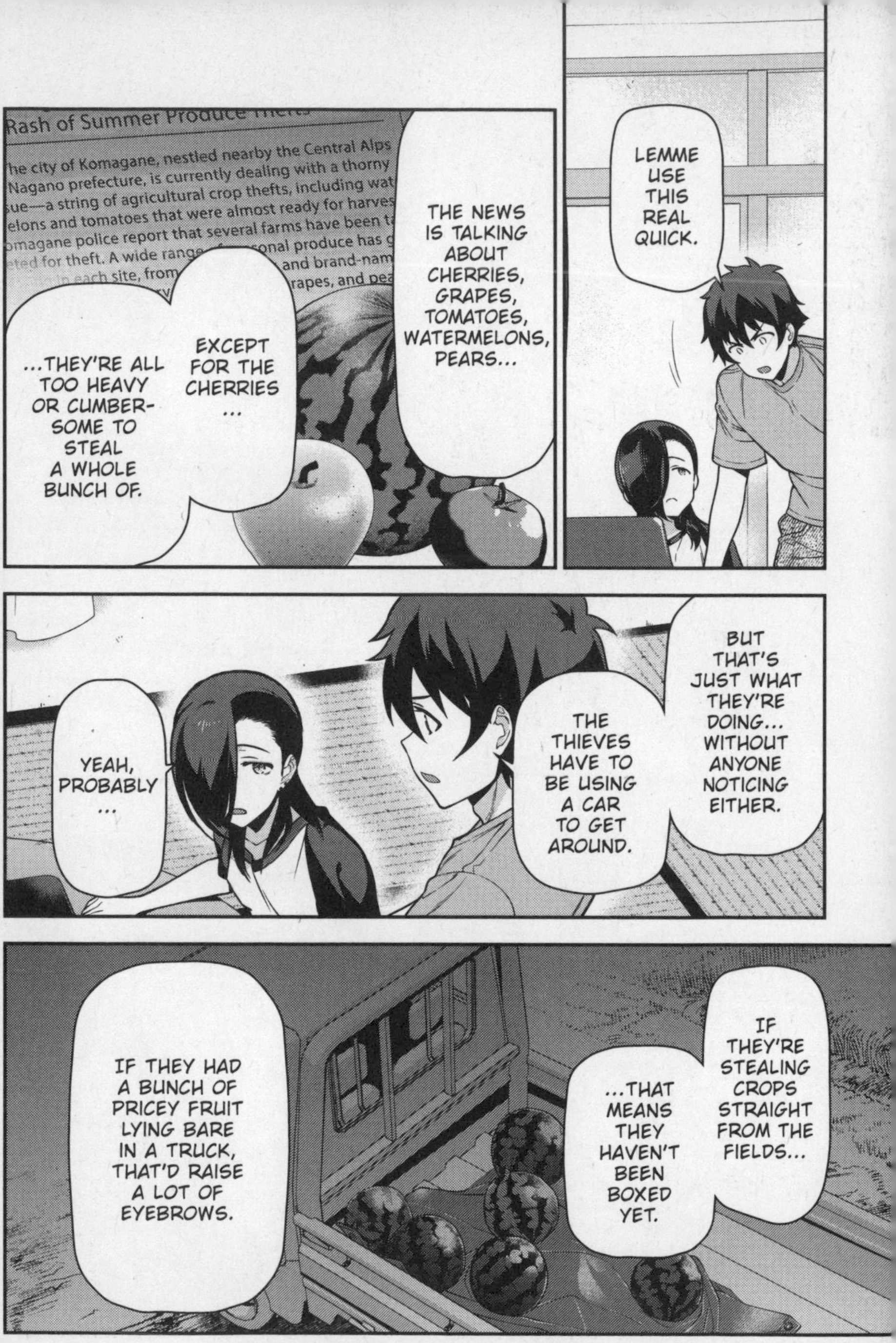
LEMME USE THIS REAL QUICK.
Rash of Summer Produce
he city of Komagane, nestled nearby the Central Alps
Nagano prefecture, is currently dealing with a thorny
sue—a string of agricultural crop thefts, including wat
elons and tomatoes that were almost ready for harves
omagane police report that several farms have been t
THE NEWS IS TALKING ABOUT CHERRIES, GRAPES, TOMATOES, WATERMELONS, PEARS...
EXCEPT FOR THE CHERRIES...
...THEY'RE ALL TOO HEAVY OR CUMBER-SOME TO STEAL A WHOLE BUNCH OF.
BUT THAT'S JUST WHAT THEY'RE DOING... WITHOUT ANYONE NOTICING EITHER.
THE THIEVES HAVE TO BE USING A CAR TO GET AROUND.
YEAH, PROBABLY...
IF THEY'RE STEALING CROPS STRAIGHT FROM THE FIELDS...
...THAT MEANS THEY HAVEN'T BEEN BOXED YET.
IF THEY HAD A BUNCH OF PRICEY FRUIT LYING BARE IN A TRUCK, THAT'D RAISE A LOT OF EYEBROWS.

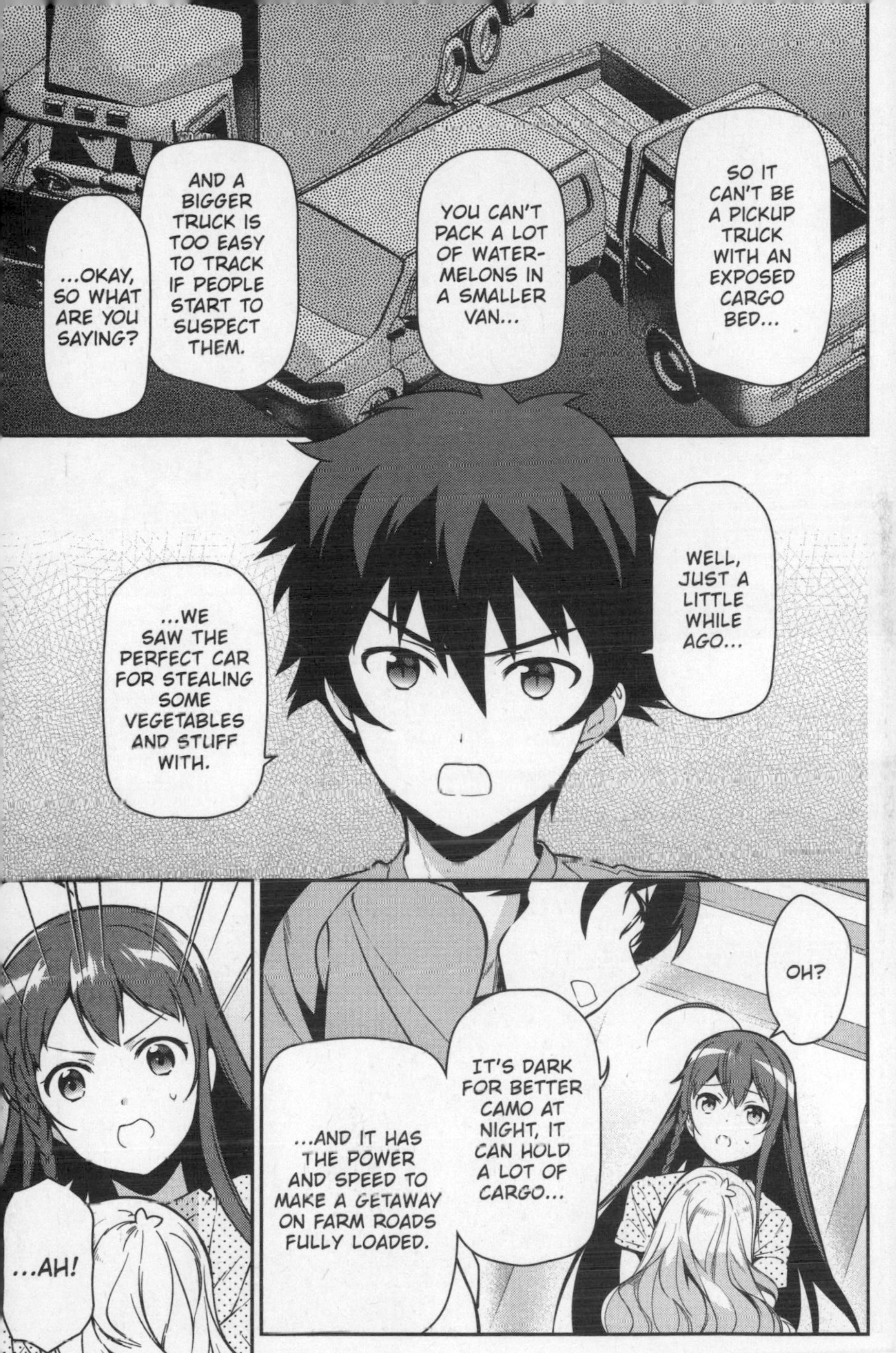
SO IT CAN'T BE A PICKUP TRUCK WITH AN EXPOSED CARGO BED...
YOU CAN'T PACK A LOT OF WATER-MELONS IN A SMALLER VAN...
AND A BIGGER TRUCK IS TOO EASY TO TRACK IF PEOPLE START TO SUSPECT THEM.
...OKAY, SO WHAT ARE YOU SAYING?
WELL, JUST A LITTLE WHILE AGO...
...WE SAW THE PERFECT CAR FOR STEALING SOME VEGETABLES AND STUFF WITH.
OH?
IT'S DARK FOR BETTER CAMO AT NIGHT, IT CAN HOLD A LOT OF CARGO...
...AND IT HAS THE POWER AND SPEED TO MAKE A GETAWAY ON FARM ROADS FULLY LOADED.
...AH!

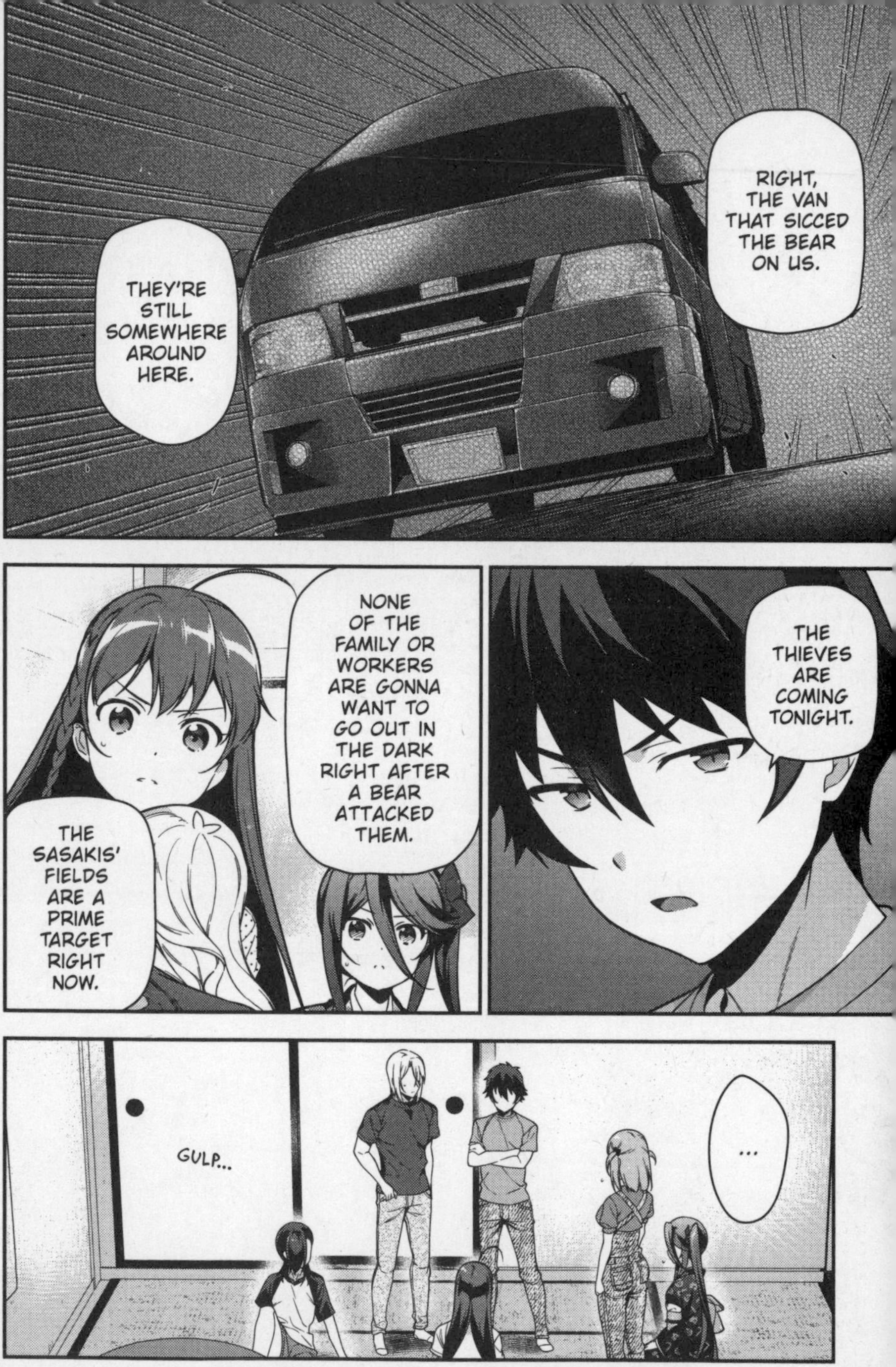
RIGHT, THE VAN THAT SICCED THE BEAR ON US.
THEY'RE STILL SOMEWHERE AROUND HERE.
THE THIEVES ARE COMING TONIGHT.
NONE OF THE FAMILY OR WORKERS ARE GONNA WANT TO GO OUT IN THE DARK RIGHT AFTER A BEAR ATTACKED THEM.
THE SASAKIS' FIELDS ARE A PRIME TARGET RIGHT NOW.
...
GULP...

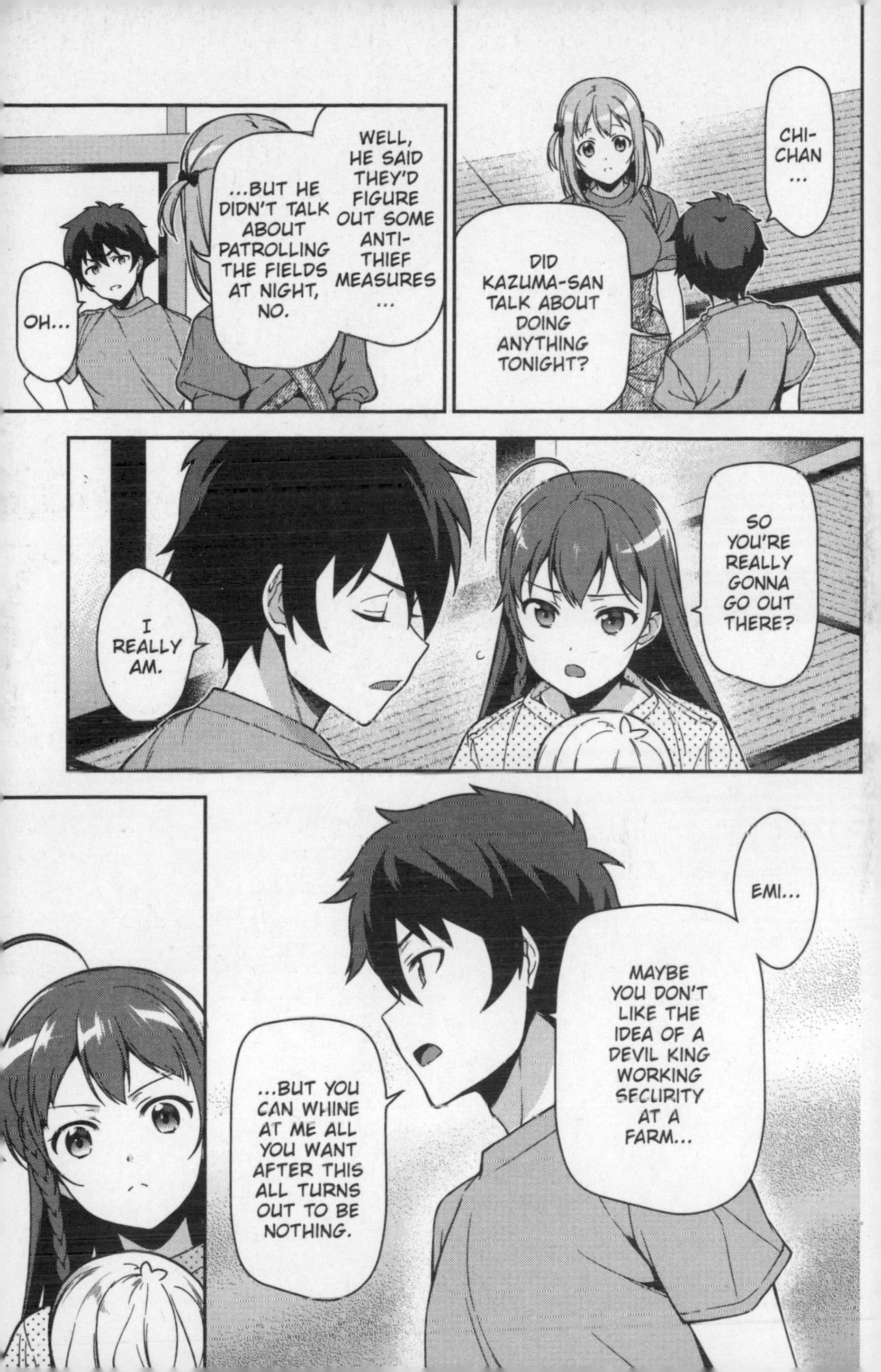
CHI-CHAN...
DID KAZUMA-SAN TALK ABOUT DOING ANYTHING TONIGHT?
WELL, HE SAID THEY'D FIGURE OUT SOME ANTI-THIEF MEASURES...
...BUT HE DIDN'T TALK ABOUT PATROLLING THE FIELDS AT NIGHT, NO.
OH...
SO YOU'RE REALLY GONNA GO OUT THERE?
I REALLY AM.
EMI...
MAYBE YOU DON'T LIKE THE IDEA OF A DEVIL KING WORKING SECURITY AT A FARM...
...BUT YOU CAN WHINE AT ME ALL YOU WANT AFTER THIS ALL TURNS OUT TO BE NOTHING.

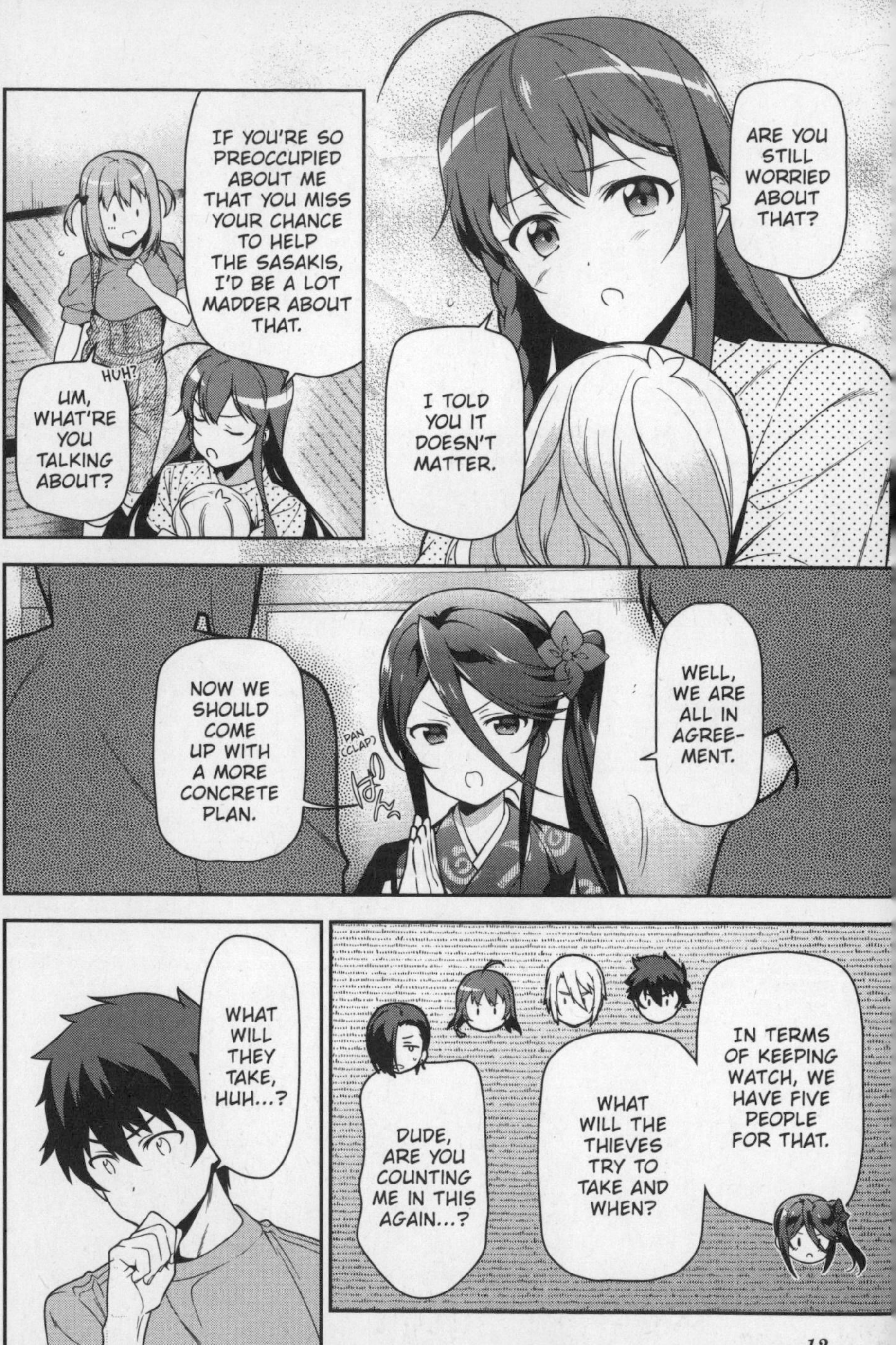
ARE YOU STILL WORRIED ABOUT THAT?
I TOLD YOU IT DOESN'T MATTER.
IF YOU'RE SO PREOCCUPIED ABOUT ME THAT YOU MISS YOUR CHANCE TO HELP THE SASAKIS, I'D BE A LOT MADDER ABOUT THAT.
HUH?
UM, WHAT'RE YOU TALKING ABOUT?
WELL, WE ARE ALL IN AGREE-MENT.
PAN (CLAP)
NOW WE SHOULD COME UP WITH A MORE CONCRETE PLAN.
IN TERMS OF KEEPING WATCH, WE HAVE FIVE PEOPLE FOR THAT.
WHAT WILL THE THIEVES TRY TO TAKE AND WHEN?
DUDE, ARE YOU COUNTING ME IN THIS AGAIN...?
WHAT WILL THEY TAKE, HUH...?

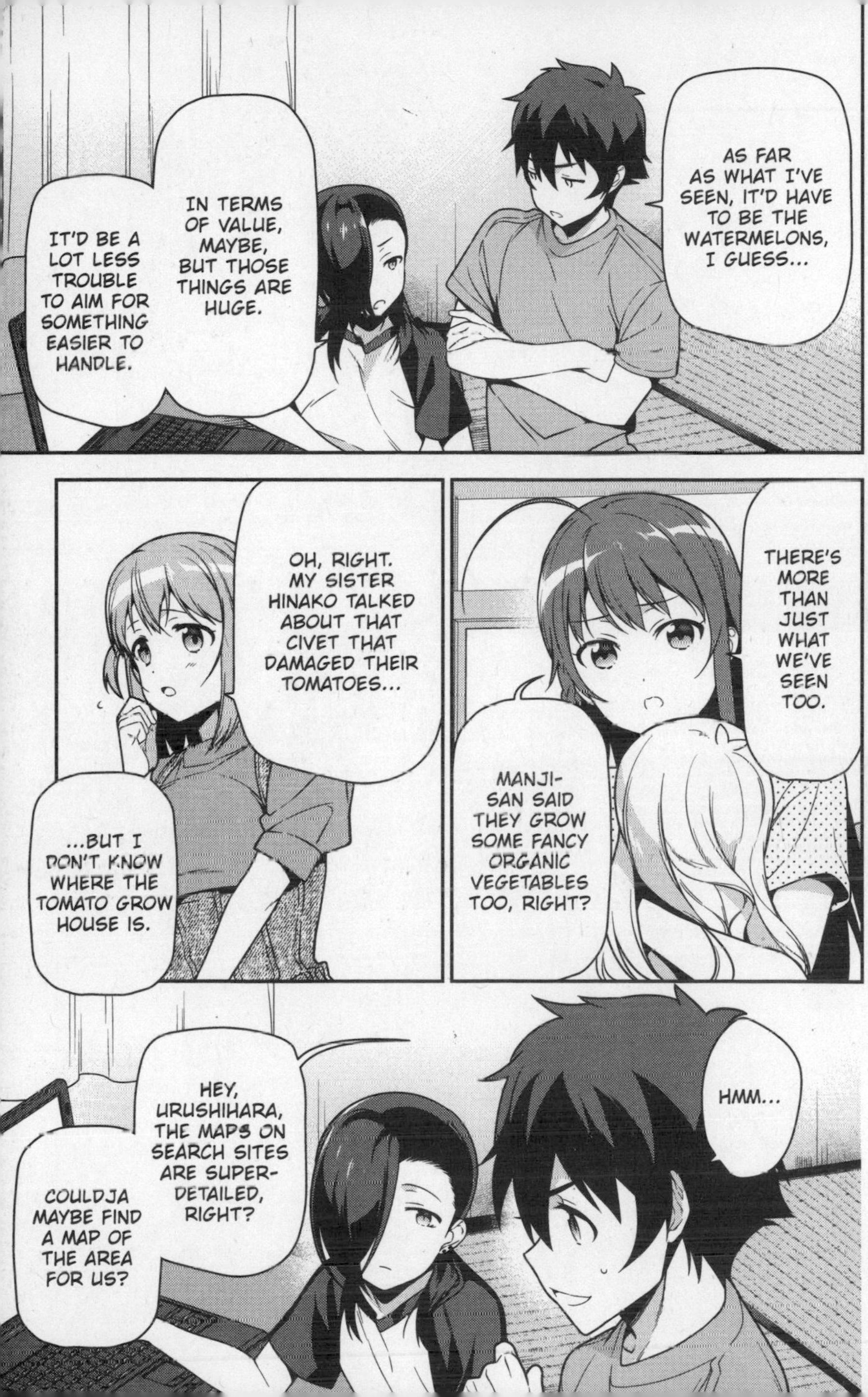
AS FAR AS WHAT I'VE SEEN, IT'D HAVE TO BE THE WATERMELONS, I GUESS...
IN TERMS OF VALUE, MAYBE, BUT THOSE THINGS ARE HUGE.
IT'D BE A LOT LESS TROUBLE TO AIM FOR SOMETHING EASIER TO HANDLE.
THERE'S MORE THAN JUST WHAT WE'VE SEEN TOO.
MANJI-SAN SAID THEY GROW SOME FANCY ORGANIC VEGETABLES TOO, RIGHT?
OH, RIGHT. MY SISTER HINAKO TALKED ABOUT THAT CIVET THAT DAMAGED THEIR TOMATOES...
...BUT I DON'T KNOW WHERE THE TOMATO GROW HOUSE IS.
HMM...
HEY, URUSHIHARA, THE MAPS ON SEARCH SITES ARE SUPER-DETAILED, RIGHT?
COULDJA MAYBE FIND A MAP OF THE AREA FOR US?

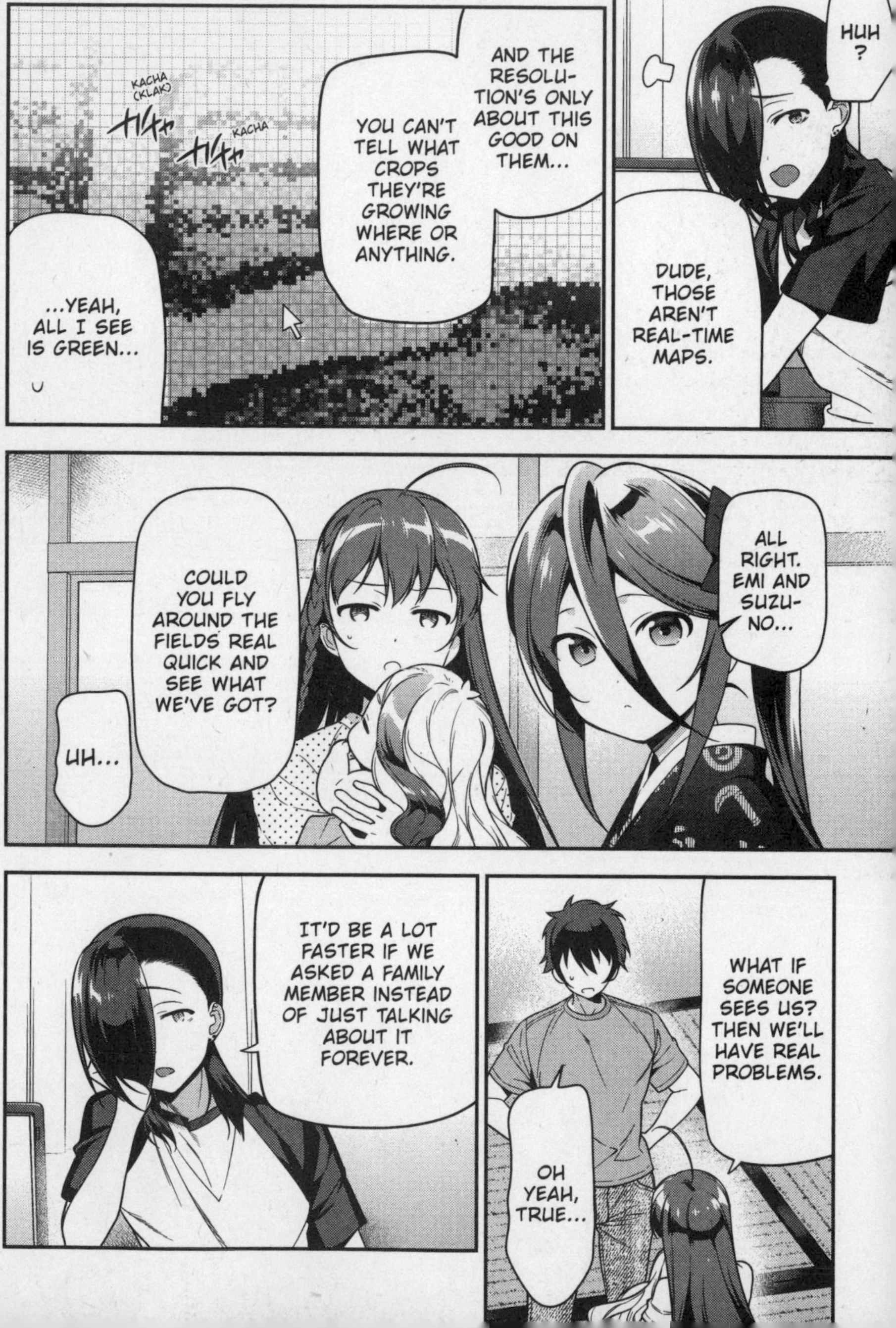
HUH?
DUDE, THOSE AREN'T REAL-TIME MAPS.
AND THE RESOLUTION'S ONLY ABOUT THIS GOOD ON THEM...
YOU CAN'T TELL WHAT CROPS THEY'RE GROWING WHERE OR ANYTHING.
KACHA
KACHA (KLAK)
...YEAH, ALL I SEE IS GREEN...
ALL RIGHT. EMI AND SUZUNO...
COULD YOU FLY AROUND THE FIELDS REAL QUICK AND SEE WHAT WE'VE GOT?
UH...
WHAT IF SOMEONE SEES US? THEN WE'LL HAVE REAL PROBLEMS.
OH YEAH, TRUE...
IT'D BE A LOT FASTER IF WE ASKED A FAMILY MEMBER INSTEAD OF JUST TALKING ABOUT IT FOREVER.

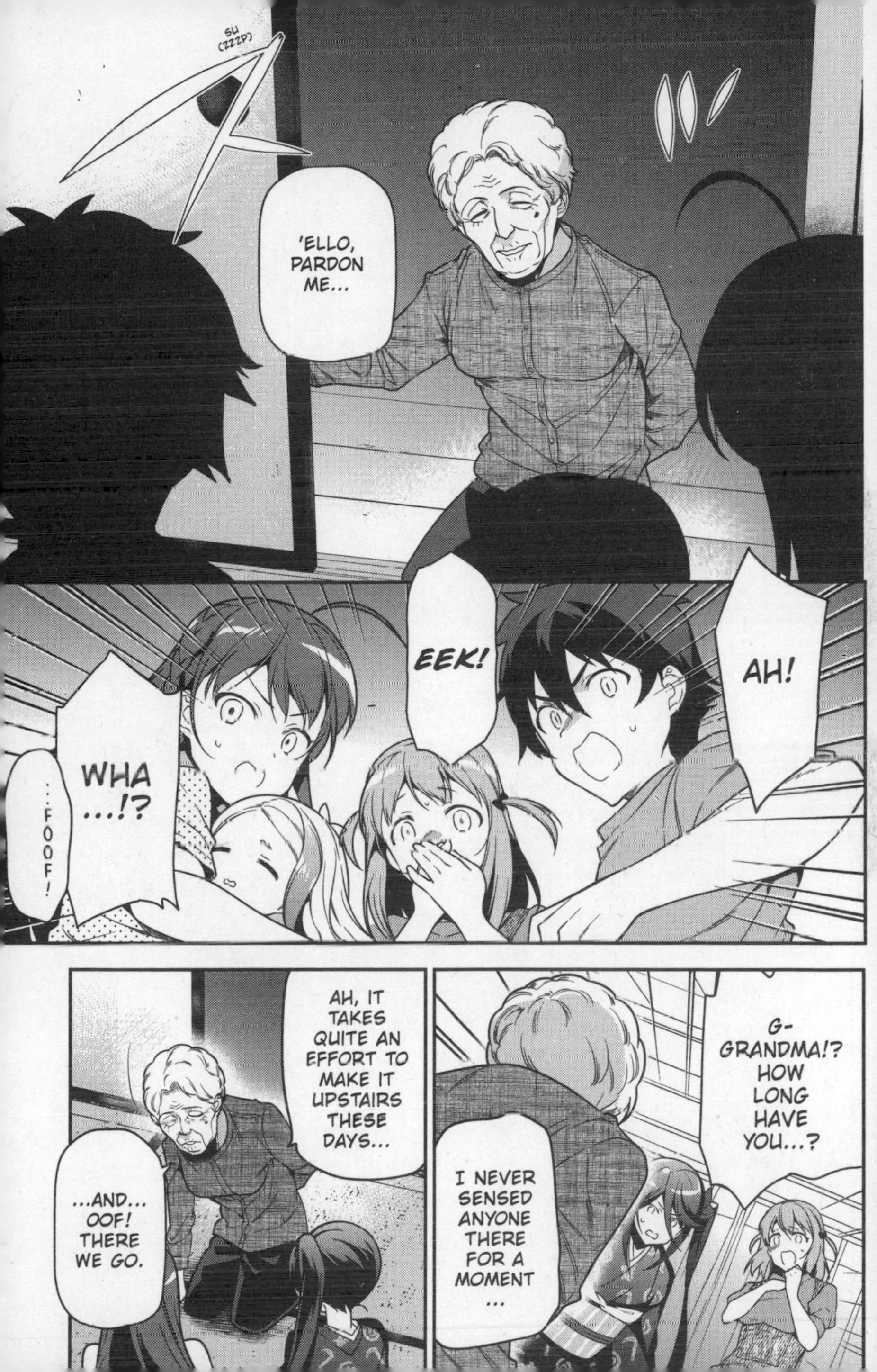
SU (ZZZP)
'ELLO, PARDON ME...
AH!
EEK!
WHA...!?
...FOOF!
G-GRANDMA!? HOW LONG HAVE YOU...?
I NEVER SENSED ANYONE THERE FOR A MOMENT...
AH, IT TAKES QUITE AN EFFORT TO MAKE IT UPSTAIRS THESE DAYS...
...AND... OOF! THERE WE GO.

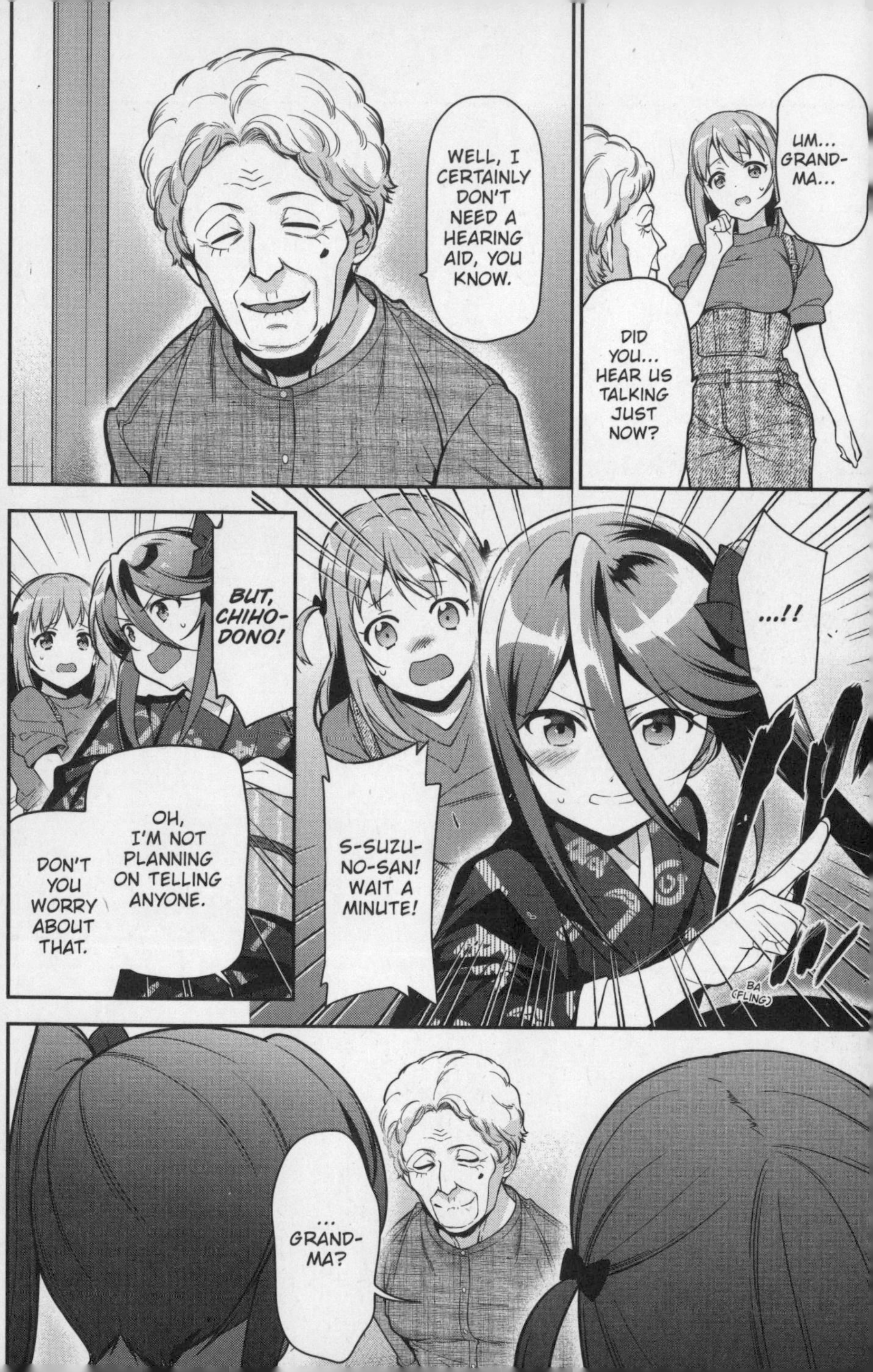
UM... GRAND-MA...
DID YOU... HEAR US TALKING JUST NOW?
WELL, I CERTAINLY DON'T NEED A HEARING AID, YOU KNOW.
...!!
S-SUZU-NO-SAN! WAIT A MINUTE!
BA (FLING)
BUT, CHIHO-DONO!
OH, I'M NOT PLANNING ON TELLING ANYONE.
DON'T YOU WORRY ABOUT THAT.
... GRAND-MA?

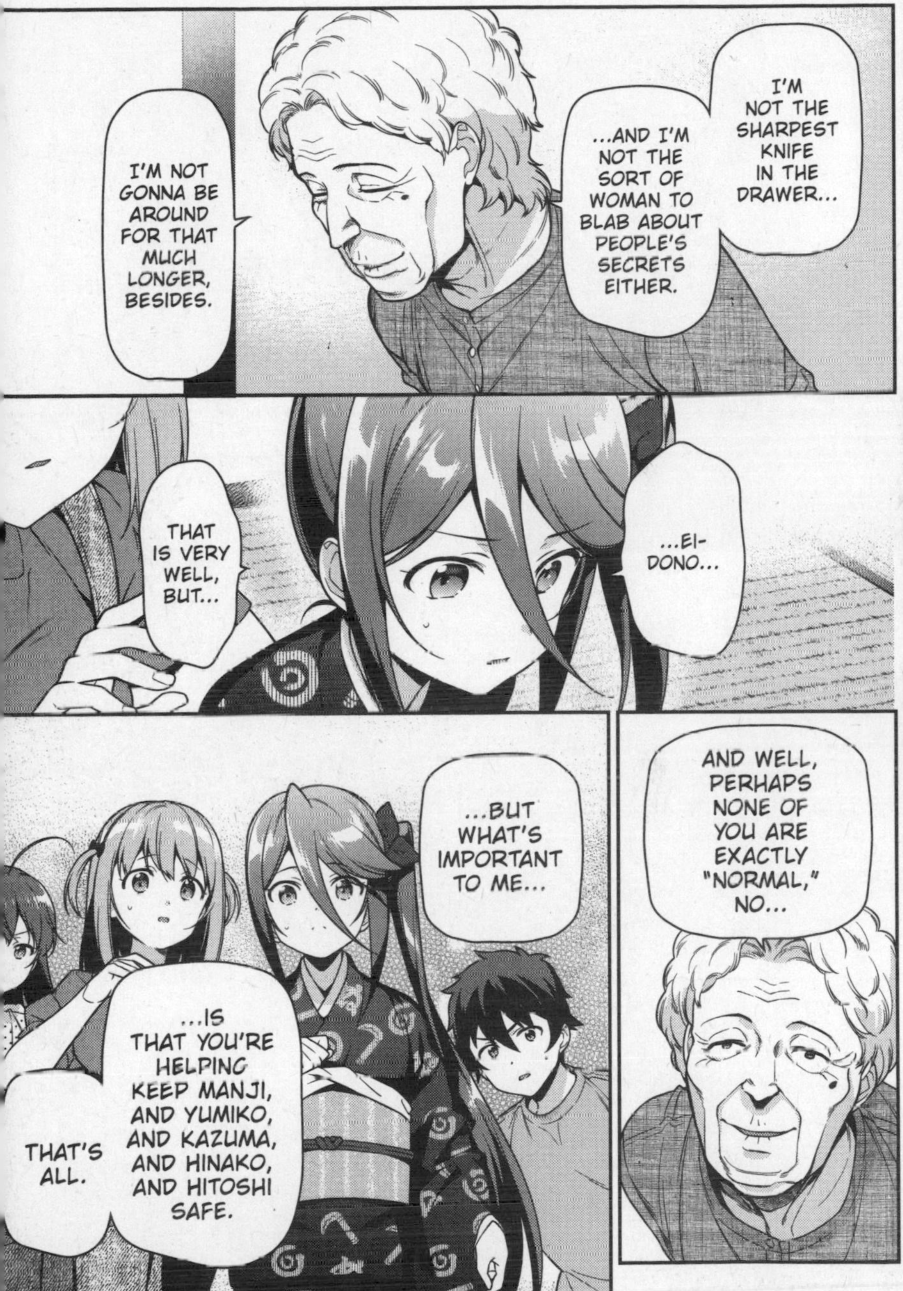
I'M NOT THE SHARPEST KNIFE IN THE DRAWER...
...AND I'M NOT THE SORT OF WOMAN TO BLAB ABOUT PEOPLE'S SECRETS EITHER.
I'M NOT GONNA BE AROUND FOR THAT MUCH LONGER, BESIDES.
...EI-DONO...
THAT IS VERY WELL, BUT...
AND WELL, PERHAPS NONE OF YOU ARE EXACTLY "NORMAL," NO...
...BUT WHAT'S IMPORTANT TO ME...
...IS THAT YOU'RE HELPING KEEP MANJI, AND YUMIKO, AND KAZUMA, AND HINAKO, AND HITOSHI SAFE.
THAT'S ALL.

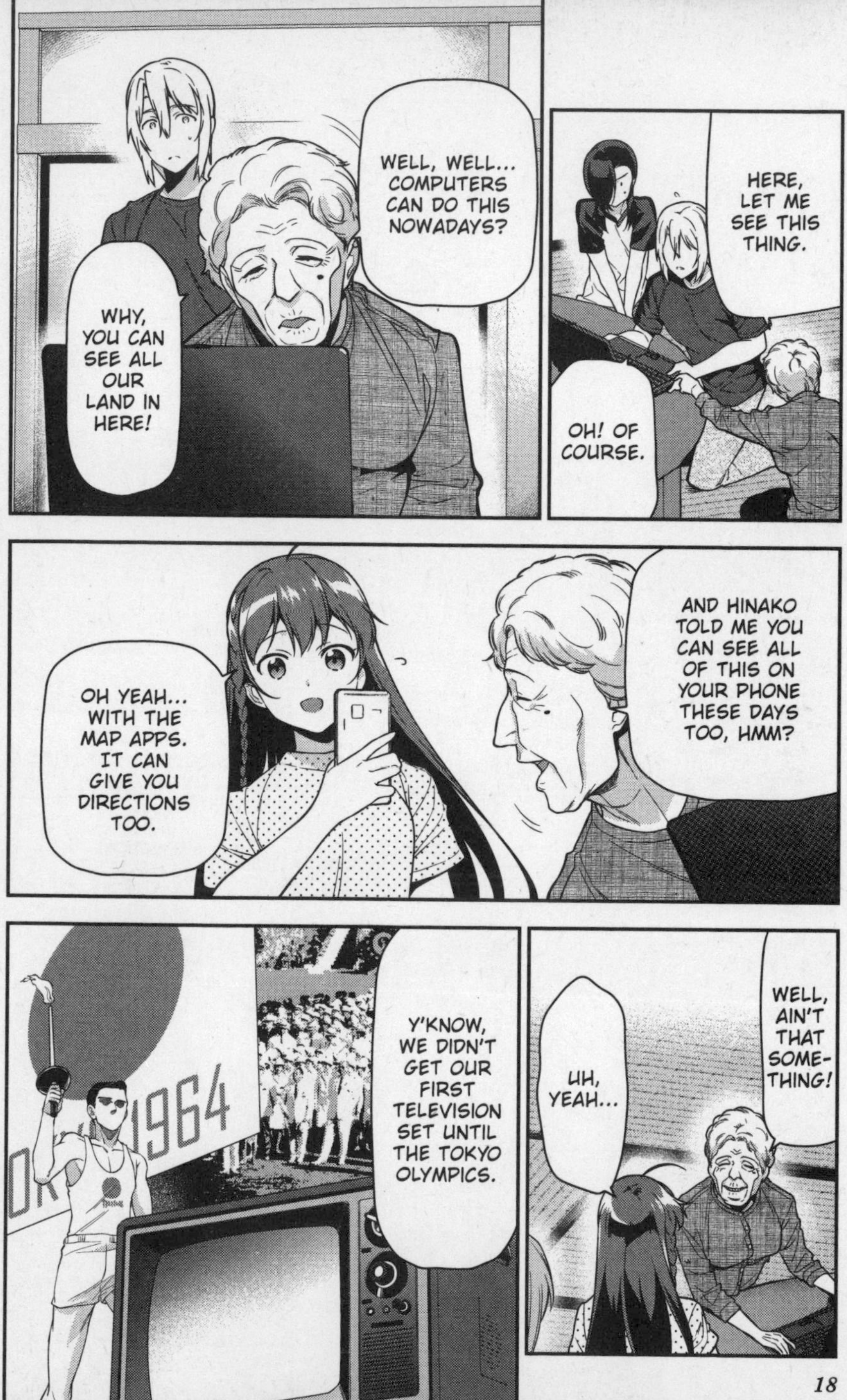
HERE, LET ME SEE THIS THING.
OH! OF COURSE.
WELL, WELL... COMPUTERS CAN DO THIS NOWADAYS?
WHY, YOU CAN SEE ALL OUR LAND IN HERE!
AND HINAKO TOLD ME YOU CAN SEE ALL OF THIS ON YOUR PHONE THESE DAYS TOO, HMM?
OH YEAH... WITH THE MAP APPS. IT CAN GIVE YOU DIRECTIONS TOO.
WELL, AIN'T THAT SOME-THING!
UH, YEAH...
Y'KNOW, WE DIDN'T GET OUR FIRST TELEVISION SET UNTIL THE TOKYO OLYMPICS.
1964

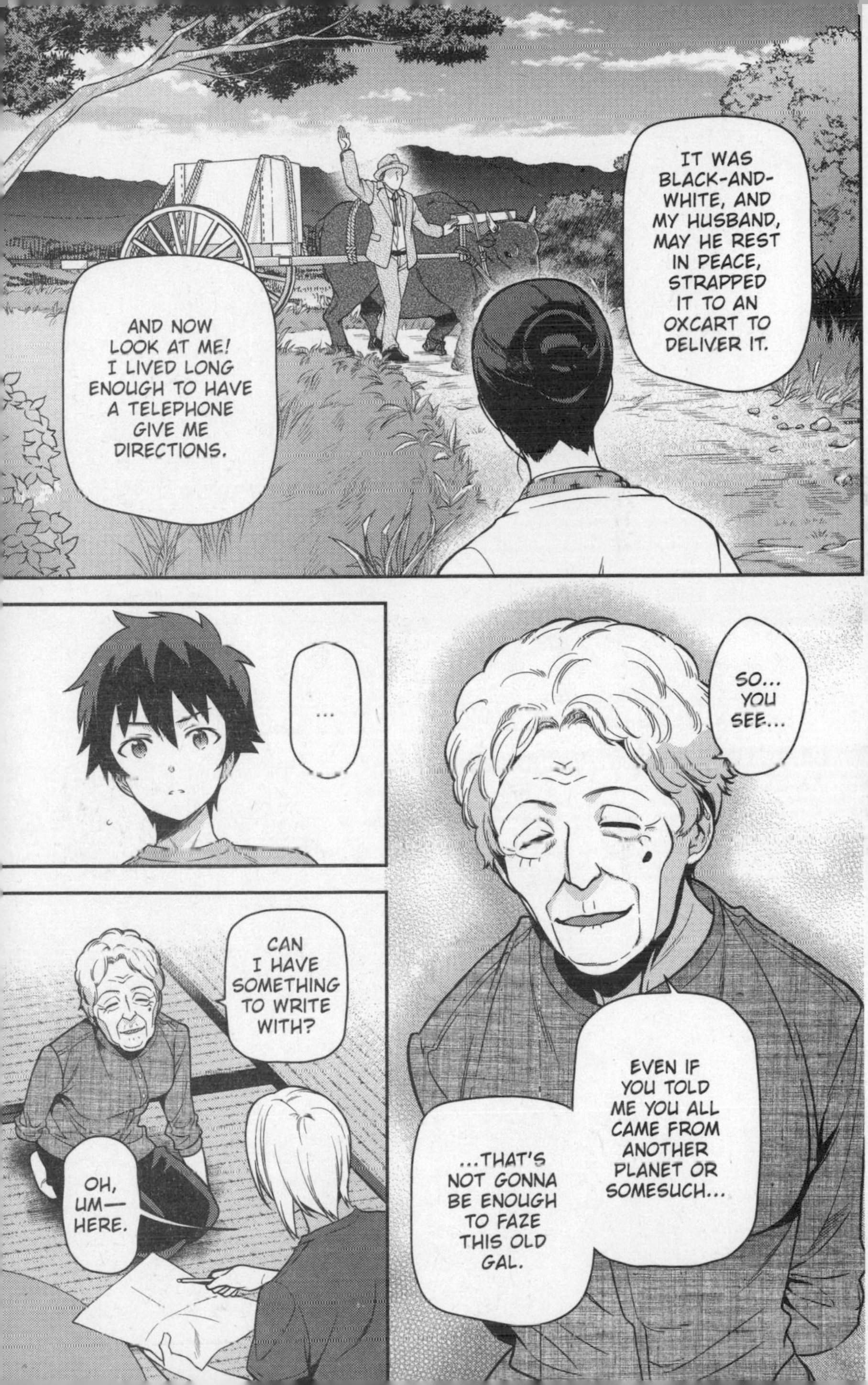
IT WAS BLACK-AND-WHITE, AND MY HUSBAND, MAY HE REST IN PEACE, STRAPPED IT TO AN OXCART TO DELIVER IT.
AND NOW LOOK AT ME! I LIVED LONG ENOUGH TO HAVE A TELEPHONE GIVE ME DIRECTIONS.
SO... YOU SEE...
EVEN IF YOU TOLD ME YOU ALL CAME FROM ANOTHER PLANET OR SOMESUCH...
...THAT'S NOT GONNA BE ENOUGH TO FAZE THIS OLD GAL.
...
CAN I HAVE SOMETHING TO WRITE WITH?
OH, UM— HERE.

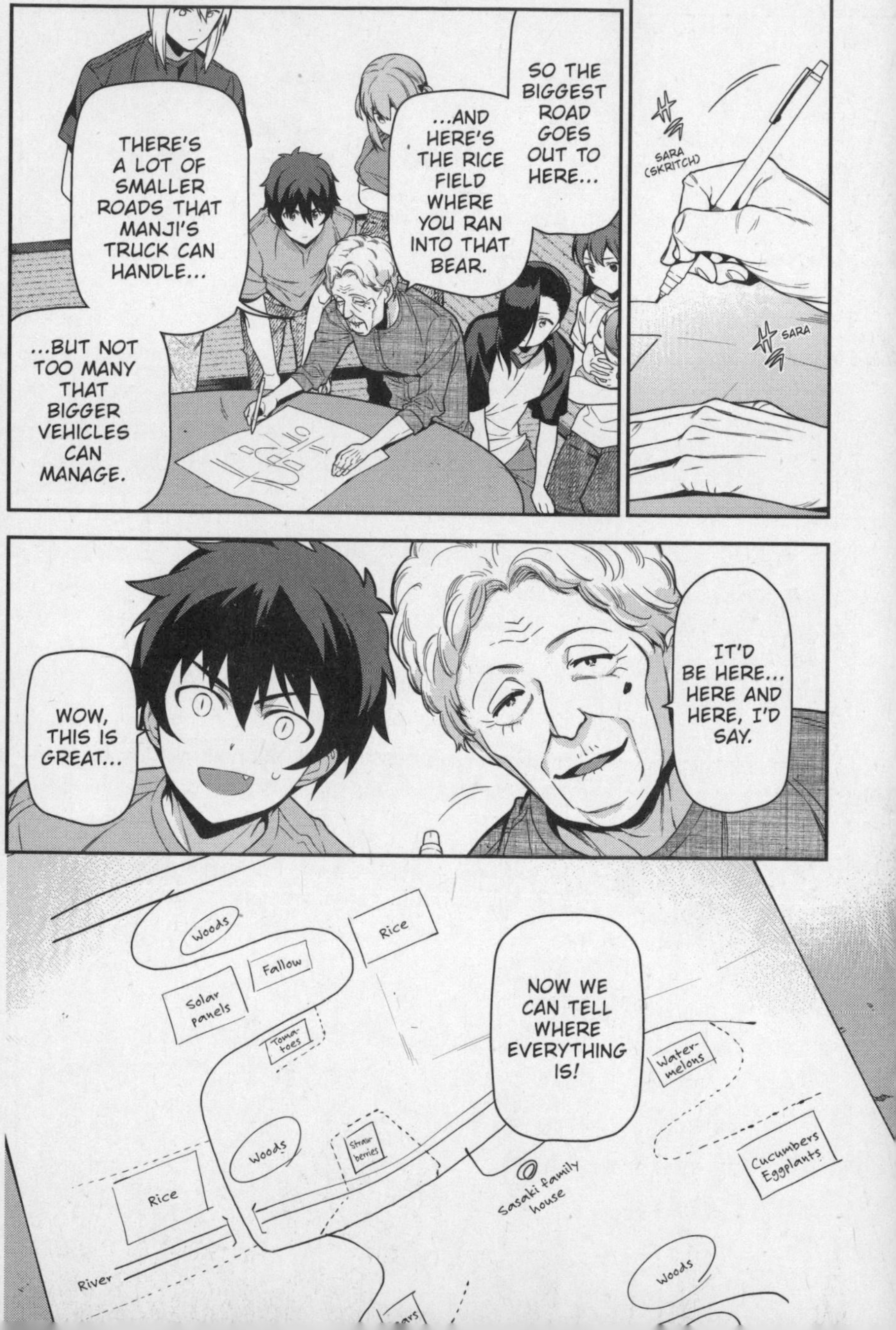
SARA (SKRITCH)
SARA
SO THE BIGGEST ROAD GOES OUT TO HERE...
...AND HERE'S THE RICE FIELD WHERE YOU RAN INTO THAT BEAR.
THERE'S A LOT OF SMALLER ROADS THAT MANJI'S TRUCK CAN HANDLE...
...BUT NOT TOO MANY THAT BIGGER VEHICLES CAN MANAGE.
IT'D BE HERE... HERE AND HERE, I'D SAY.
WOW, THIS IS GREAT...
NOW WE CAN TELL WHERE EVERYTHING IS!
Woods
Rice
Fallow
Solar panels
Toma-toes
Water-melons
Woods
Straw-berries
Cucumbers Eggplants
Rice
Sasaki family house
River
Woods

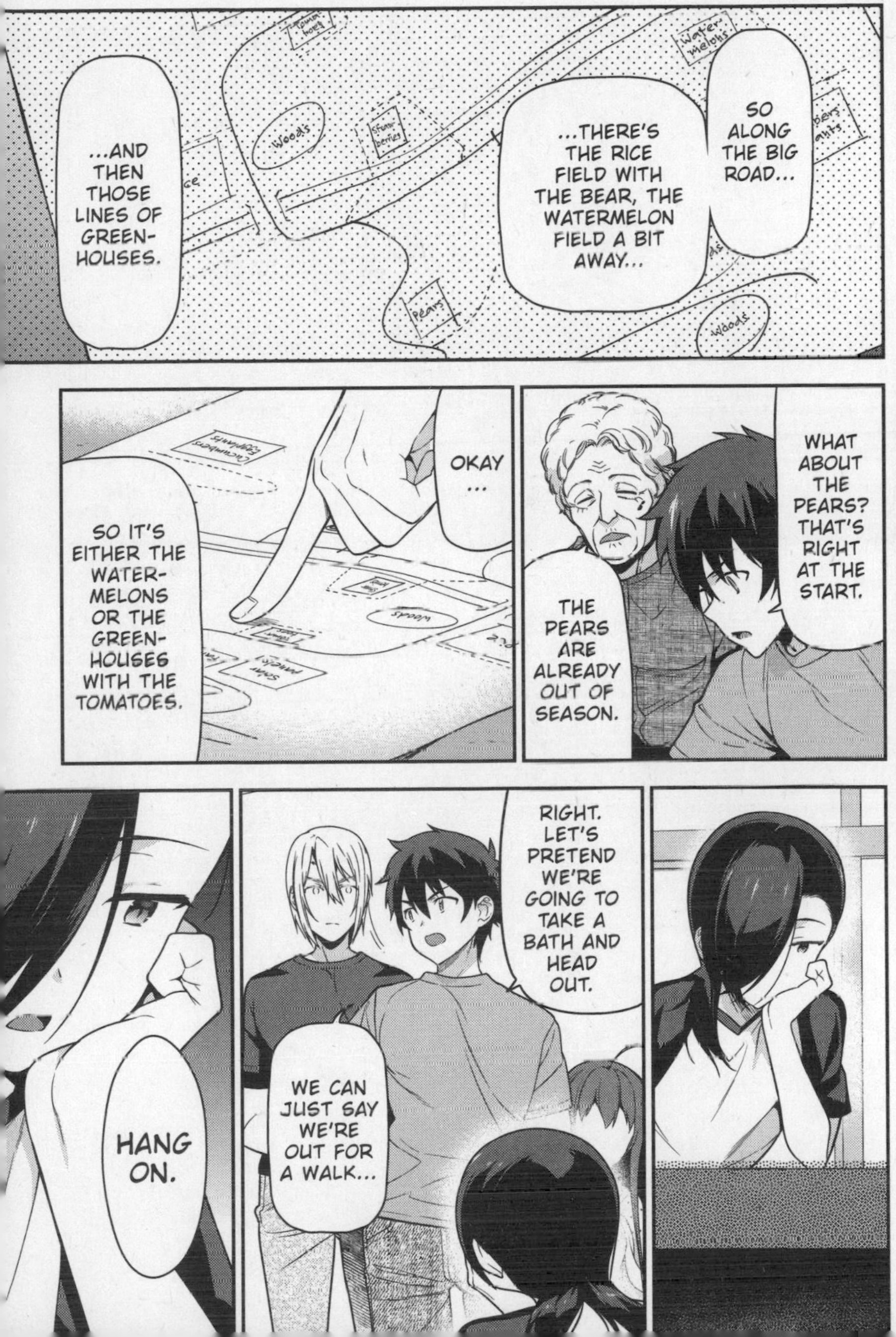
Water-melons
SO ALONG THE BIG ROAD...
...THERE'S THE RICE FIELD WITH THE BEAR, THE WATERMELON FIELD A BIT AWAY...
Straw-berries
Woods
...AND THEN THOSE LINES OF GREEN-HOUSES.
Pears
Woods
WHAT ABOUT THE PEARS? THAT'S RIGHT AT THE START.
THE PEARS ARE ALREADY OUT OF SEASON.
OKAY...
SO IT'S EITHER THE WATER-MELONS OR THE GREEN-HOUSES WITH THE TOMATOES.
RIGHT. LET'S PRETEND WE'RE GOING TO TAKE A BATH AND HEAD OUT.
WE CAN JUST SAY WE'RE OUT FOR A WALK...
HANG ON.

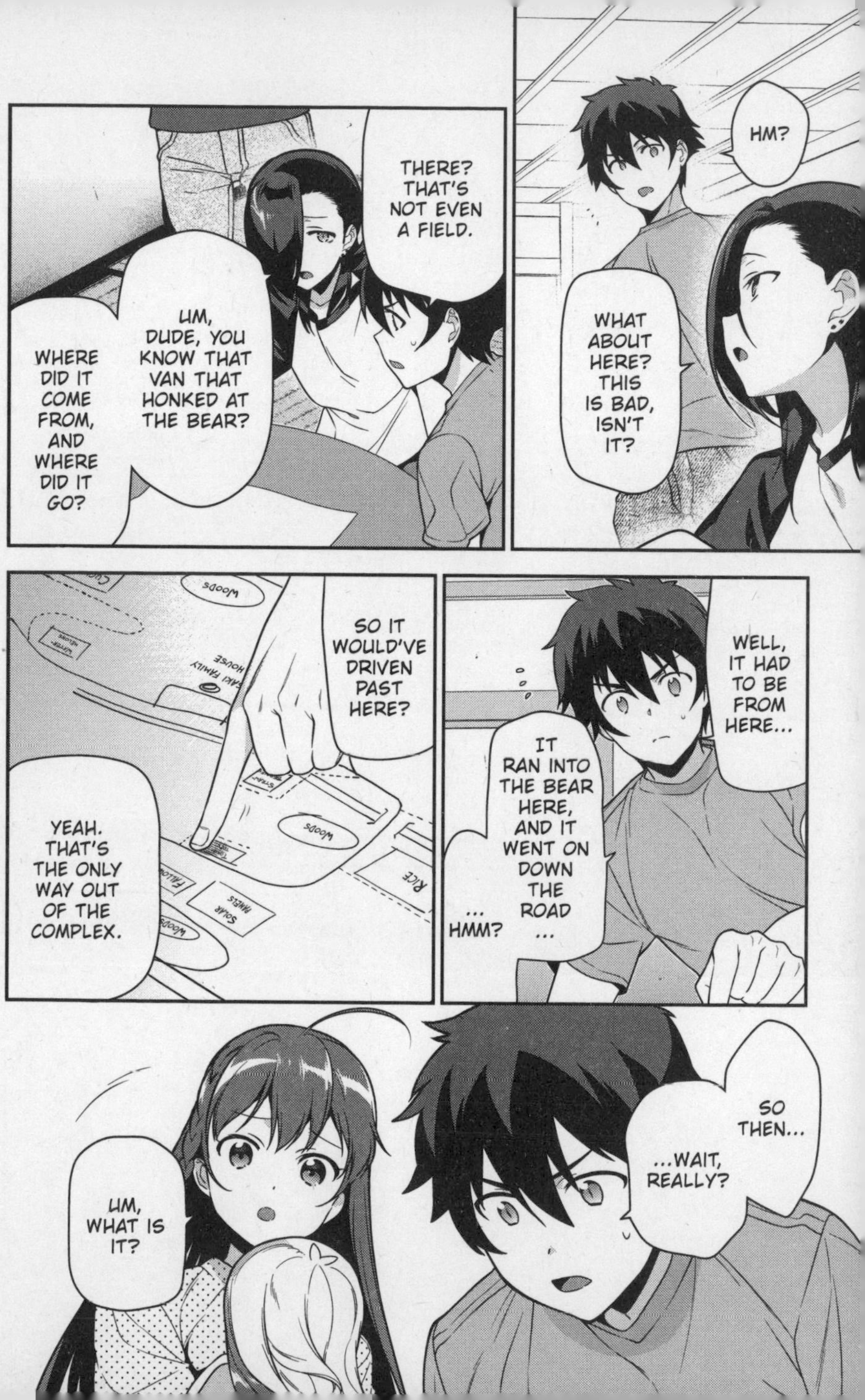
HM?
WHAT ABOUT HERE? THIS IS BAD, ISN'T IT?
THERE? THAT'S NOT EVEN A FIELD.
UM, DUDE, YOU KNOW THAT VAN THAT HONKED AT THE BEAR?
WHERE DID IT COME FROM, AND WHERE DID IT GO?
WELL, IT HAD TO BE FROM HERE...
IT RAN INTO THE BEAR HERE, AND IT WENT ON DOWN THE ROAD ...
... HMM?
SO IT WOULD'VE DRIVEN PAST HERE?
YEAH. THAT'S THE ONLY WAY OUT OF THE COMPLEX.
SO THEN...
...WAIT, REALLY?
UM, WHAT IS IT?

PERSONALLY, I'D BE A LOT MORE ATTRACTED TO THIS OVER A BUNCH OF VEGETABLES.
TAKE ONE OR TWO OF 'EM, AND EVEN IF YOU SELL 'EM DIRT CHEAP, IT'D BE WORTH A TON MORE THAN SOME PRODUCE.
BUT THAT'S A DEV SETUP FROM THE COLLEGE, RIGHT?
YEAH, I DOUBT IT'S THAT ROBUST AN INSTALLATION, REALLY.
IF THEY STOLE THEM, THAT COULD WIPE OUT ALL THE CROPS IN THE GREEN-HOUSES.
AND EVEN IF IT DIDN'T...
...IT'D PROBABLY TAKE A TON OF MONEY TO RESTORE THE SYSTEM.
Woods
Wate
melo
Fallow
Solar panels
Toma-toes

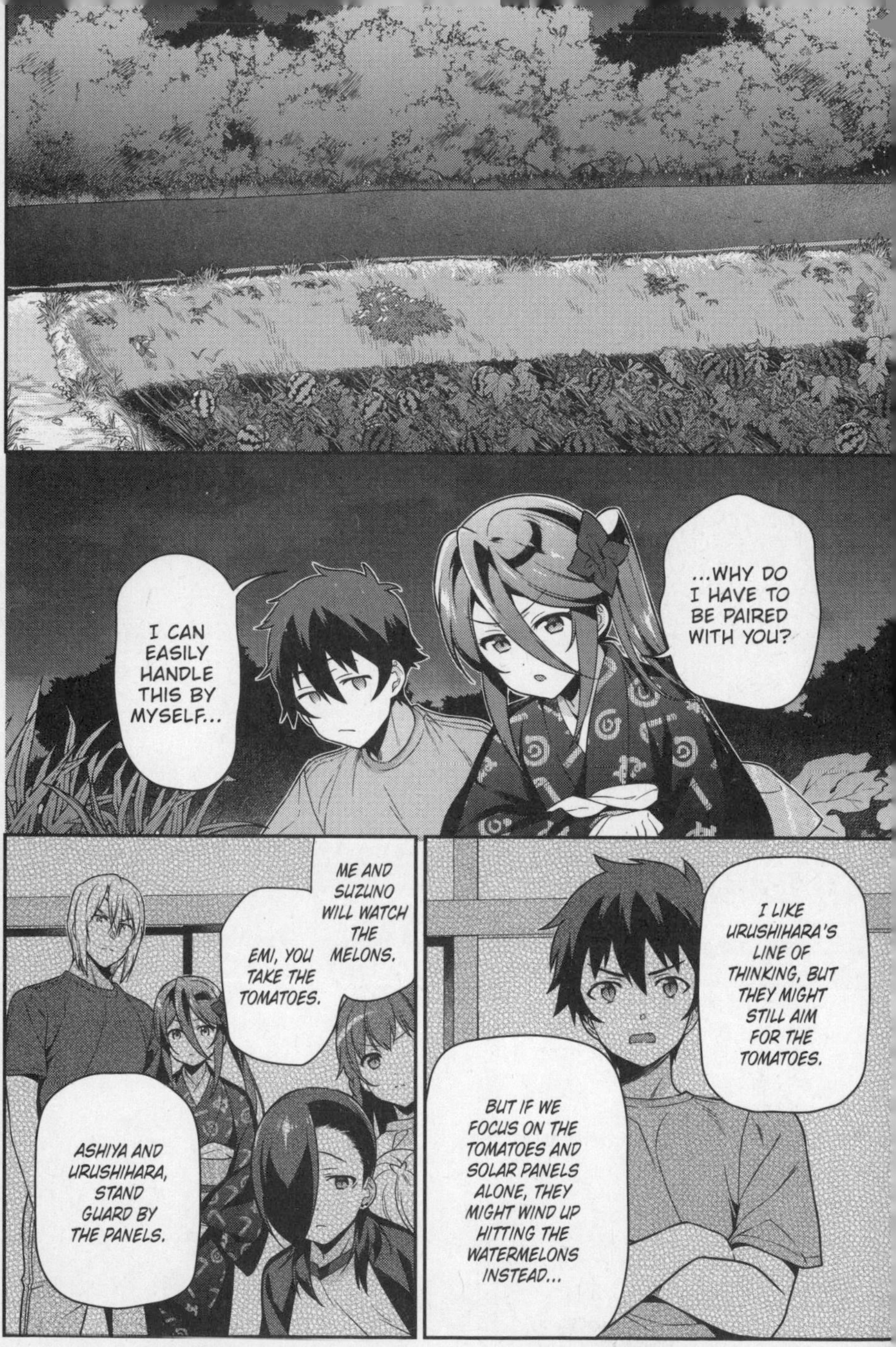
...WHY DO I HAVE TO BE PAIRED WITH YOU?
I CAN EASILY HANDLE THIS BY MYSELF...
I LIKE URUSHIHARA'S LINE OF THINKING, BUT THEY MIGHT STILL AIM FOR THE TOMATOES.
BUT IF WE FOCUS ON THE TOMATOES AND SOLAR PANELS ALONE, THEY MIGHT WIND UP HITTING THE WATERMELONS INSTEAD...
ME AND SUZUNO WILL WATCH THE MELONS.
EMI, YOU TAKE THE TOMATOES.
ASHIYA AND URUSHIHARA, STAND GUARD BY THE PANELS.

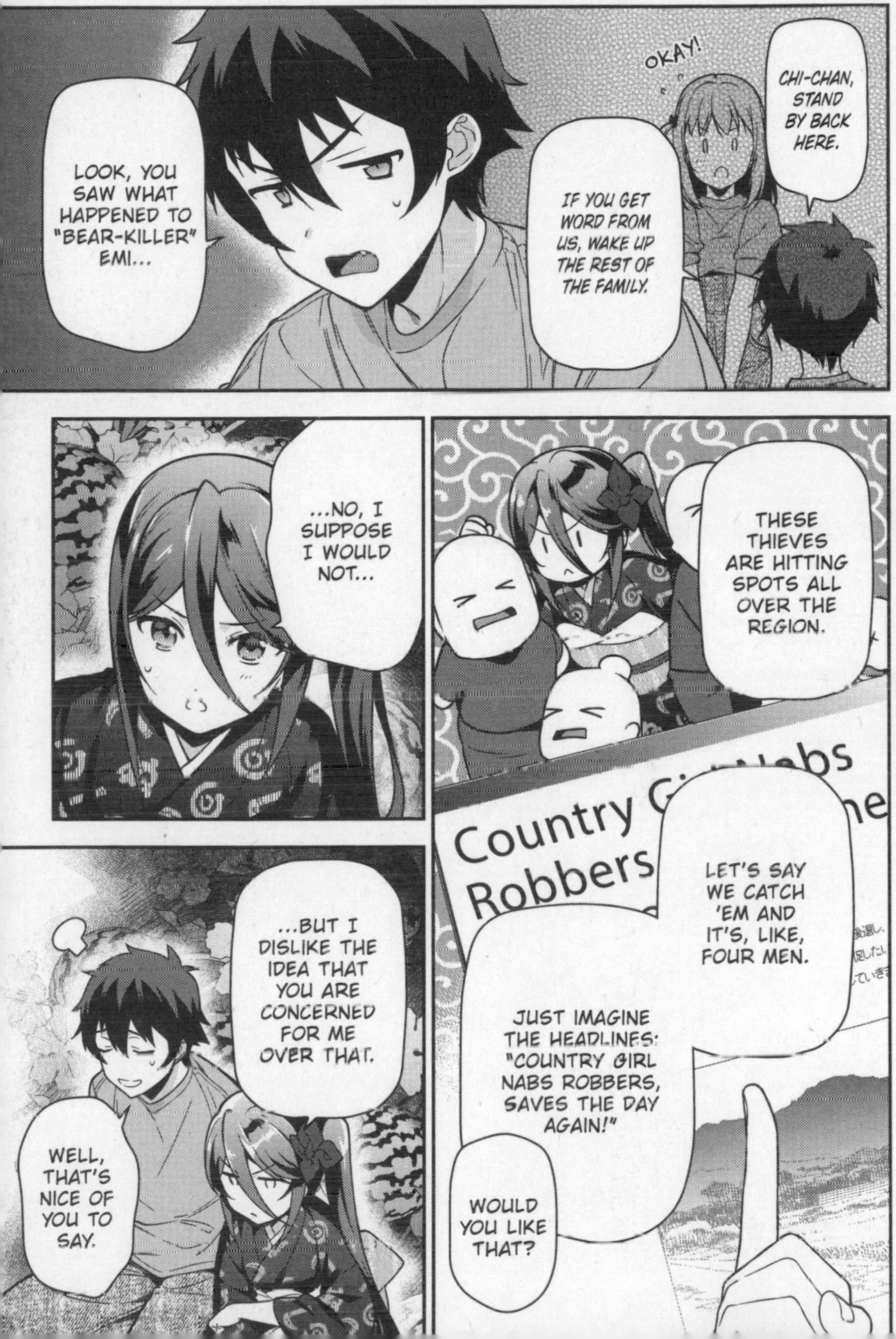
CHI-CHAN, STAND BY BACK HERE.
OKAY!
IF YOU GET WORD FROM US, WAKE UP THE REST OF THE FAMILY.
LOOK, YOU SAW WHAT HAPPENED TO "BEAR-KILLER" EMI...
THESE THIEVES ARE HITTING SPOTS ALL OVER THE REGION.
LET'S SAY WE CATCH 'EM AND IT'S, LIKE, FOUR MEN.
JUST IMAGINE THE HEADLINES: "COUNTRY GIRL NABS ROBBERS, SAVES THE DAY AGAIN!"
WOULD YOU LIKE THAT?
...NO, I SUPPOSE I WOULD NOT...
...BUT I DISLIKE THE IDEA THAT YOU ARE CONCERNED FOR ME OVER THAT.
WELL, THAT'S NICE OF YOU TO SAY.

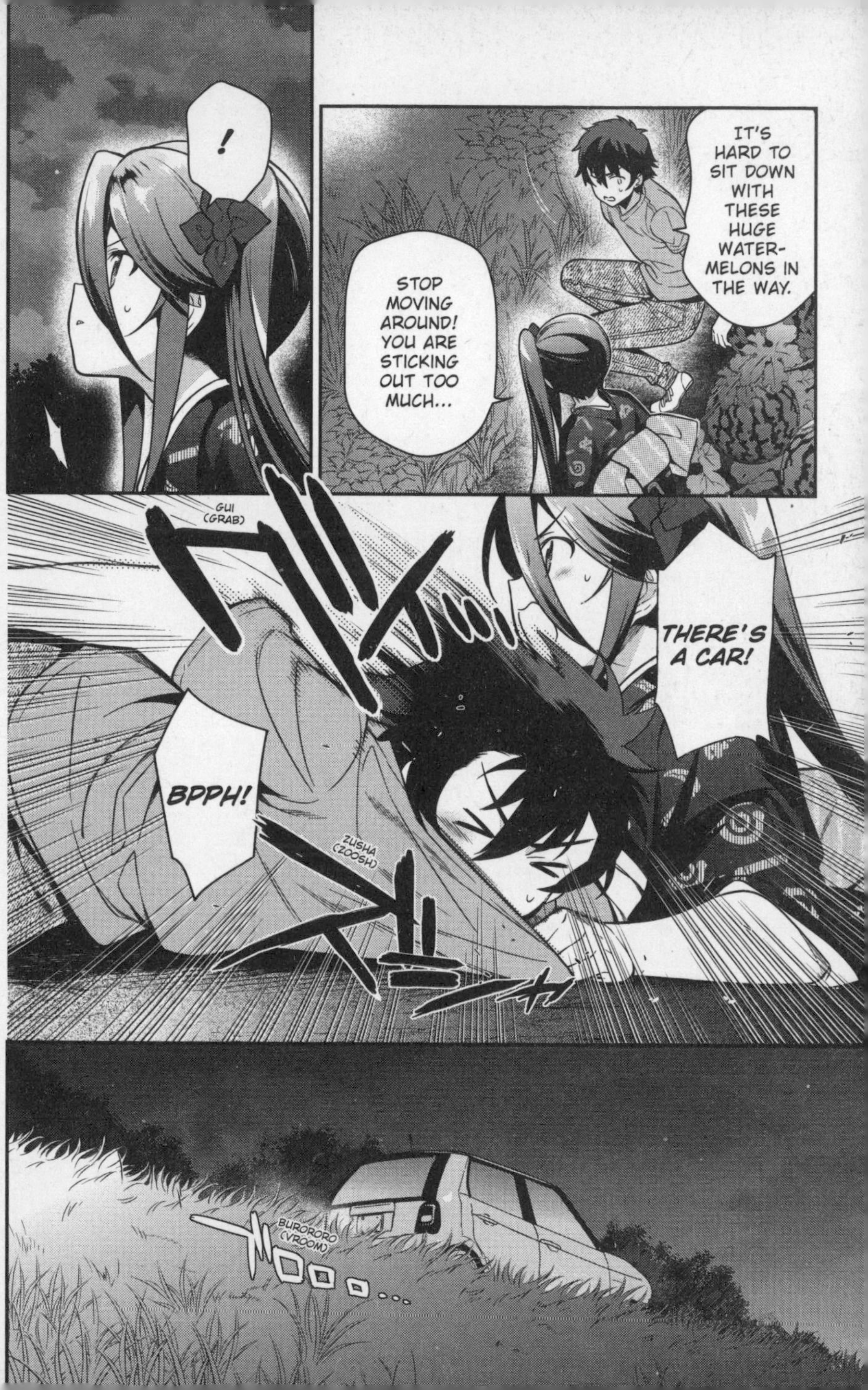
IT'S HARD TO SIT DOWN WITH THESE HUGE WATER-MELONS IN THE WAY.
STOP MOVING AROUND! YOU ARE STICKING OUT TOO MUCH...
!
THERE'S A CAR!
GUI (GRAB)
BPPH!
ZUSHA (ZOOSH)
BURORORO (VROOM)

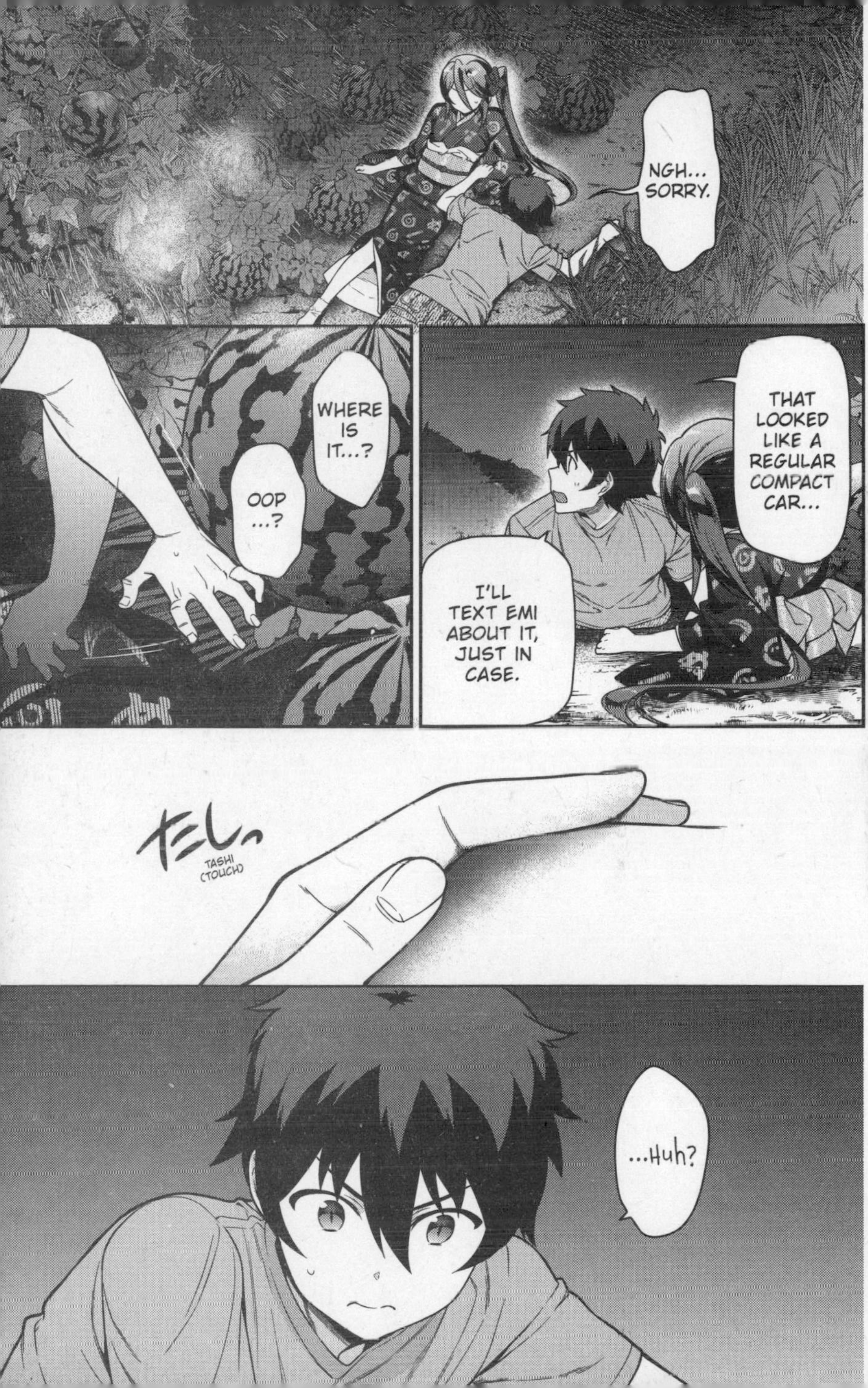
NGH... SORRY.
THAT LOOKED LIKE A REGULAR COMPACT CAR...
I'LL TEXT EMI ABOUT IT, JUST IN CASE.
WHERE IS IT...?
OOP...?
たしっ
TASHI (TOUCH)
...Huh?

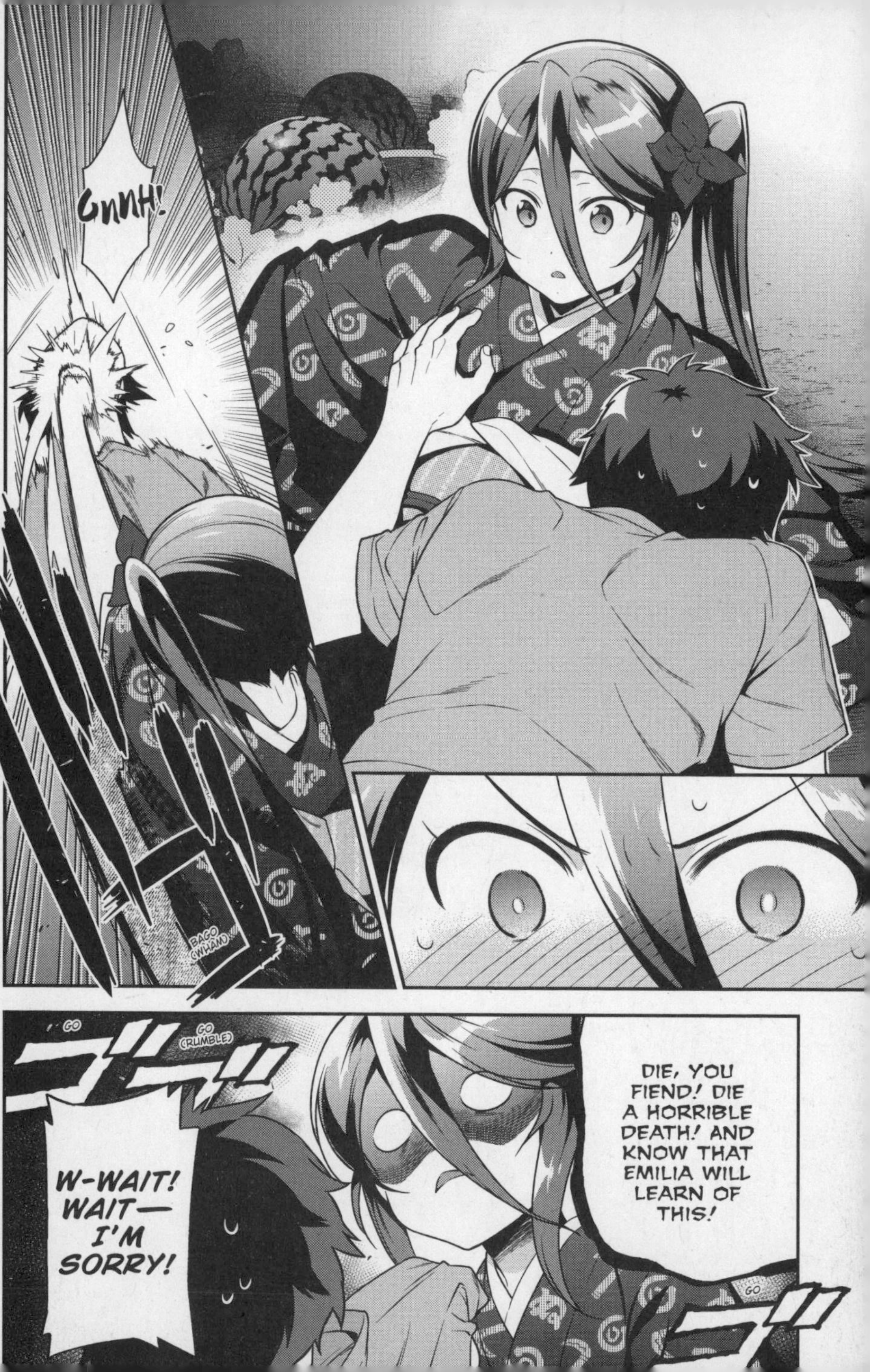
GNNH!
BAGO (WHAM)
DIE, YOU FIEND! DIE A HORRIBLE DEATH! AND KNOW THAT EMILIA WILL LEARN OF THIS!
GO
GO (RUMBLE)
W-WAIT! WAIT— I'M SORRY!
GO

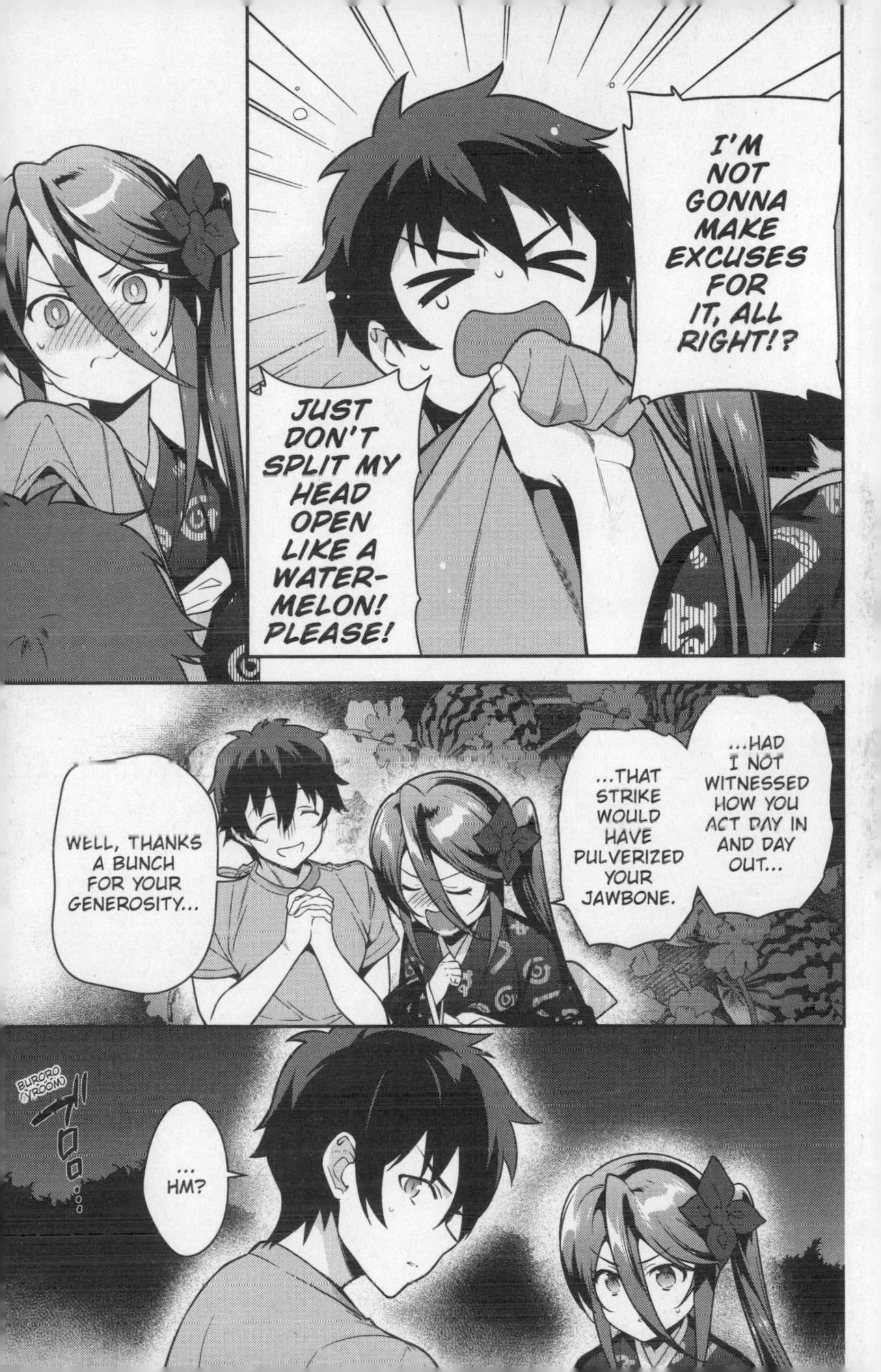
I'M NOT GONNA MAKE EXCUSES FOR IT, ALL RIGHT!?
JUST DON'T SPLIT MY HEAD OPEN LIKE A WATER-MELON! PLEASE!
...HAD I NOT WITNESSED HOW YOU ACT DAY IN AND DAY OUT...
...THAT STRIKE WOULD HAVE PULVERIZED YOUR JAWBONE.
WELL, THANKS A BUNCH FOR YOUR GENEROSITY...
... HM?
BURORO (VROOM)

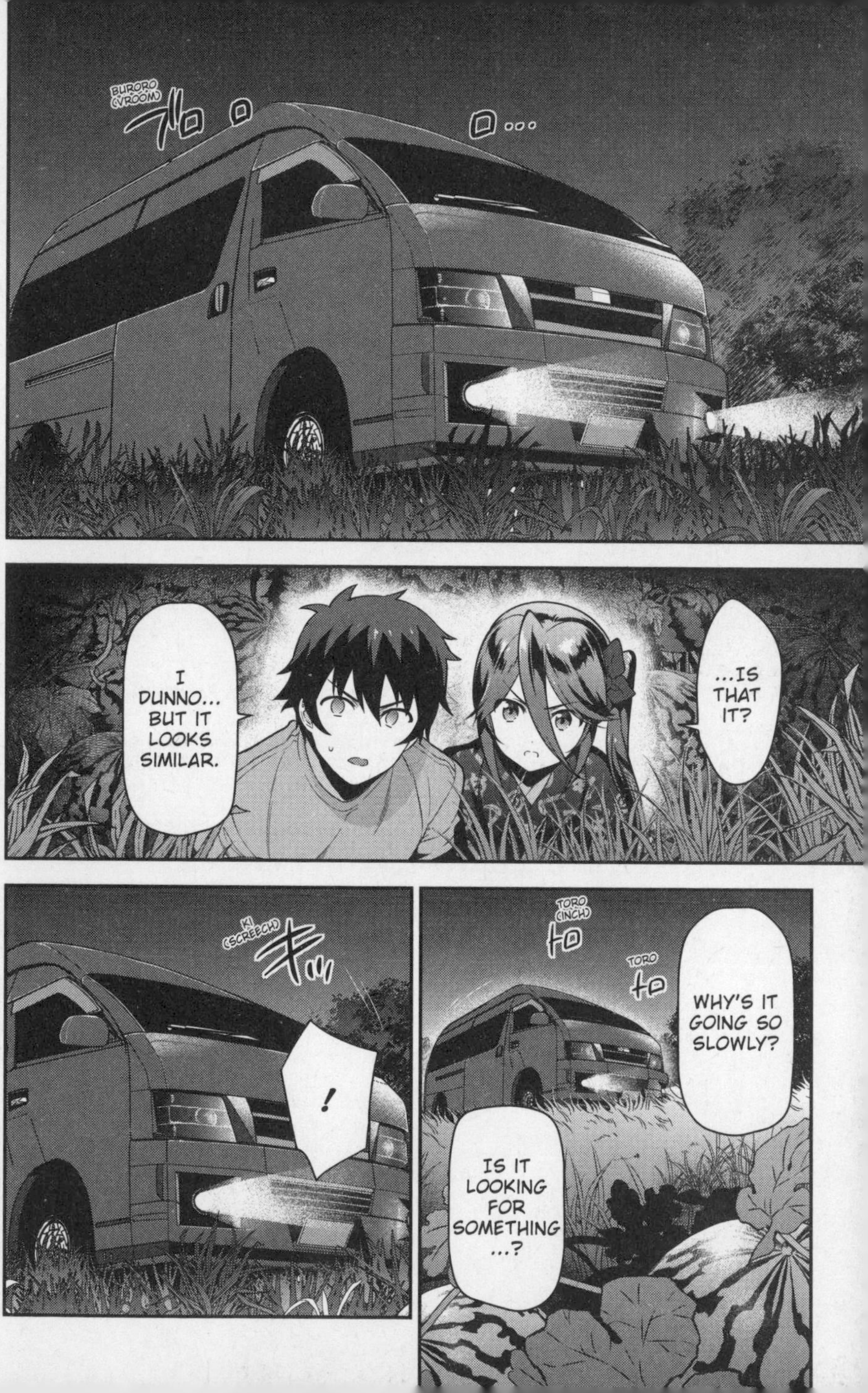
BURORO (VROOM)
...IS THAT IT?
I DUNNO... BUT IT LOOKS SIMILAR.
TORO (INCH)
TORO
WHY'S IT GOING SO SLOWLY?
IS IT LOOKING FOR SOMETHING ...?
KI (SCREECH)
!

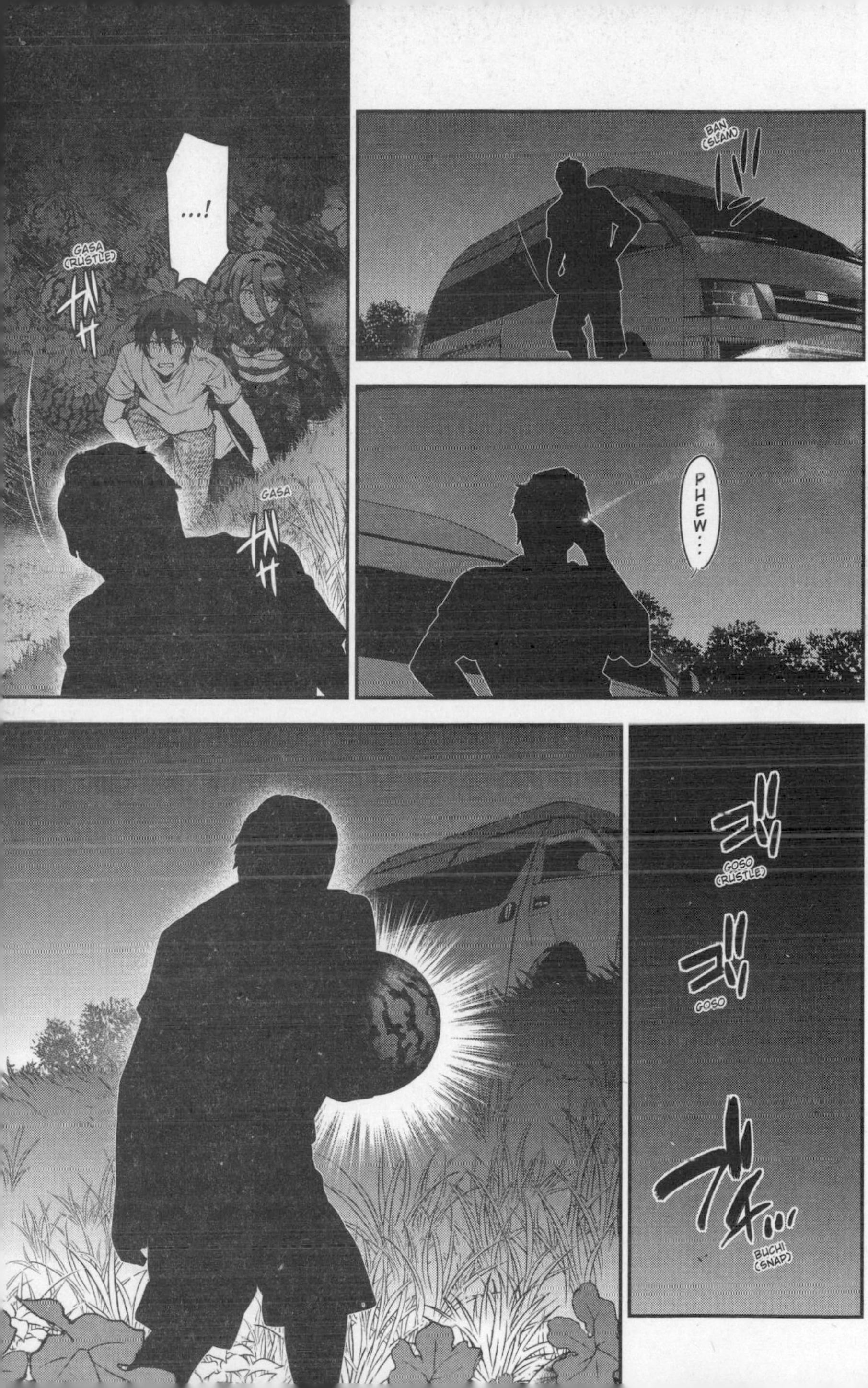
BAN (SLAM)
PHEW...
...!
GASA (RUSTLE)
GASA
GOSO (RUSTLE)
GOSO
BUCHI (SNAP)

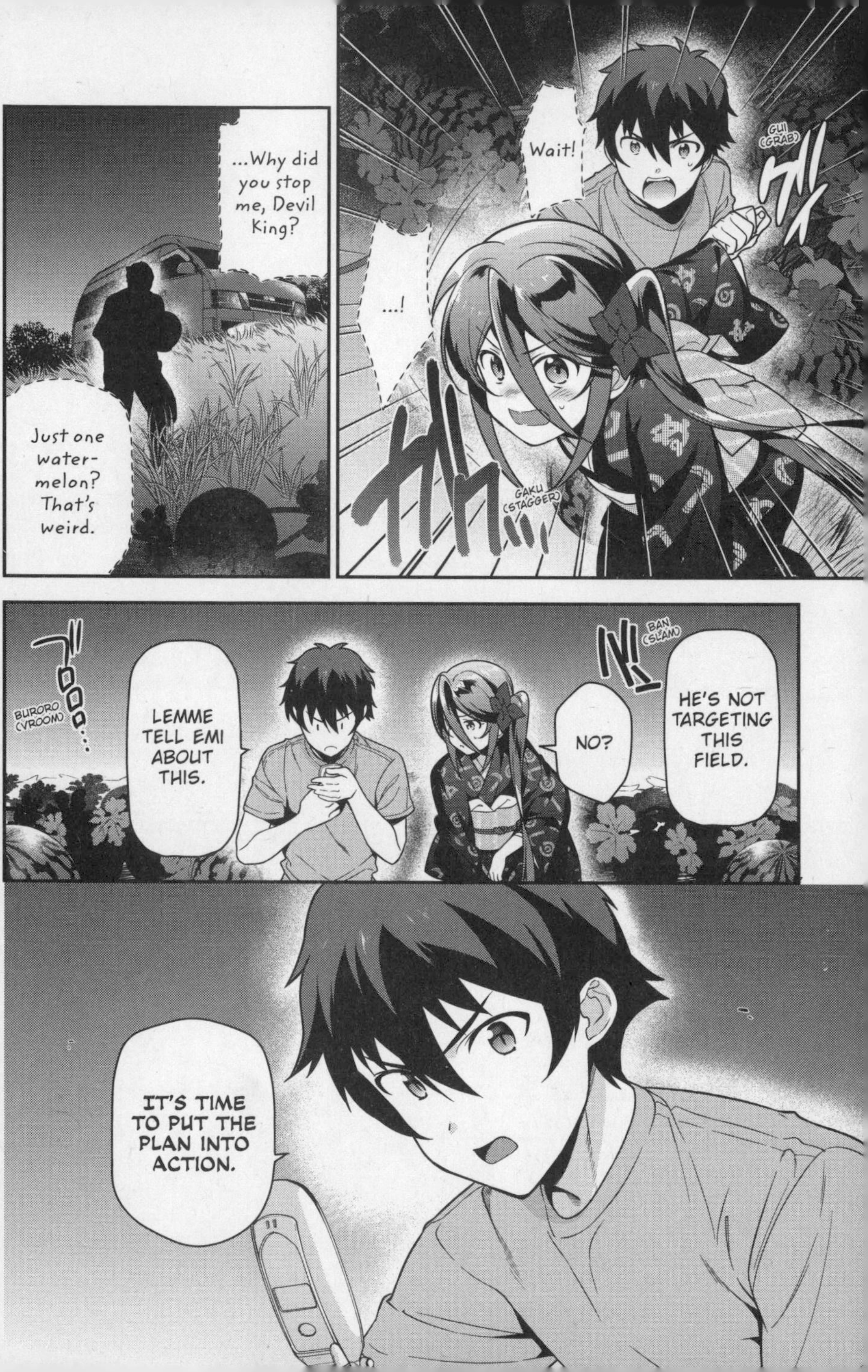
Wait!
...!
GUI (GRAB)
GAKU (STAGGER)
...Why did you stop me, Devil King?
Just one water-melon? That's weird.
BAN (SLAM)
HE'S NOT TARGETING THIS FIELD.
NO?
LEMME TELL EMI ABOUT THIS.
BURORO (VROOM)
IT'S TIME TO PUT THE PLAN INTO ACTION.

Suzuno
Kamazuki

THE DEVIL IS A PART-TIMER!

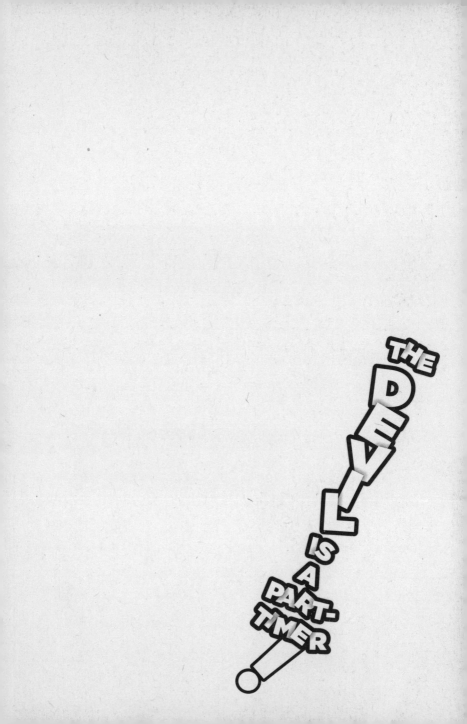

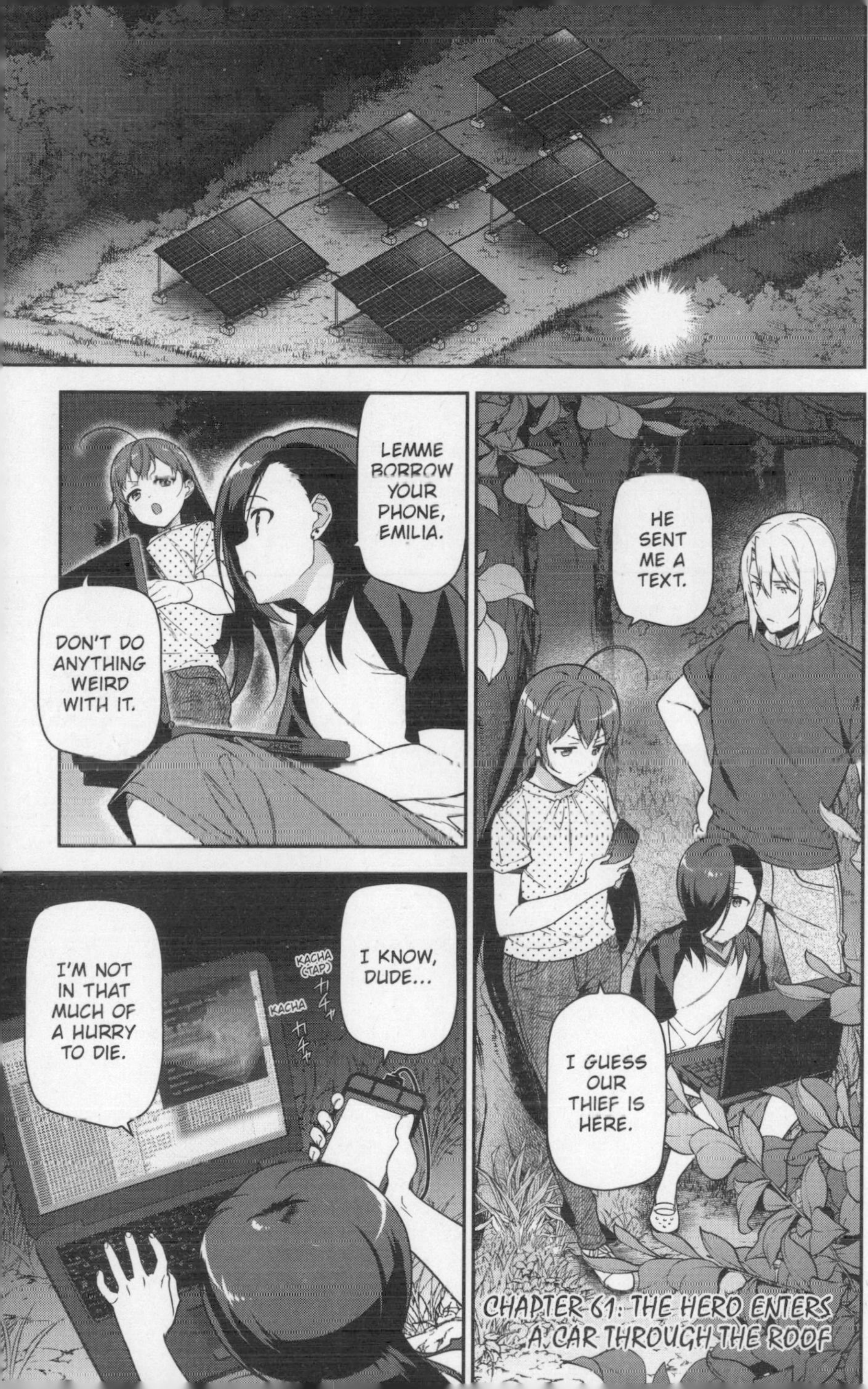
HE SENT ME A TEXT.
I GUESS OUR THIEF IS HERE.
CHAPTER 61: THE HERO ENTERS A CAR THROUGH THE ROOF
LEMME BORROW YOUR PHONE, EMILIA.
DON'T DO ANYTHING WEIRD WITH IT.
I KNOW, DUDE...
KACHA (TAP) カチャ
KACHA カチャ
I'M NOT IN THAT MUCH OF A HURRY TO DIE.

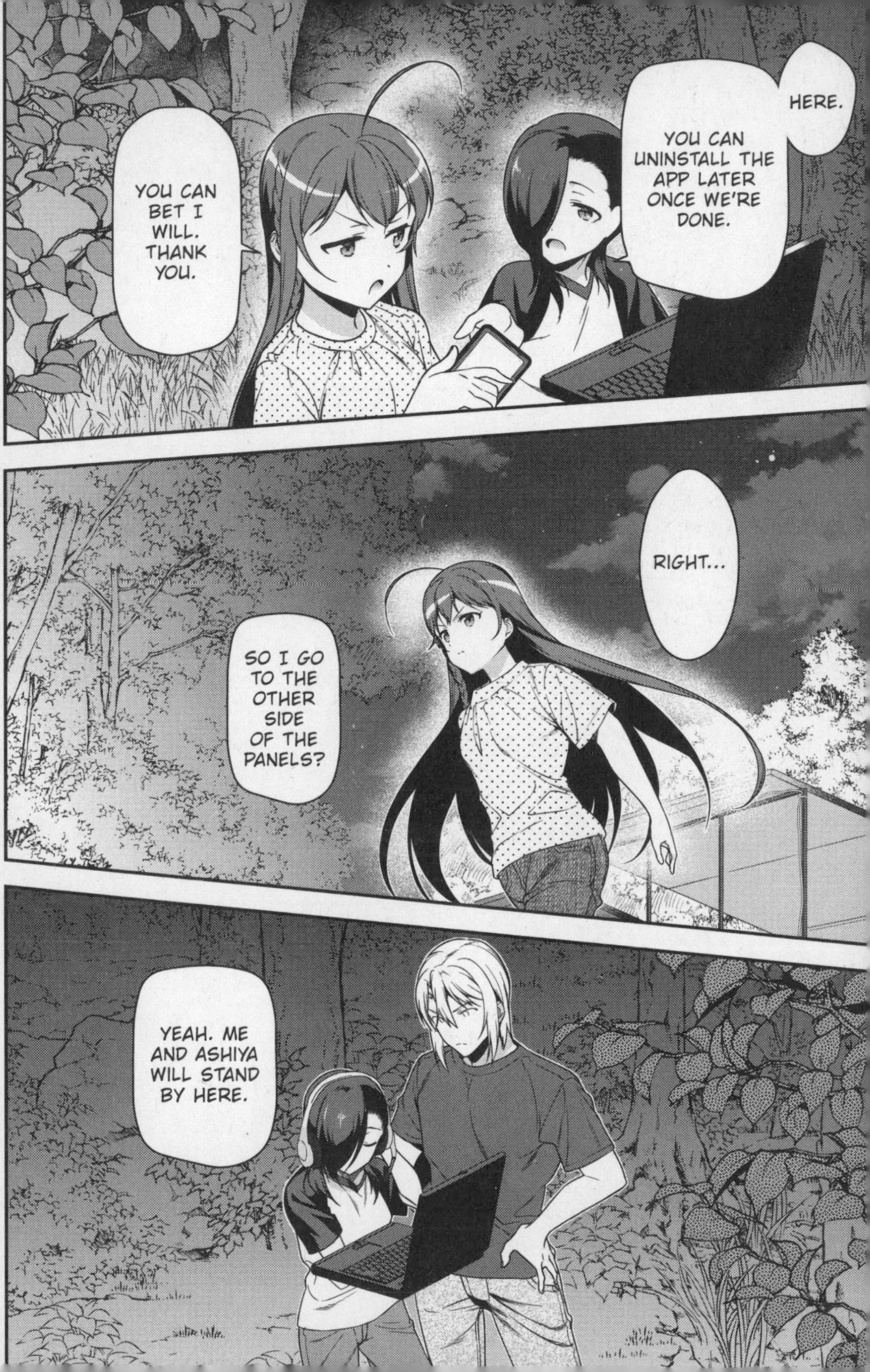
HERE.
YOU CAN UNINSTALL THE APP LATER ONCE WE'RE DONE.
YOU CAN BET I WILL. THANK YOU.
RIGHT...
SO I GO TO THE OTHER SIDE OF THE PANELS?
YEAH. ME AND ASHIYA WILL STAND BY HERE.

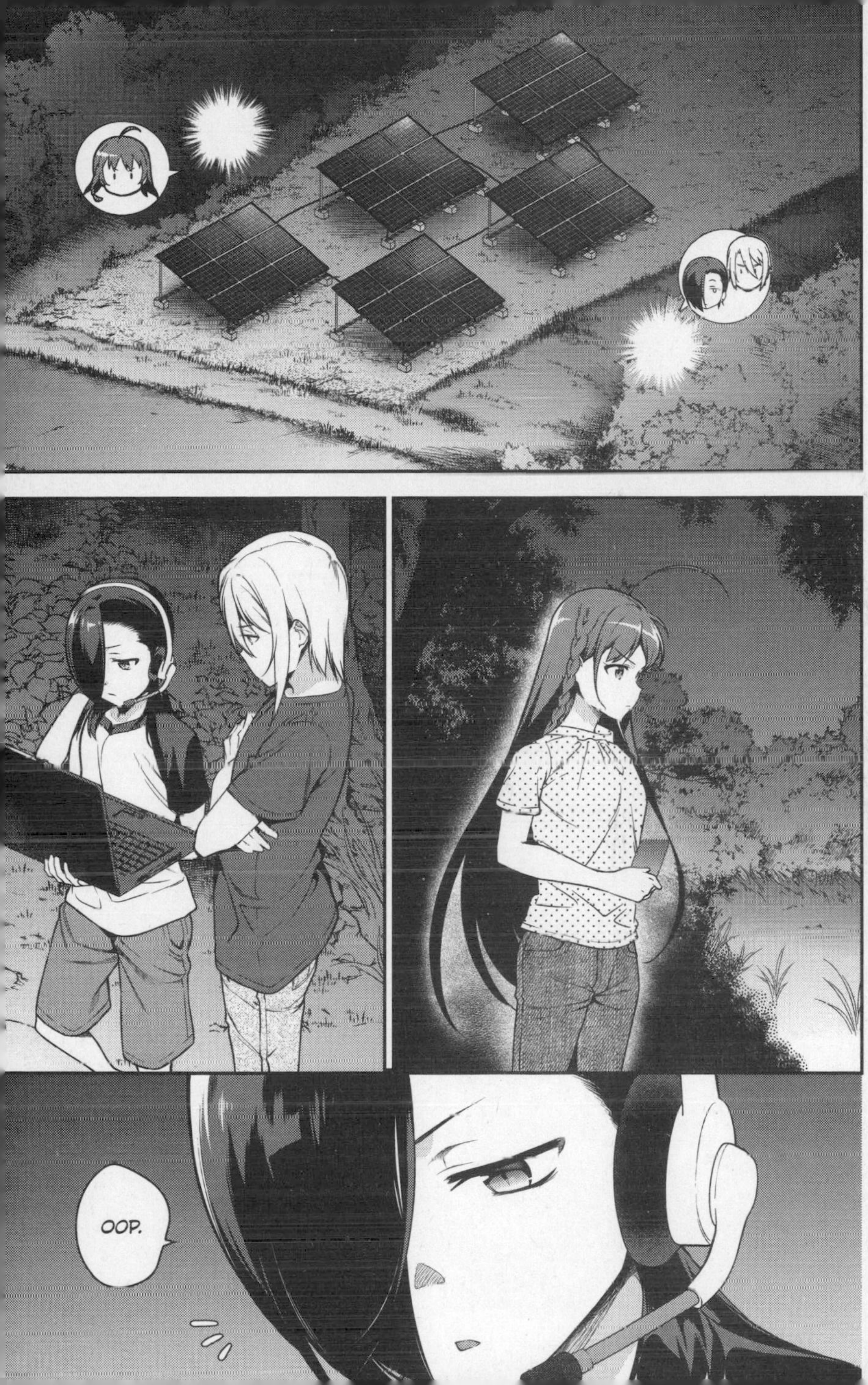
OOP.

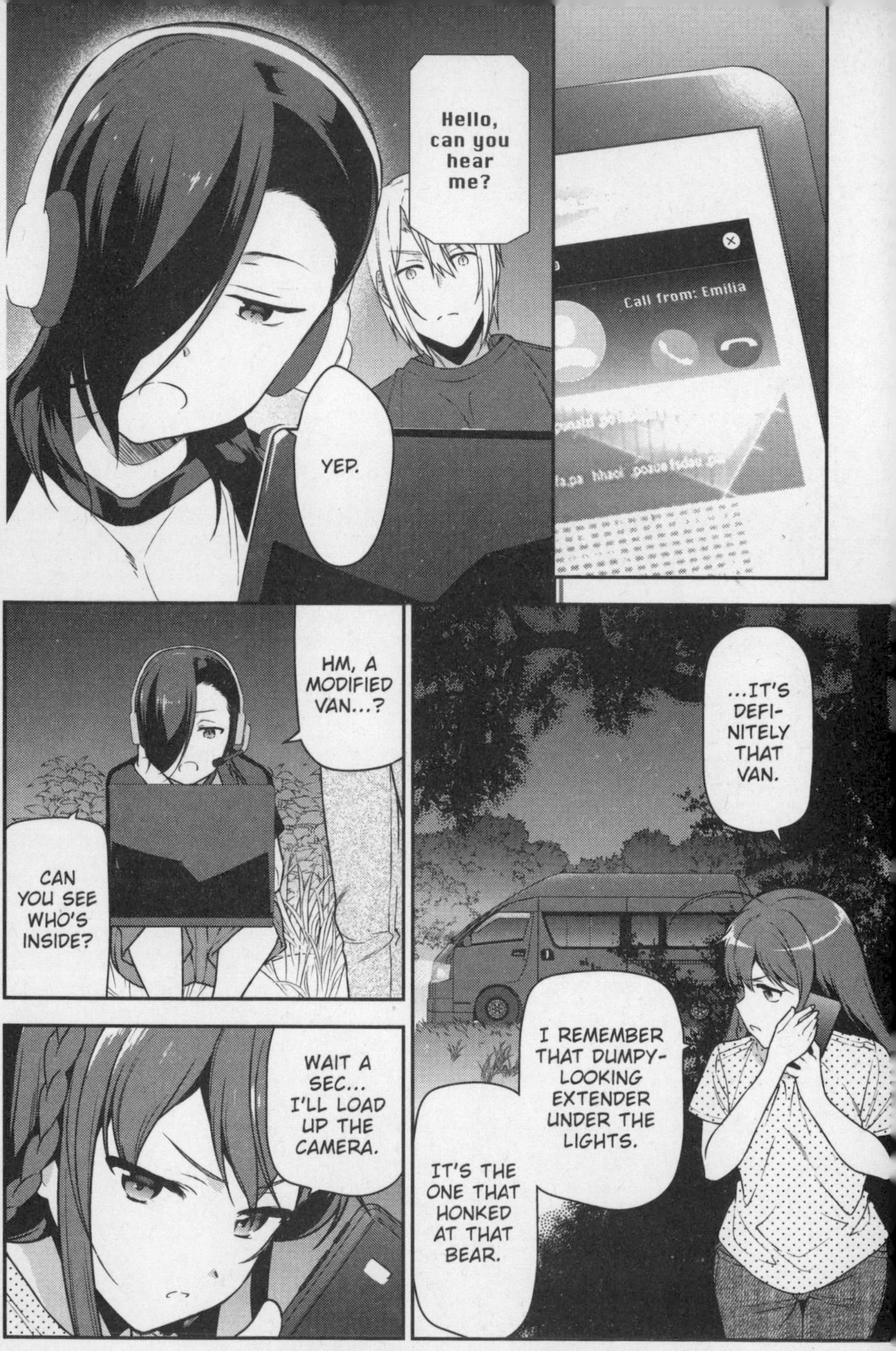
Call from: Emilia
Hello, can you hear me?
YEP.
...IT'S DEFI-NITELY THAT VAN.
I REMEMBER THAT DUMPY-LOOKING EXTENDER UNDER THE LIGHTS.
IT'S THE ONE THAT HONKED AT THAT BEAR.
HM, A MODIFIED VAN...?
CAN YOU SEE WHO'S INSIDE?
WAIT A SEC... I'LL LOAD UP THE CAMERA.

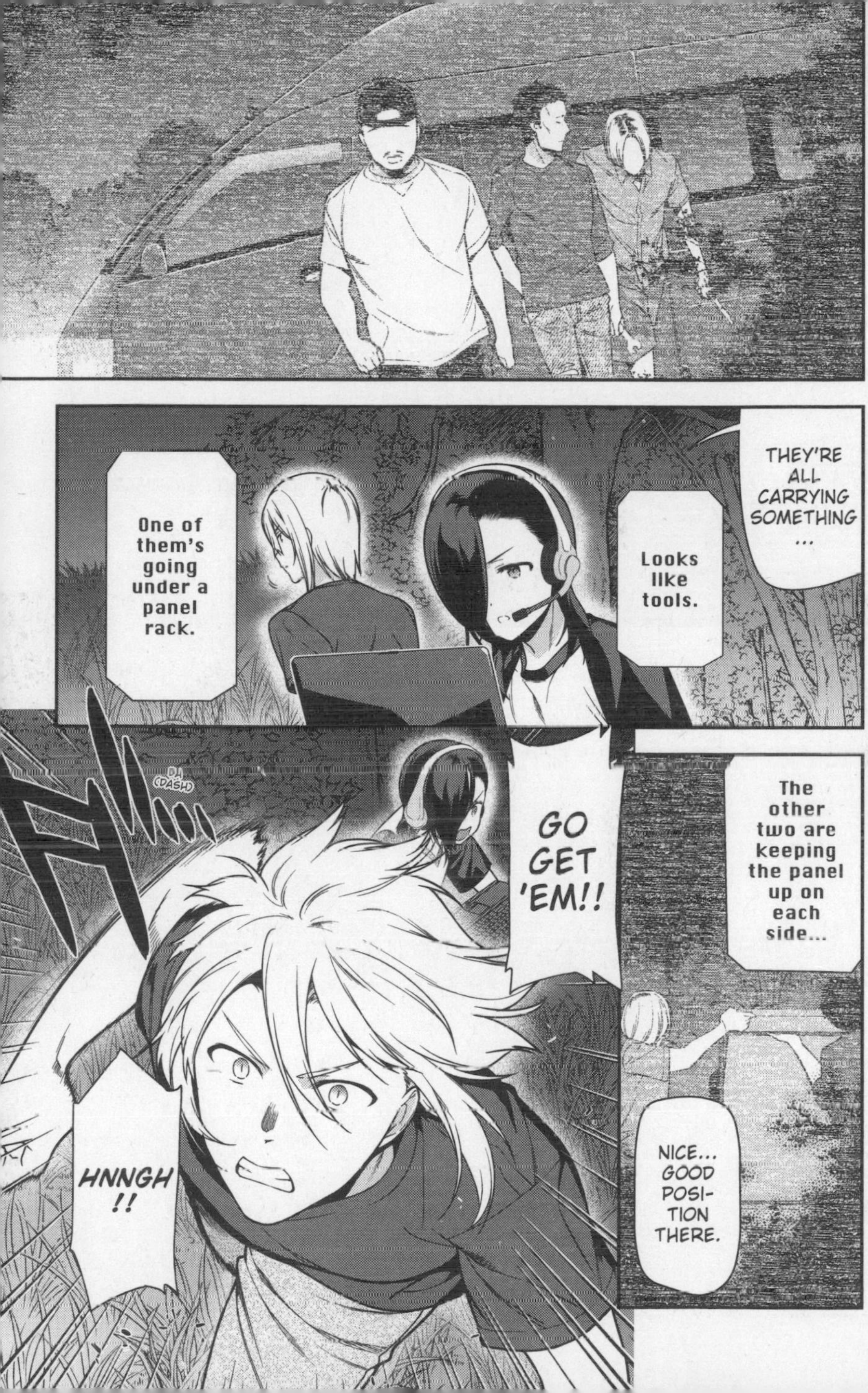
THEY'RE ALL CARRYING SOMETHING...
Looks like tools.
One of them's going under a panel rack.
The other two are keeping the panel up on each side...
NICE... GOOD POSI-TION THERE.
GO GET 'EM!!
DA (DASH)
HNNGH!!

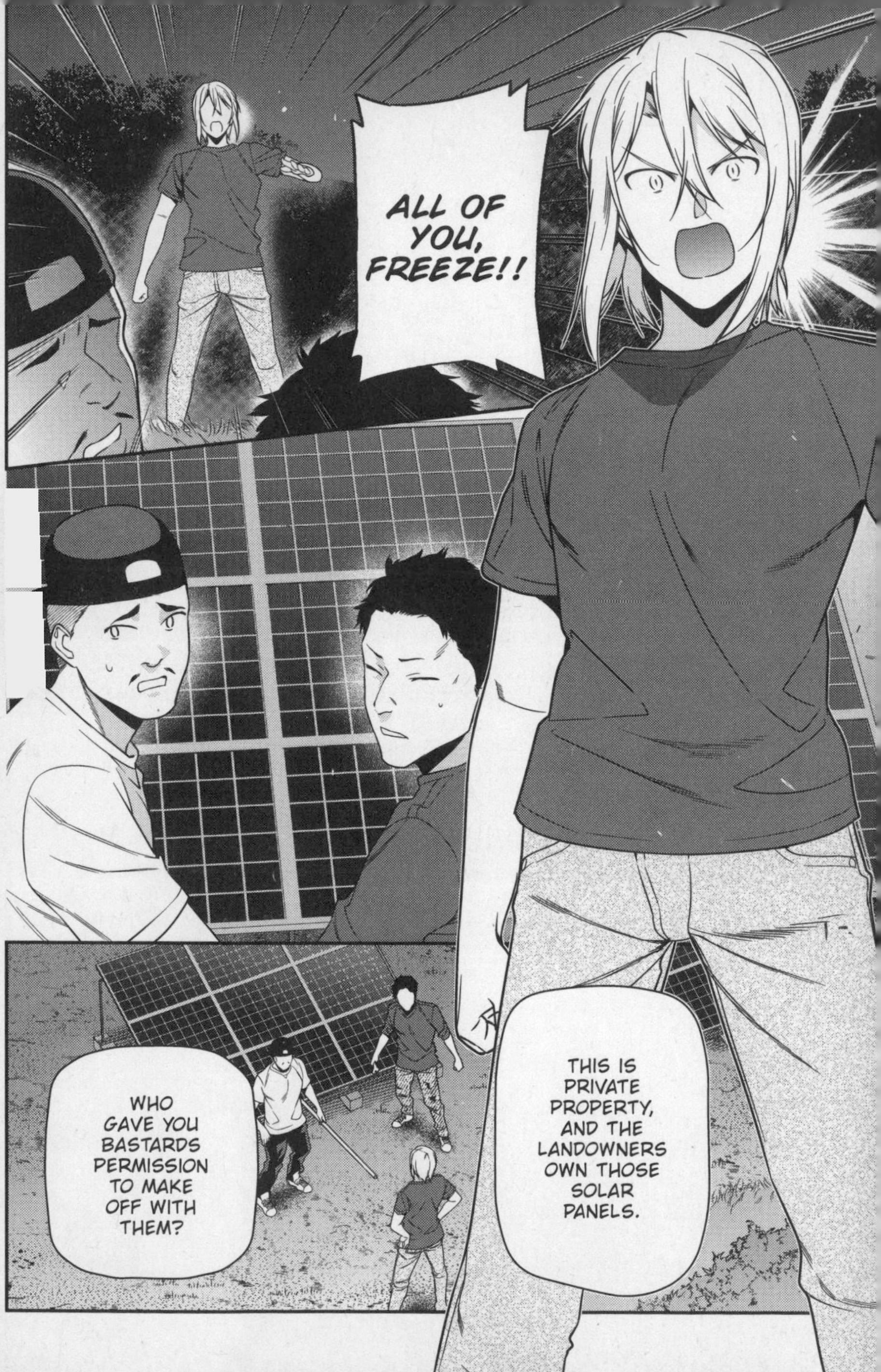
ALL OF YOU, FREEZE!!
THIS IS PRIVATE PROPERTY, AND THE LANDOWNERS OWN THOSE SOLAR PANELS.
WHO GAVE YOU BASTARDS PERMISSION TO MAKE OFF WITH THEM?

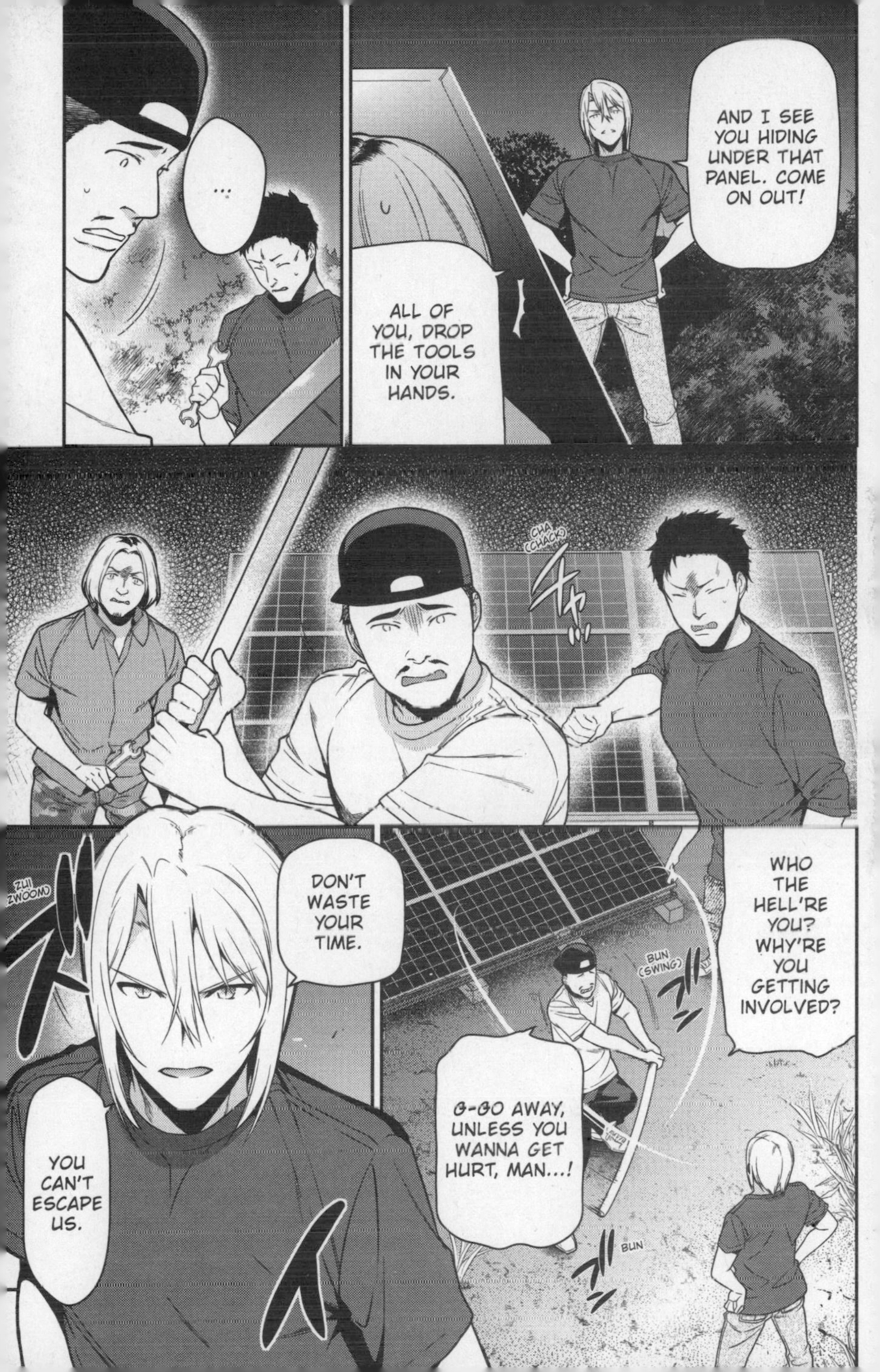
AND I SEE YOU HIDING UNDER THAT PANEL. COME ON OUT!
ALL OF YOU, DROP THE TOOLS IN YOUR HANDS.
...
CHA (CHACK)
WHO THE HELL'RE YOU? WHY'RE YOU GETTING INVOLVED?
BUN (SWING)
G-GO AWAY, UNLESS YOU WANNA GET HURT, MAN...!
BUN
ZUI (ZWOOM)
DON'T WASTE YOUR TIME.
YOU CAN'T ESCAPE US.

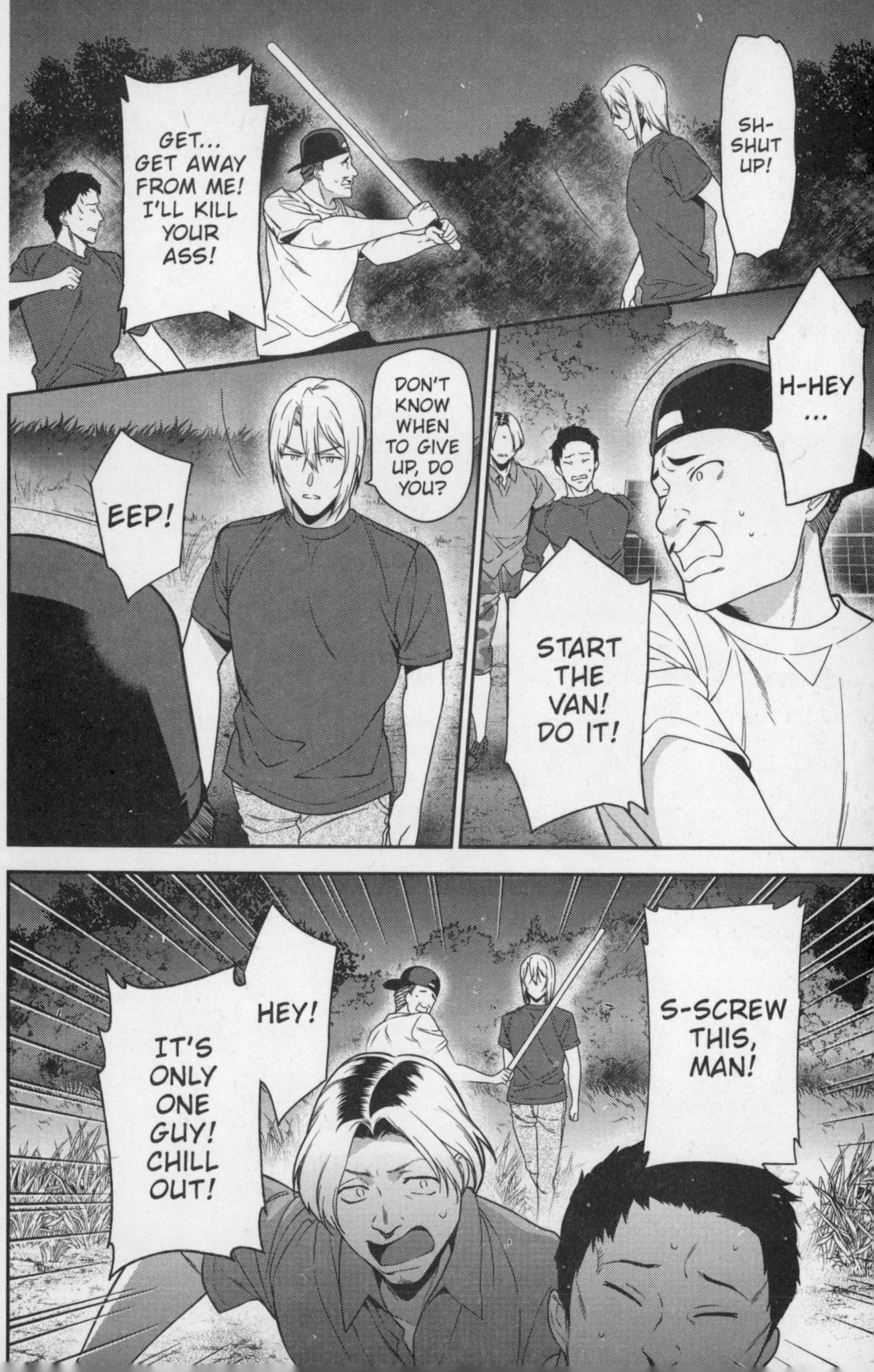
SH-SHUT UP!
GET... GET AWAY FROM ME! I'LL KILL YOUR ASS!
H-HEY...
START THE VAN! DO IT!
DON'T KNOW WHEN TO GIVE UP, DO YOU?
EEP!
S-SCREW THIS, MAN!
HEY!
IT'S ONLY ONE GUY! CHILL OUT!

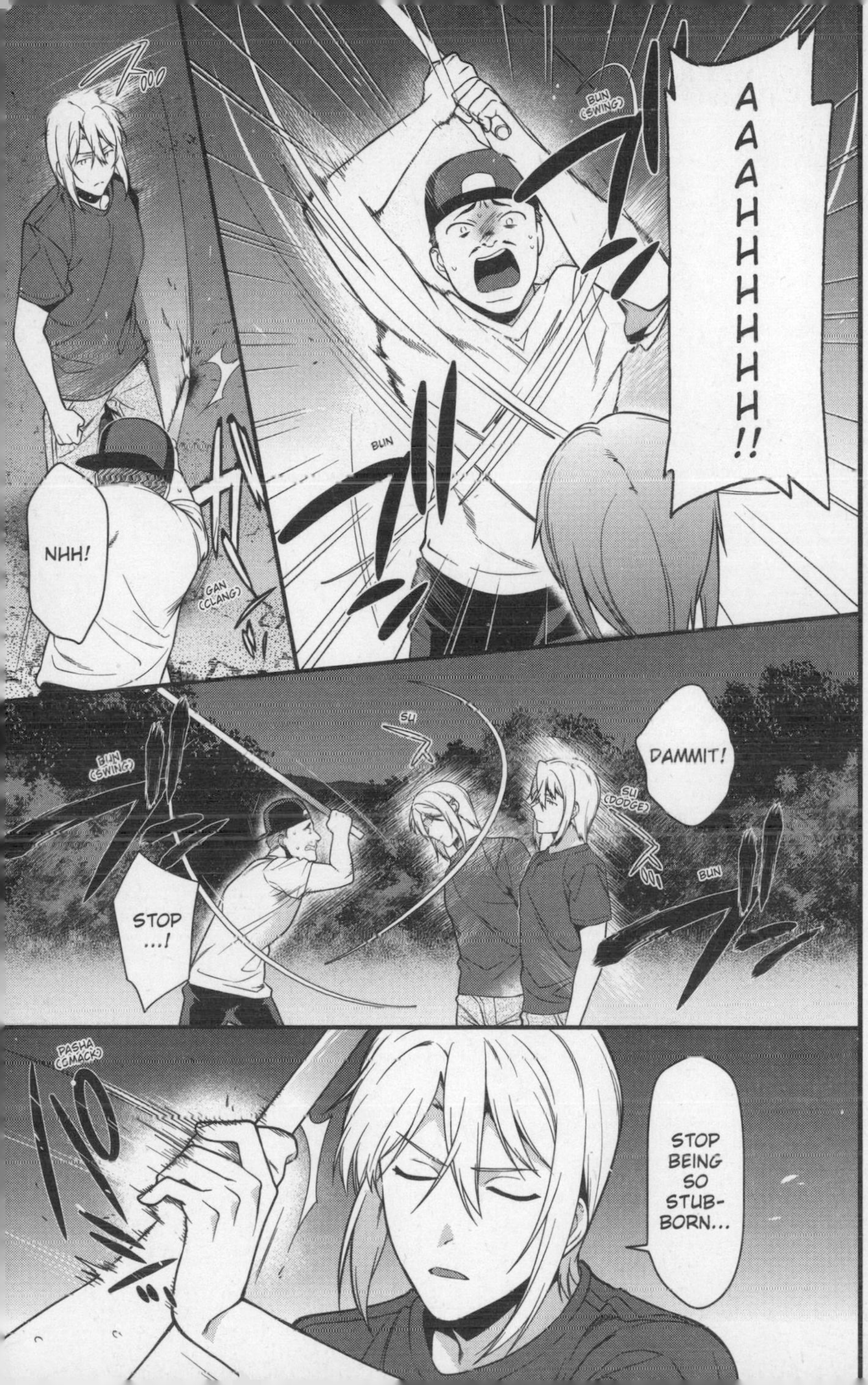
AAAHHHHHH!!
BUN (SWING)
BUN
NHH!
GAN (CLANG)
DAMMIT!
SU (DODGE)
BUN
SU
BUN (SWING)
STOP ...!
STOP BEING SO STUB-BORN...
PASHA (SMACK)

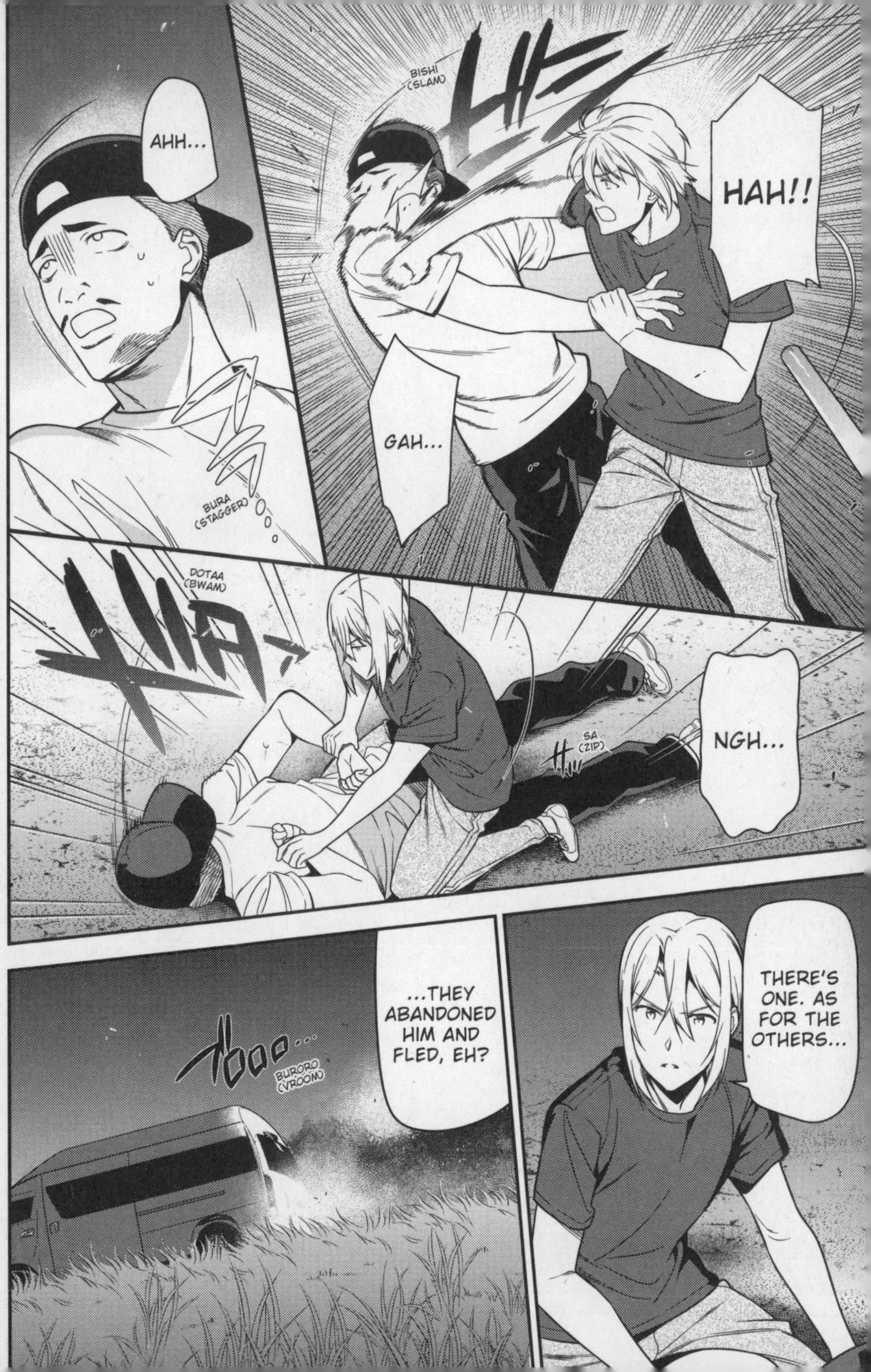
HAH!!
BISHI (SLAM)
GAH...
AHH...
BURA (STAGGER)
NGH...
SA (ZIP)
DOTAA (BWAM)
THERE'S ONE. AS FOR THE OTHERS...
...THEY ABANDONED HIM AND FLED, EH?
BURORO (VROOM)

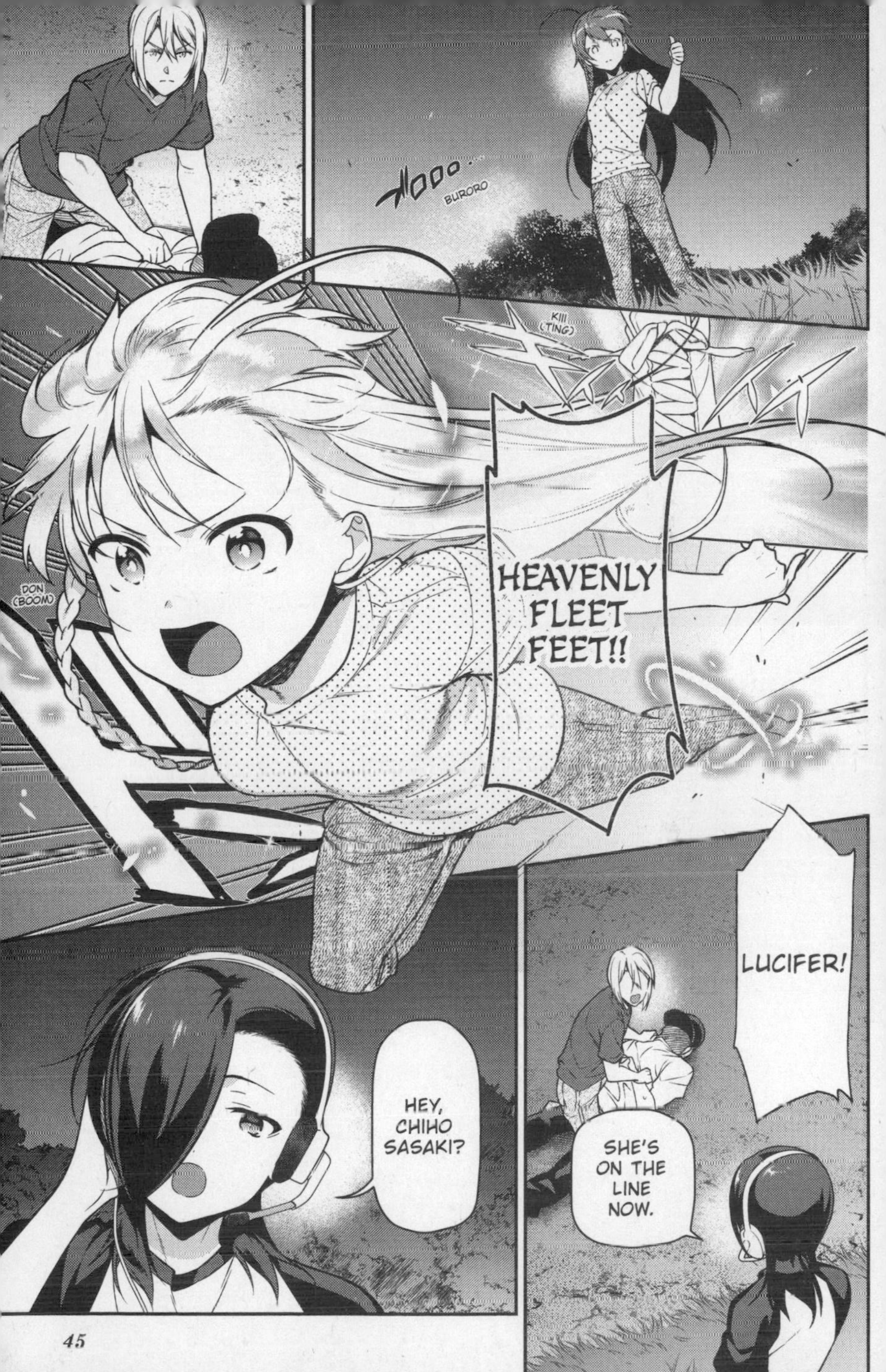
BURORO
KIII (TING)
HEAVENLY FLEET FEET!!
DON (BOOM)
LUCIFER!
SHE'S ON THE LINE NOW.
HEY, CHIHO SASAKI?

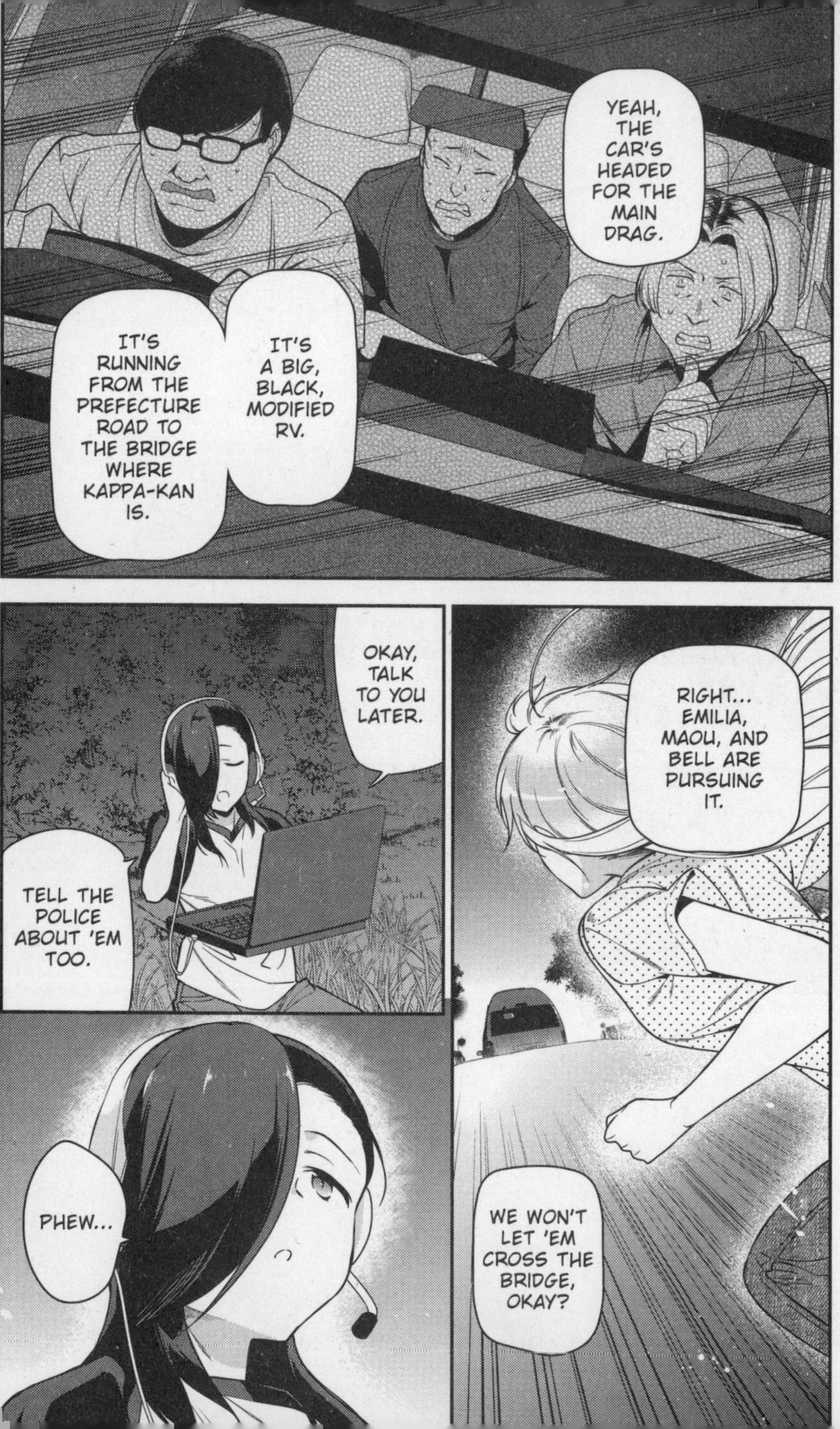
YEAH, THE CAR'S HEADED FOR THE MAIN DRAG.
IT'S A BIG, BLACK, MODIFIED RV.
IT'S RUNNING FROM THE PREFECTURE ROAD TO THE BRIDGE WHERE KAPPA-KAN IS.
RIGHT... EMILIA, MAOU, AND BELL ARE PURSUING IT.
WE WON'T LET 'EM CROSS THE BRIDGE, OKAY?
OKAY, TALK TO YOU LATER.
TELL THE POLICE ABOUT 'EM TOO.
PHEW...

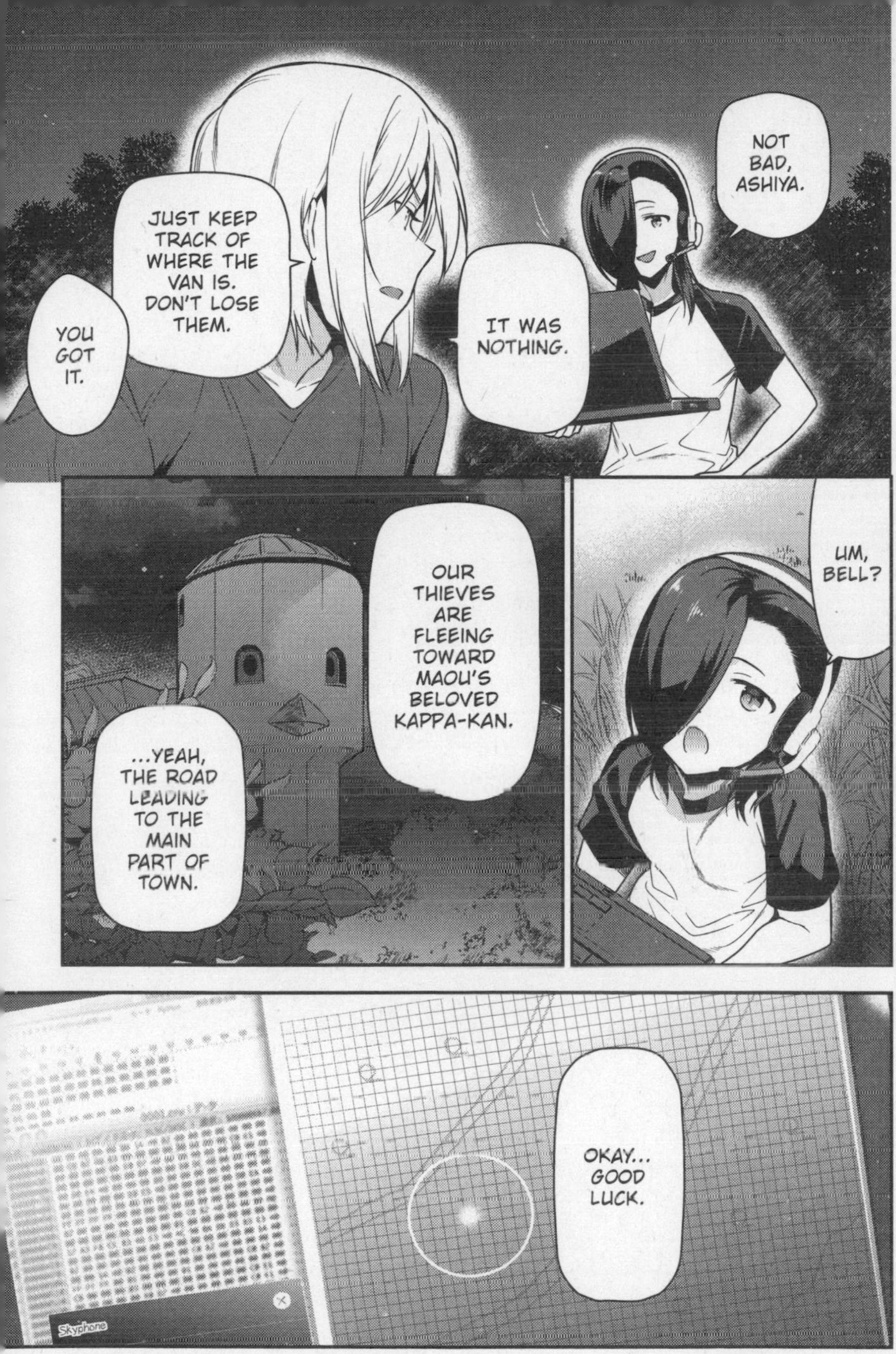
NOT BAD, ASHIYA.
IT WAS NOTHING.
JUST KEEP TRACK OF WHERE THE VAN IS. DON'T LOSE THEM.
YOU GOT IT.
UM, BELL?
OUR THIEVES ARE FLEEING TOWARD MAOU'S BELOVED KAPPA-KAN.
...YEAH, THE ROAD LEADING TO THE MAIN PART OF TOWN.
OKAY... GOOD LUCK.
Skyphone

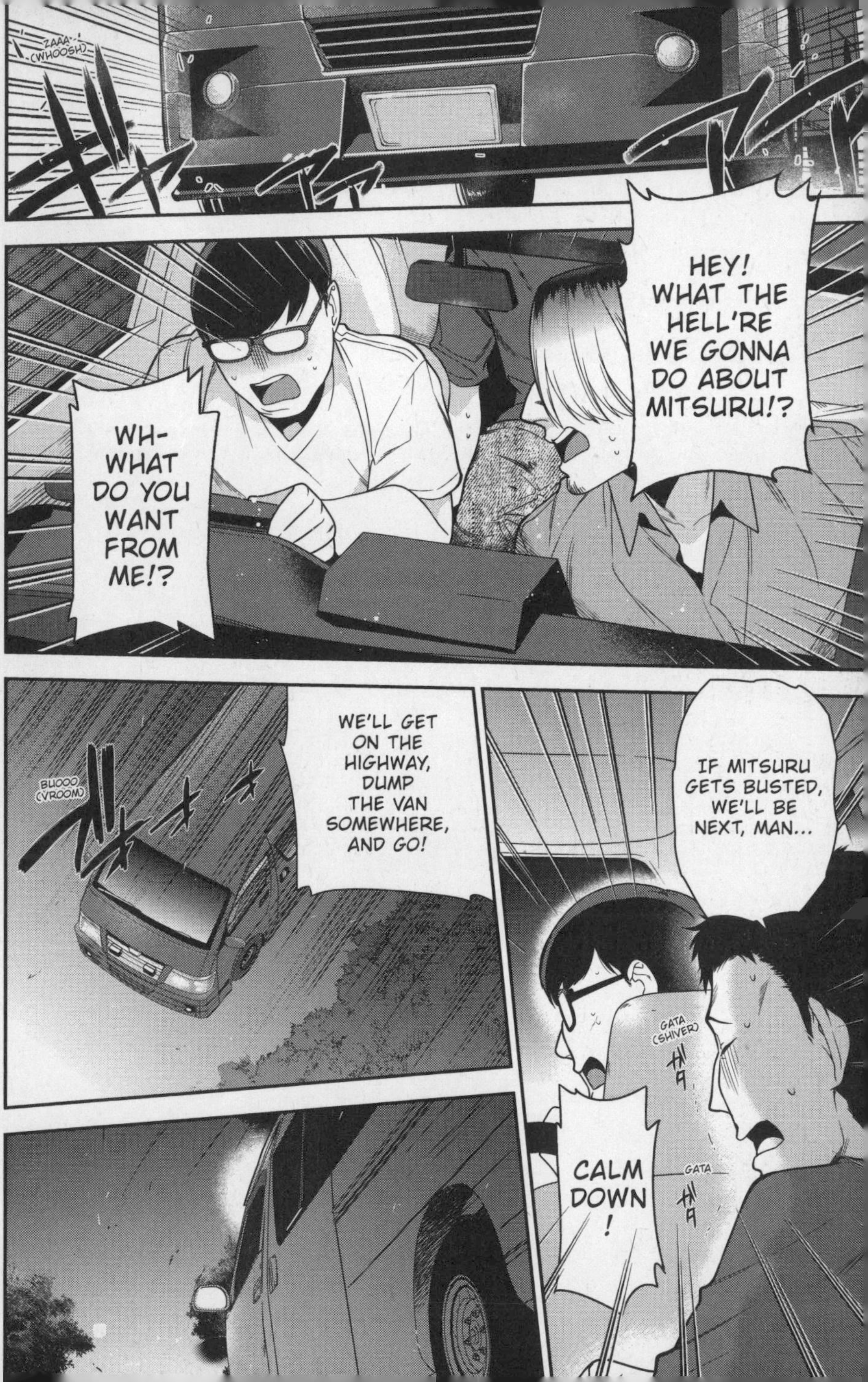
ZAAA (WHOOSH)
HEY! WHAT THE HELL'RE WE GONNA DO ABOUT MITSURU!?
WH-WHAT DO YOU WANT FROM ME!?
IF MITSURU GETS BUSTED, WE'LL BE NEXT, MAN...
GATA (SHIVER)
GATA
CALM DOWN!
WE'LL GET ON THE HIGHWAY, DUMP THE VAN SOMEWHERE, AND GO!
BUOOO (VROOM)

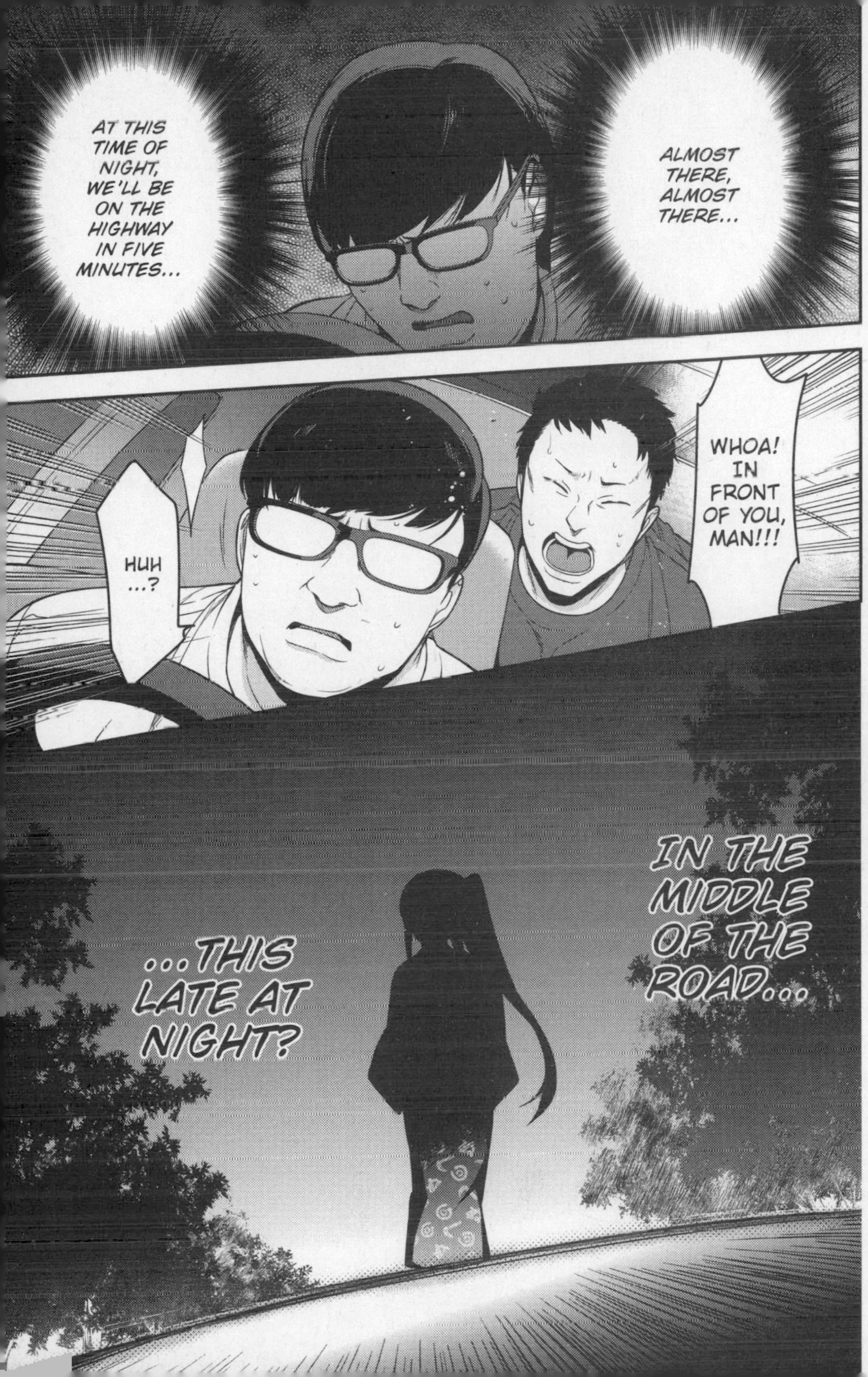
ALMOST THERE, ALMOST THERE...
AT THIS TIME OF NIGHT, WE'LL BE ON THE HIGHWAY IN FIVE MINUTES...
WHOA! IN FRONT OF YOU, MAN!!!
HUH ...?
IN THE MIDDLE OF THE ROAD...
...THIS LATE AT NIGHT?

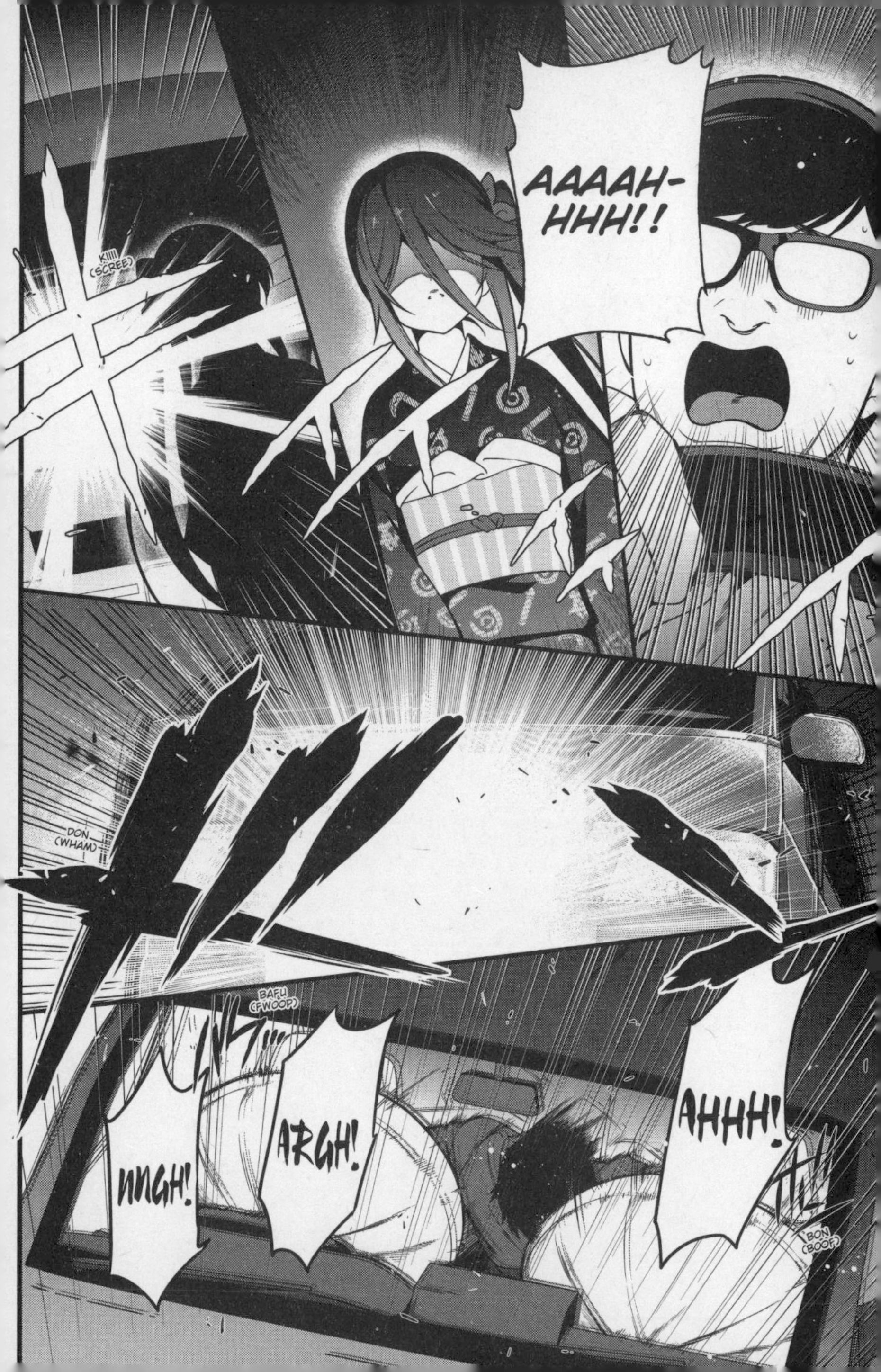
AAAAH-HHH!!
KIIII (SCREE)
DON (WHAM)
BAFU (FWOOP)
AHHH!
BON (BOOP)
ARGH!
UNGH!

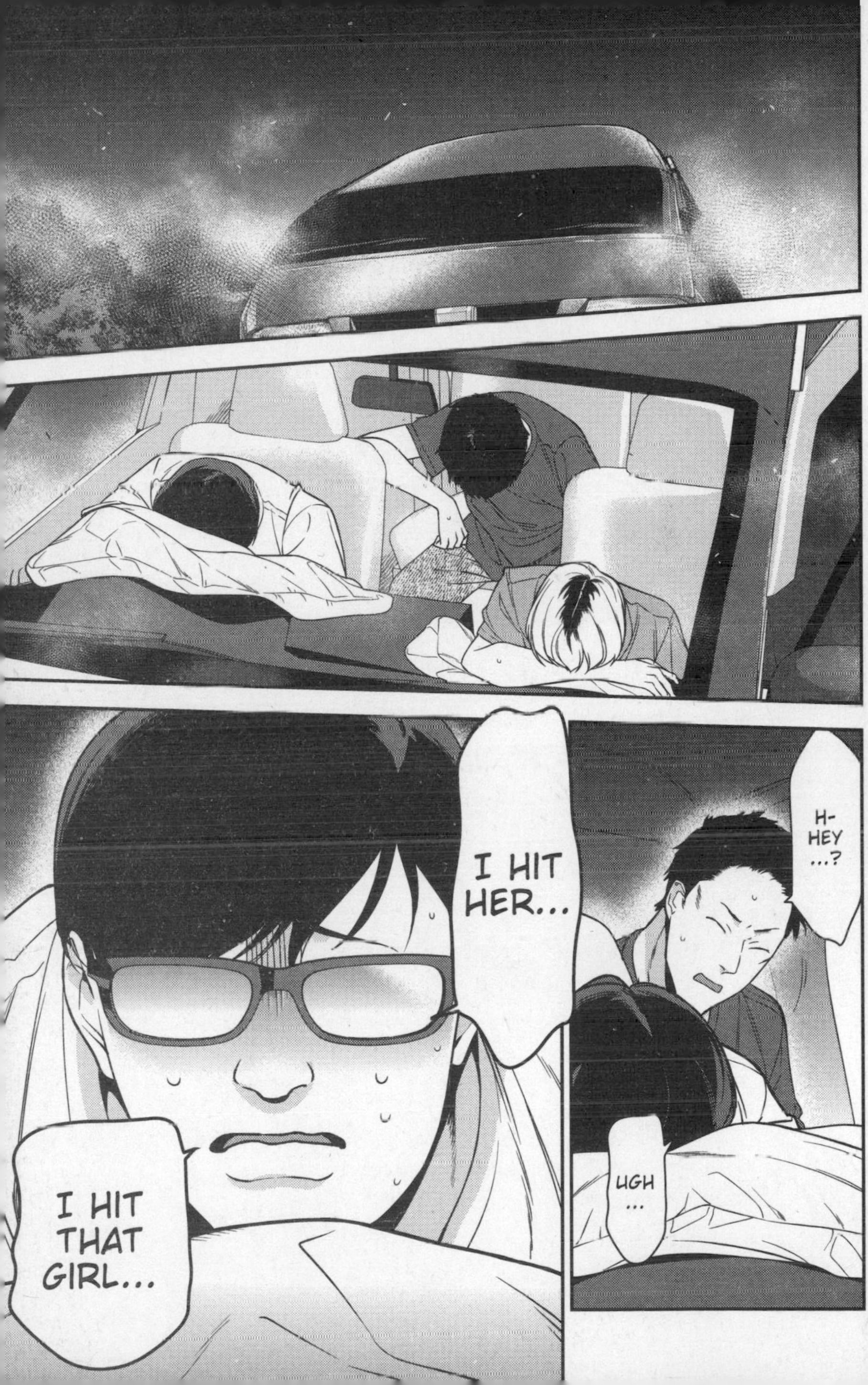
H-HEY ...?
UGH ...
I HIT HER...
I HIT THAT GIRL...

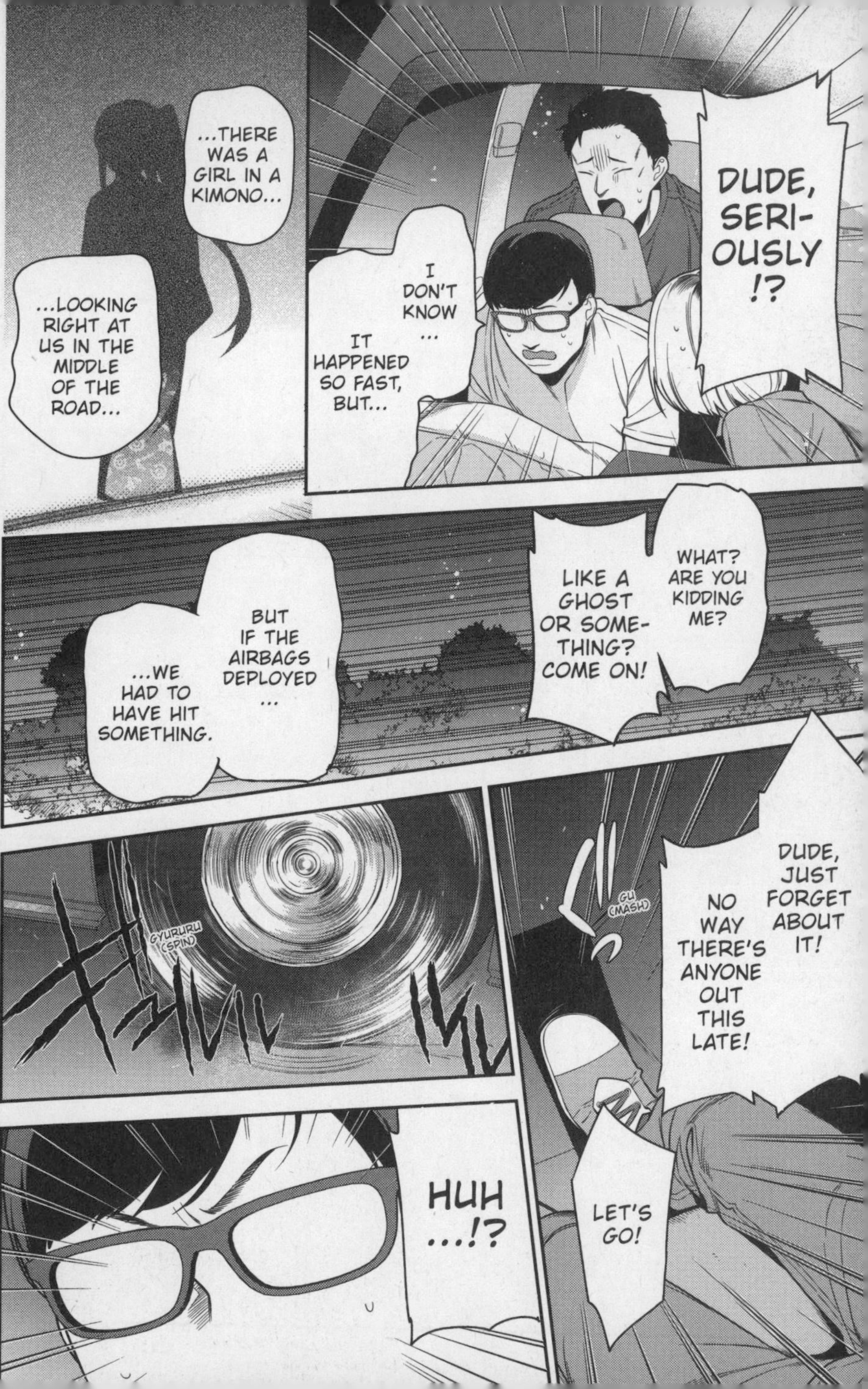
DUDE, SERIOUSLY!?
I DON'T KNOW...
IT HAPPENED SO FAST, BUT...
...THERE WAS A GIRL IN A KIMONO...
...LOOKING RIGHT AT US IN THE MIDDLE OF THE ROAD...
WHAT? ARE YOU KIDDING ME?
LIKE A GHOST OR SOMETHING? COME ON!
BUT IF THE AIRBAGS DEPLOYED...
...WE HAD TO HAVE HIT SOMETHING.
DUDE, JUST FORGET ABOUT IT!
NO WAY THERE'S ANYONE OUT THIS LATE!
GU (MASH)
LET'S GO!
GYURURU (SPIN)
HUH...!?

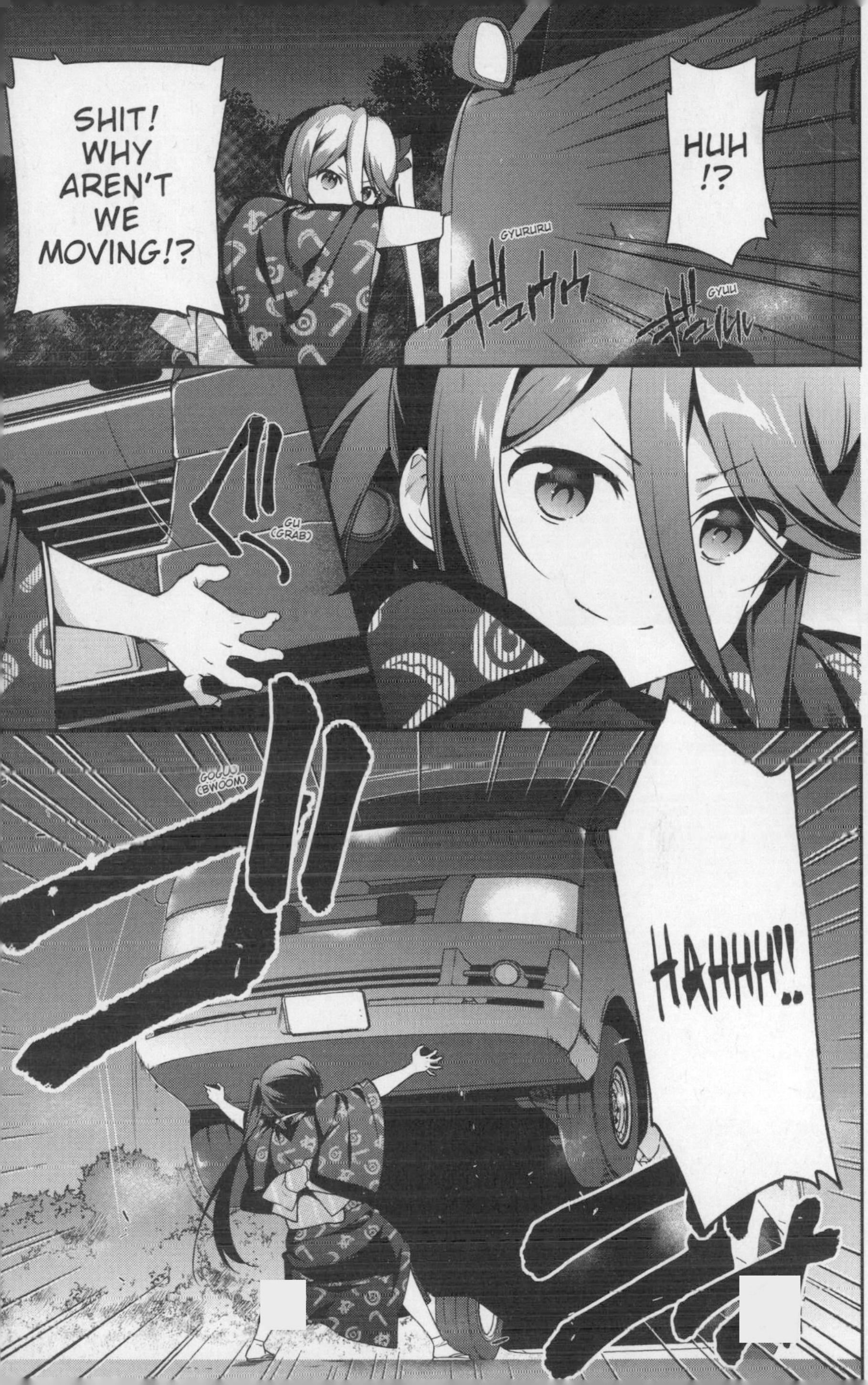
HUH !?
SHIT! WHY AREN'T WE MOVING!?
GYURURU
GYUU
GU (GRAB)
(BWOOM)
HAHHH!!

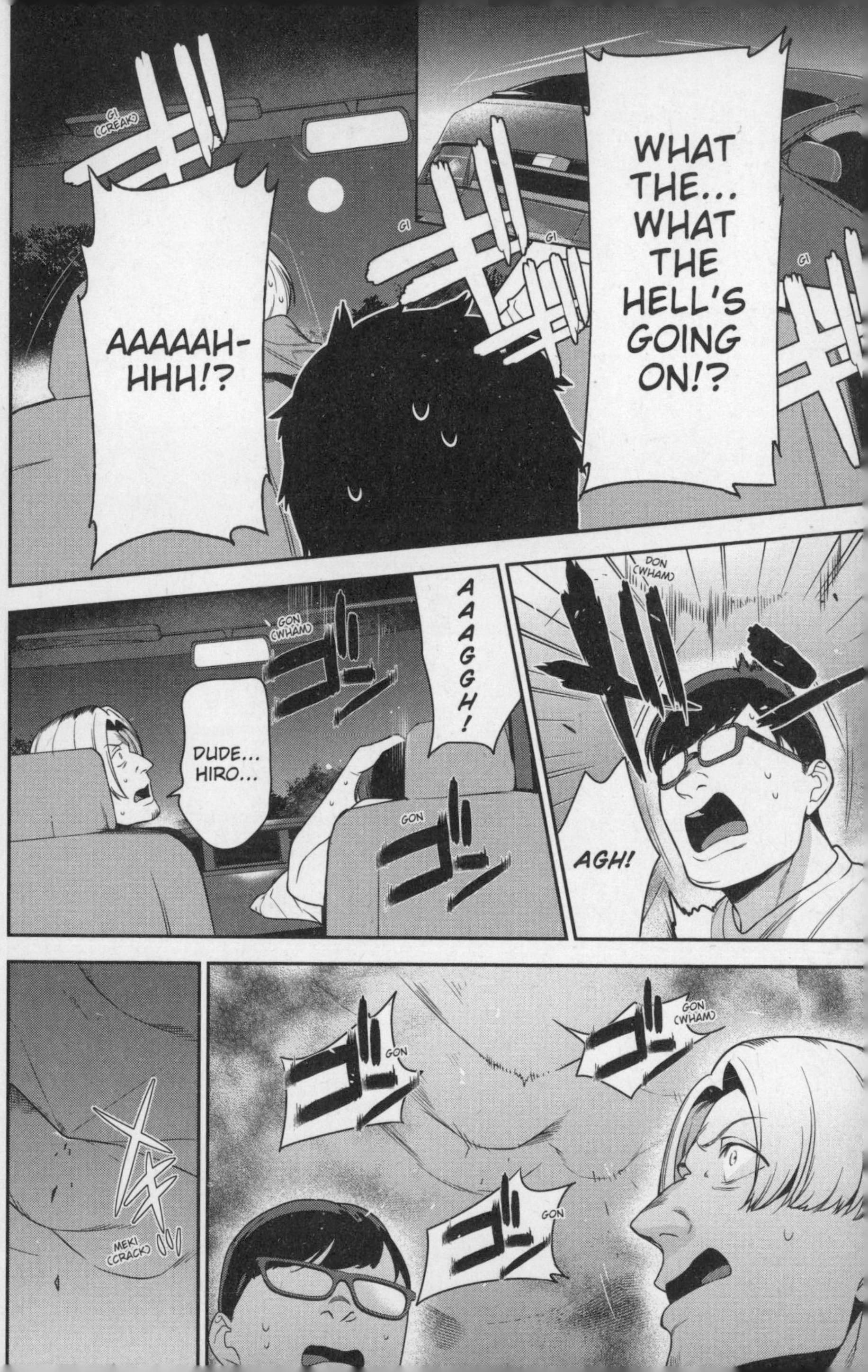
WHAT THE... WHAT THE HELL'S GOING ON!?
GI
GI
GI
GI (CREAK)
AAAAAH-HHH!?
DON (WHAM)
AGH!
AAAGGH!
GON (WHAM)
DUDE... HIRO...
GON
GON (WHAM)
GON
GON
MEKI (CRACK)

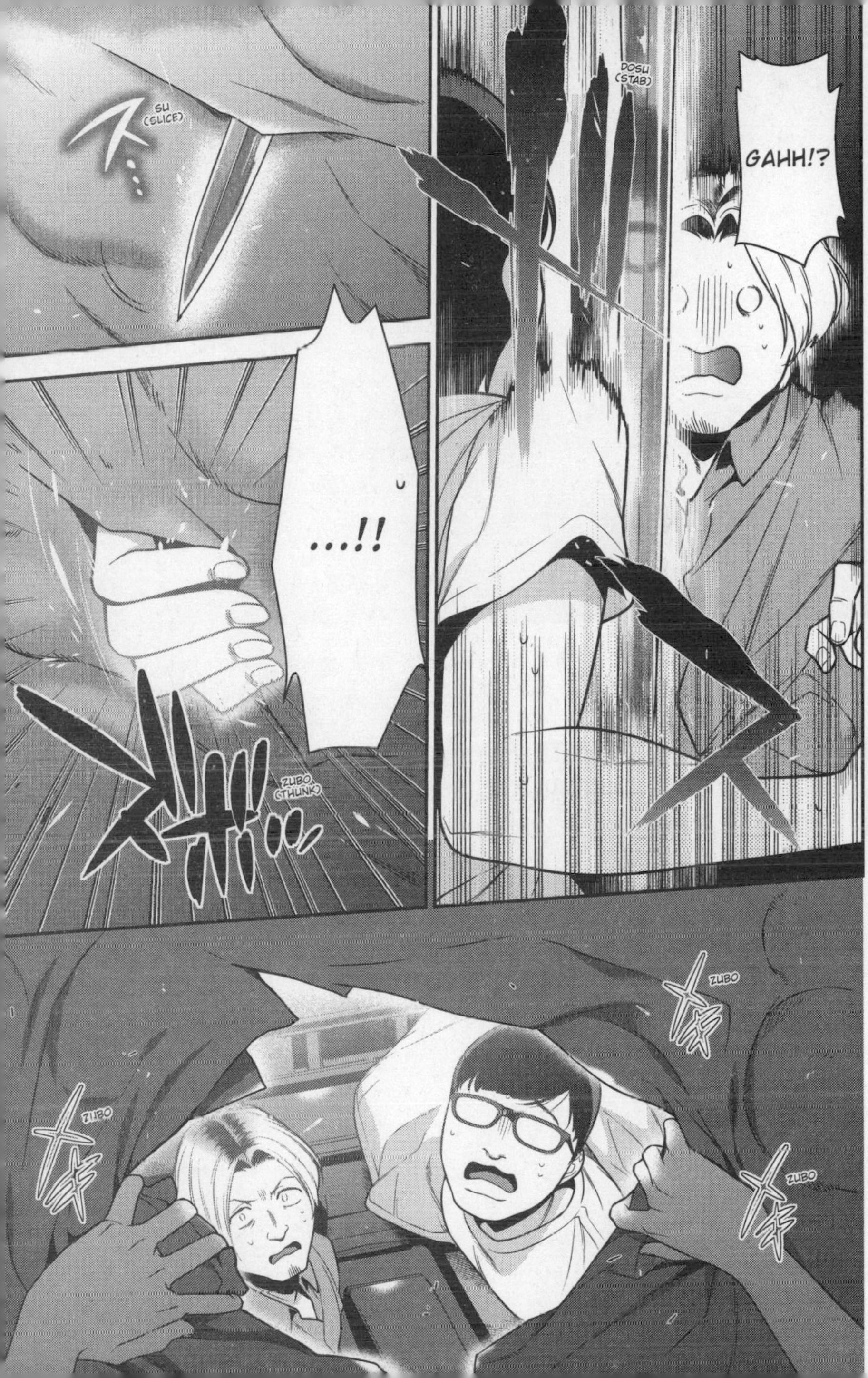
GAHH!?
DOSU (STAB)
SU (SLICE)
...!!
ZUBO (THUNK)
ZUBO
ZUBO
ZUBO

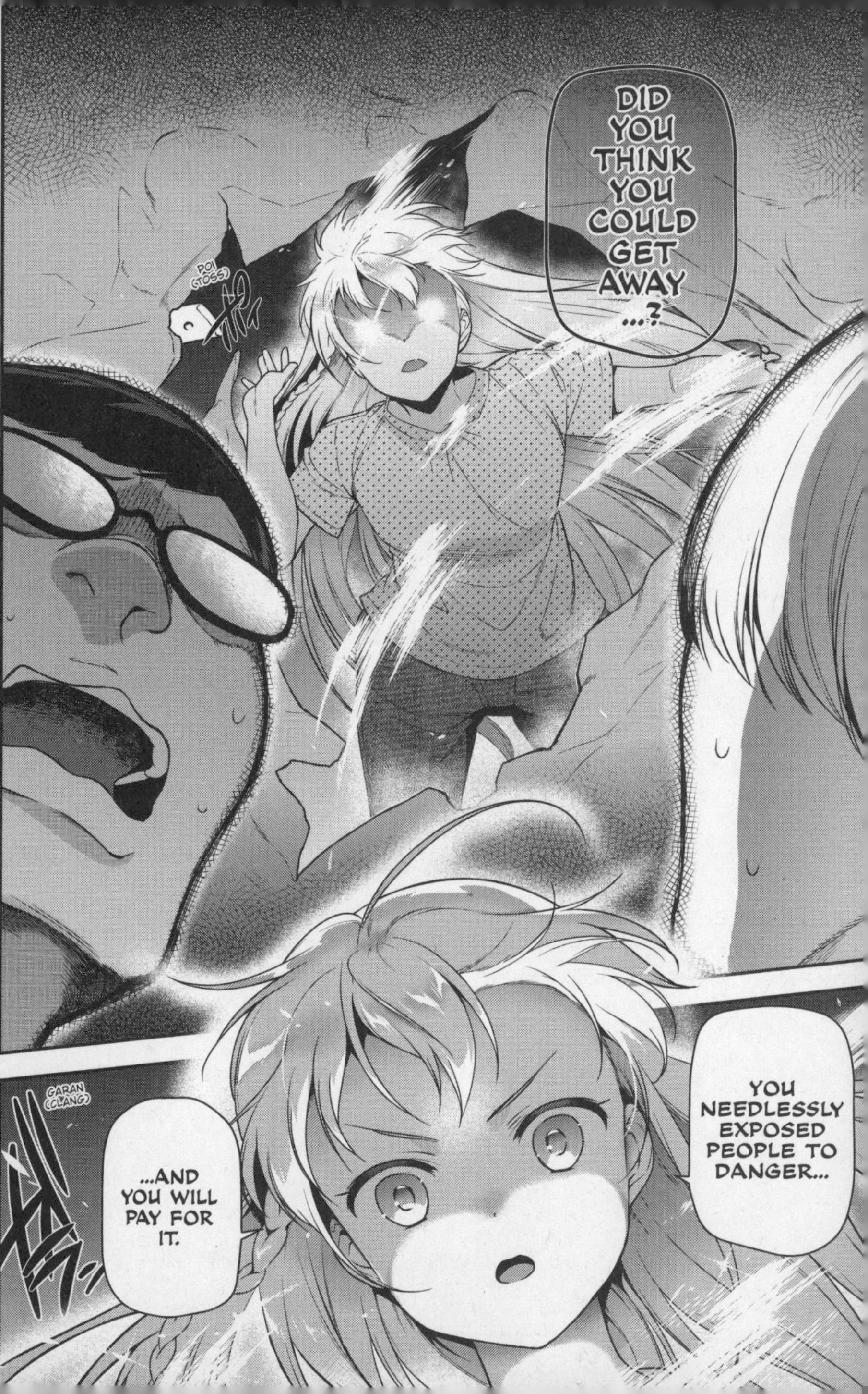
DID YOU THINK YOU COULD GET AWAY ...?
POI (TOSS)
YOU NEEDLESSLY EXPOSED PEOPLE TO DANGER...
...AND YOU WILL PAY FOR IT.
GARAN (CLANG)

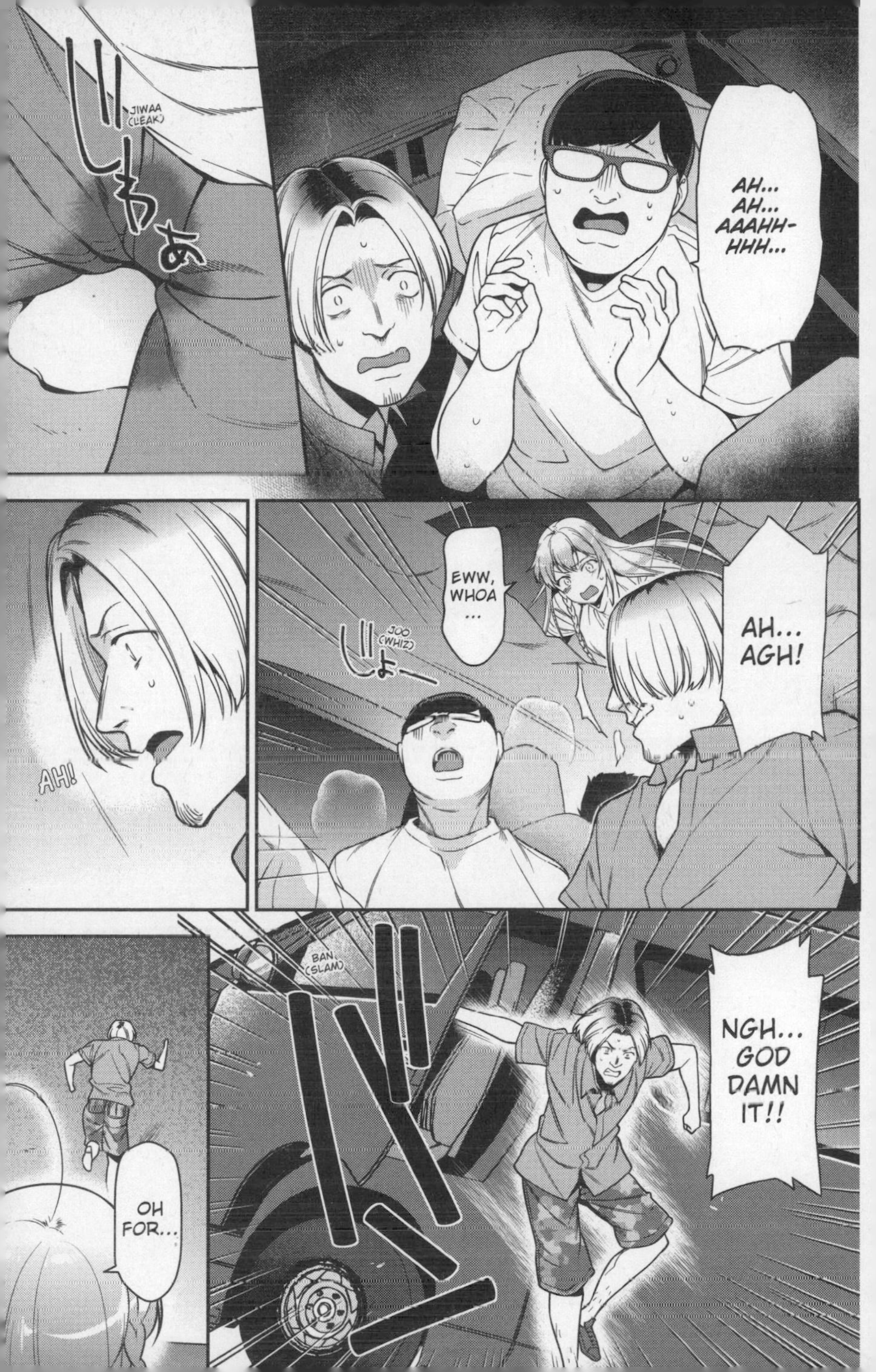
AH... AH... AAAHH-HHH...
じわぁ
JIWAA (LEAK)
AH... AGH!
EWW, WHOA ...
じょー
JOO (WHIZ)
AH!
NGH... GOD DAMN IT!!
BAN (SLAM)
OH FOR...

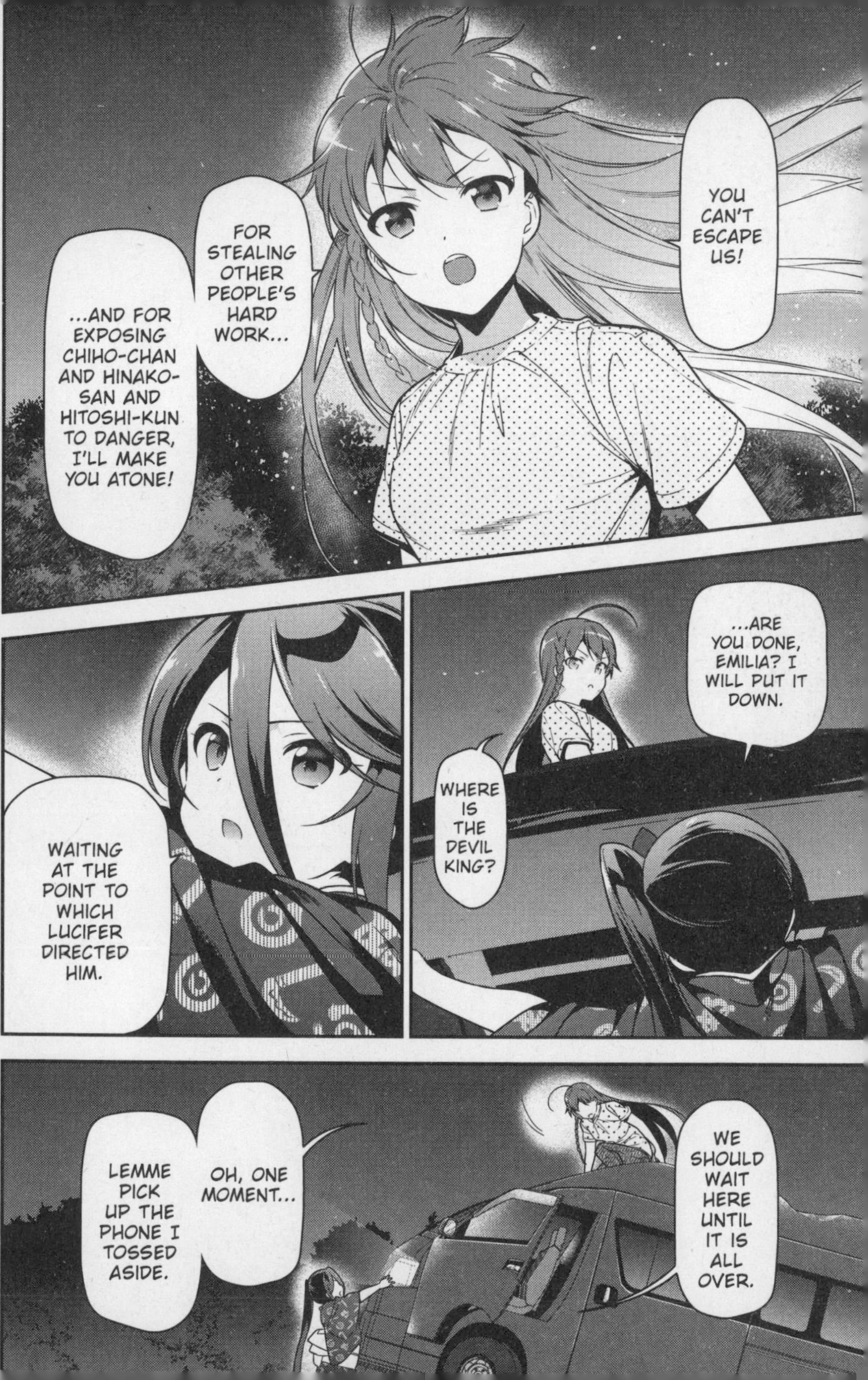
YOU CAN'T ESCAPE US!
FOR STEALING OTHER PEOPLE'S HARD WORK...
...AND FOR EXPOSING CHIHO-CHAN AND HINAKO-SAN AND HITOSHI-KUN TO DANGER, I'LL MAKE YOU ATONE!
...ARE YOU DONE, EMILIA? I WILL PUT IT DOWN.
WHERE IS THE DEVIL KING?
WAITING AT THE POINT TO WHICH LUCIFER DIRECTED HIM.
WE SHOULD WAIT HERE UNTIL IT IS ALL OVER.
OH, ONE MOMENT...
LEMME PICK UP THE PHONE I TOSSED ASIDE.

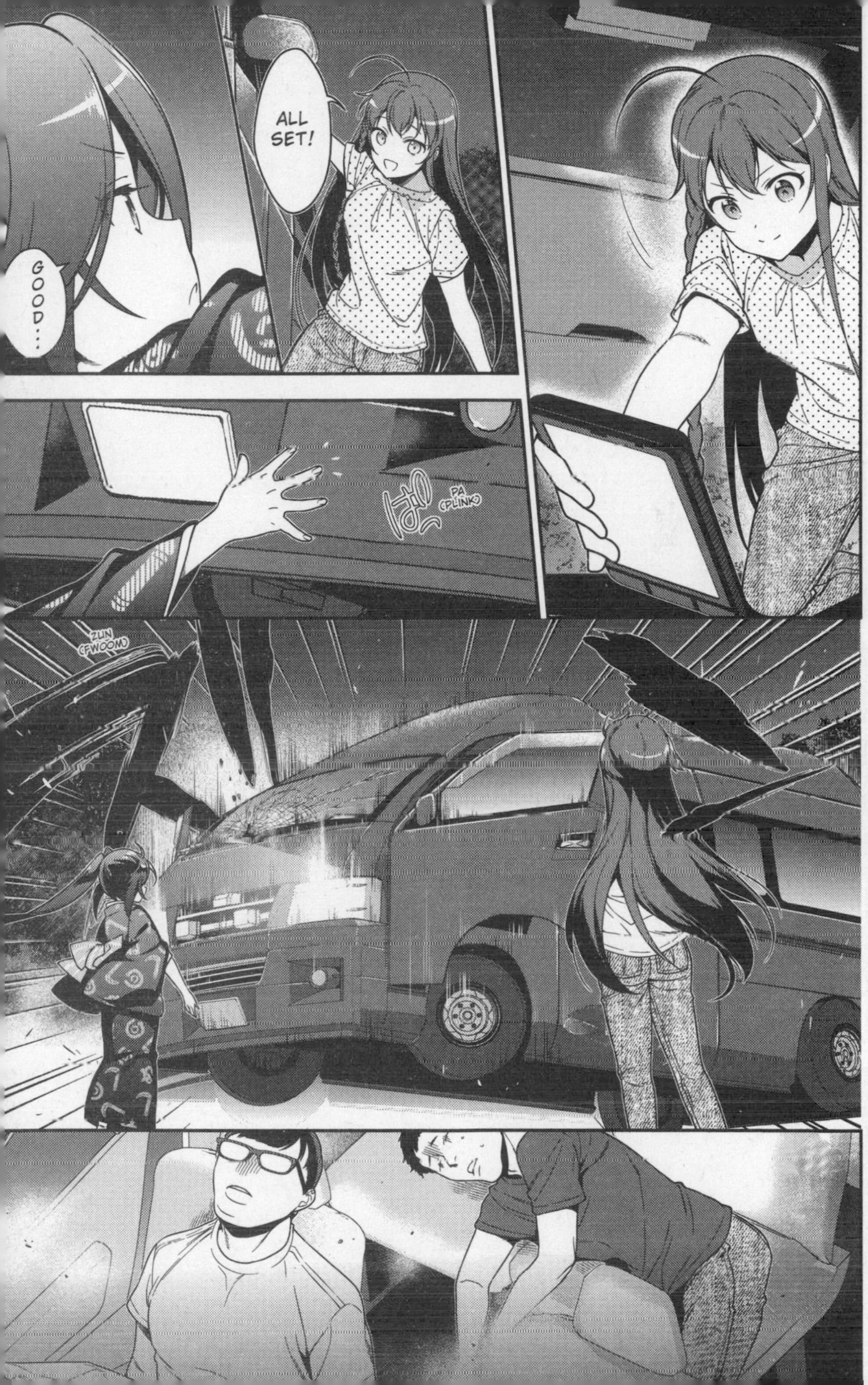
ALL SET!
GOOD...
ぱっ
PA (PLINK)
ZUN (FWOOM)

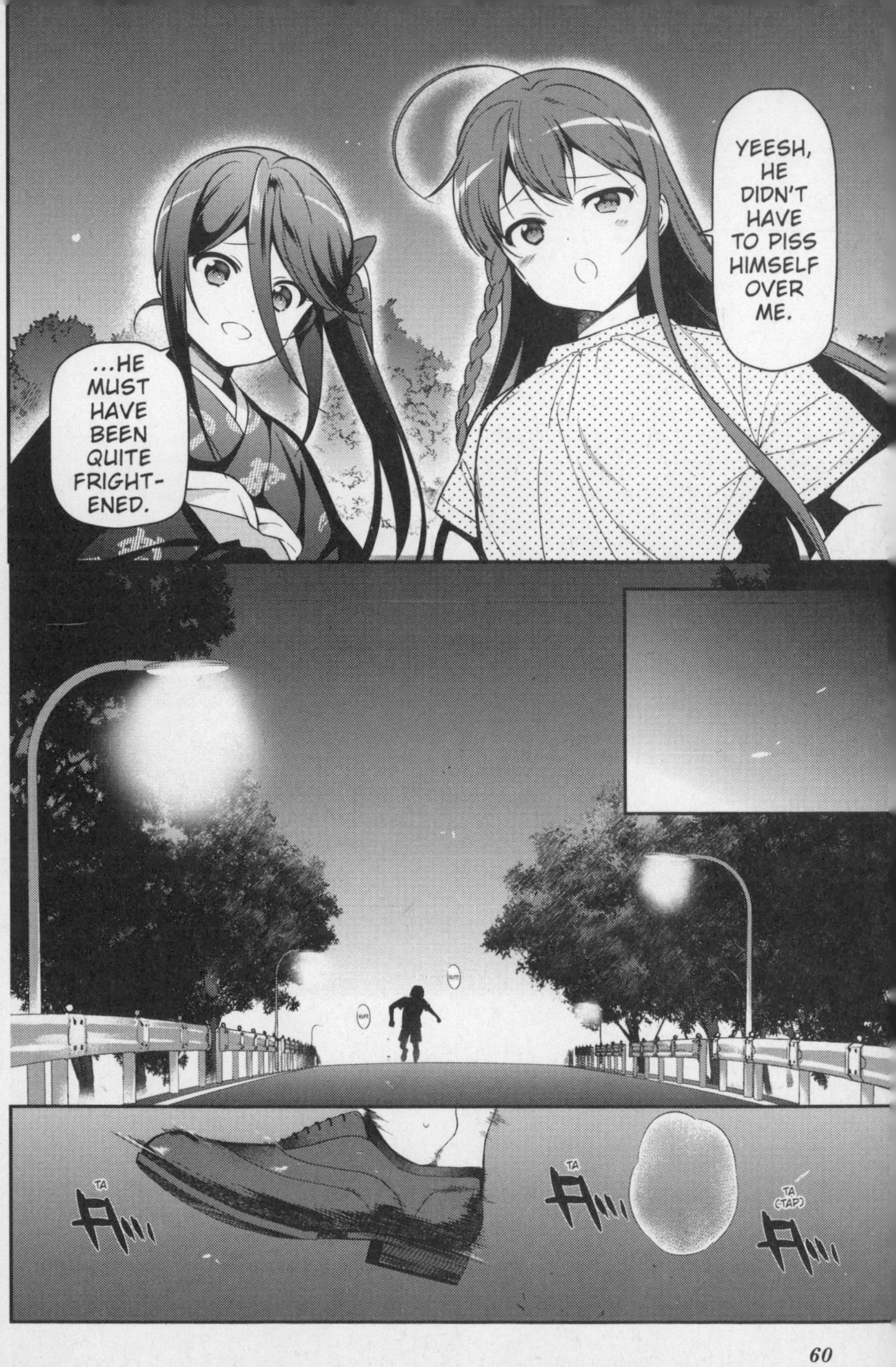
YEESH, HE DIDN'T HAVE TO PISS HIMSELF OVER ME.
...HE MUST HAVE BEEN QUITE FRIGHT-ENED.
HUFF
HUFF
TA (TAP)
TA
TA

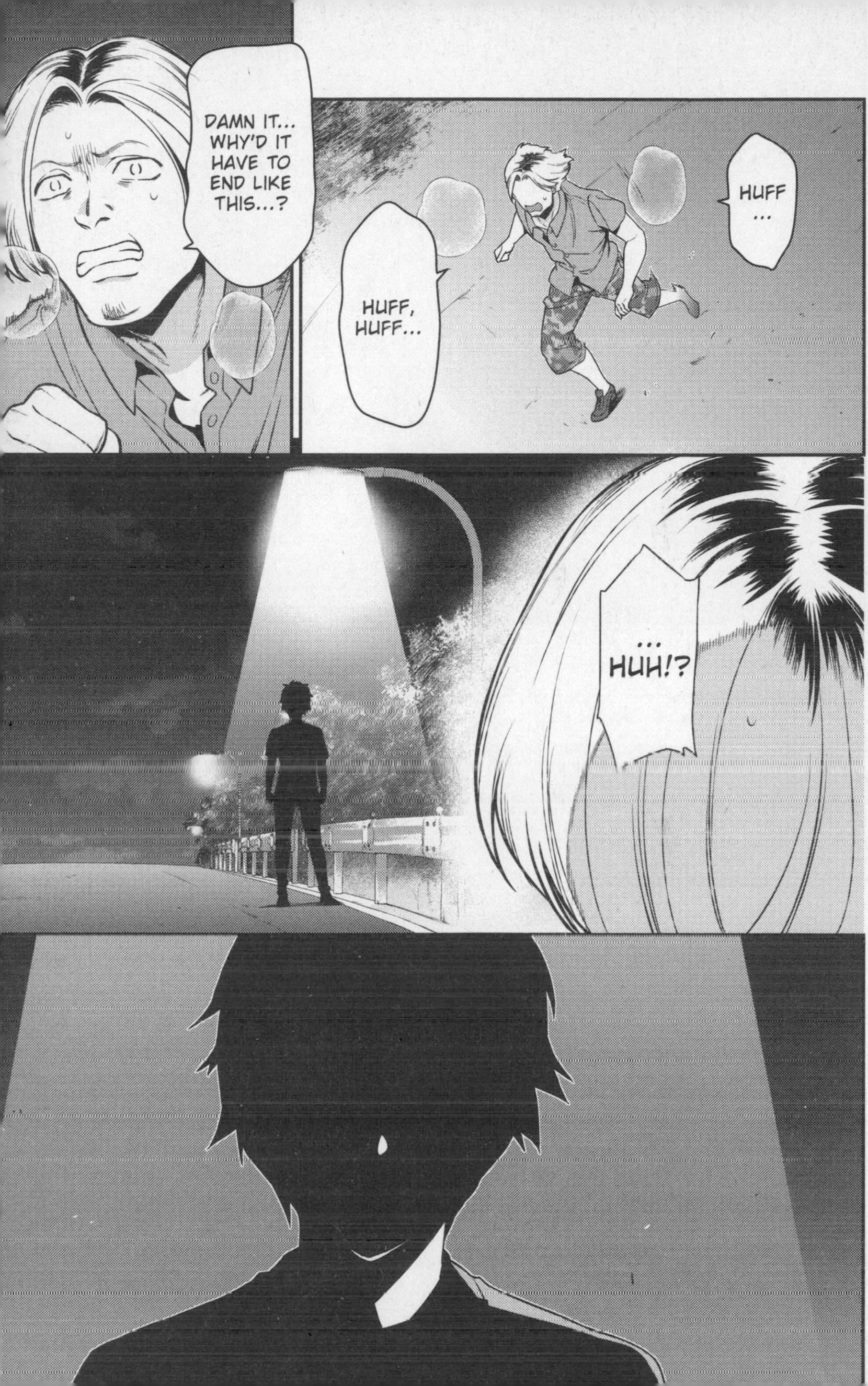
HUFF ...
HUFF, HUFF...
DAMN IT... WHY'D IT HAVE TO END LIKE THIS...?
... HUH!?

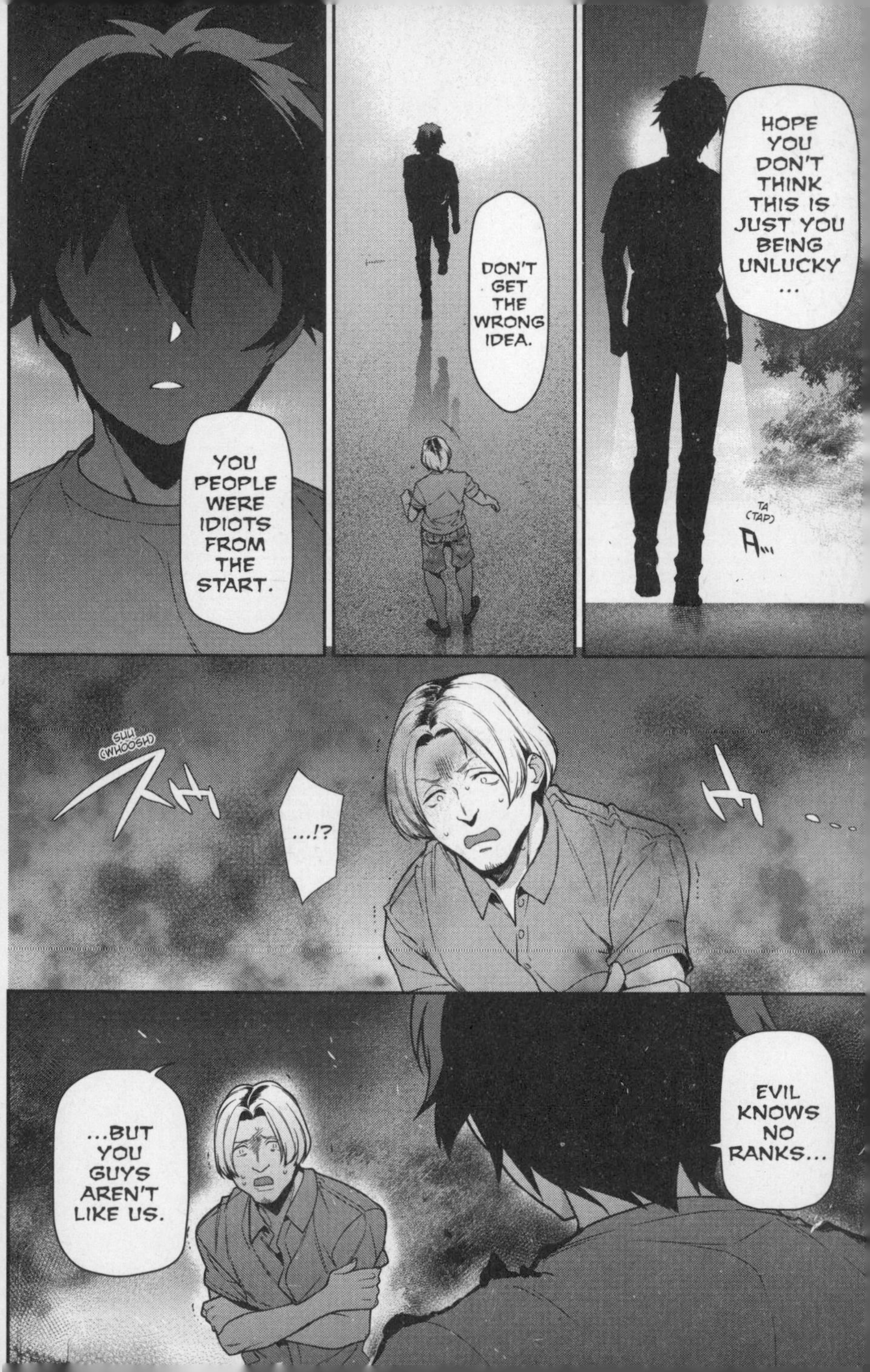
HOPE YOU DON'T THINK THIS IS JUST YOU BEING UNLUCKY ...
TA (TAP)
DON'T GET THE WRONG IDEA.
YOU PEOPLE WERE IDIOTS FROM THE START.
...!?
SUU (WHOOSH)
EVIL KNOWS NO RANKS...
...BUT YOU GUYS AREN'T LIKE US.

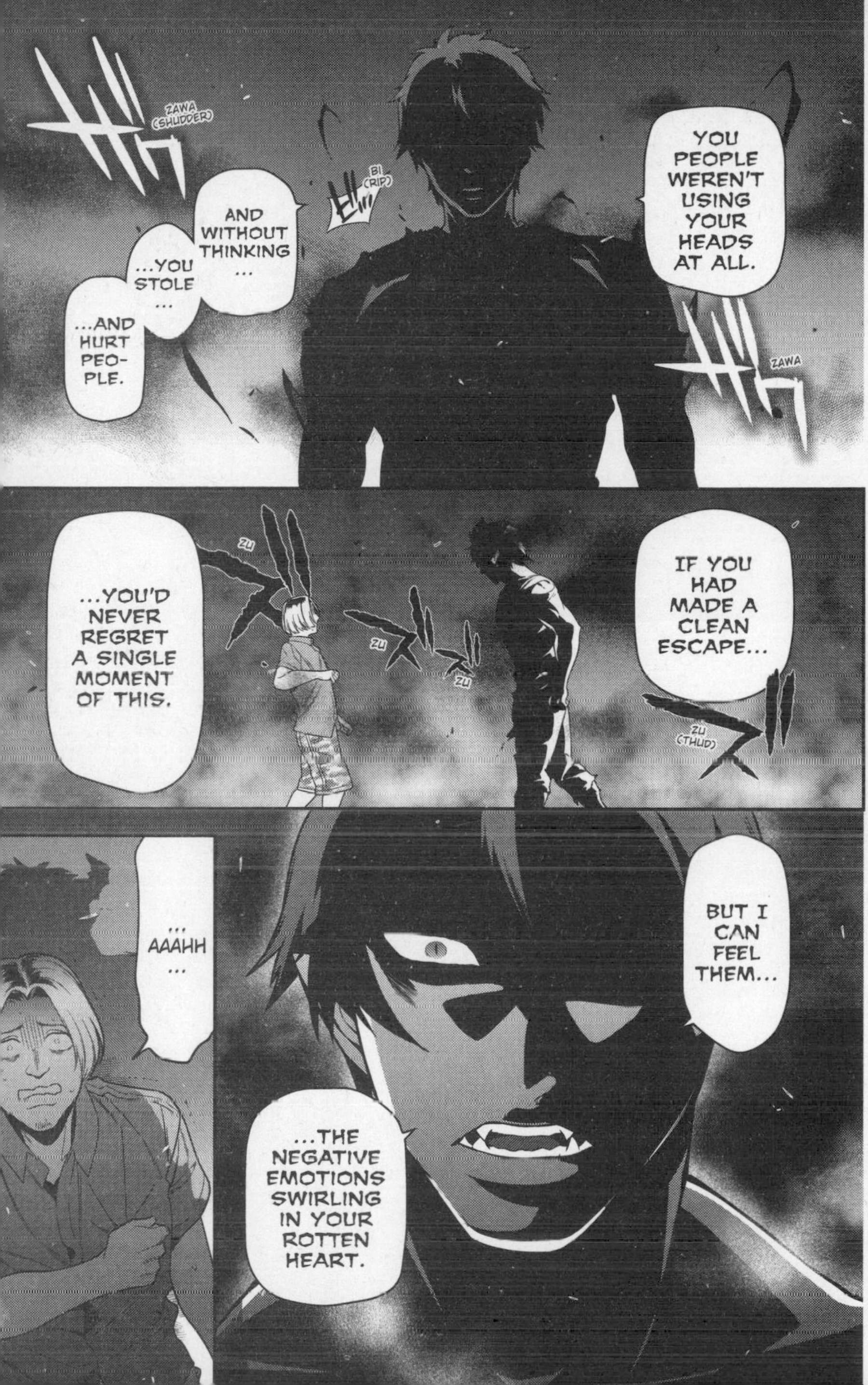
YOU PEOPLE WEREN'T USING YOUR HEADS AT ALL.
ZAWA
BI (RIP)
AND WITHOUT THINKING...
...YOU STOLE...
...AND HURT PEO-PLE.
ZAWA (SHUDDER)
IF YOU HAD MADE A CLEAN ESCAPE...
ZU (THUD)
ZU
ZU
ZU
...YOU'D NEVER REGRET A SINGLE MOMENT OF THIS.
BUT I CAN FEEL THEM...
...THE NEGATIVE EMOTIONS SWIRLING IN YOUR ROTTEN HEART.
... AAAHH ...

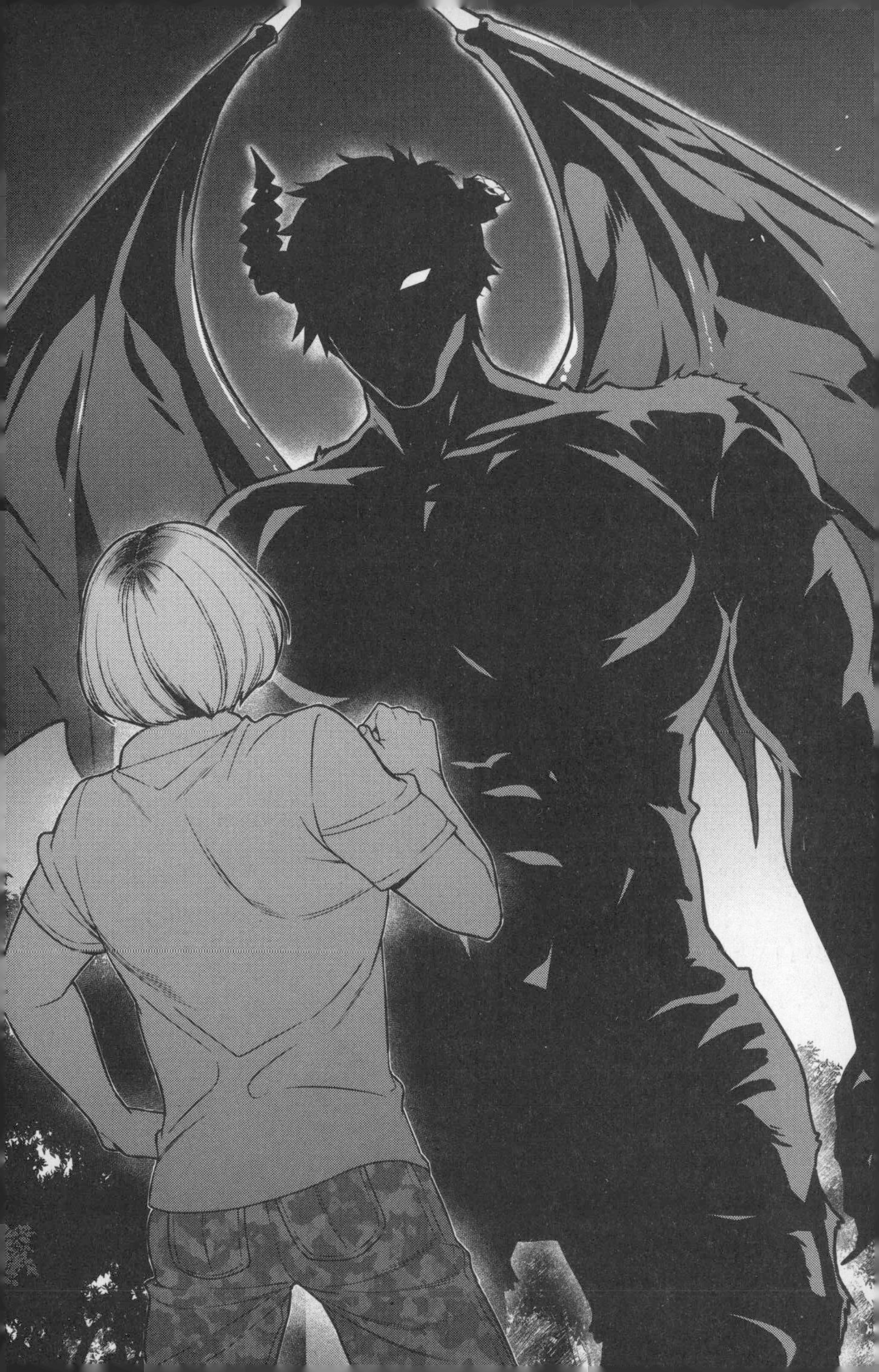

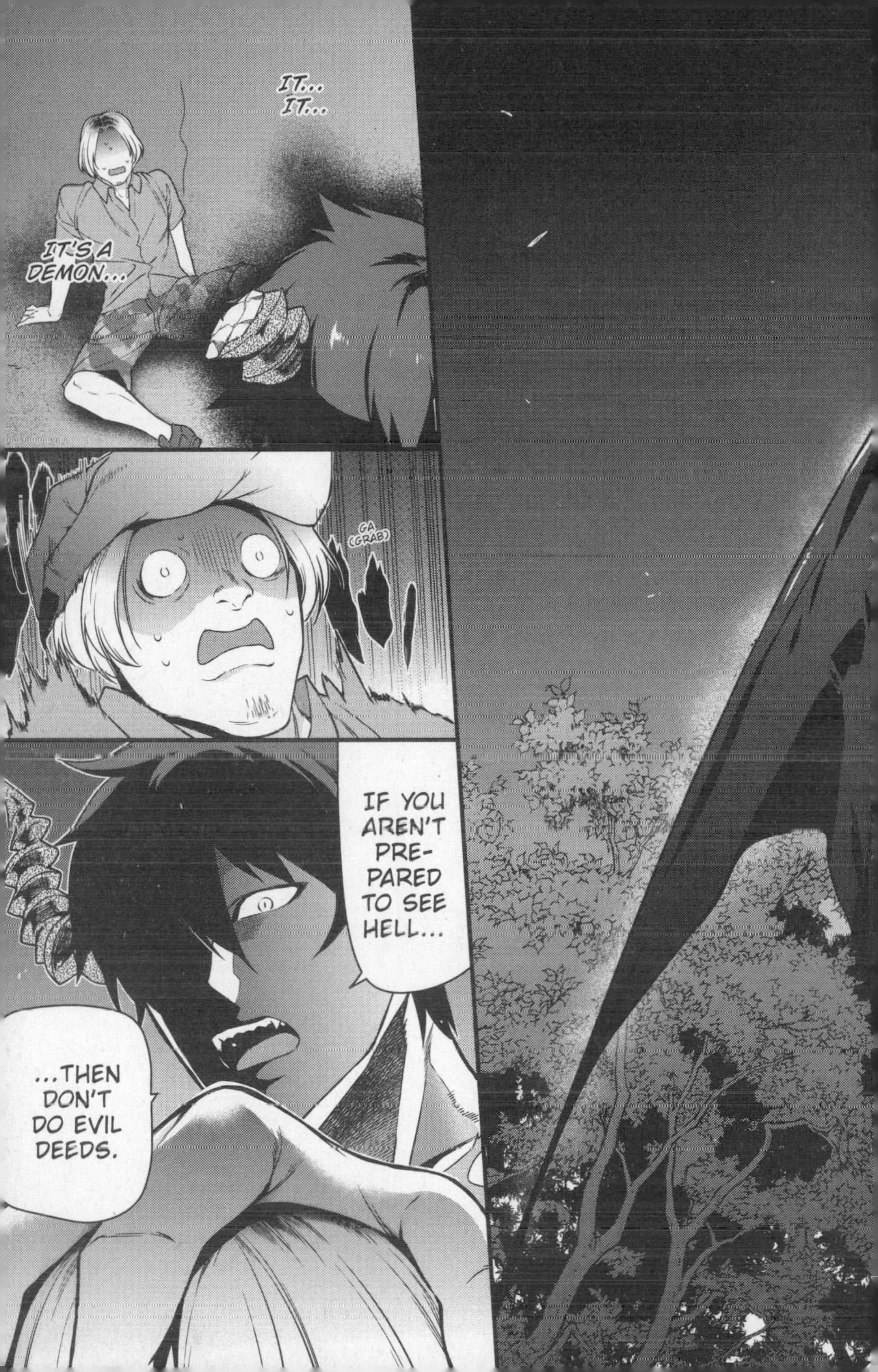
IT... IT...
IT'S A DEMON...
GA (GRAB)
IF YOU AREN'T PRE-PARED TO SEE HELL...
...THEN DON'T DO EVIL DEEDS.

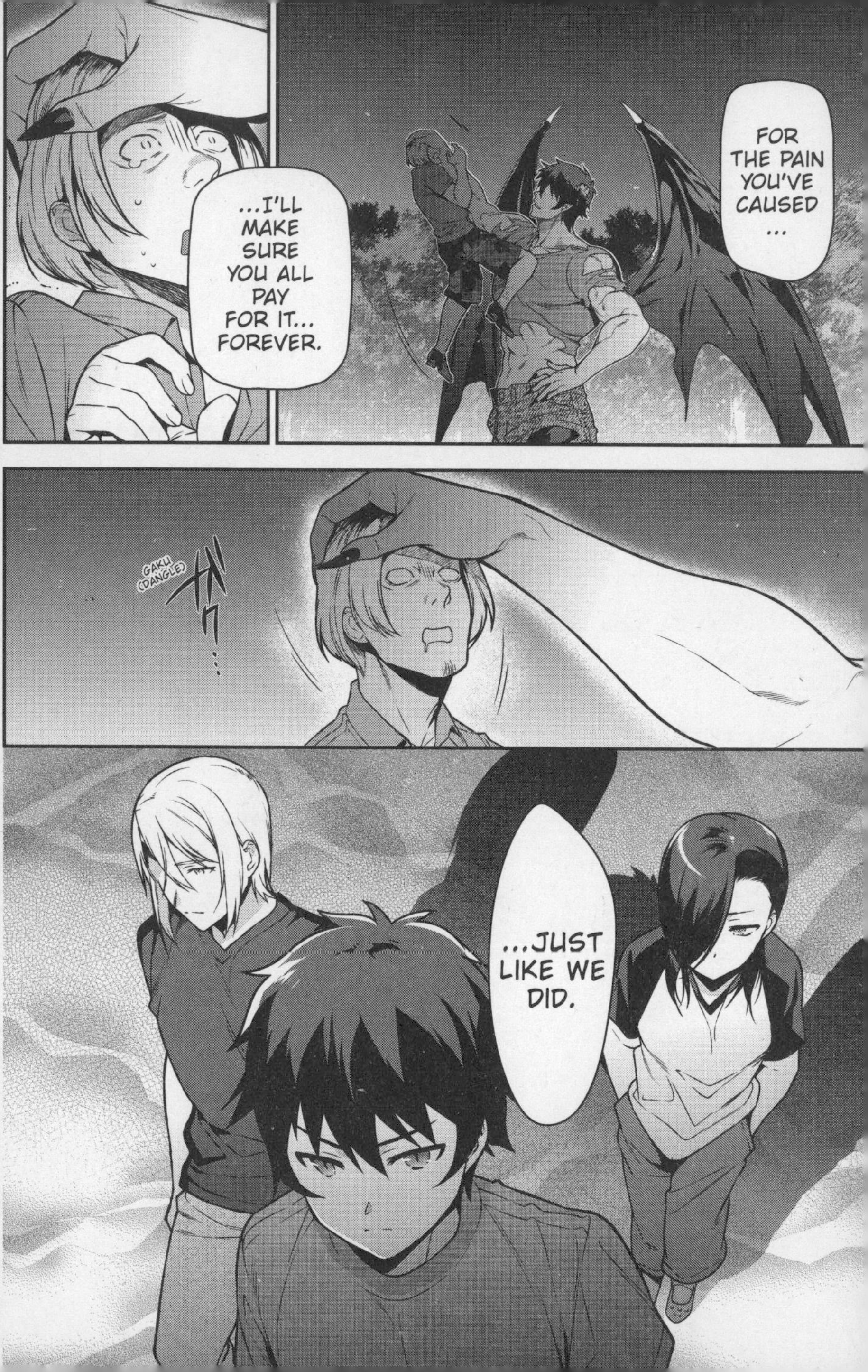
FOR THE PAIN YOU'VE CAUSED ...
...I'LL MAKE SURE YOU ALL PAY FOR IT... FOREVER.
GAKU (DANGLE)
...JUST LIKE WE DID.

THE DEVIL IS A PART-TIMER!

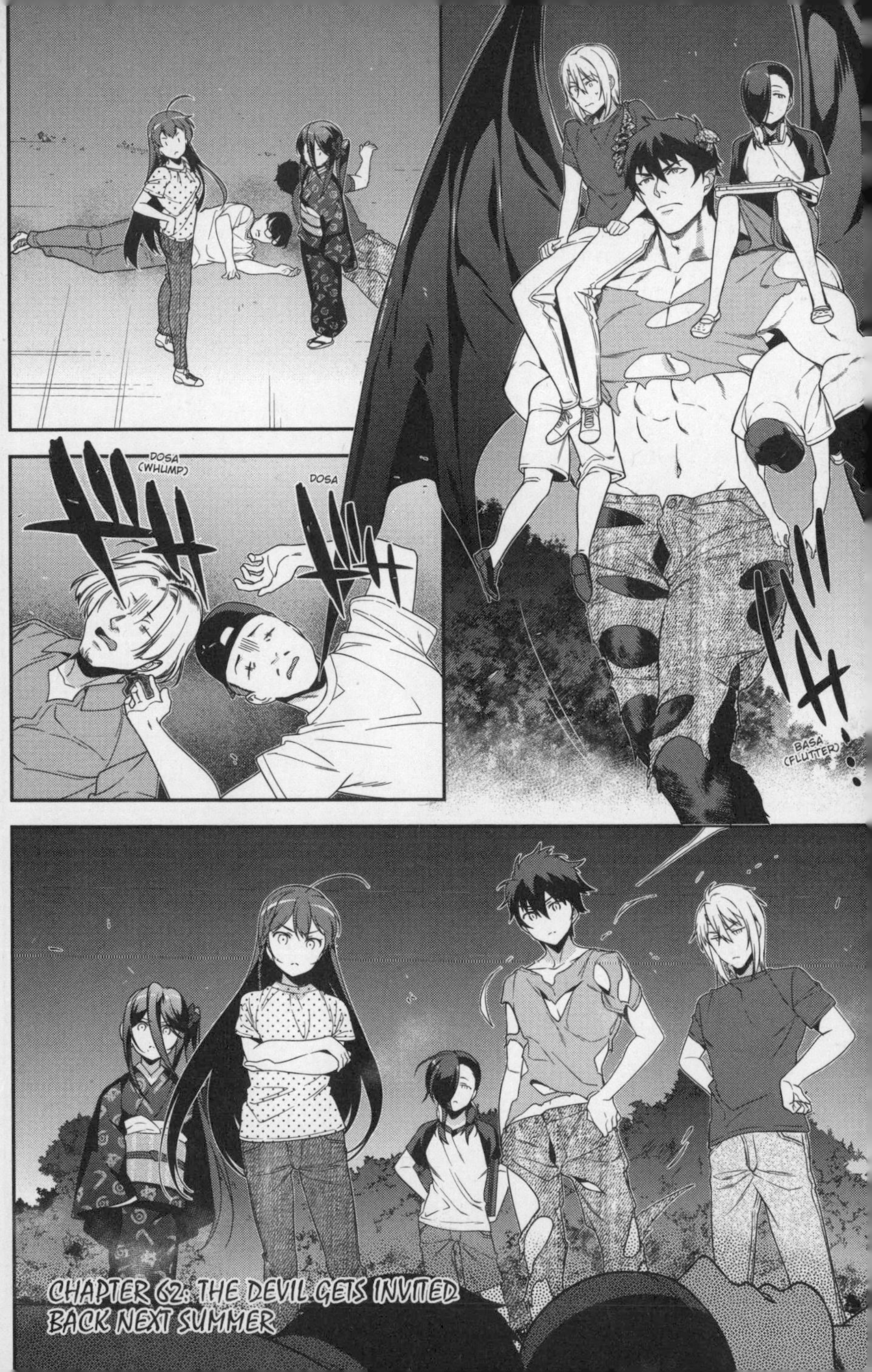
BASA (FLUTTER)
DOSA (WHUMP)
DOSA
CHAPTER 62: THE DEVIL GETS INVITED BACK NEXT SUMMER

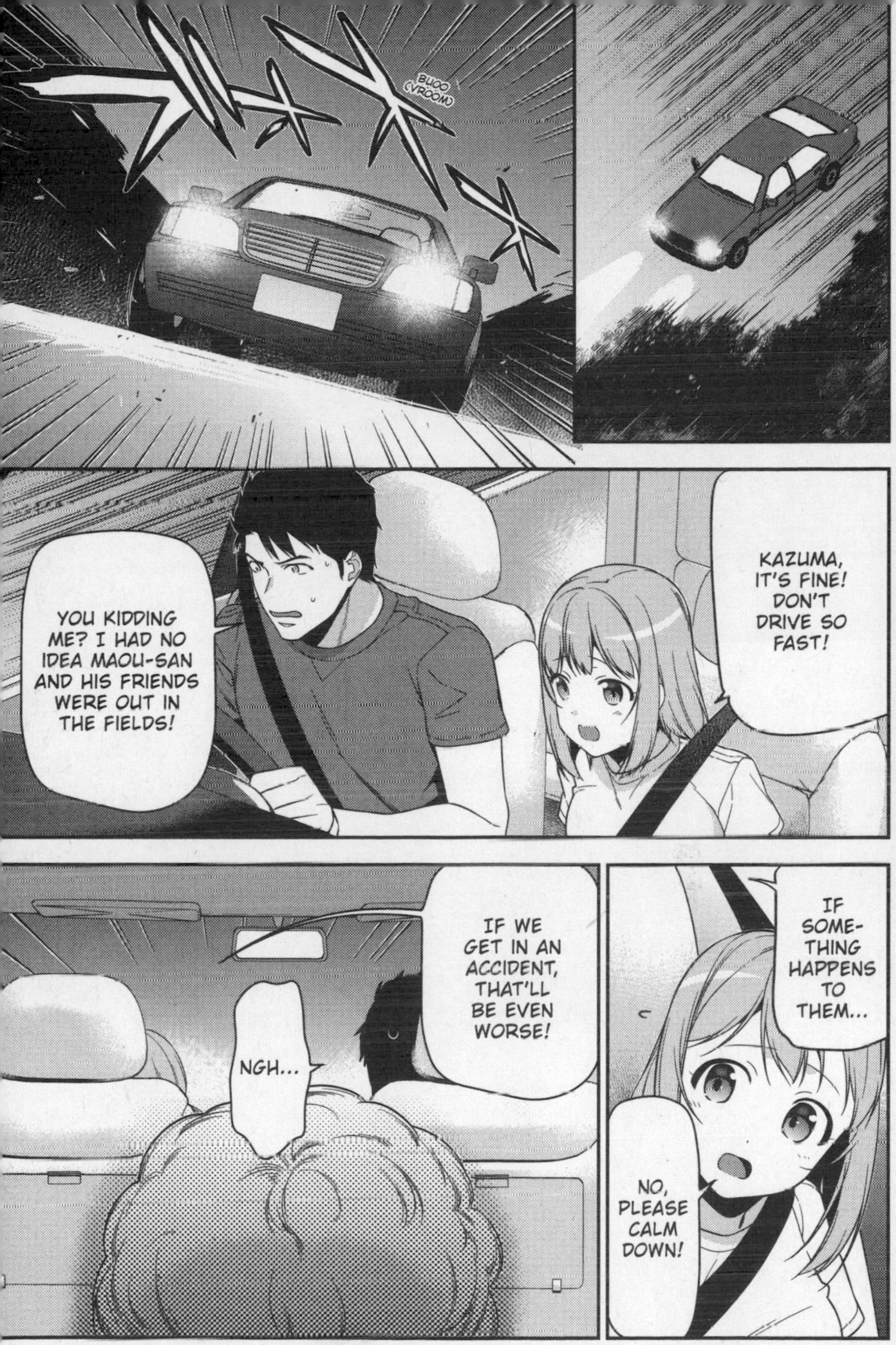
BUOO (VROOM)
KAZUMA, IT'S FINE! DON'T DRIVE SO FAST!
YOU KIDDING ME? I HAD NO IDEA MAOU-SAN AND HIS FRIENDS WERE OUT IN THE FIELDS!
IF SOMETHING HAPPENS TO THEM...
NO, PLEASE CALM DOWN!
IF WE GET IN AN ACCIDENT, THAT'LL BE EVEN WORSE!
NGH...

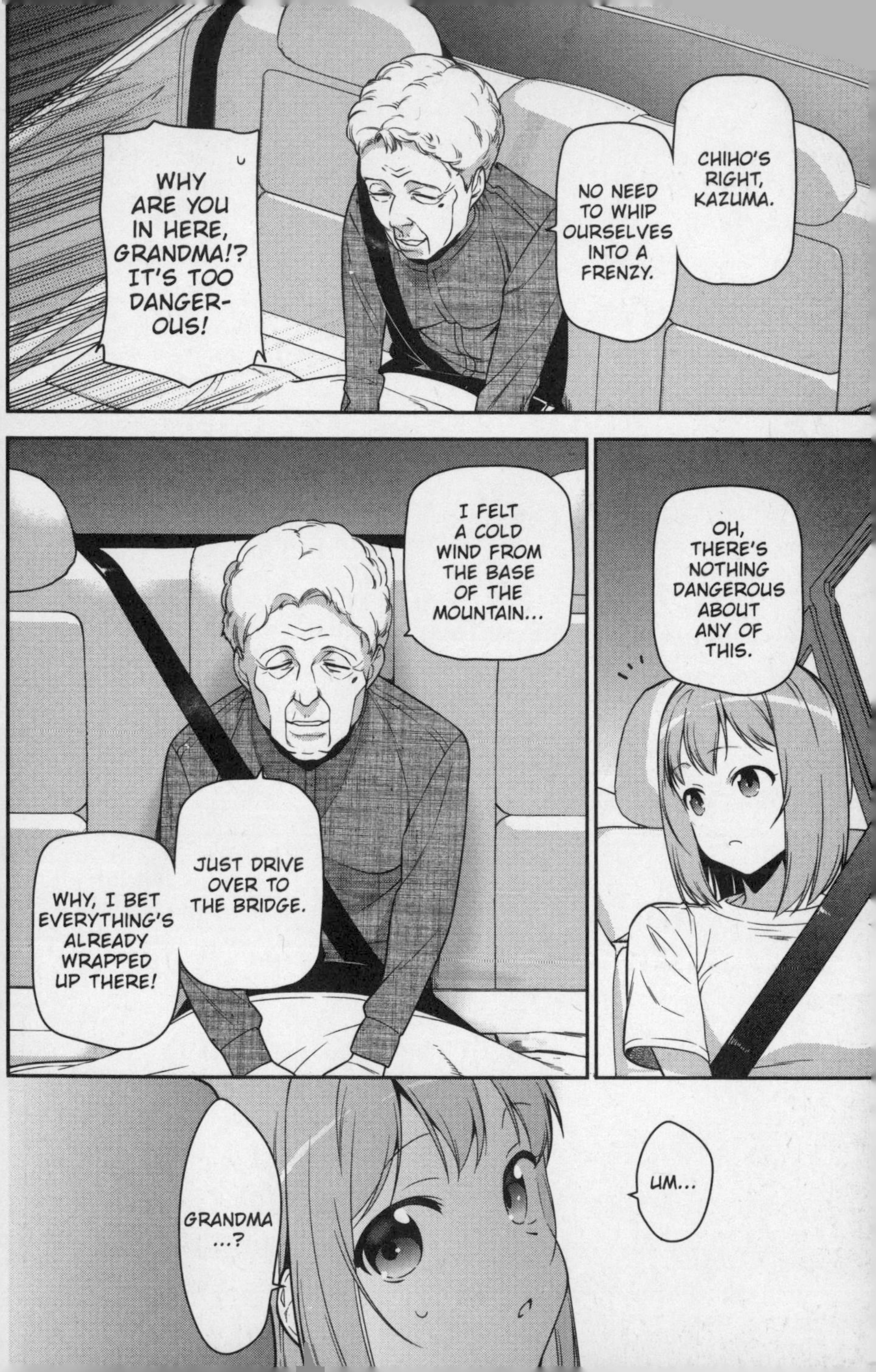
CHIHO'S RIGHT, KAZUMA.
NO NEED TO WHIP OURSELVES INTO A FRENZY.
WHY ARE YOU IN HERE, GRANDMA!? IT'S TOO DANGEROUS!
OH, THERE'S NOTHING DANGEROUS ABOUT ANY OF THIS.
I FELT A COLD WIND FROM THE BASE OF THE MOUNTAIN...
JUST DRIVE OVER TO THE BRIDGE.
WHY, I BET EVERYTHING'S ALREADY WRAPPED UP THERE!
UM...
GRANDMA ...?

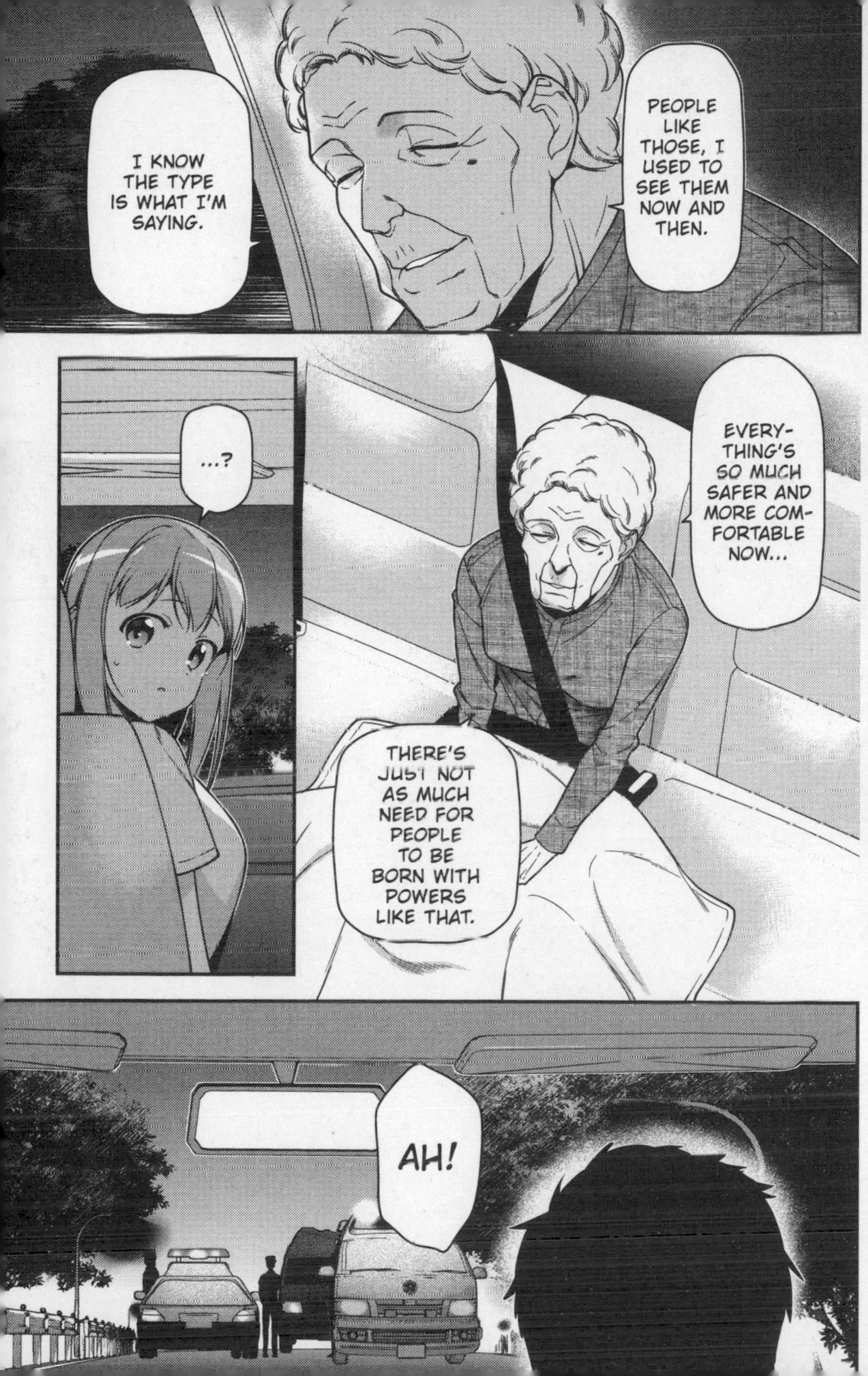
PEOPLE LIKE THOSE, I USED TO SEE THEM NOW AND THEN.
I KNOW THE TYPE IS WHAT I'M SAYING.
EVERY-THING'S SO MUCH SAFER AND MORE COM-FORTABLE NOW...
THERE'S JUST NOT AS MUCH NEED FOR PEOPLE TO BE BORN WITH POWERS LIKE THAT.
...?
AH!

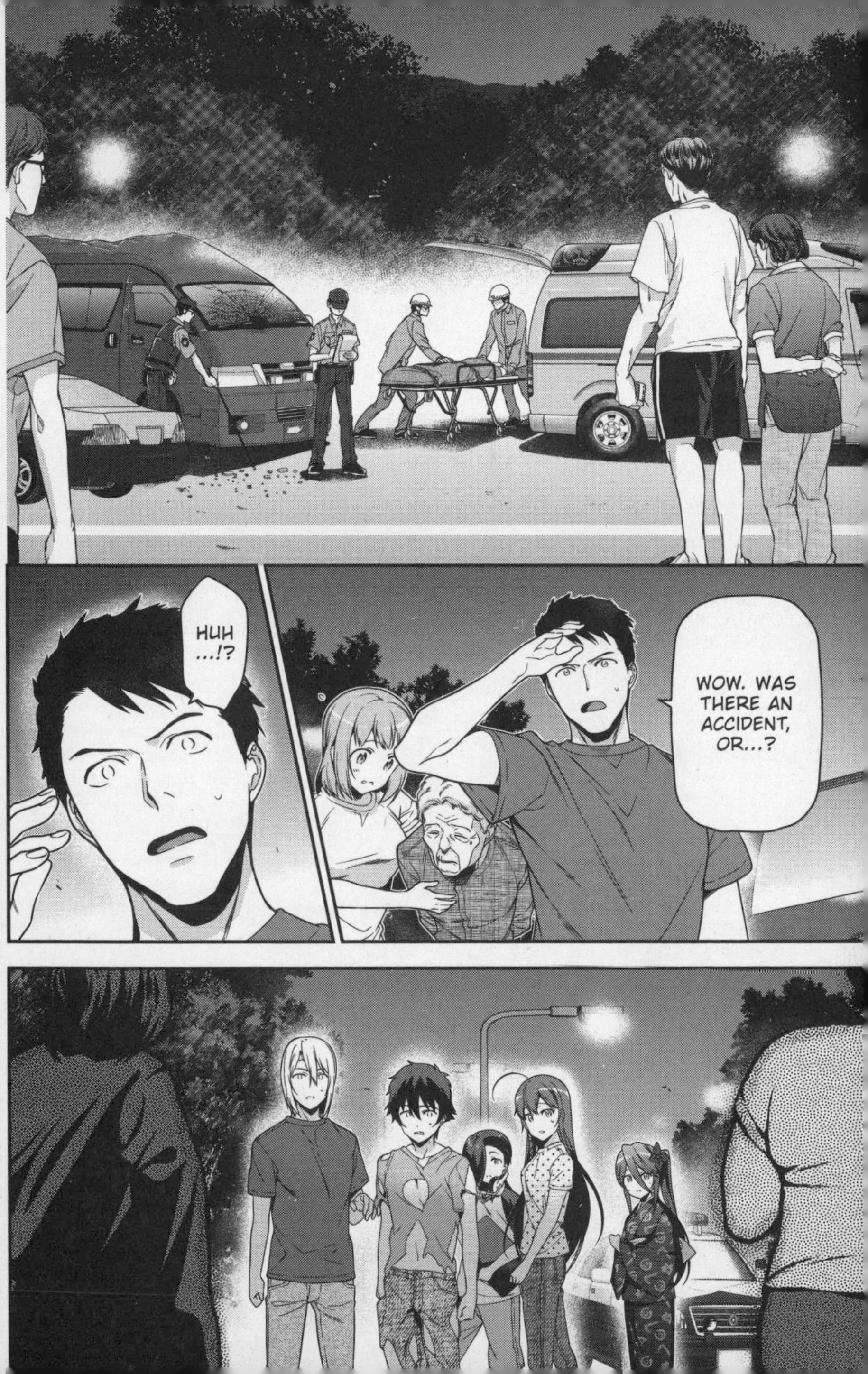
WOW. WAS THERE AN ACCIDENT, OR...?
HUH ...!?

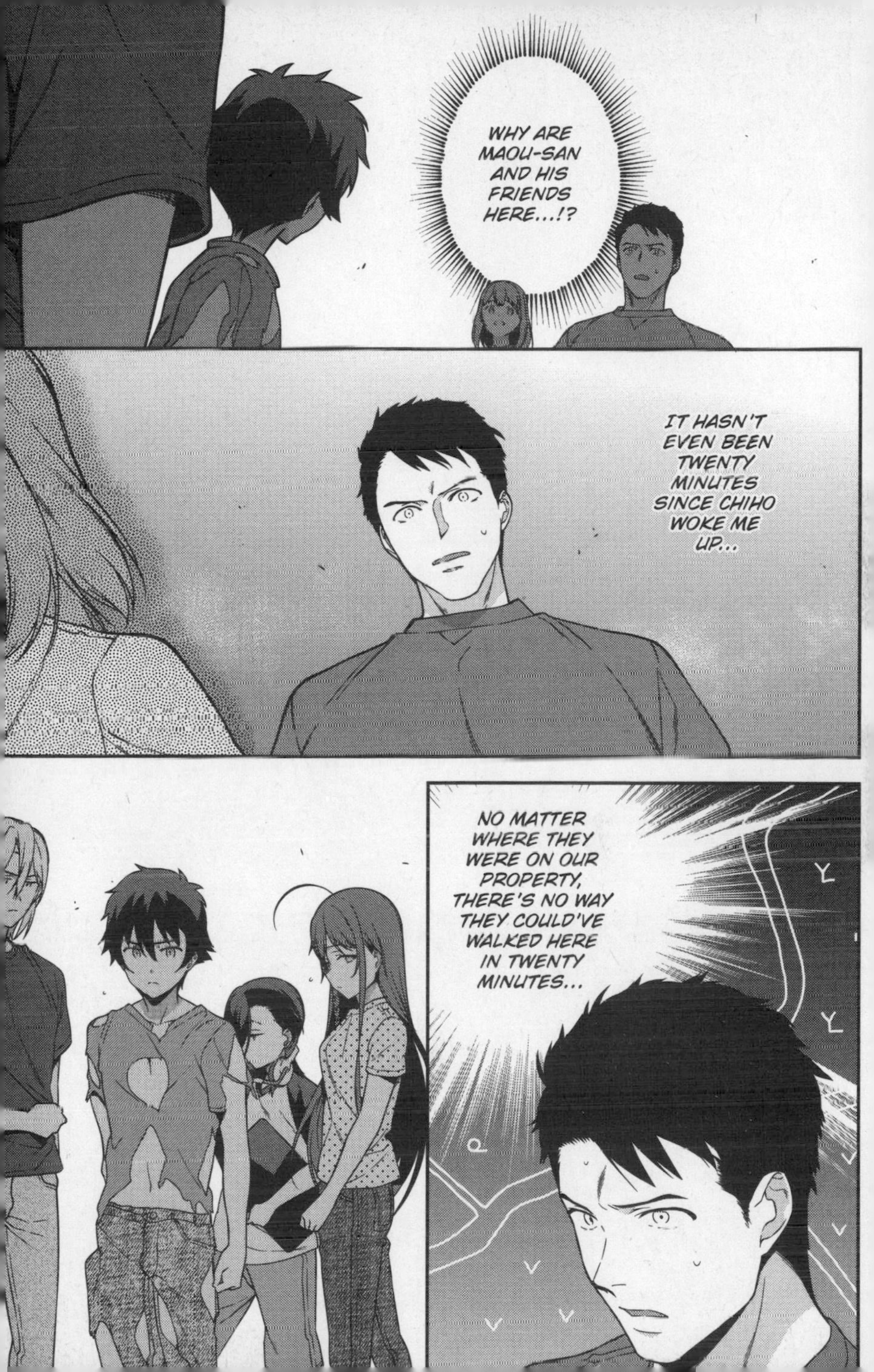
WHY ARE MAOU-SAN AND HIS FRIENDS HERE...!?
IT HASN'T EVEN BEEN TWENTY MINUTES SINCE CHIHO WOKE ME UP...
NO MATTER WHERE THEY WERE ON OUR PROPERTY, THERE'S NO WAY THEY COULD'VE WALKED HERE IN TWENTY MINUTES...

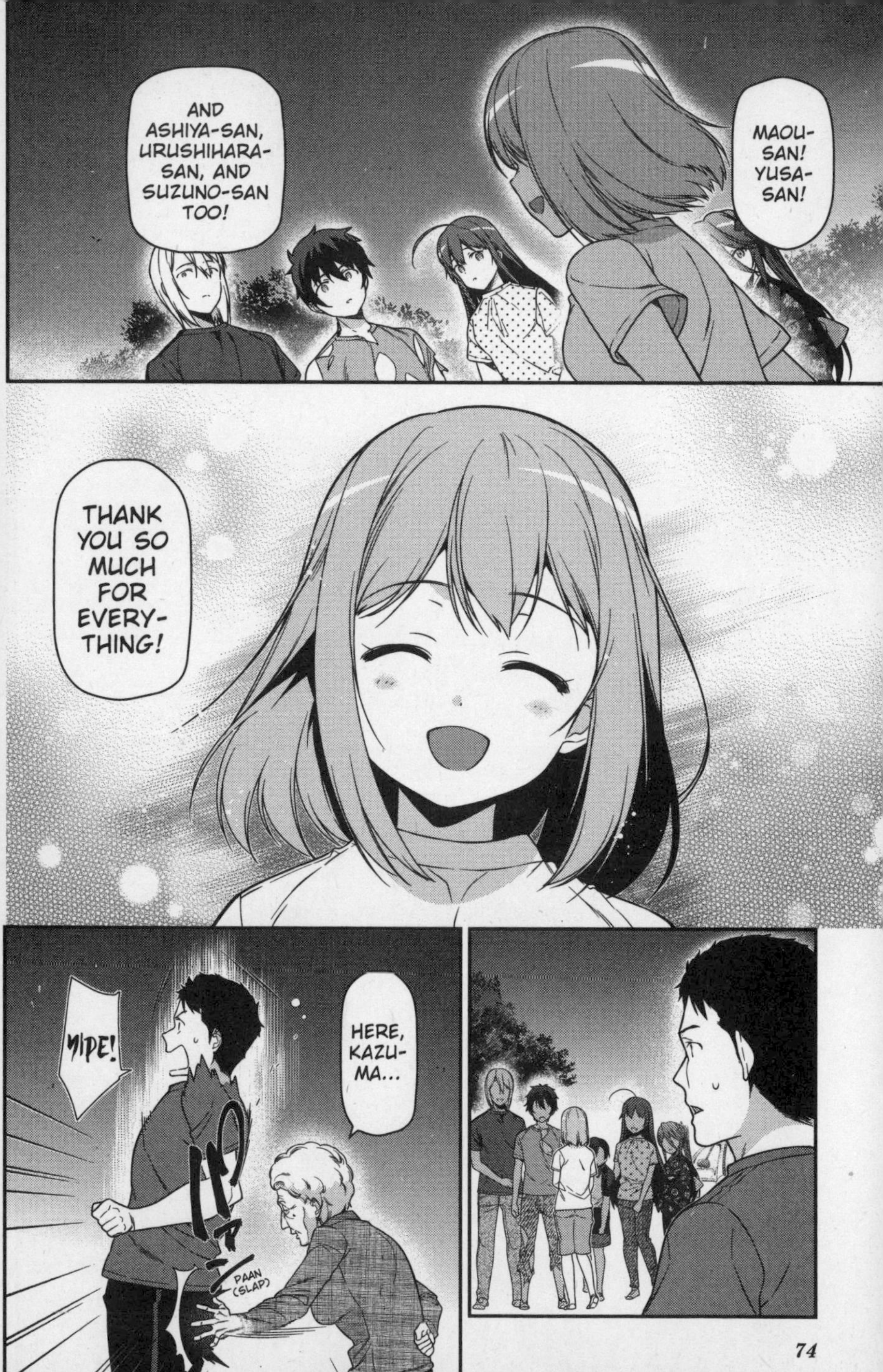
MAOU-SAN! YUSA-SAN!
AND ASHIYA-SAN, URUSHIHARA-SAN, AND SUZUNO-SAN TOO!
THANK YOU SO MUCH FOR EVERYTHING!
HERE, KAZUMA...
YIPE!
PAAN (SLAP)

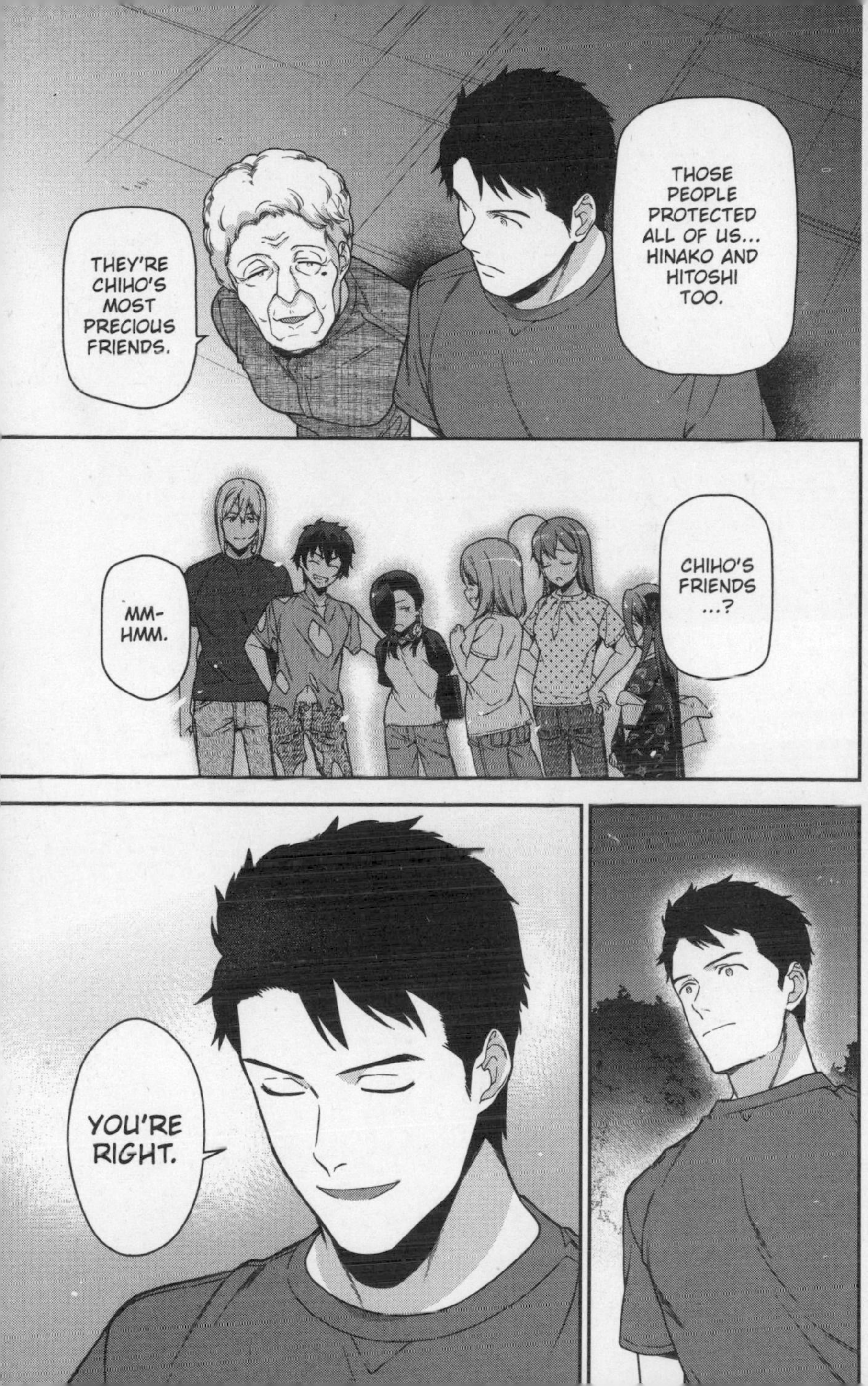
THOSE PEOPLE PROTECTED ALL OF US... HINAKO AND HITOSHI TOO.
THEY'RE CHIHO'S MOST PRECIOUS FRIENDS.
CHIHO'S FRIENDS ...?
MM-HMM.
YOU'RE RIGHT.

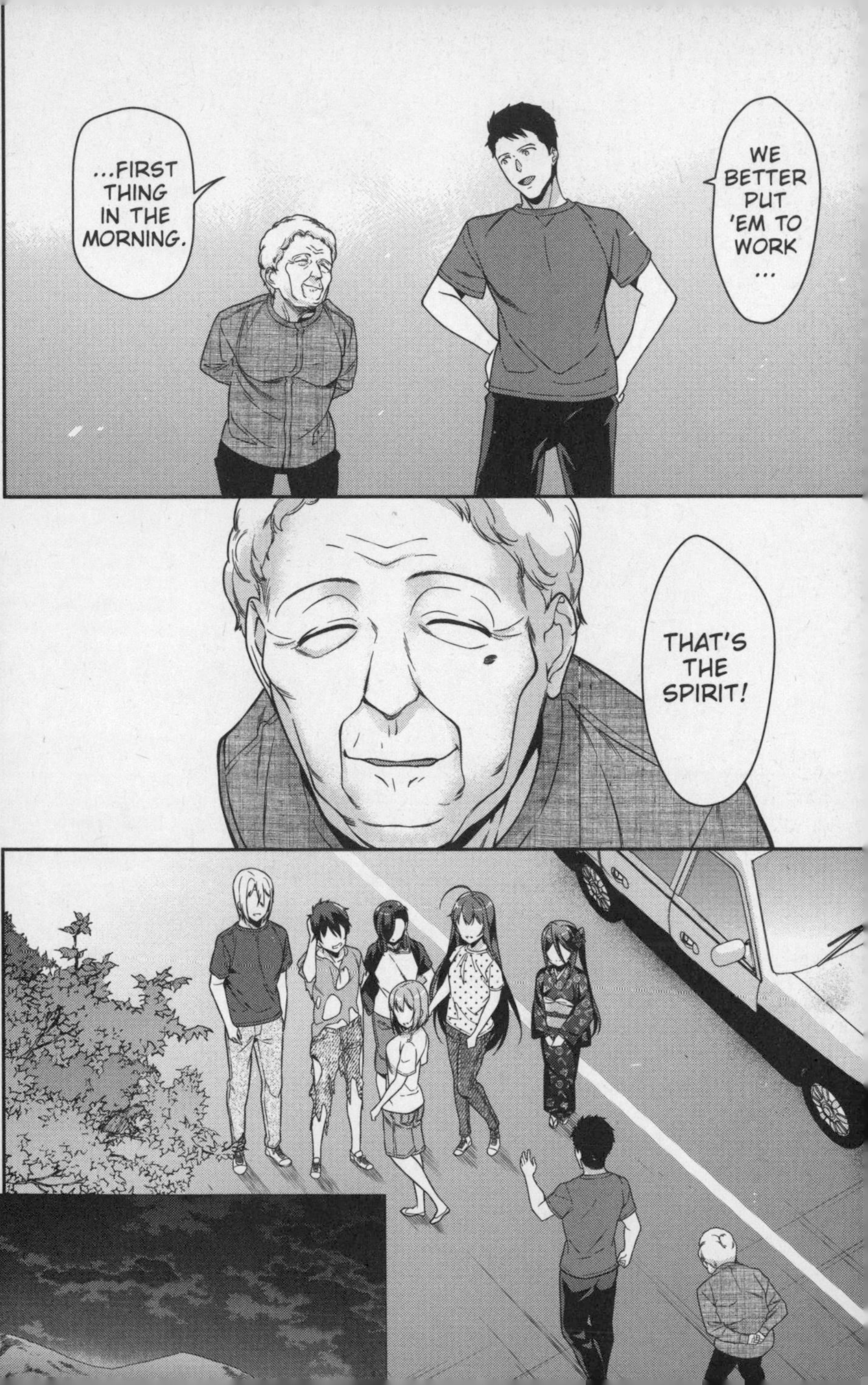
WE BETTER PUT 'EM TO WORK ...
...FIRST THING IN THE MORNING.
THAT'S THE SPIRIT!

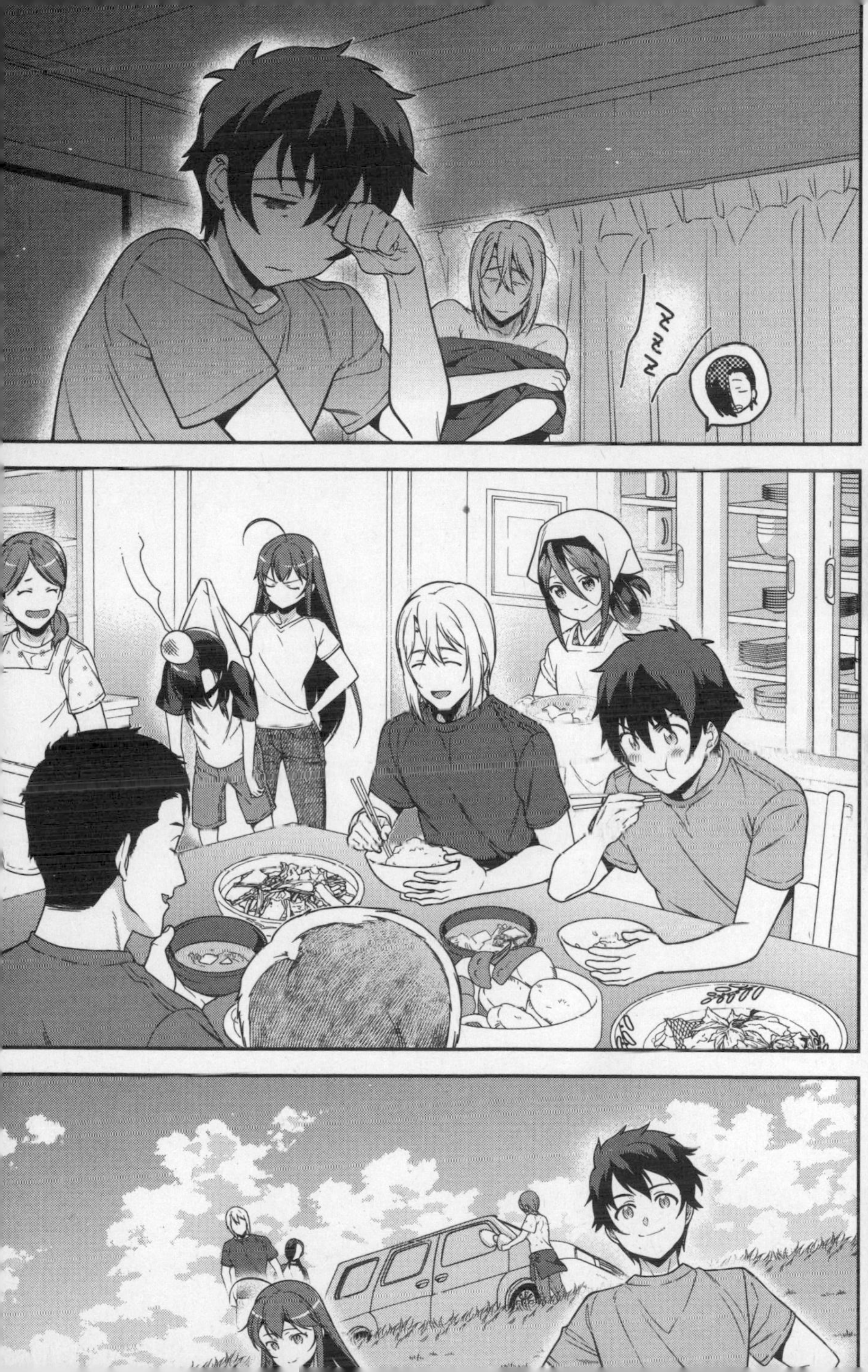
zzz

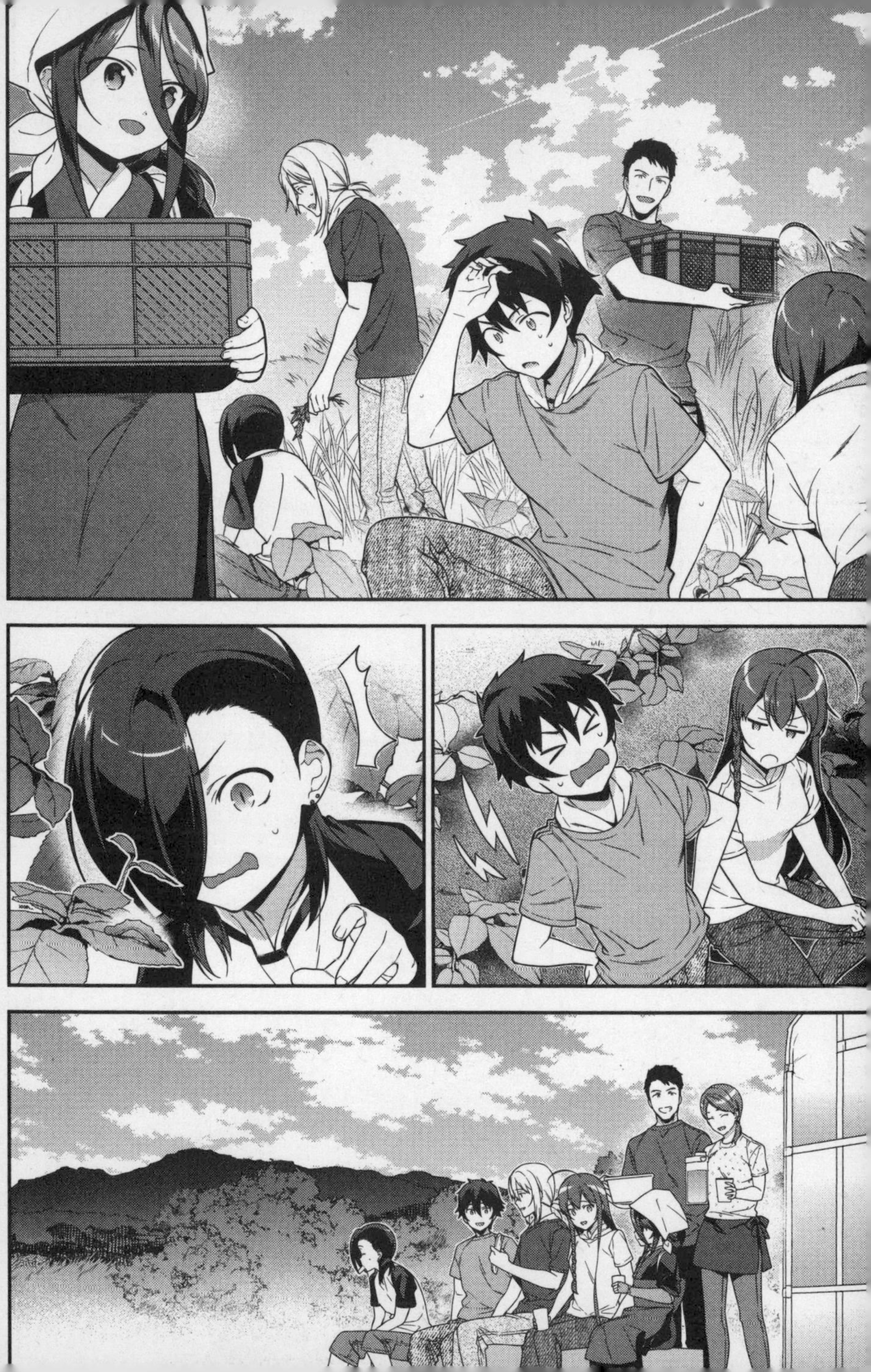

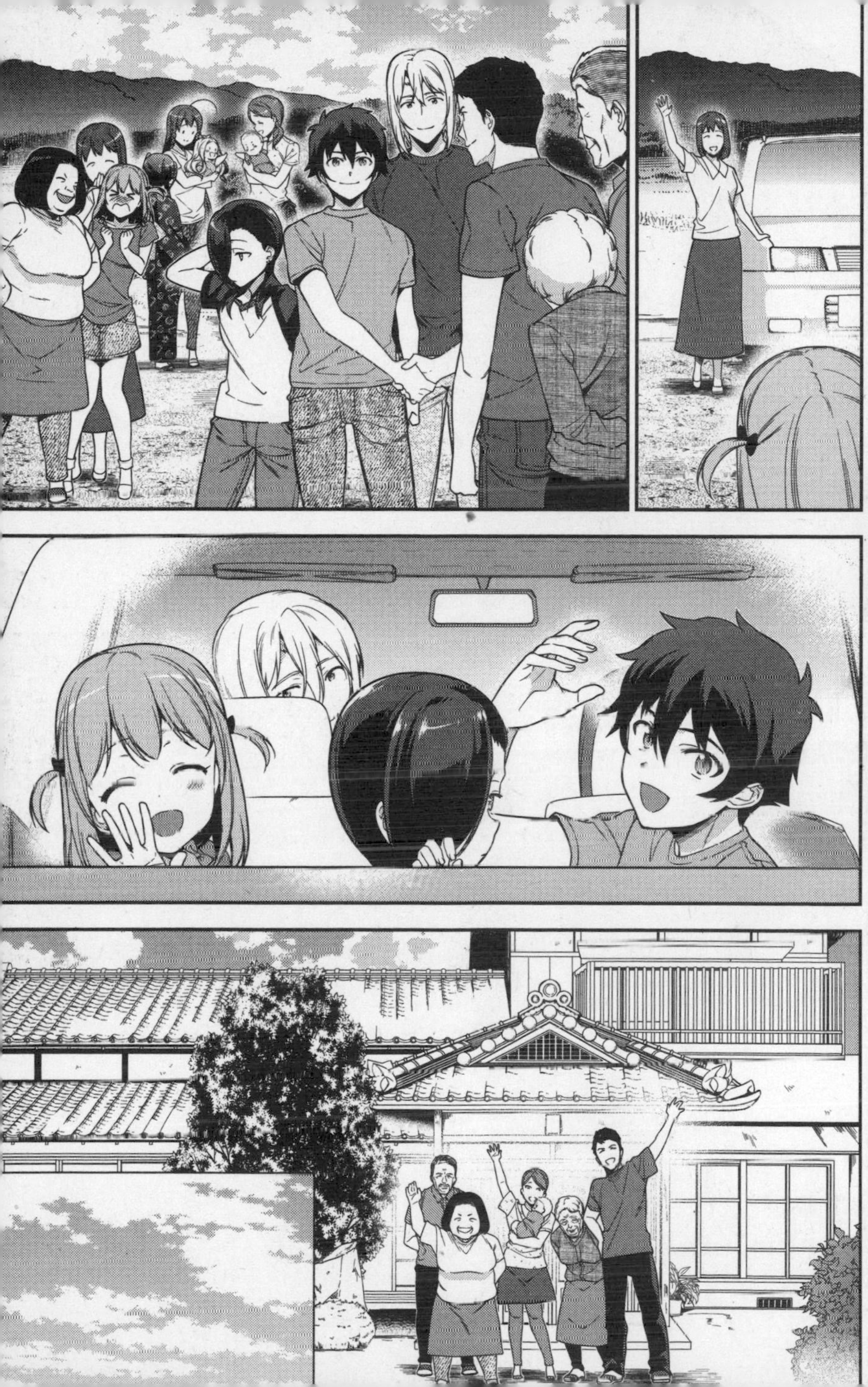

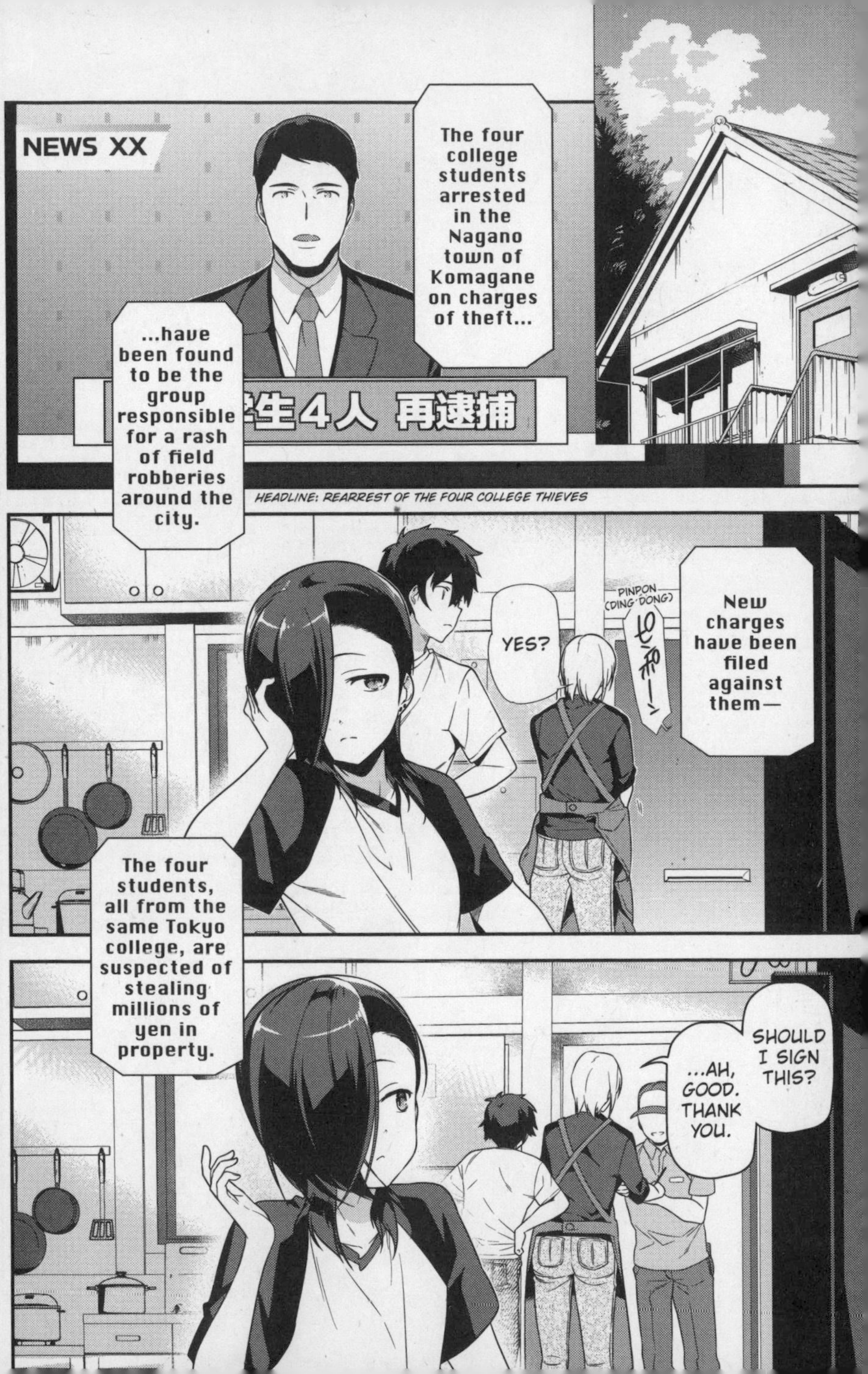
NEWS XX
The four college students arrested in the Nagano town of Komagane on charges of theft...
生4人 再逮捕
...have been found to be the group responsible for a rash of field robberies around the city.
HEADLINE: REARREST OF THE FOUR COLLEGE THIEVES
New charges have been filed against them—
PINPON (DING DONG)
YES?
The four students, all from the same Tokyo college, are suspected of stealing millions of yen in property.
SHOULD I SIGN THIS?
...AH, GOOD. THANK YOU.

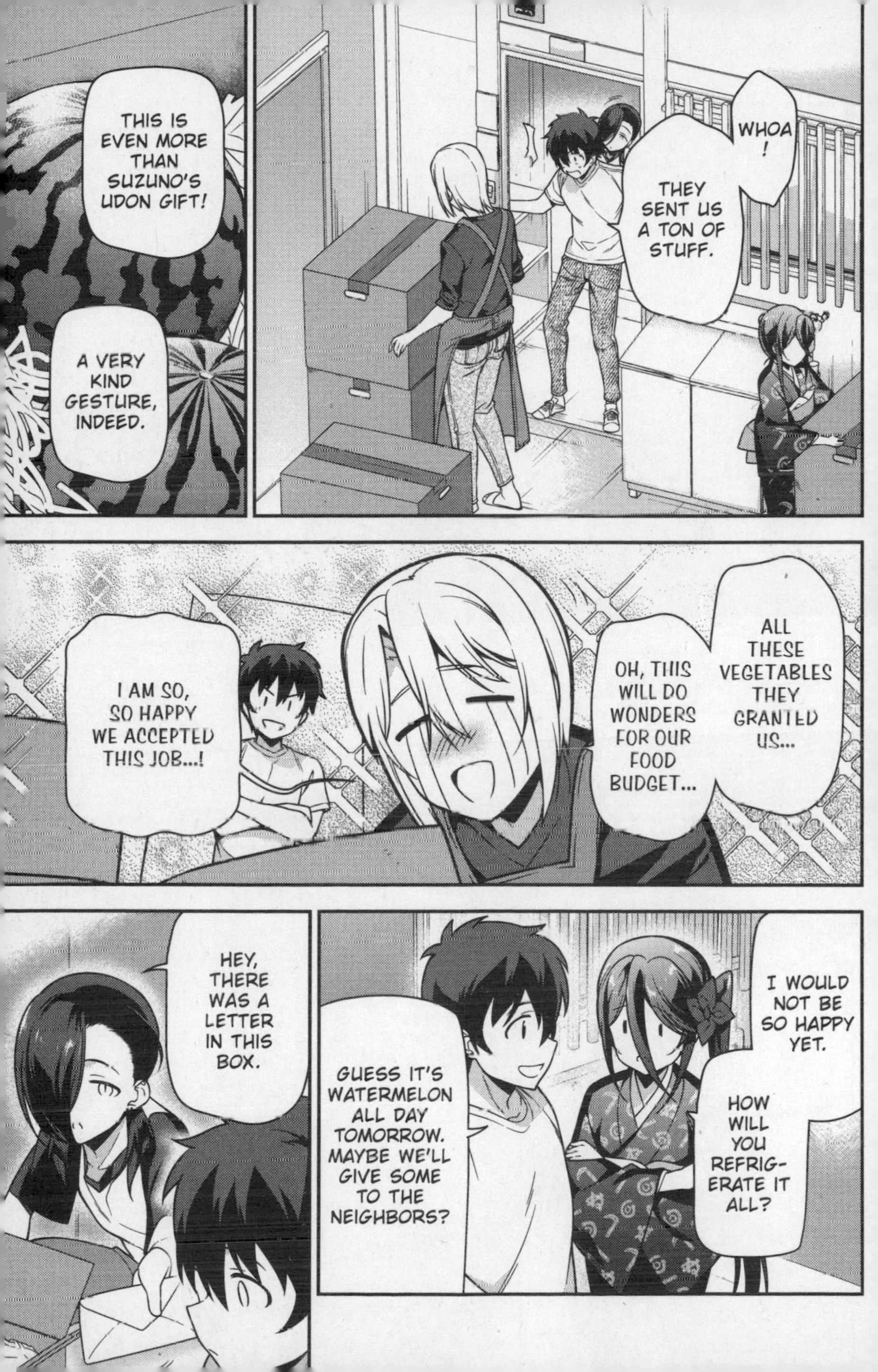
WHOA!
THEY SENT US A TON OF STUFF.
THIS IS EVEN MORE THAN SUZUNO'S UDON GIFT!
A VERY KIND GESTURE, INDEED.
ALL THESE VEGETABLES THEY GRANTED US...
OH, THIS WILL DO WONDERS FOR OUR FOOD BUDGET...
I AM SO, SO HAPPY WE ACCEPTED THIS JOB...!
I WOULD NOT BE SO HAPPY YET.
HOW WILL YOU REFRIGERATE IT ALL?
GUESS IT'S WATERMELON ALL DAY TOMORROW. MAYBE WE'LL GIVE SOME TO THE NEIGHBORS?
HEY, THERE WAS A LETTER IN THIS BOX.

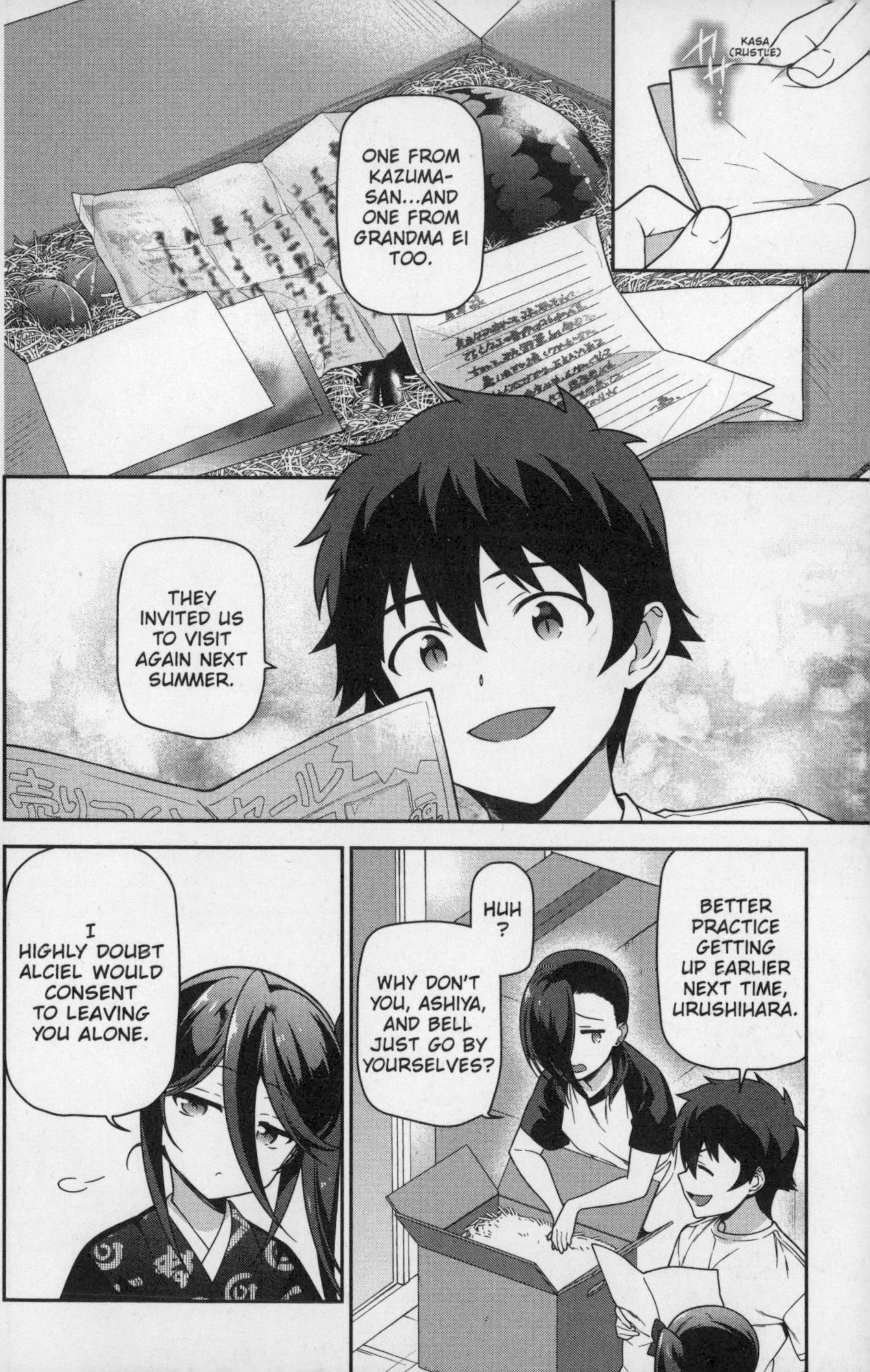
KASA (RUSTLE)
ONE FROM KAZUMA-SAN...AND ONE FROM GRANDMA EI TOO.
THEY INVITED US TO VISIT AGAIN NEXT SUMMER.
BETTER PRACTICE GETTING UP EARLIER NEXT TIME, URUSHIHARA.
HUH?
WHY DON'T YOU, ASHIYA, AND BELL JUST GO BY YOURSELVES?
I HIGHLY DOUBT ALCIEL WOULD CONSENT TO LEAVING YOU ALONE.

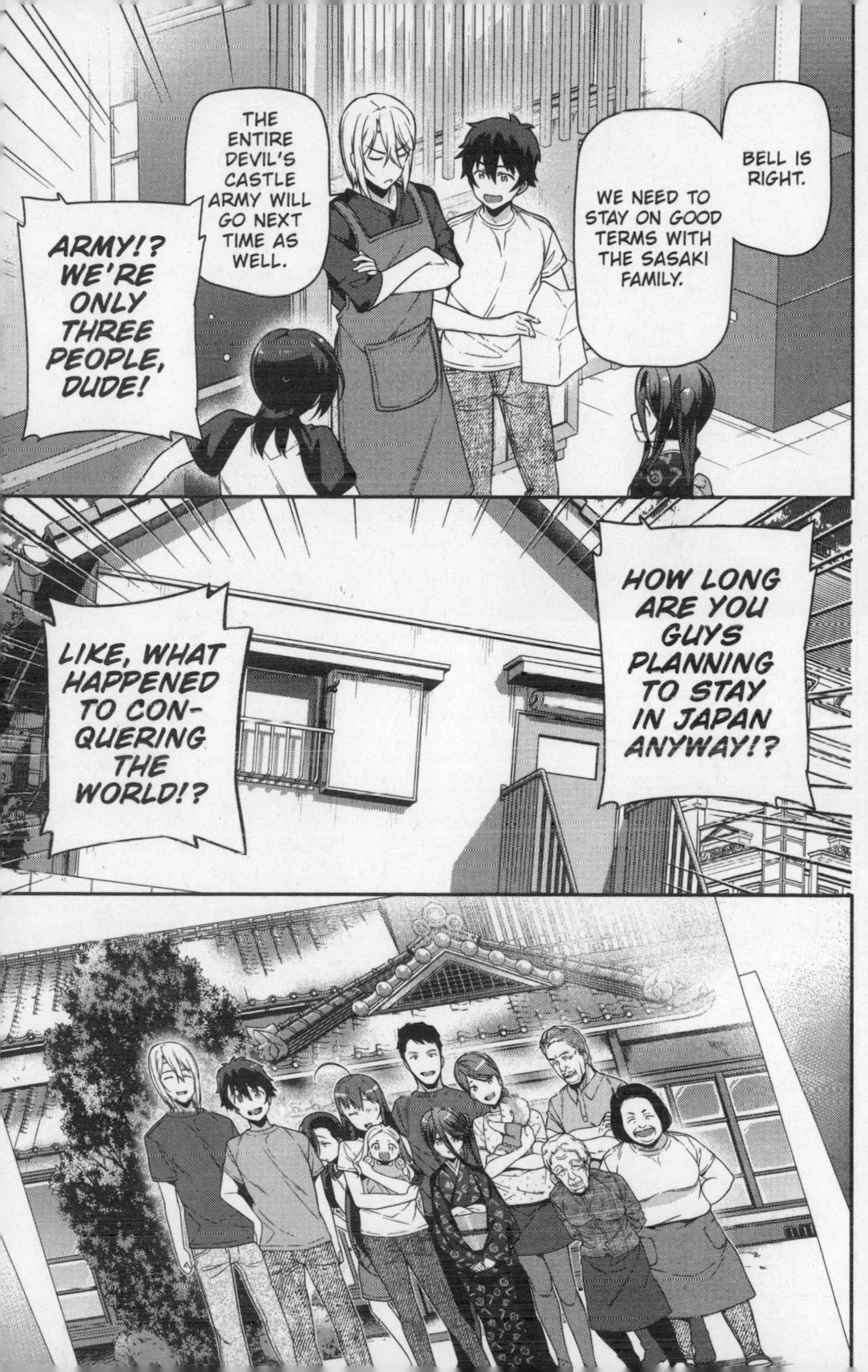
BELL IS RIGHT.
WE NEED TO STAY ON GOOD TERMS WITH THE SASAKI FAMILY.
THE ENTIRE DEVIL'S CASTLE ARMY WILL GO NEXT TIME AS WELL.
ARMY!? WE'RE ONLY THREE PEOPLE, DUDE!
HOW LONG ARE YOU GUYS PLANNING TO STAY IN JAPAN ANYWAY!?
LIKE, WHAT HAPPENED TO CON-QUERING THE WORLD!?

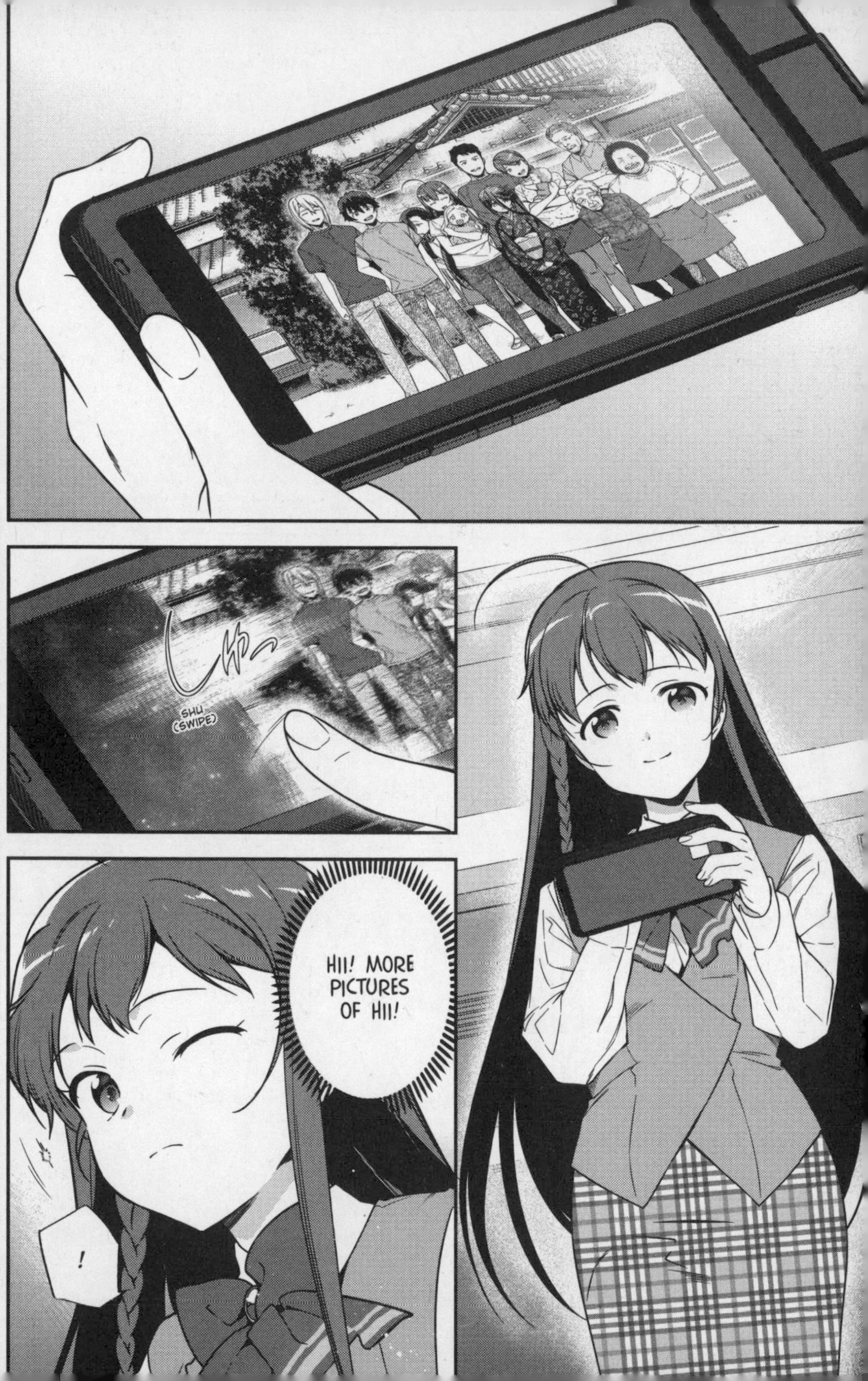
しゅっ
SHU (SWIPE)
HII! MORE PICTURES OF HII!
!

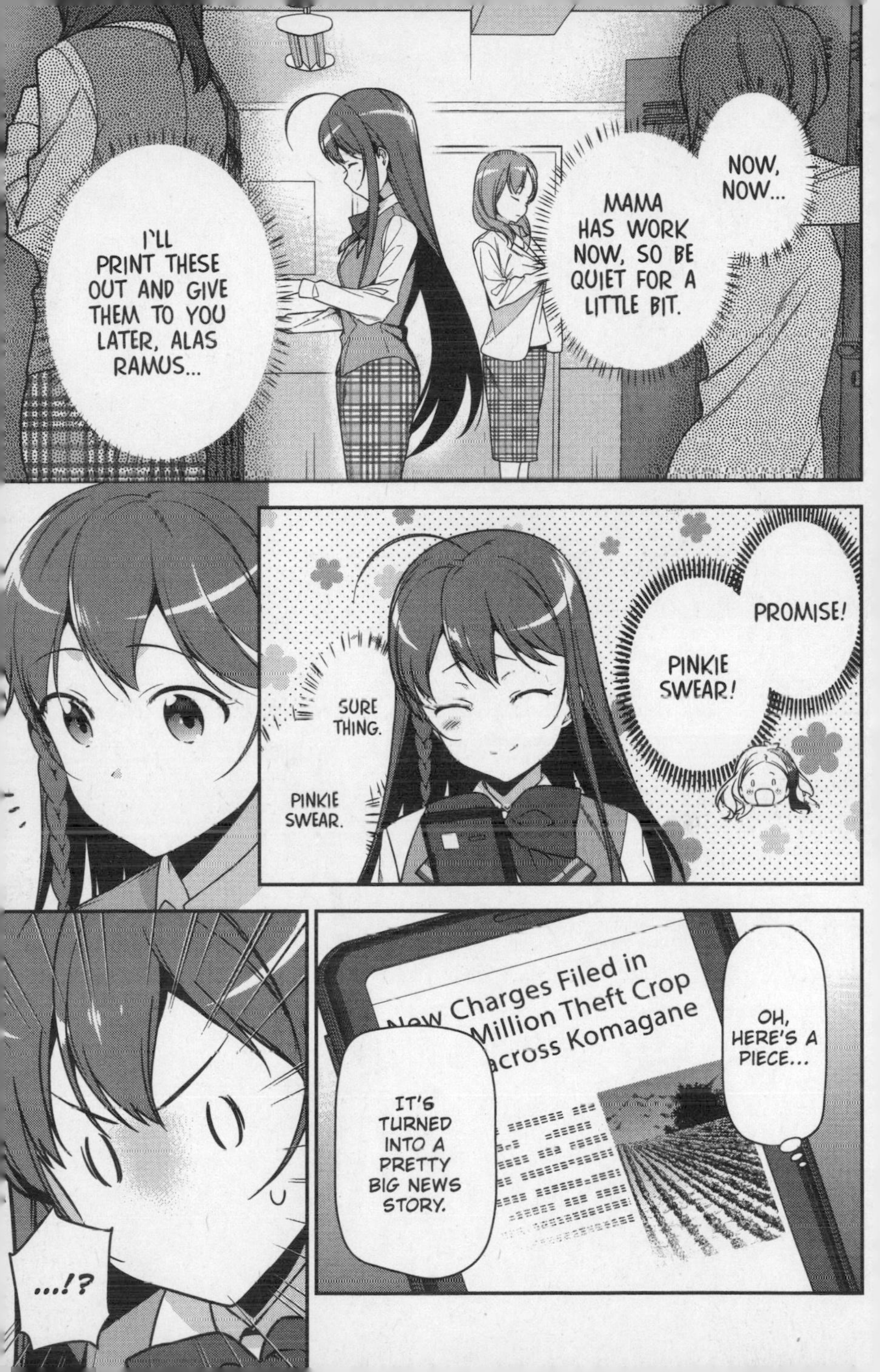
NOW, NOW...
MAMA HAS WORK NOW, SO BE QUIET FOR A LITTLE BIT.
I'LL PRINT THESE OUT AND GIVE THEM TO YOU LATER, ALAS RAMUS...
PROMISE!
PINKIE SWEAR!
SURE THING.
PINKIE SWEAR.
OH, HERE'S A PIECE...
New Charges Filed in
Million Theft Crop
across Komagane
IT'S TURNED INTO A PRETTY BIG NEWS STORY.
...!?

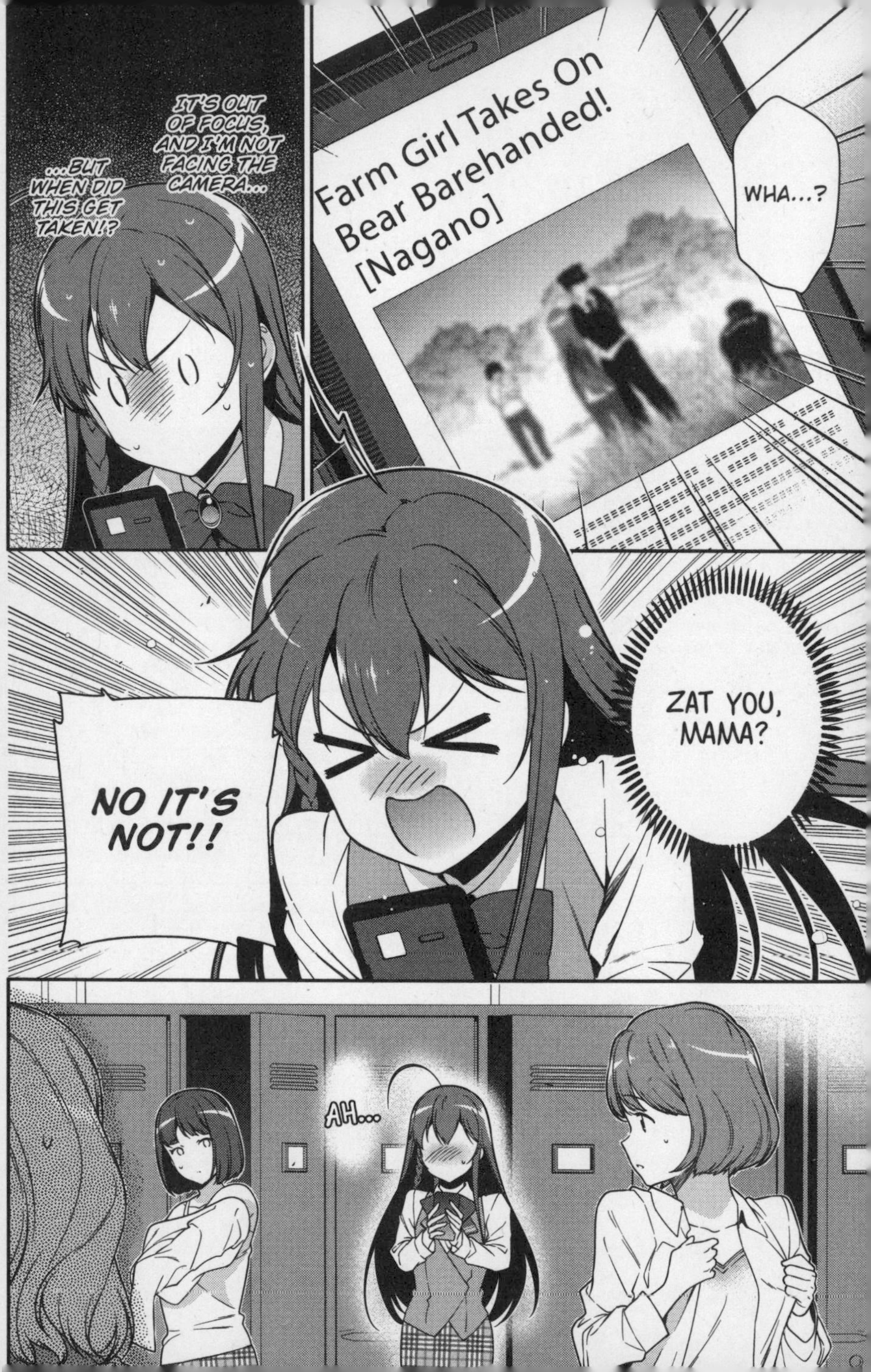
Farm Girl Takes On Bear Barehanded! [Nagano]
WHA...?
IT'S OUT OF FOCUS, AND I'M NOT FACING THE CAMERA...
...BUT WHEN DID THIS GET TAKEN!?
ZAT YOU, MAMA?
NO IT'S NOT!!
AH...

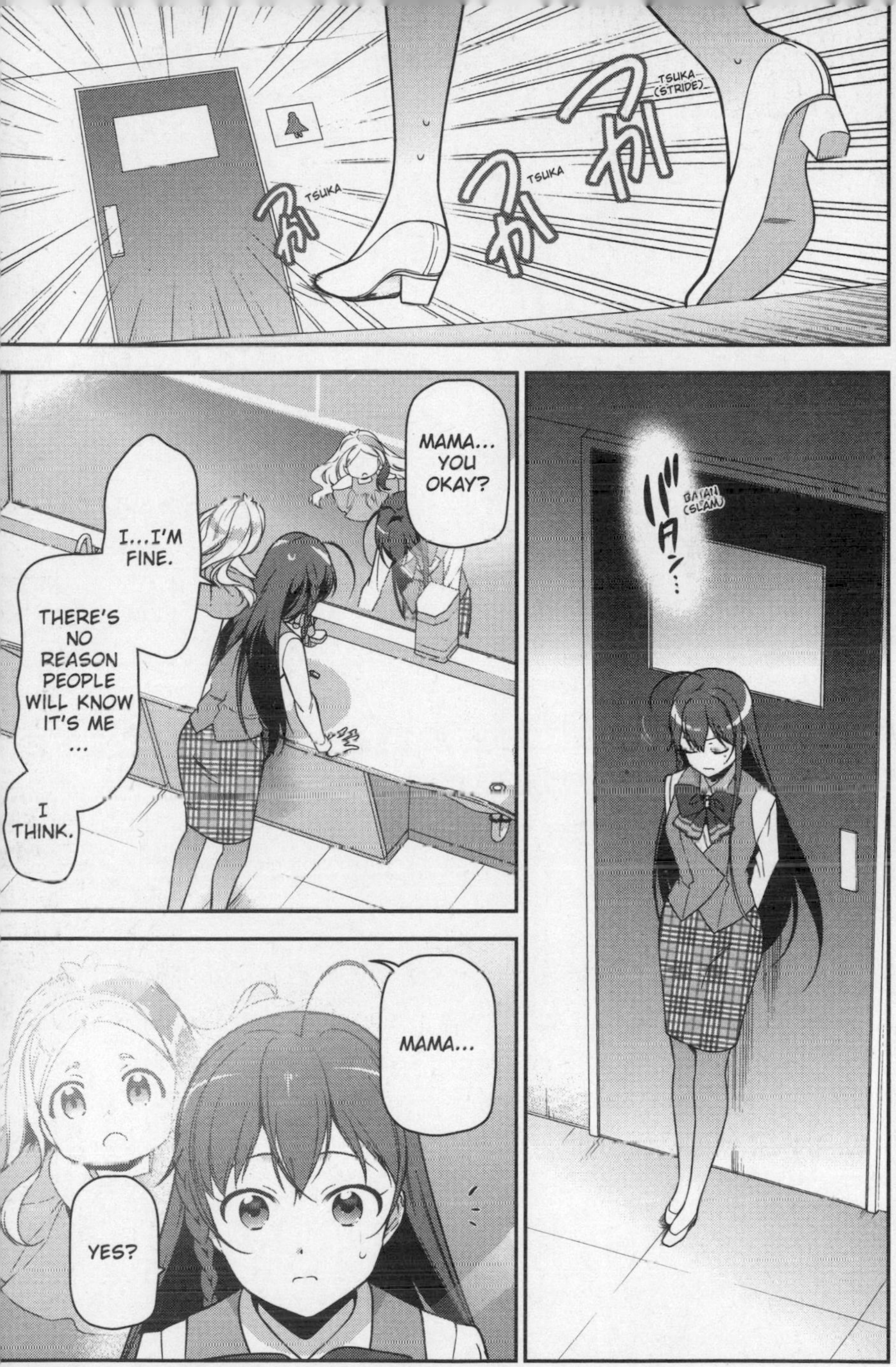
TSUKA (STRIDE)
TSUKA
TSUKA
BATAN (SLAM)
MAMA... YOU OKAY?
I...I'M FINE.
THERE'S NO REASON PEOPLE WILL KNOW IT'S ME ...
I THINK.
MAMA...
YES?

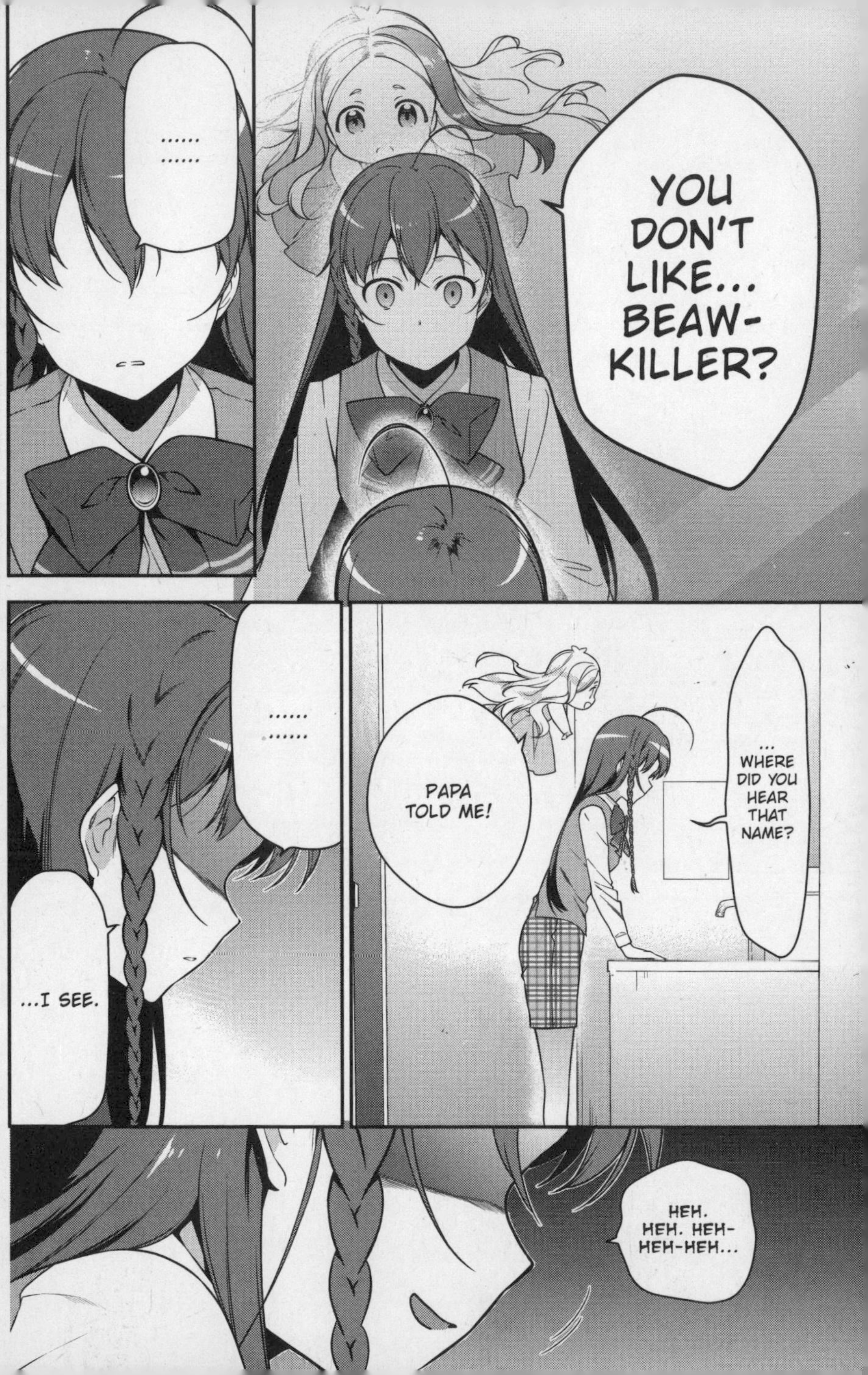
YOU DON'T LIKE... BEAW-KILLER?
......
......
... WHERE DID YOU HEAR THAT NAME?
PAPA TOLD ME!
......
......
...I SEE.
HEH. HEH. HEH-HEH-HEH...

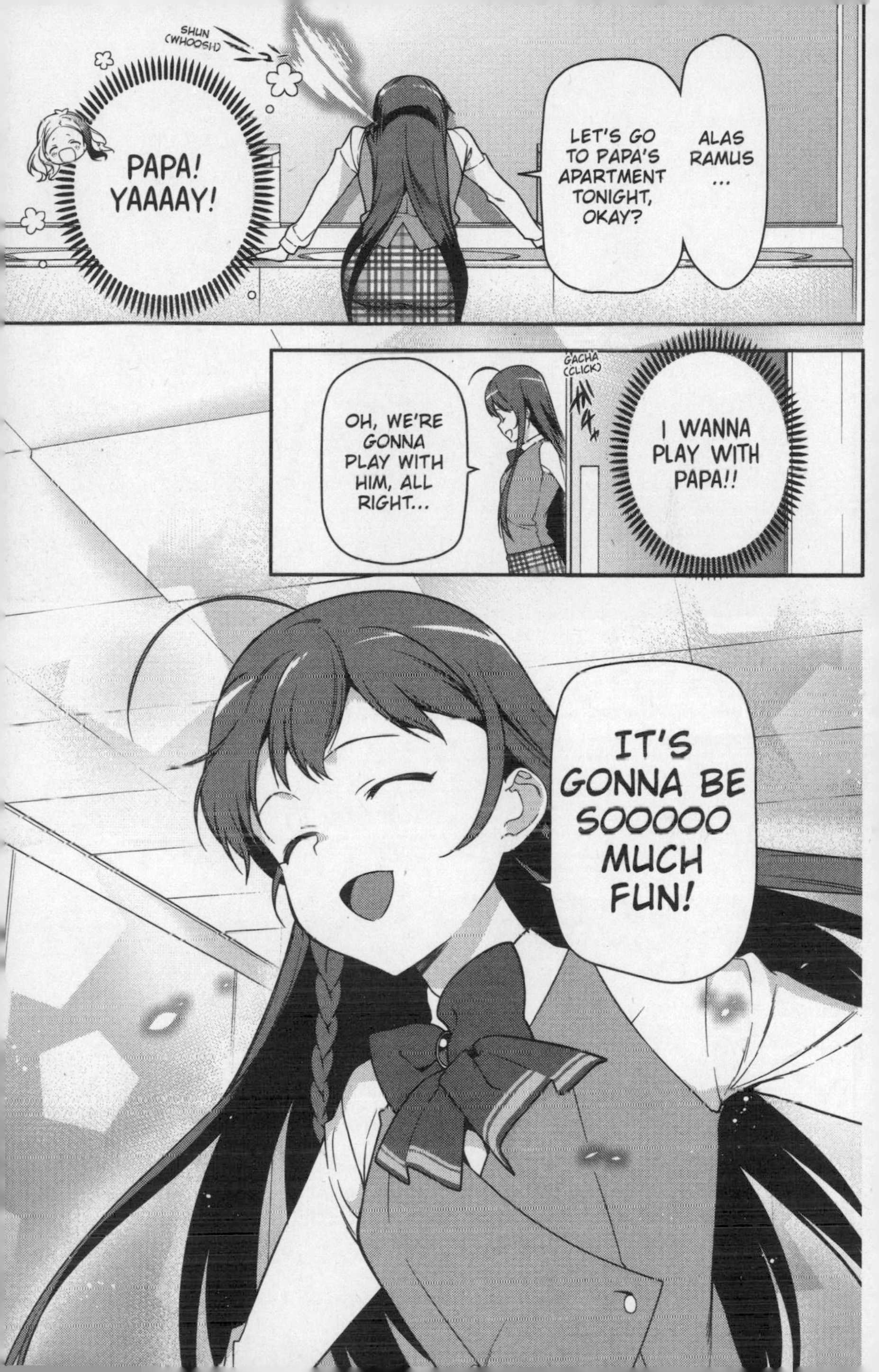
ALAS RAMUS ...
LET'S GO TO PAPA'S APARTMENT TONIGHT, OKAY?
SHUN (WHOOSH)
PAPA! YAAAAY!
I WANNA PLAY WITH PAPA!!
GACHA (CLICK)
OH, WE'RE GONNA PLAY WITH HIM, ALL RIGHT...
IT'S GONNA BE SOOOOO MUCH FUN!

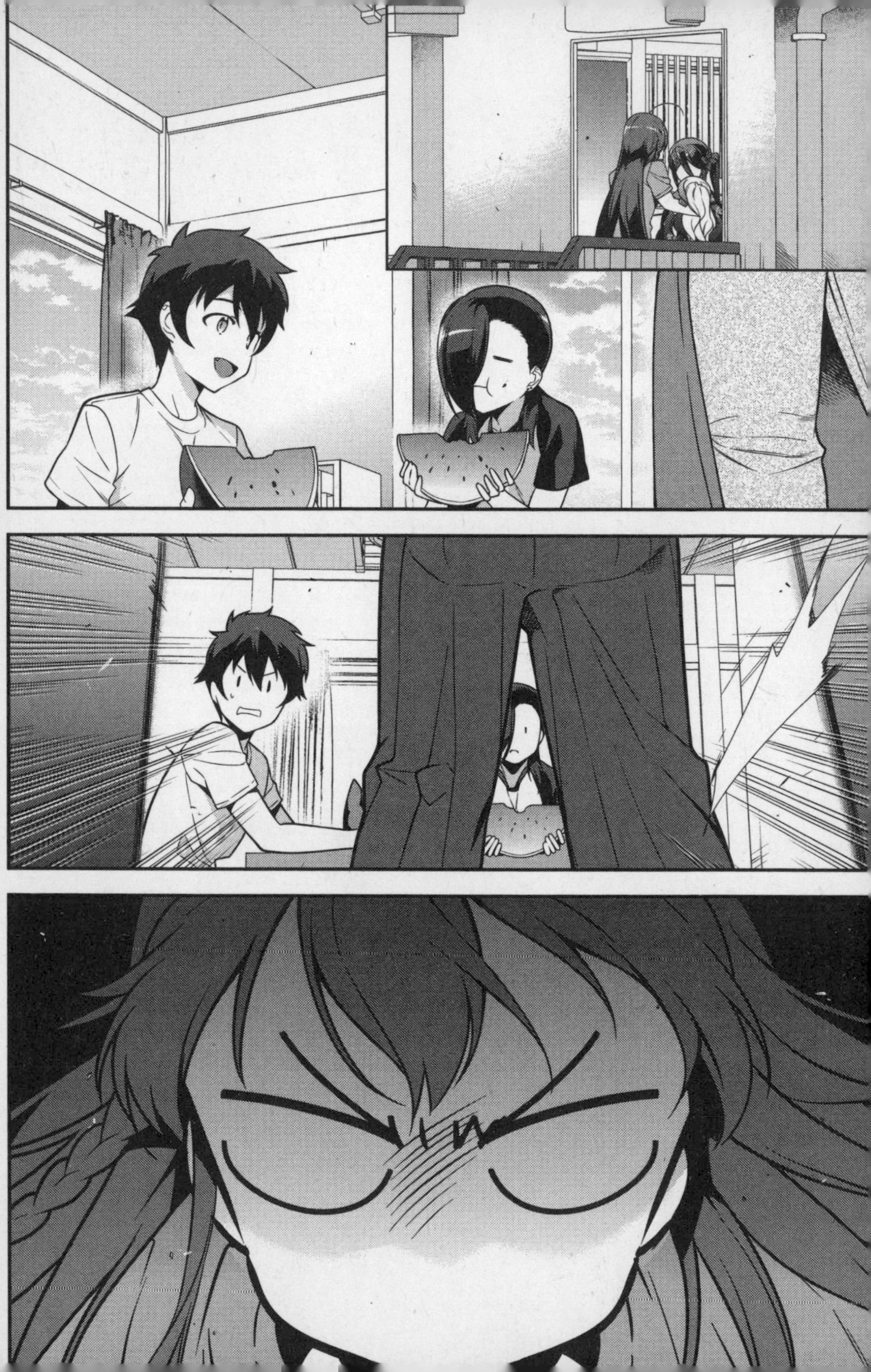

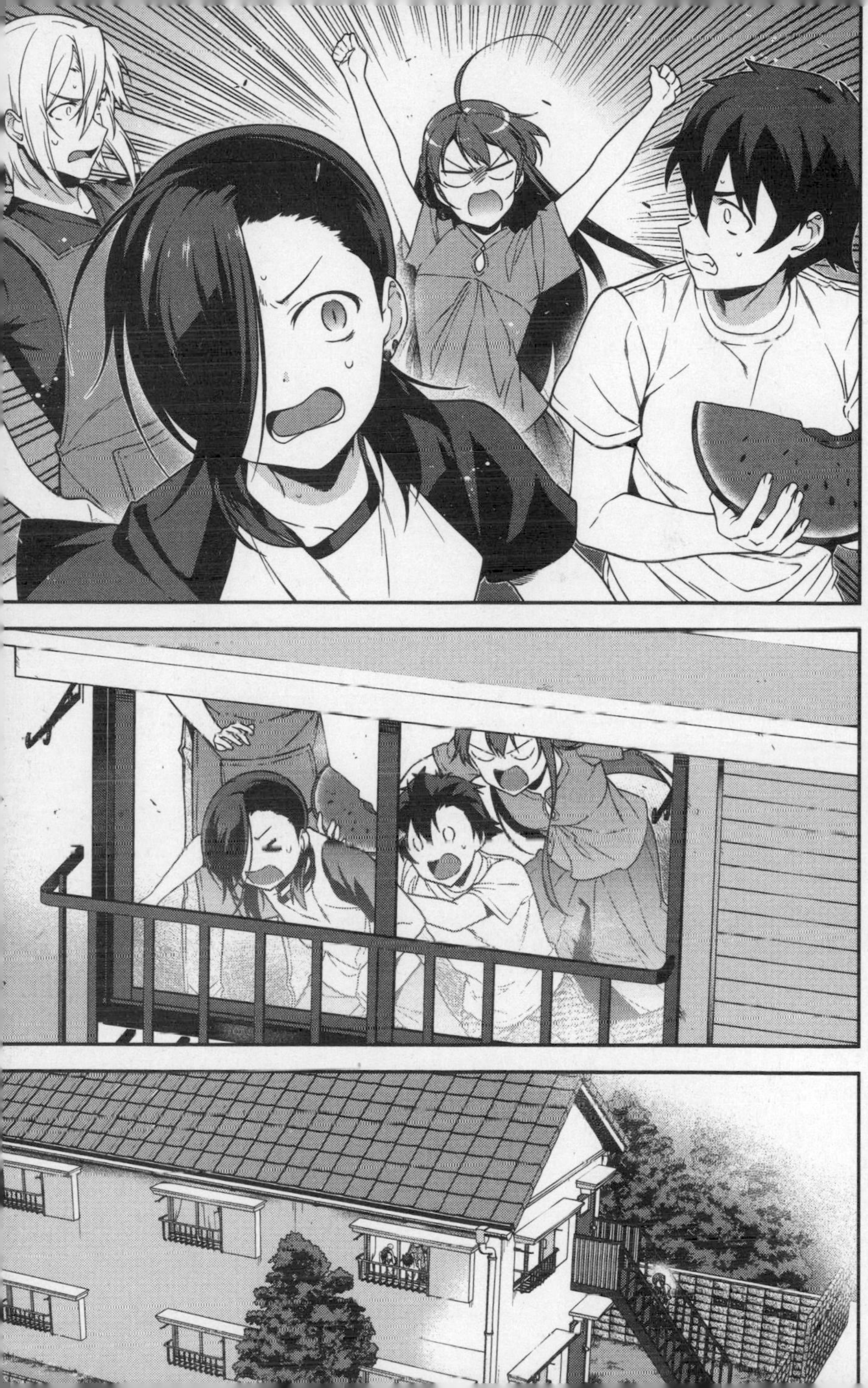

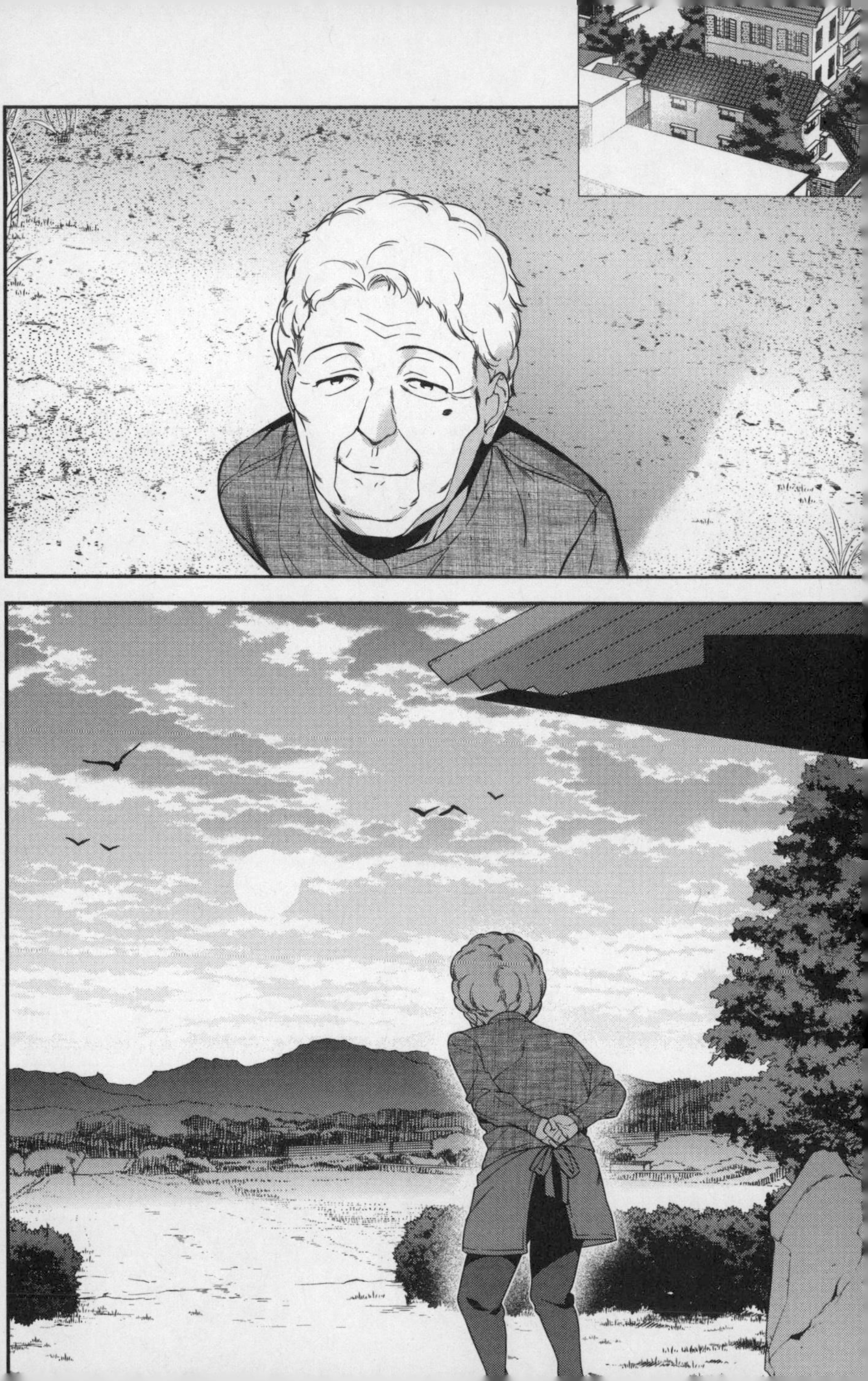

Ei
Sasaki

THE DEVIL IS A PART-TIMER!

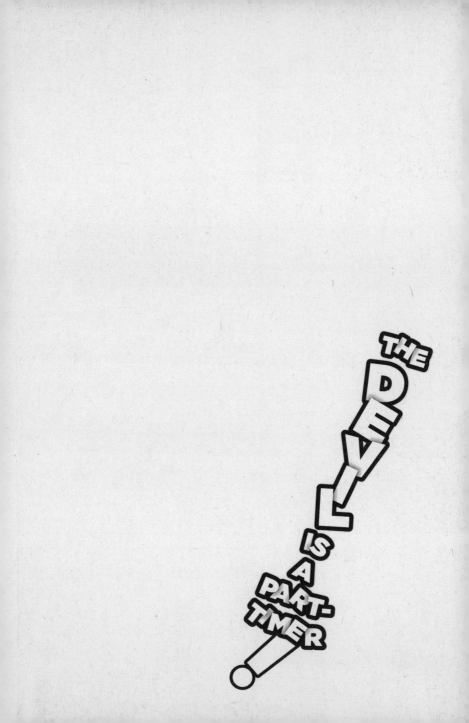

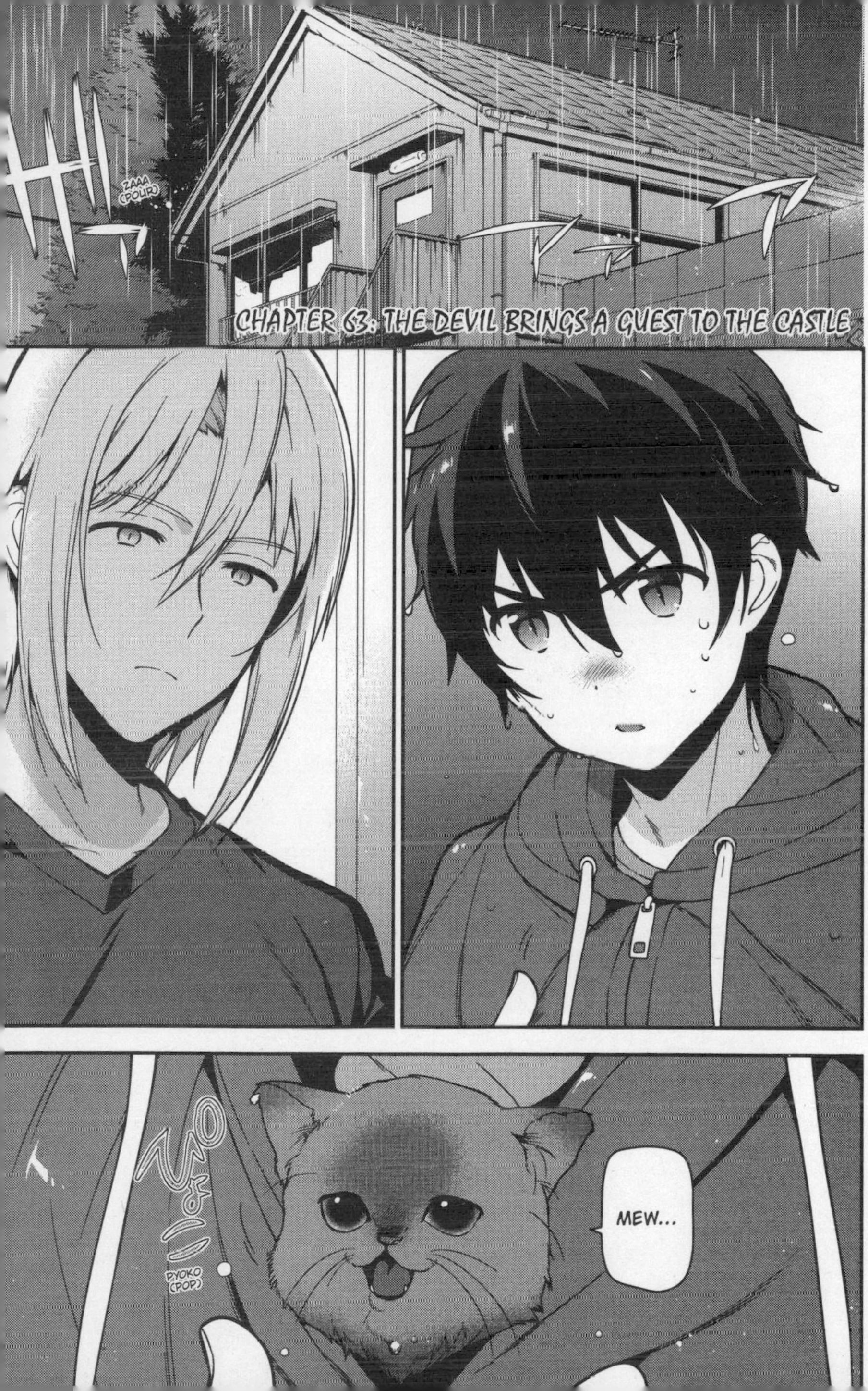
ZAAA (POUR)
CHAPTER 63: THE DEVIL BRINGS A GUEST TO THE CASTLE
MEW...
PYOKO (POP)

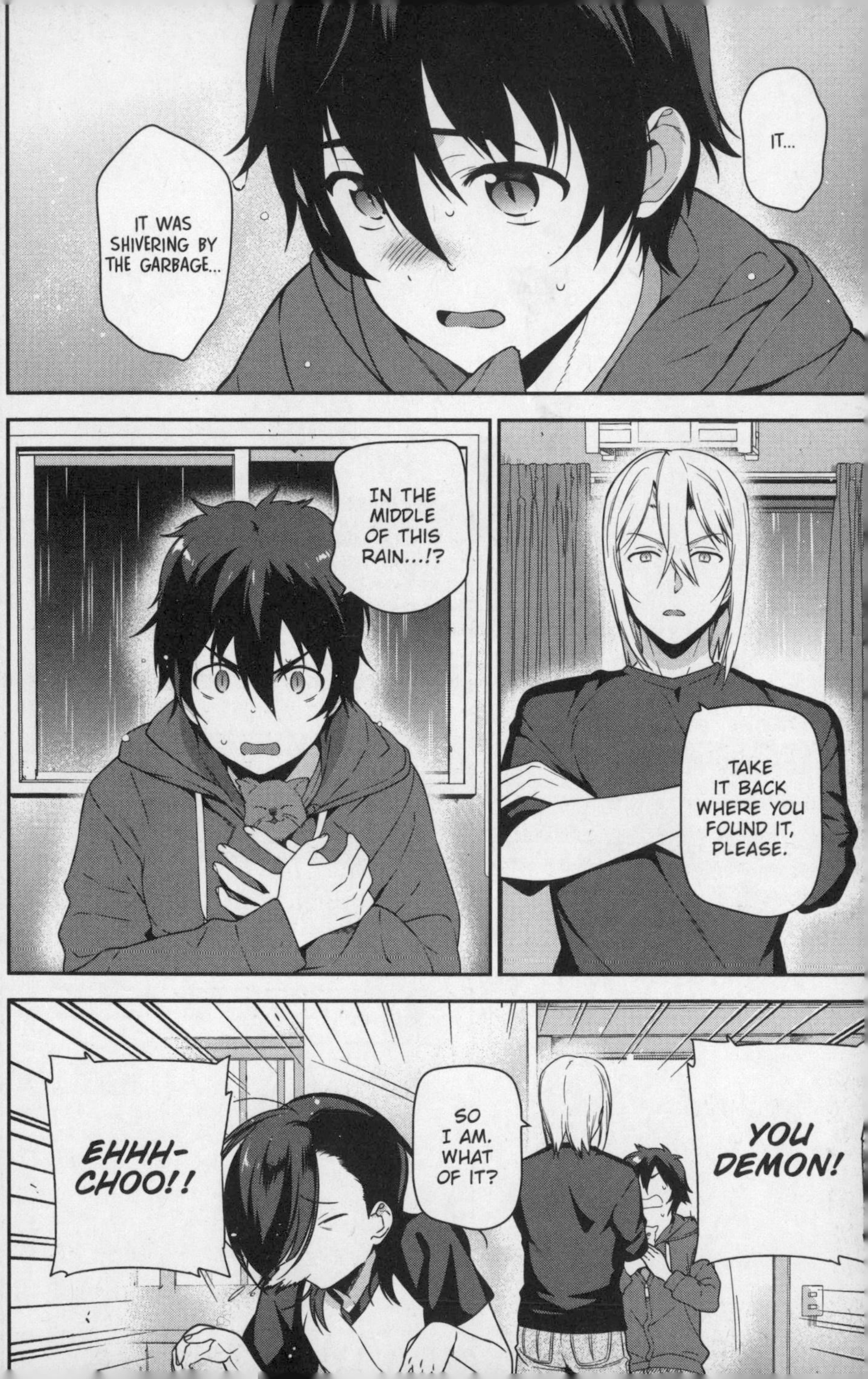
IT...
IT WAS SHIVERING BY THE GARBAGE...
TAKE IT BACK WHERE YOU FOUND IT, PLEASE.
IN THE MIDDLE OF THIS RAIN...!?
YOU DEMON!
SO I AM. WHAT OF IT?
EHHH-CHOO!!

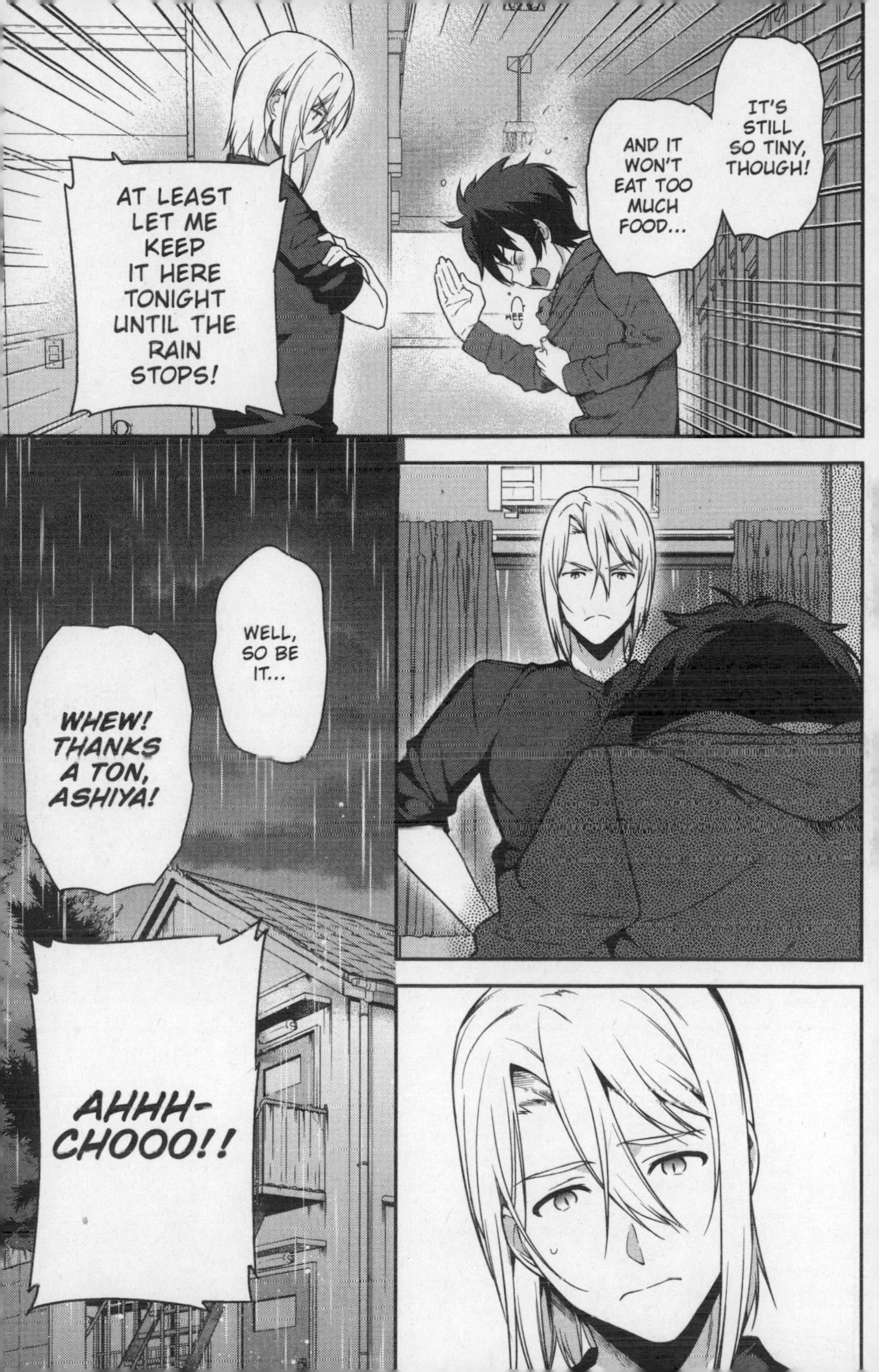
IT'S STILL SO TINY, THOUGH!
AND IT WON'T EAT TOO MUCH FOOD...
MEE
AT LEAST LET ME KEEP IT HERE TONIGHT UNTIL THE RAIN STOPS!
WELL, SO BE IT...
WHEW! THANKS A TON, ASHIYA!
AHHH-CHOOO!!

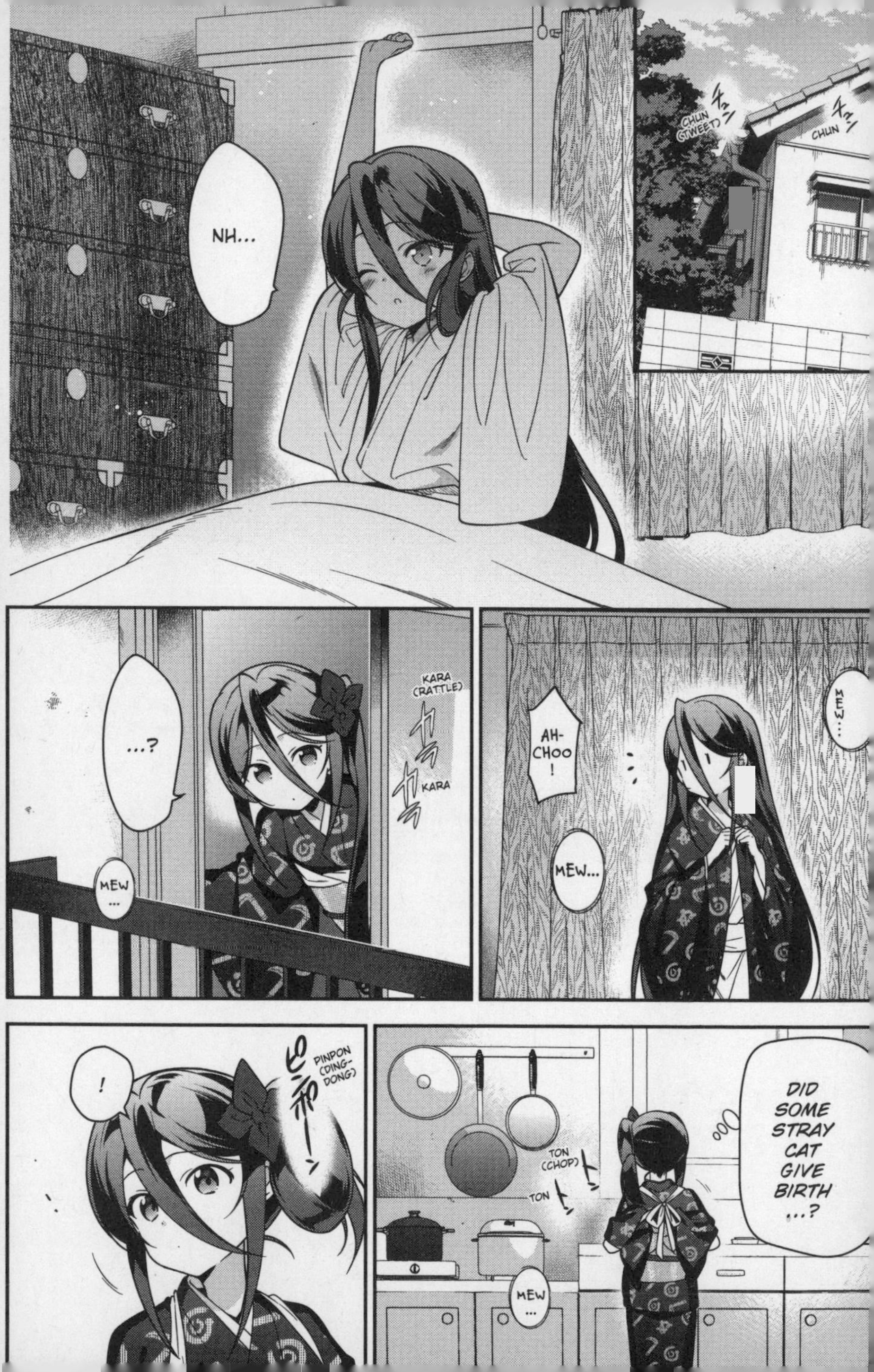
CHUN (TWEET)
CHUN
NH...
MEW...
AH-CHOO!
MEW...
KARA (RATTLE)
KARA
...?
MEW...
DID SOME STRAY CAT GIVE BIRTH...?
TON (CHOP)
TON
MEW...
PINPON (DING-DONG)
!

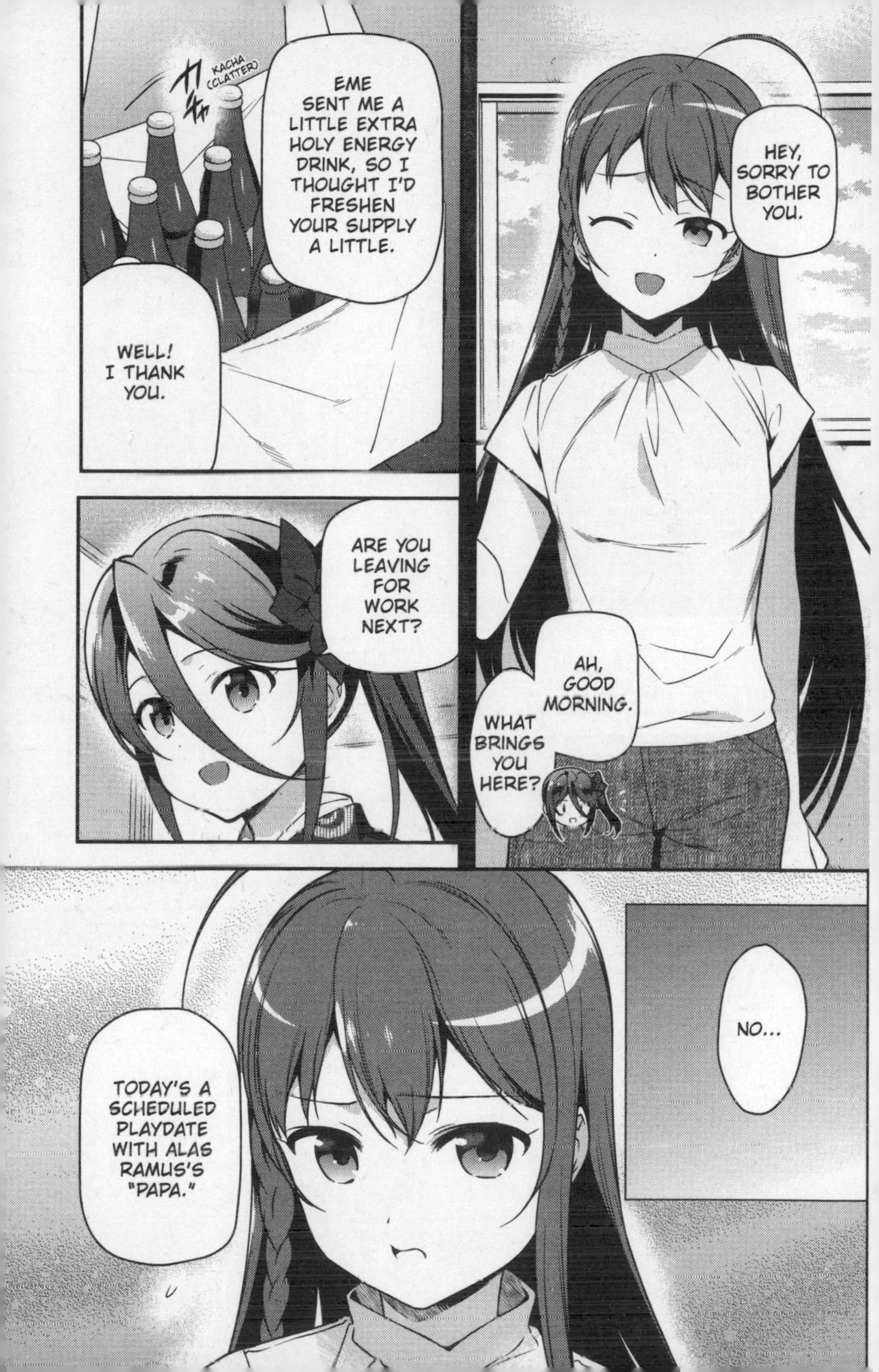
HEY, SORRY TO BOTHER YOU.
AH, GOOD MORNING.
WHAT BRINGS YOU HERE?
EME SENT ME A LITTLE EXTRA HOLY ENERGY DRINK, SO I THOUGHT I'D FRESHEN YOUR SUPPLY A LITTLE.
KACHA (CLATTER)
WELL! I THANK YOU.
ARE YOU LEAVING FOR WORK NEXT?
NO...
TODAY'S A SCHEDULED PLAYDATE WITH ALAS RAMUS'S "PAPA."

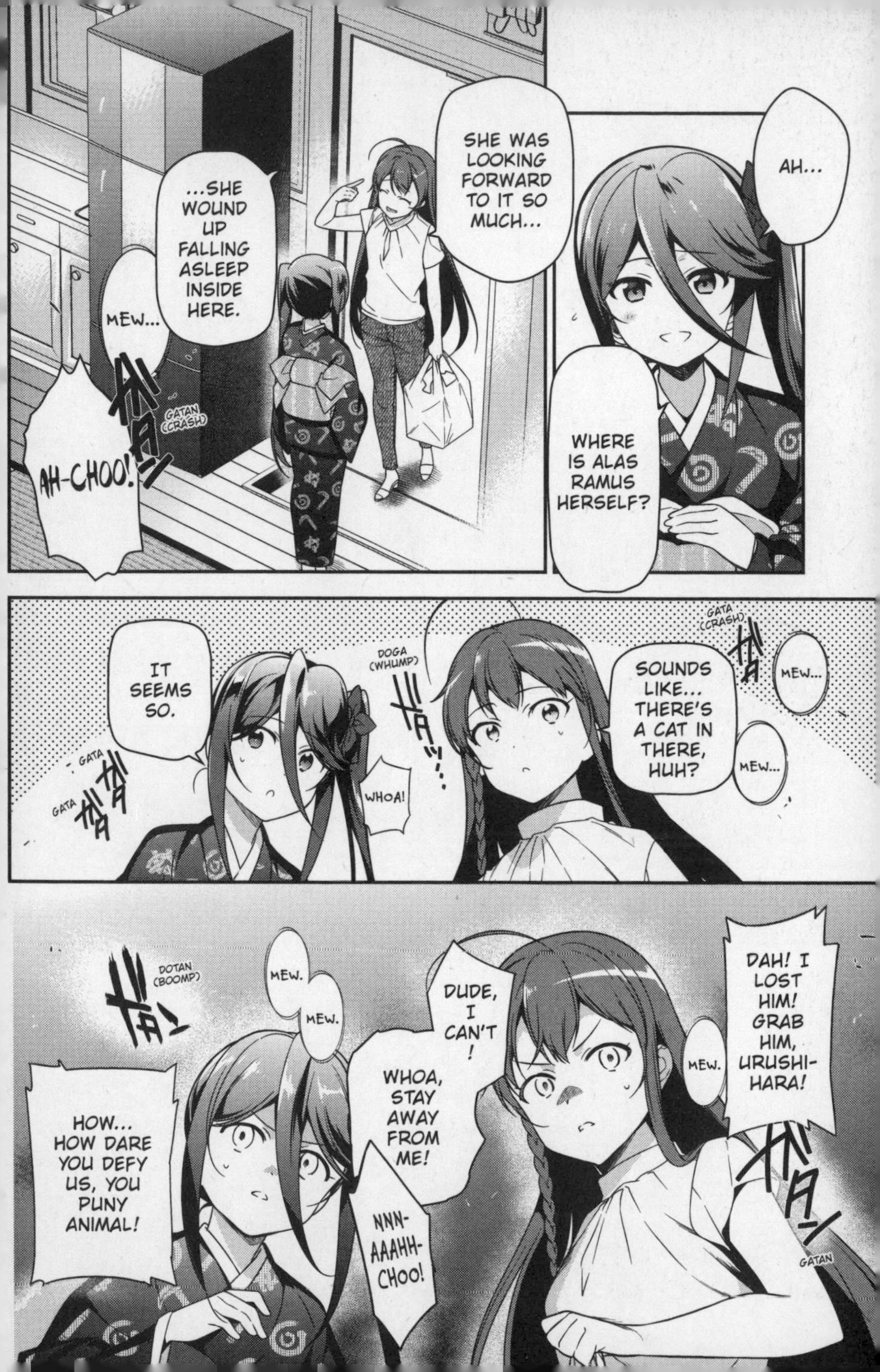
AH...
WHERE IS ALAS RAMUS HERSELF?
SHE WAS LOOKING FORWARD TO IT SO MUCH...
...SHE WOUND UP FALLING ASLEEP INSIDE HERE.
MEW...
GATAN (CRASH)
AH-CHOO!
GATA (CRASH)
MEW...
SOUNDS LIKE... THERE'S A CAT IN THERE, HUH?
MEW...
DOGA (WHUMP)
IT SEEMS SO.
WHOA!
GATA
GATA
DAH! I LOST HIM! GRAB HIM, URUSHIHARA!
MEW.
DUDE, I CAN'T!
WHOA, STAY AWAY FROM ME!
MEW.
MEW.
DOTAN (BOOMP)
HOW... HOW DARE YOU DEFY US, YOU PUNY ANIMAL!
NNN-AAAHH-CHOO!
GATAN

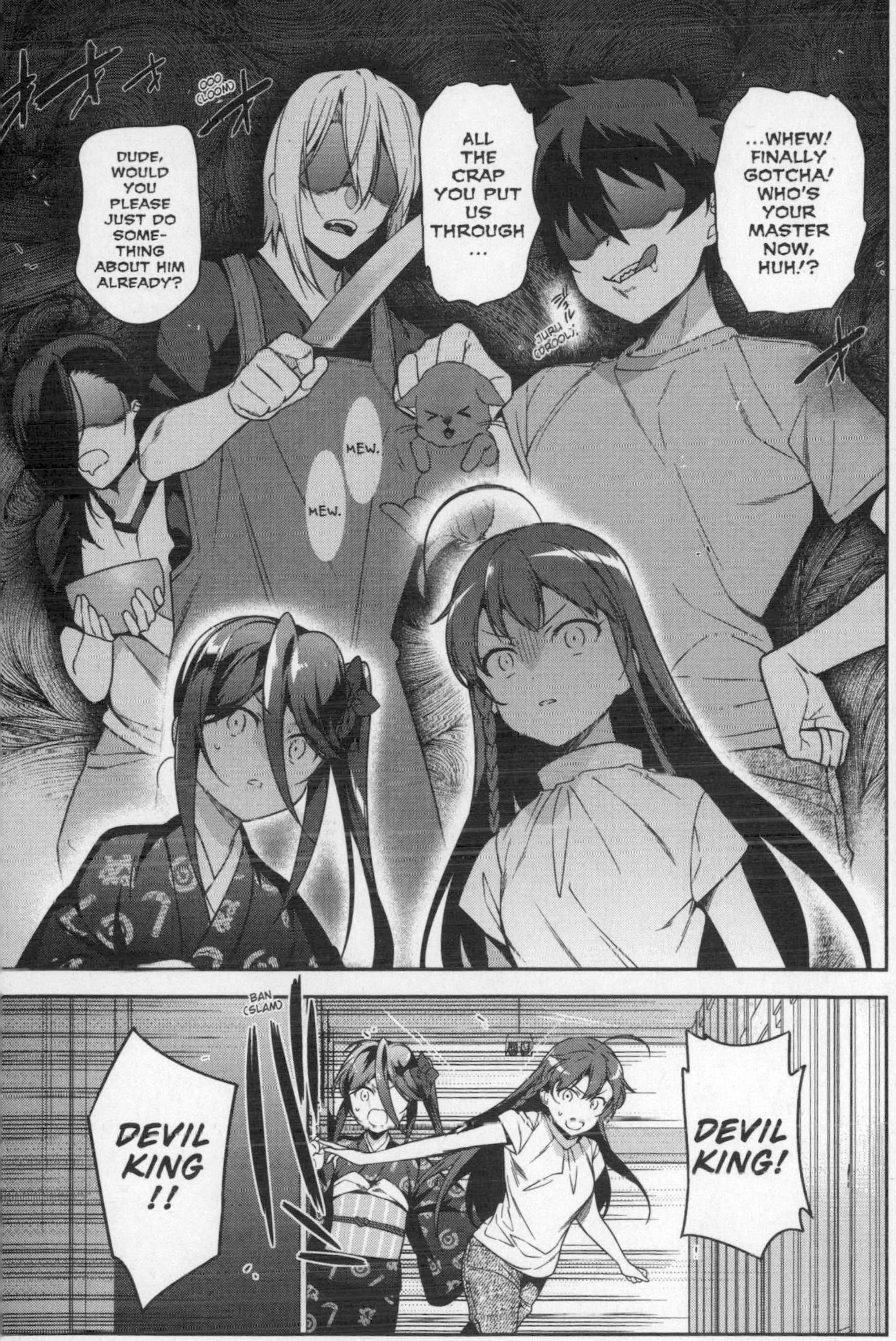
...WHEW! FINALLY GOTCHA! WHO'S YOUR MASTER NOW, HUH!?
JURU (DROOL)
ALL THE CRAP YOU PUT US THROUGH...
OOO (LOOM)
DUDE, WOULD YOU PLEASE JUST DO SOMETHING ABOUT HIM ALREADY?
MEW.
MEW.
DEVIL KING!
BAN (SLAM)
DEVIL KING!!

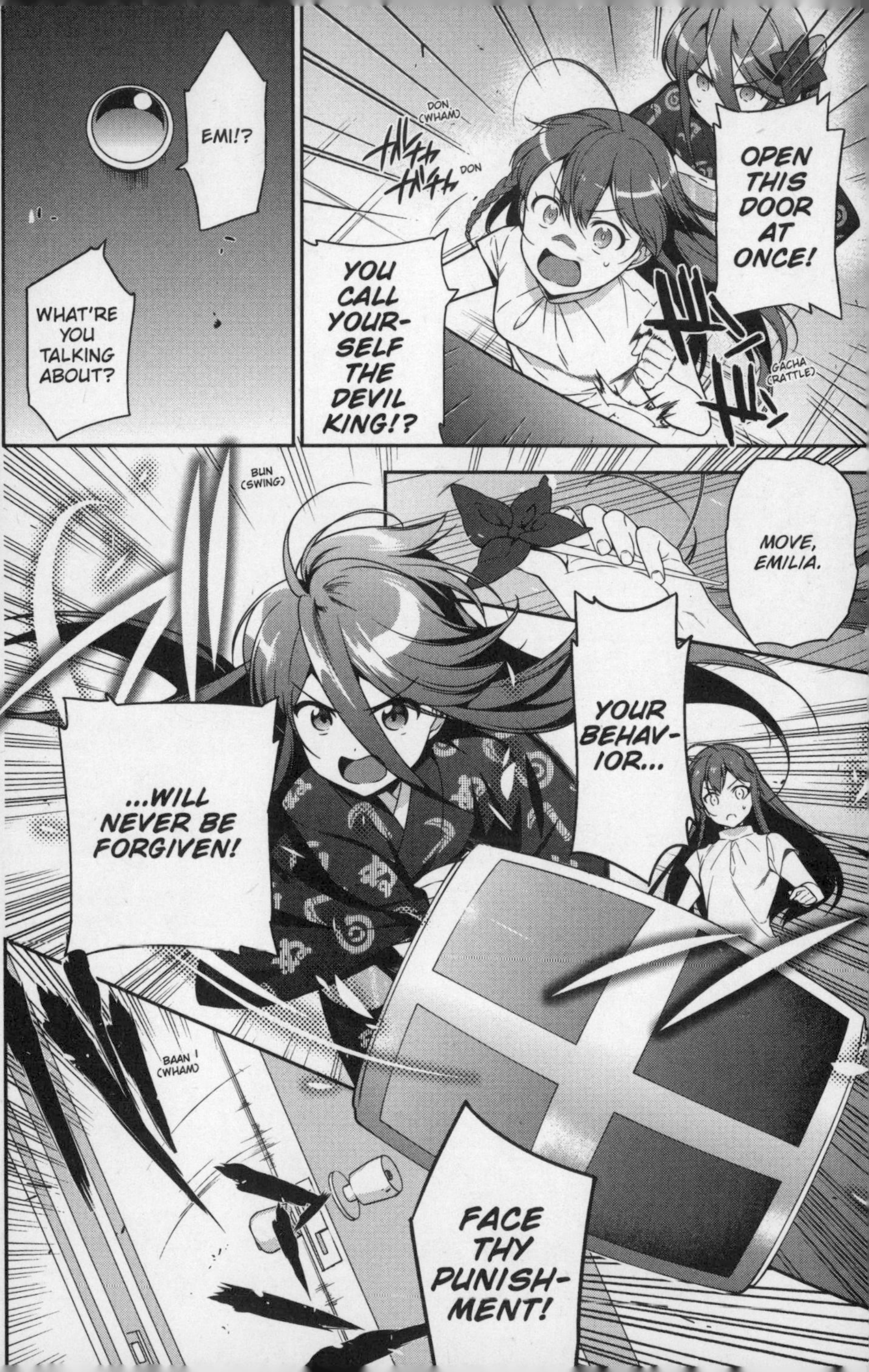
OPEN THIS DOOR AT ONCE!
DON (WHAM)
DON
YOU CALL YOURSELF THE DEVIL KING!?
GACHA (RATTLE)
EMI!?
WHAT'RE YOU TALKING ABOUT?
MOVE, EMILIA.
BUN (SWING)
YOUR BEHAVIOR...
...WILL NEVER BE FORGIVEN!
FACE THY PUNISHMENT!
BAAN (WHAM)

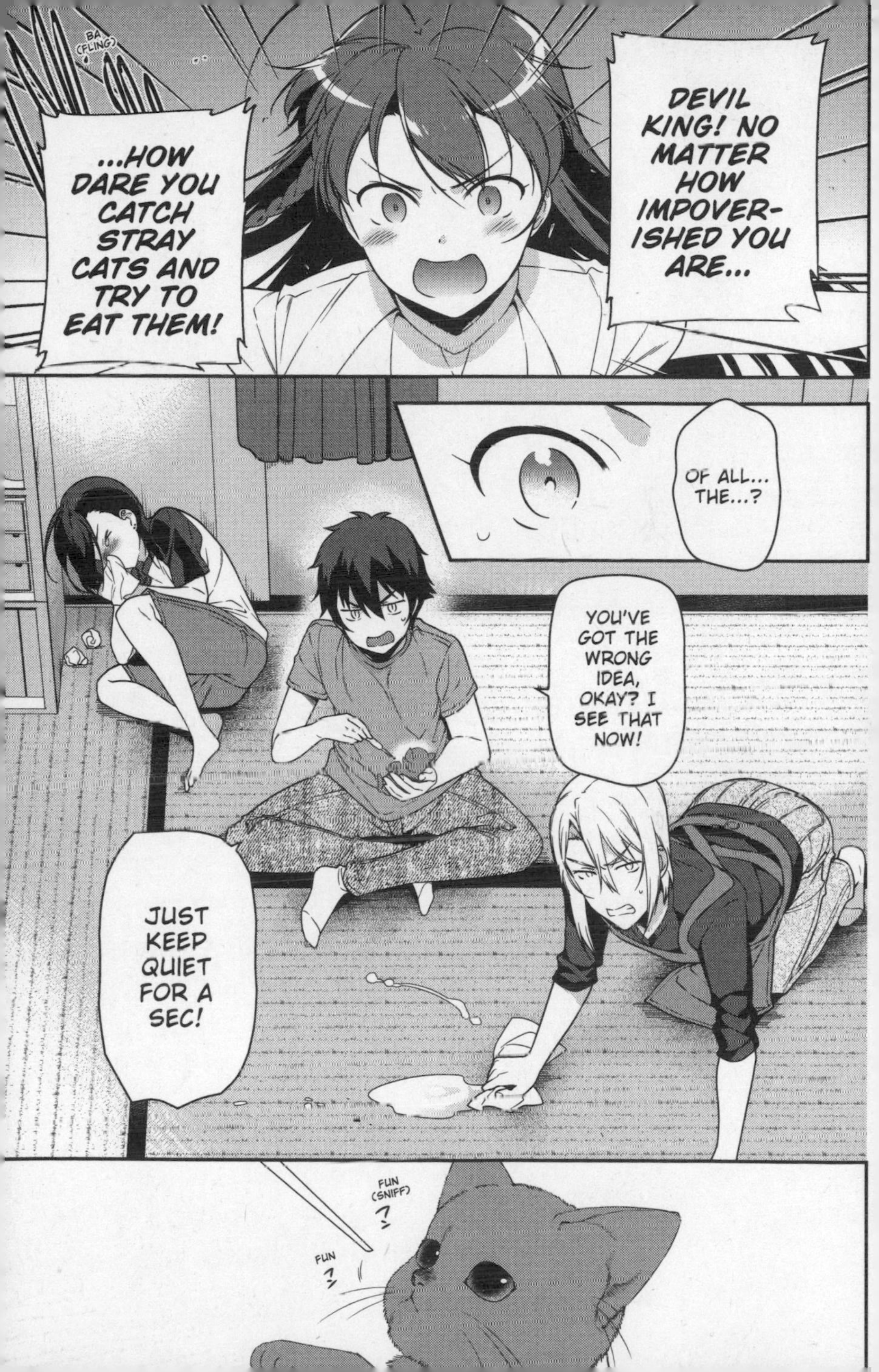
DEVIL KING! NO MATTER HOW IMPOVER-ISHED YOU ARE...
BA (FLING)
...HOW DARE YOU CATCH STRAY CATS AND TRY TO EAT THEM!
OF ALL... THE...?
YOU'VE GOT THE WRONG IDEA, OKAY? I SEE THAT NOW!
JUST KEEP QUIET FOR A SEC!
FUN (SNIFF)
FUN

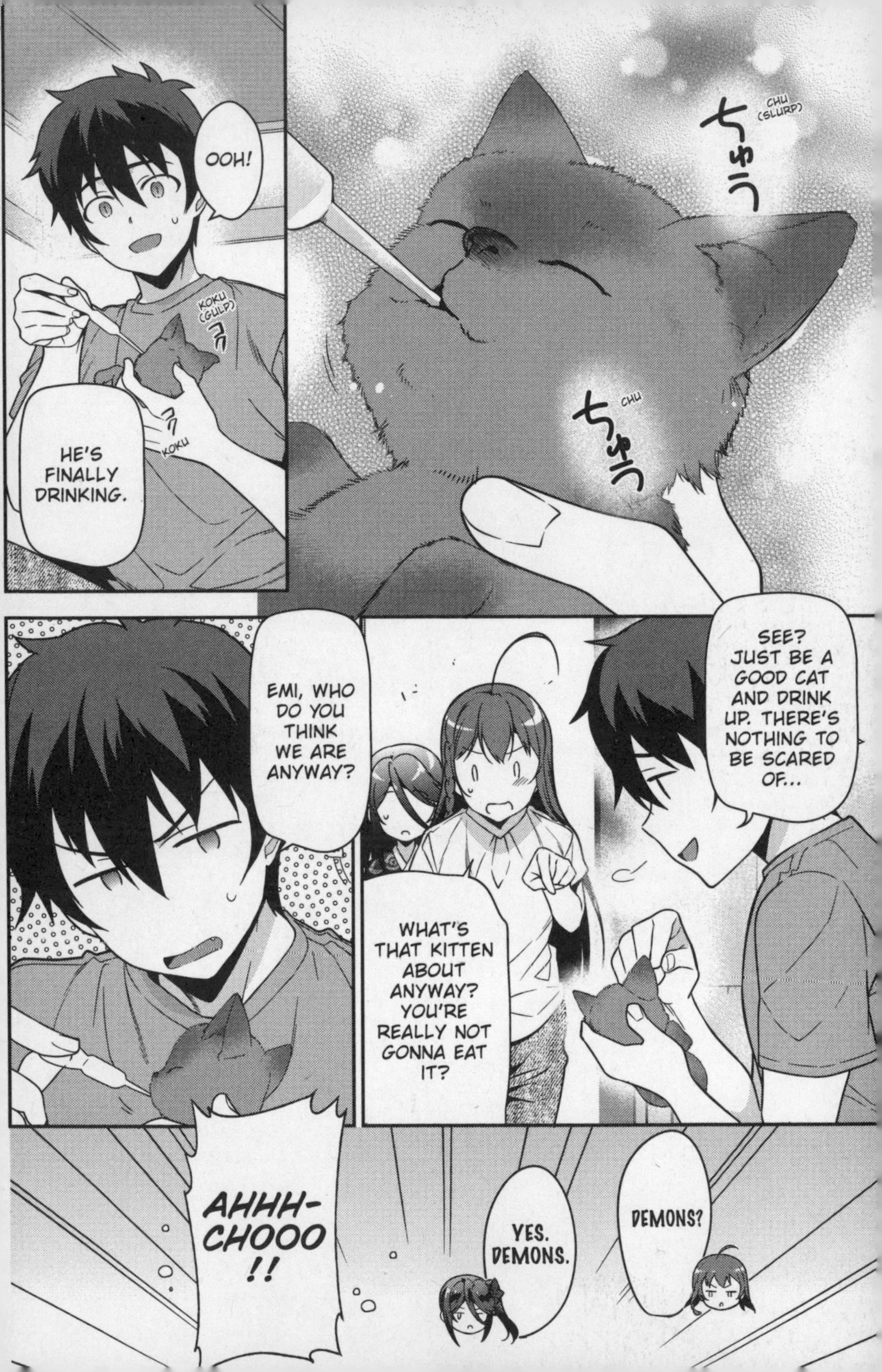
ちゅう
CHU (SLURP)
ちゅう
CHU
OOH!
KOKU (GULP)
コク
コク
KOKU
HE'S FINALLY DRINKING.
SEE? JUST BE A GOOD CAT AND DRINK UP. THERE'S NOTHING TO BE SCARED OF...
WHAT'S THAT KITTEN ABOUT ANYWAY? YOU'RE REALLY NOT GONNA EAT IT?
EMI, WHO DO YOU THINK WE ARE ANYWAY?
DEMONS?
YES. DEMONS.
AHHH-CHOOO!!

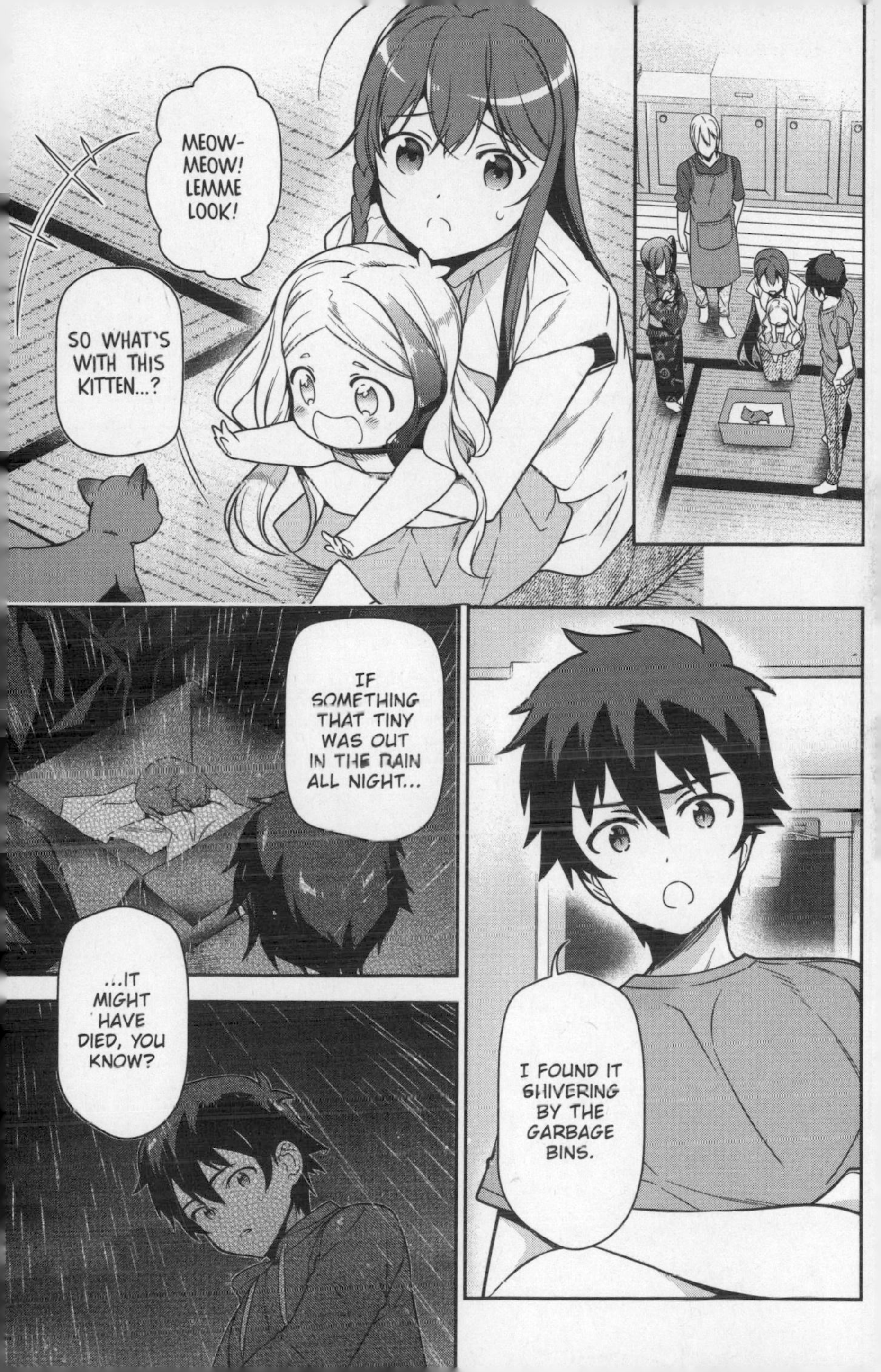
MEOW-MEOW! LEMME LOOK!
SO WHAT'S WITH THIS KITTEN...?
I FOUND IT SHIVERING BY THE GARBAGE BINS.
IF SOMETHING THAT TINY WAS OUT IN THE RAIN ALL NIGHT...
...IT MIGHT HAVE DIED, YOU KNOW?

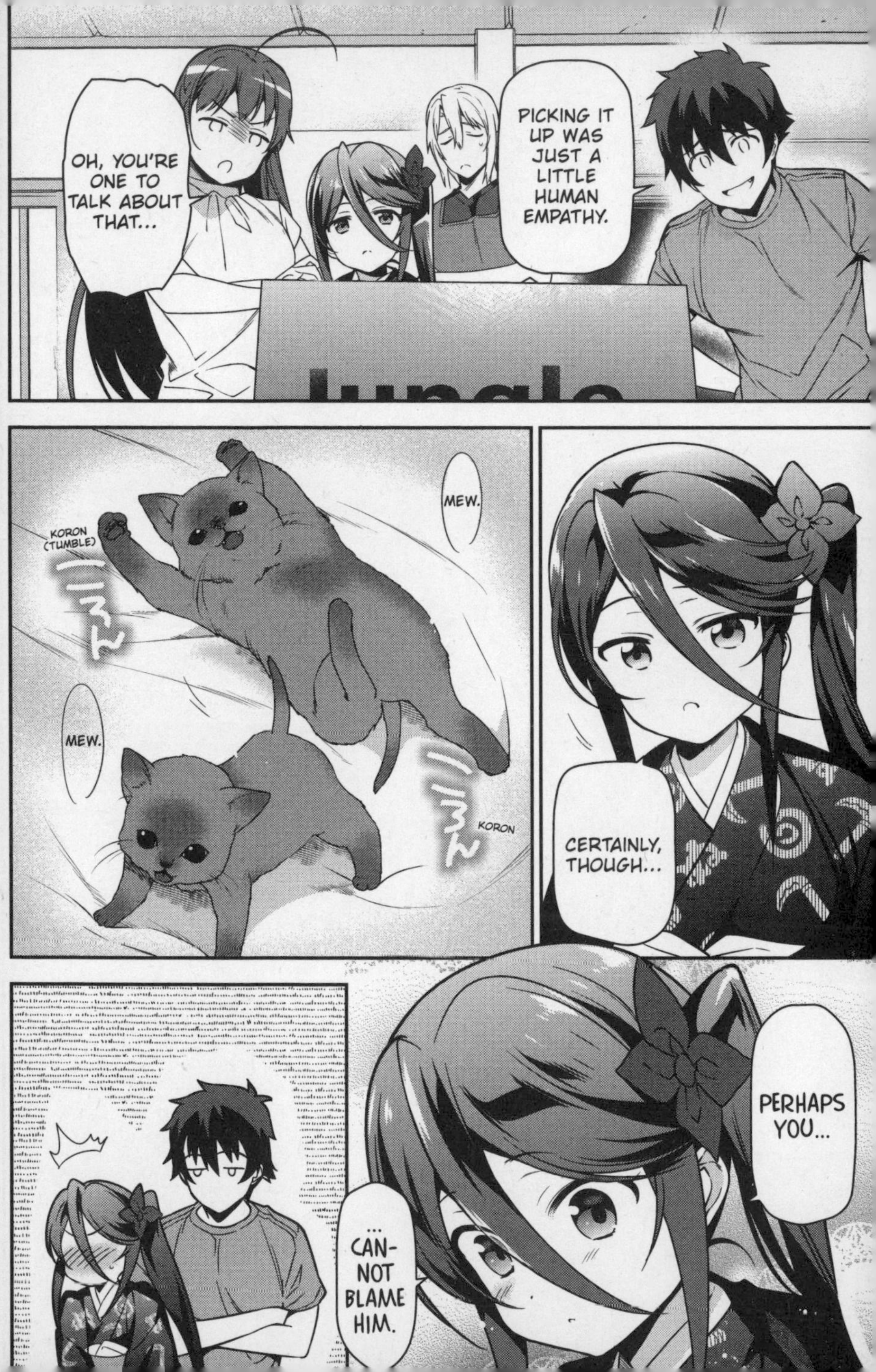
PICKING IT UP WAS JUST A LITTLE HUMAN EMPATHY.
OH, YOU'RE ONE TO TALK ABOUT THAT...
CERTAINLY, THOUGH...
MEW.
KORON (TUMBLE)
MEW.
KORON
PERHAPS YOU...
...CAN-NOT BLAME HIM.

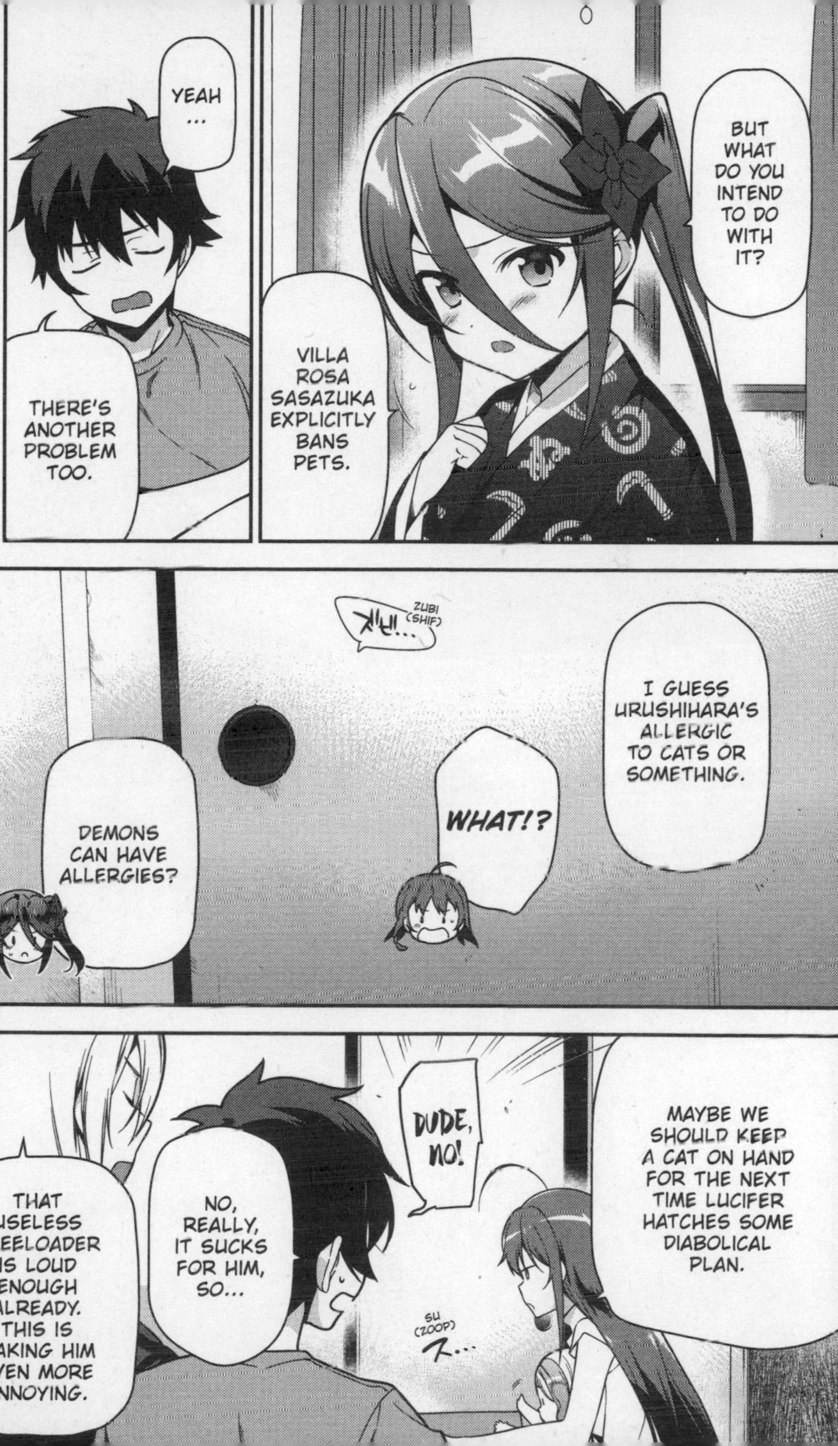
BUT WHAT DO YOU INTEND TO DO WITH IT?
VILLA ROSA SASAZUKA EXPLICITLY BANS PETS.
YEAH ...
THERE'S ANOTHER PROBLEM TOO.
I GUESS URUSHIHARA'S ALLERGIC TO CATS OR SOMETHING.
ズビ...
ZUBI (SHIF)
WHAT!?
DEMONS CAN HAVE ALLERGIES?
MAYBE WE SHOULD KEEP A CAT ON HAND FOR THE NEXT TIME LUCIFER HATCHES SOME DIABOLICAL PLAN.
DUDE, NO!
ス...
SU (ZOOP)
NO, REALLY, IT SUCKS FOR HIM, SO...
THAT USELESS FREELOADER IS LOUD ENOUGH ALREADY. THIS IS MAKING HIM EVEN MORE ANNOYING.

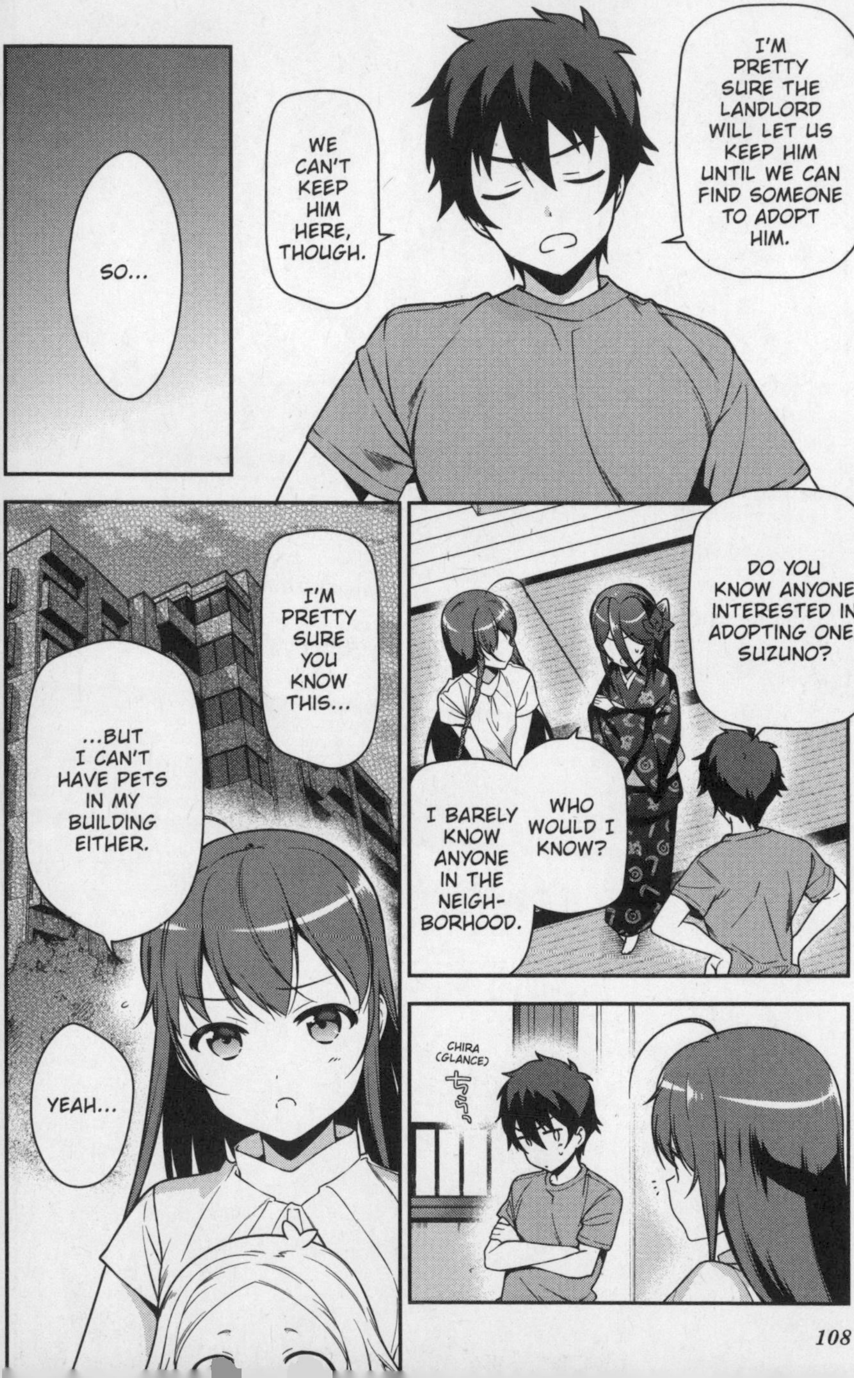
I'M PRETTY SURE THE LANDLORD WILL LET US KEEP HIM UNTIL WE CAN FIND SOMEONE TO ADOPT HIM.
WE CAN'T KEEP HIM HERE, THOUGH.
SO...
DO YOU KNOW ANYONE INTERESTED IN ADOPTING ONE, SUZUNO?
WHO WOULD I KNOW?
I BARELY KNOW ANYONE IN THE NEIGH-BORHOOD.
CHIRA (GLANCE)
I'M PRETTY SURE YOU KNOW THIS...
...BUT I CAN'T HAVE PETS IN MY BUILDING EITHER.
YEAH...

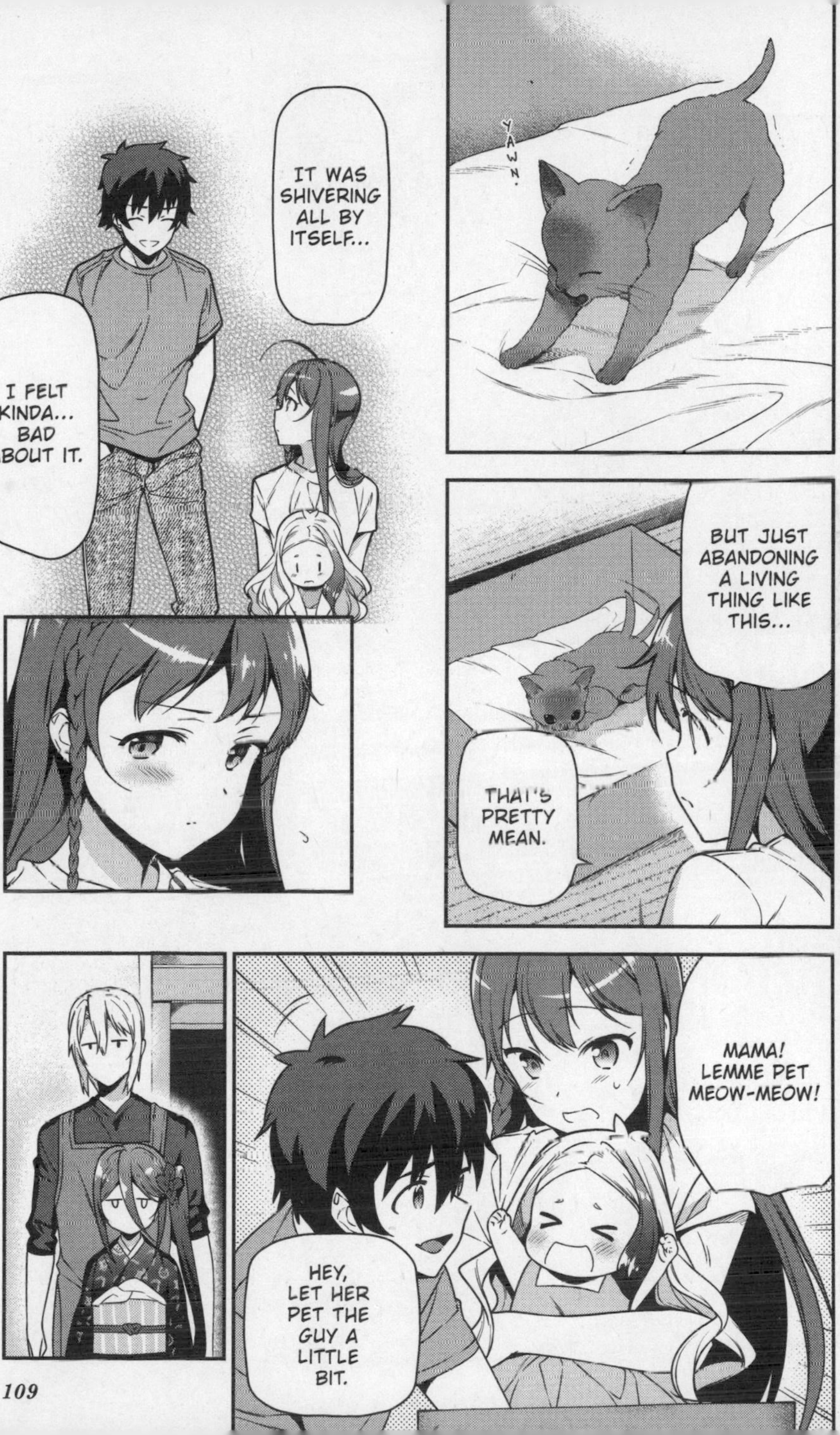
YAWN
IT WAS SHIVERING ALL BY ITSELF...
I FELT KINDA... BAD ABOUT IT.
BUT JUST ABANDONING A LIVING THING LIKE THIS...
THAT'S PRETTY MEAN.
MAMA! LEMME PET MEOW-MEOW!
HEY, LET HER PET THE GUY A LITTLE BIT.

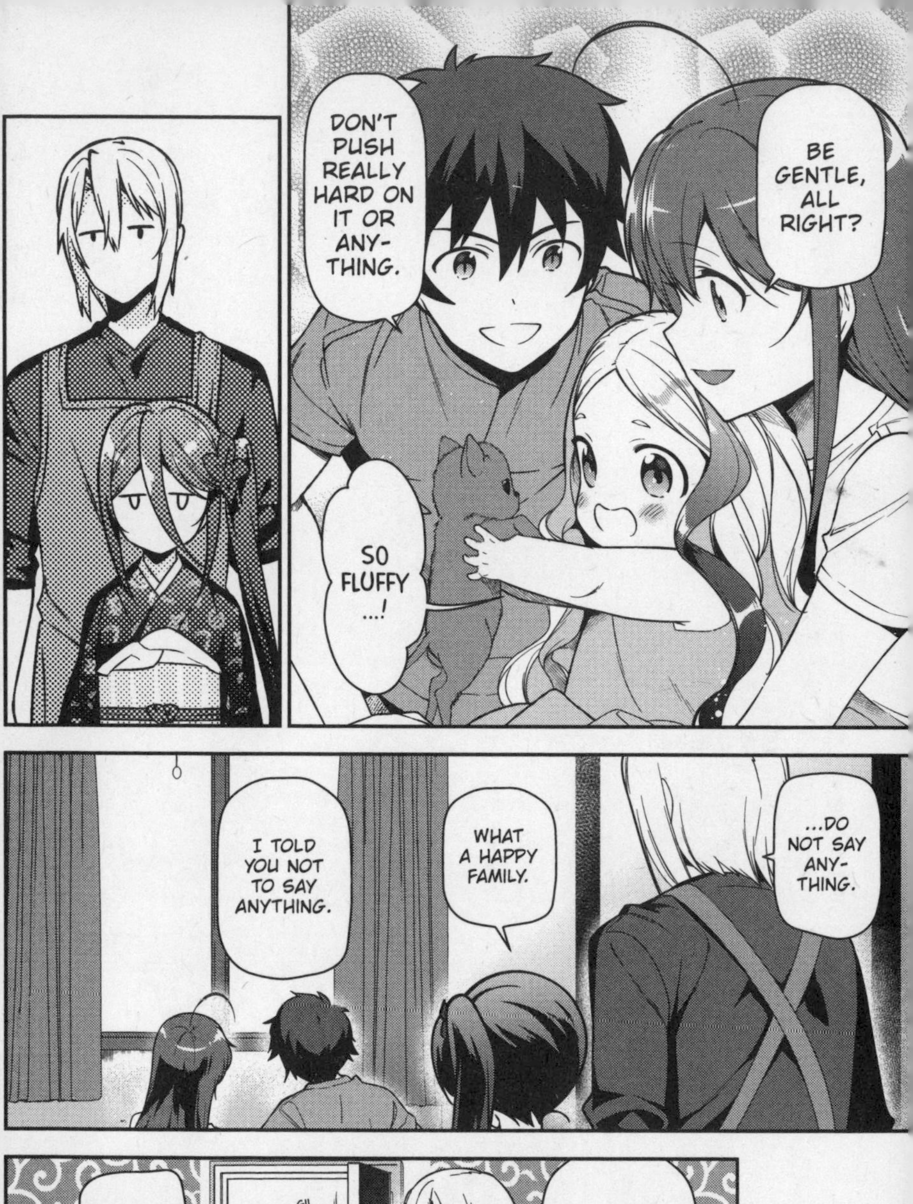
BE GENTLE, ALL RIGHT?
DON'T PUSH REALLY HARD ON IT OR ANY-THING.
SO FLUFFY ...!
...DO NOT SAY ANY-THING.
WHAT A HAPPY FAMILY.
I TOLD YOU NOT TO SAY ANYTHING.
THAT WAS QUITE A JOB YOU DID ON THE DOOR THERE...
GII (CREAK)
I...WILL PAY TO REPLACE IT.

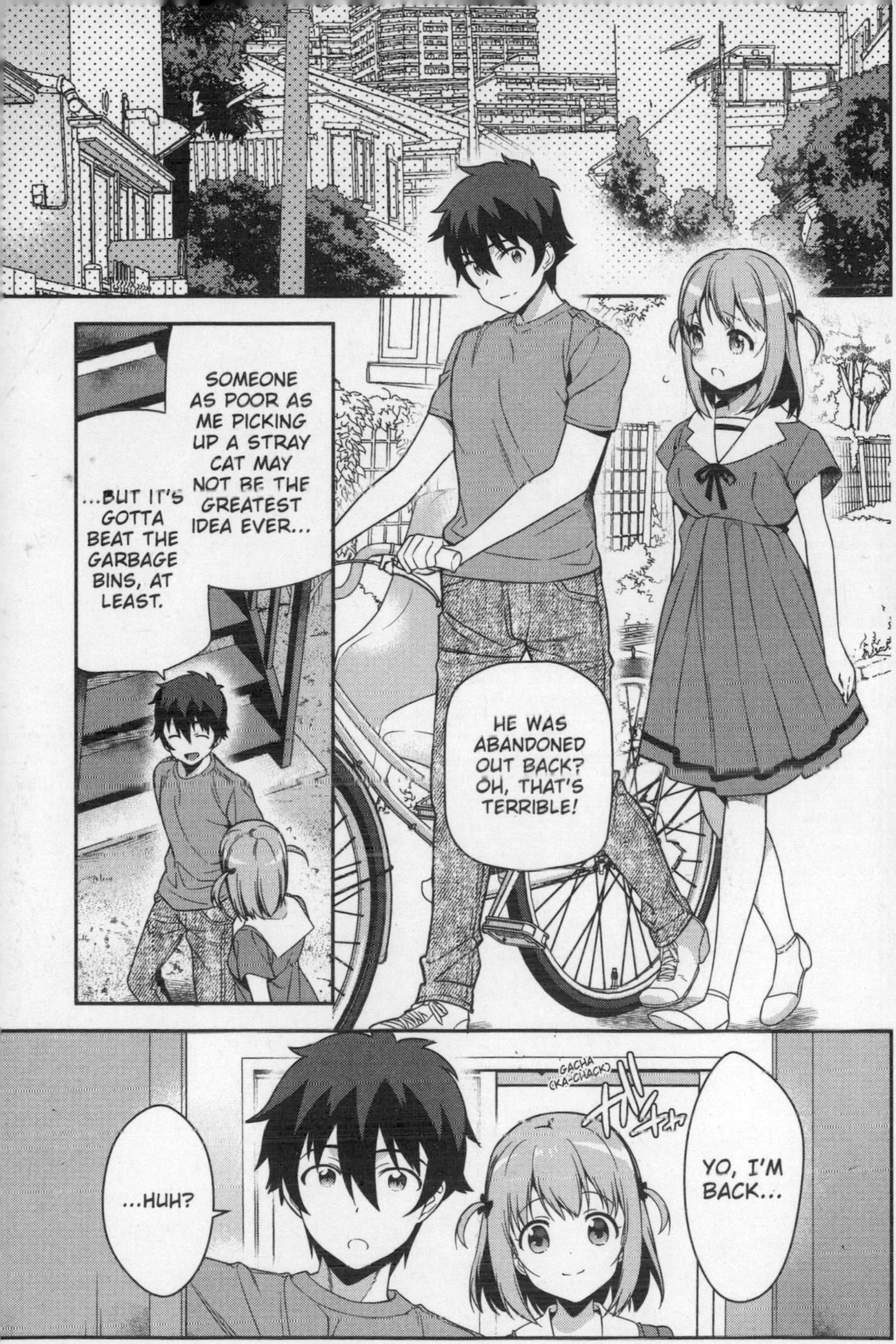
HE WAS ABANDONED OUT BACK? OH, THAT'S TERRIBLE!
SOMEONE AS POOR AS ME PICKING UP A STRAY CAT MAY NOT BE THE GREATEST IDEA EVER...
...BUT IT'S GOTTA BEAT THE GARBAGE BINS, AT LEAST.
YO, I'M BACK...
GACHA (KA-CHACK)
...HUH?

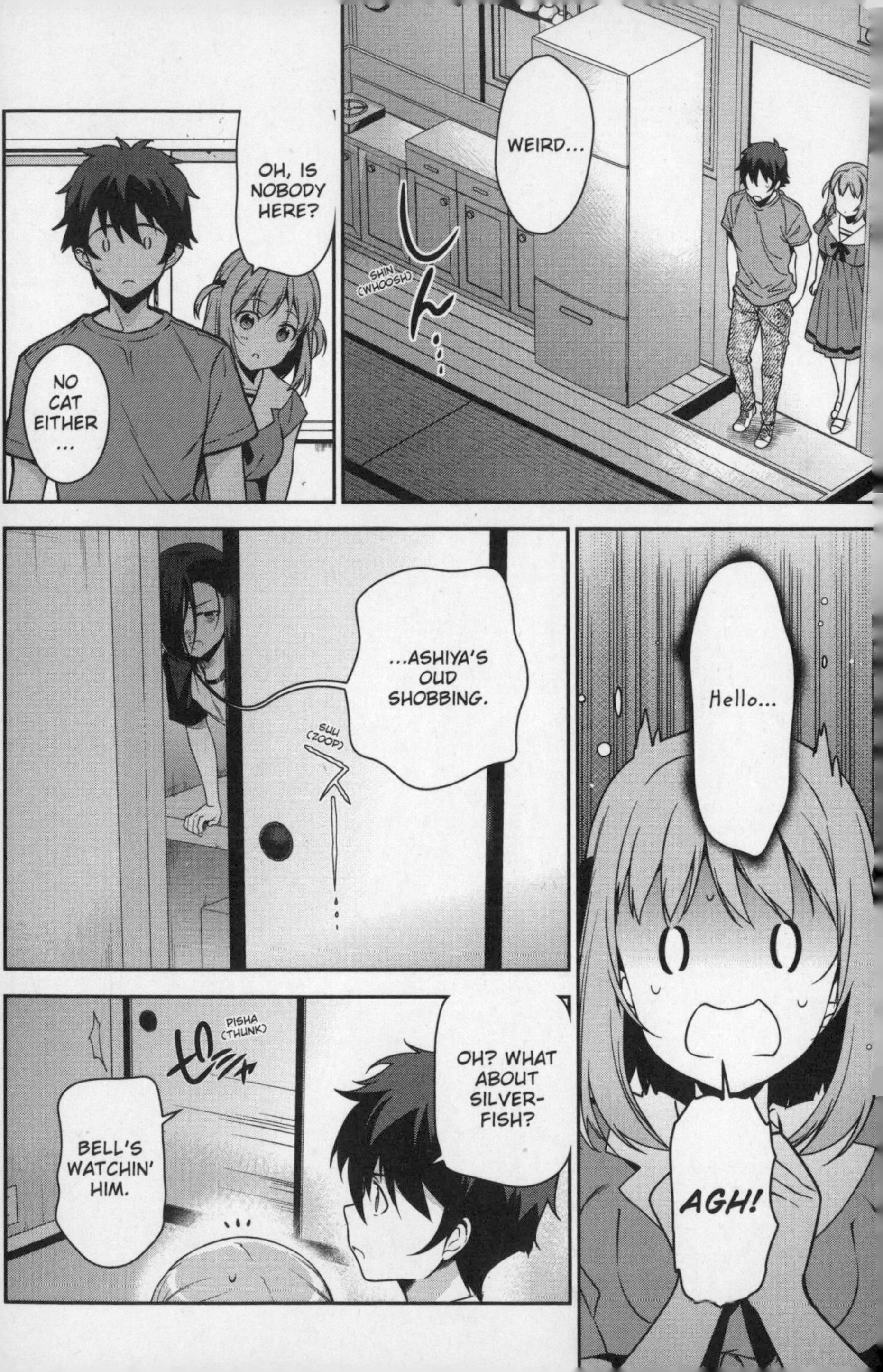
WEIRD...
SHIN (WHOOSH)
OH, IS NOBODY HERE?
NO CAT EITHER...
Hello...
AGH!
...ASHIYA'S OUD SHOBBING.
SUU (ZOOP)
OH? WHAT ABOUT SILVER-FISH?
PISHA (THUNK)
BELL'S WATCHIN' HIM.
...

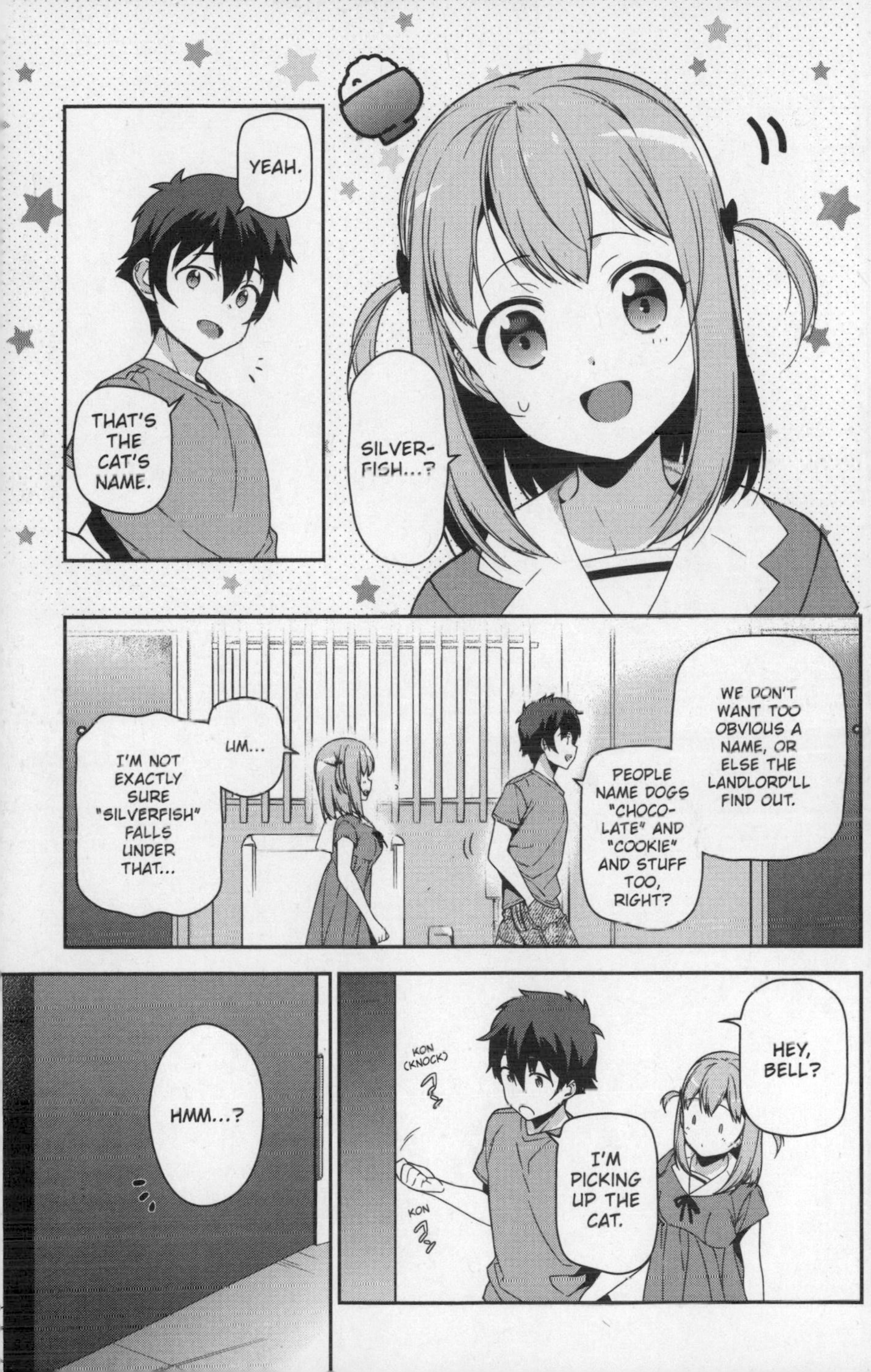
SILVER-FISH...?
YEAH.
THAT'S THE CAT'S NAME.
WE DON'T WANT TOO OBVIOUS A NAME, OR ELSE THE LANDLORD'LL FIND OUT.
PEOPLE NAME DOGS "CHOCO-LATE" AND "COOKIE" AND STUFF TOO, RIGHT?
UM...
I'M NOT EXACTLY SURE "SILVERFISH" FALLS UNDER THAT...
HEY, BELL?
I'M PICKING UP THE CAT.
KON (KNOCK)
KON
HMM...?

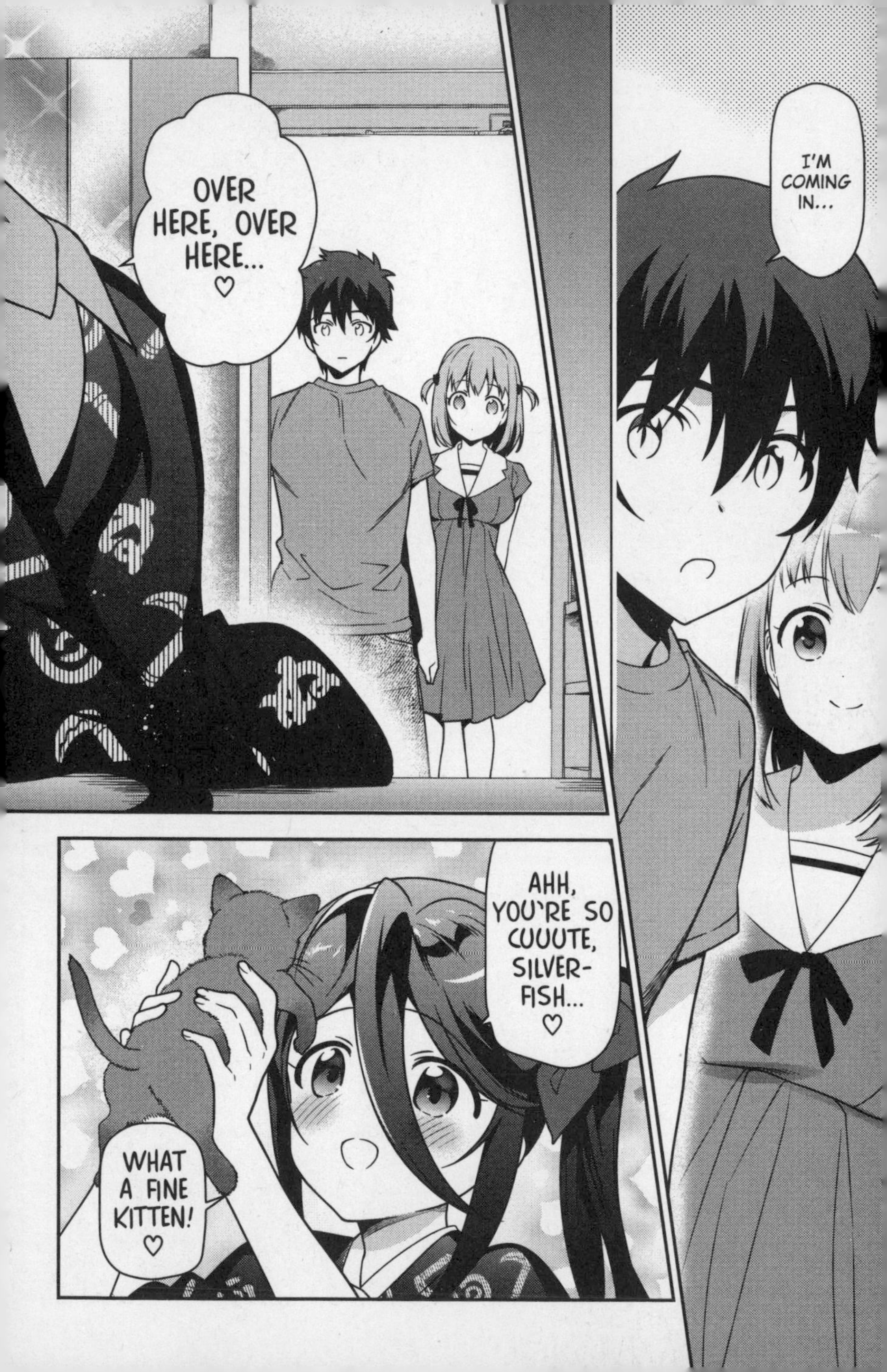
I'M COMING IN...
OVER HERE, OVER HERE... ♡
AHH, YOU'RE SO CUUUTE, SILVER-FISH... ♡
WHAT A FINE KITTEN! ♡

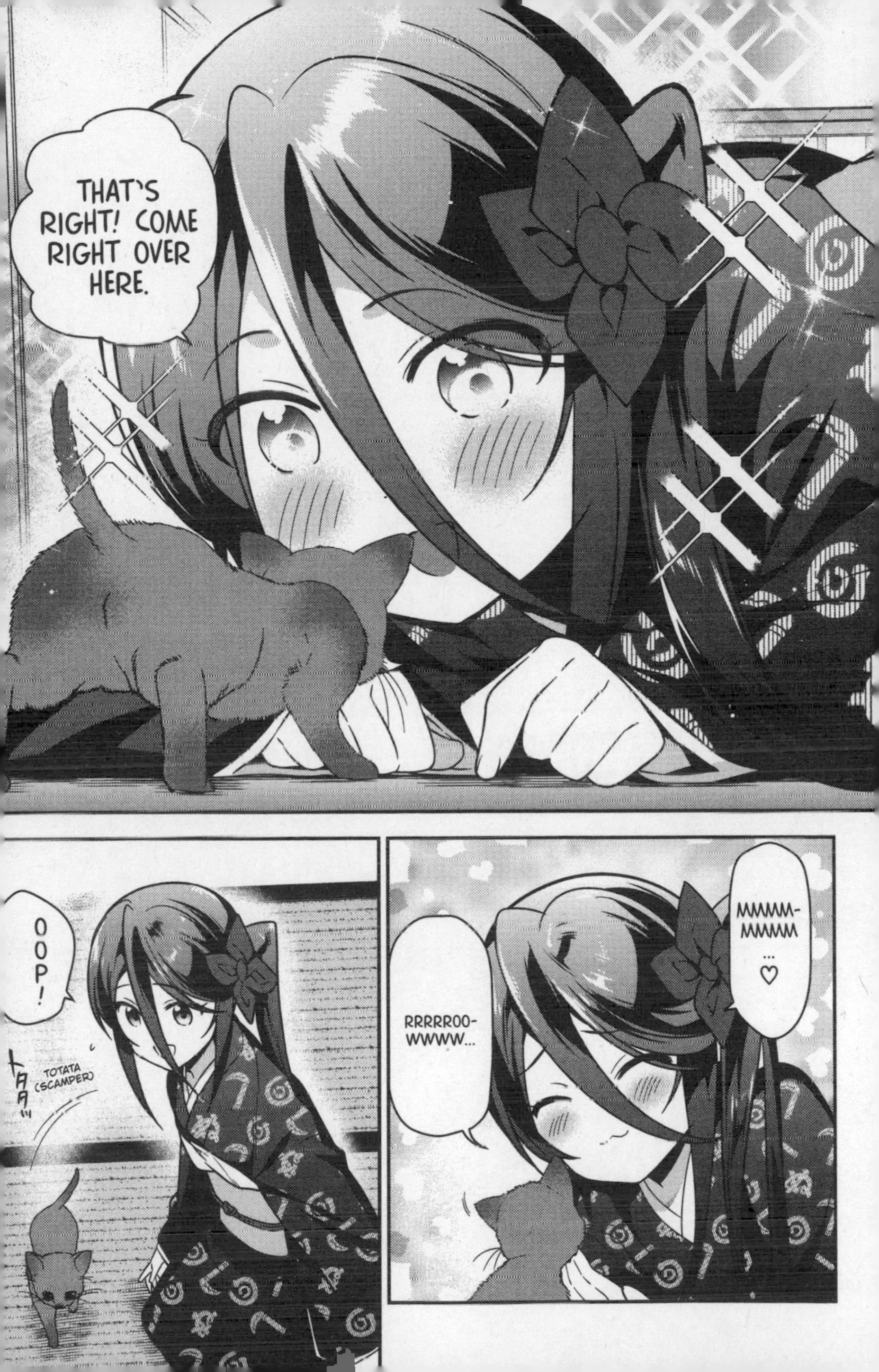
THAT'S RIGHT! COME RIGHT OVER HERE.
MMMMM-MMMMM ... ♡
RRRRROO-WWWW...
OOP!
TOTATA (SCAMPER)

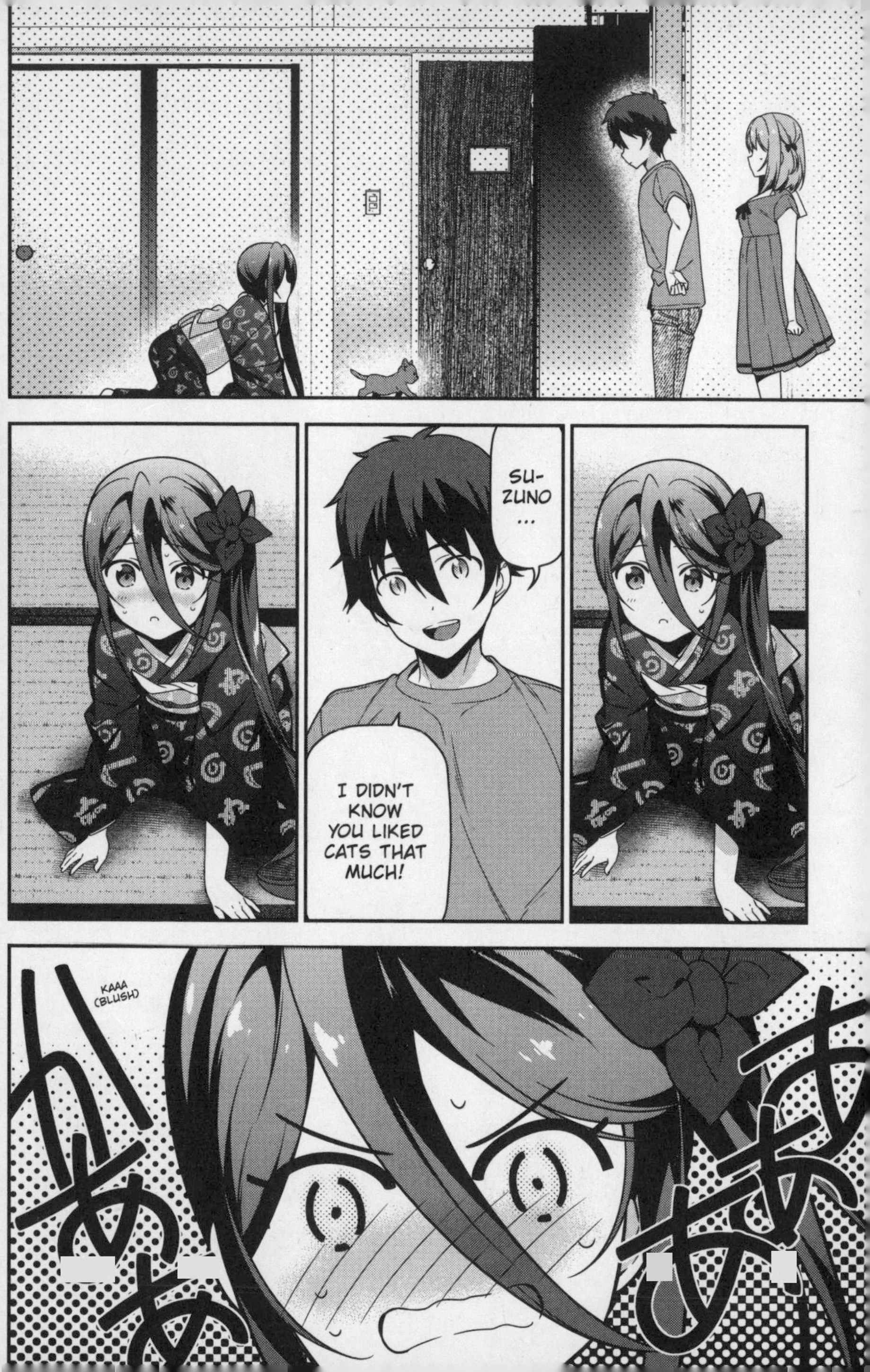
SU-ZUNO ...
I DIDN'T KNOW YOU LIKED CATS THAT MUCH!
KAAA (BLUSH)

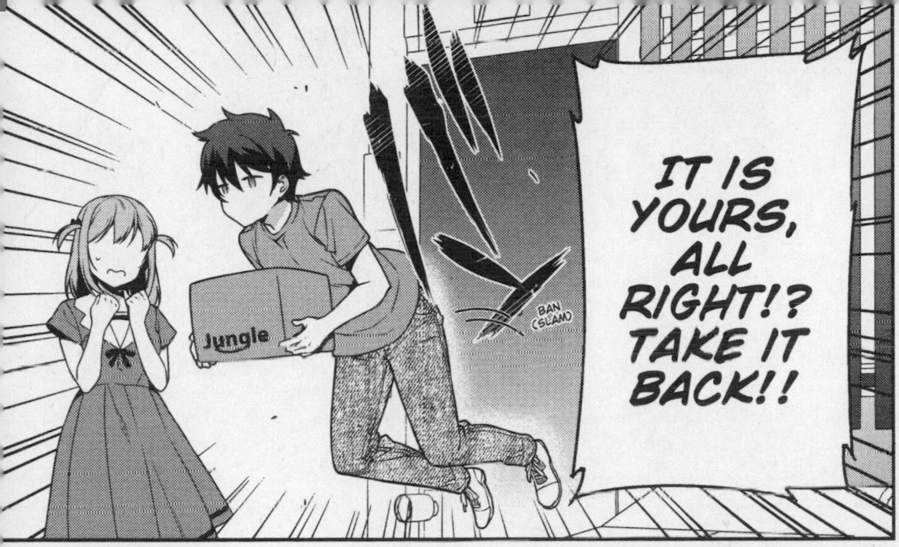
IT IS YOURS, ALL RIGHT!? TAKE IT BACK!!
BAN (SLAM)
Jungle

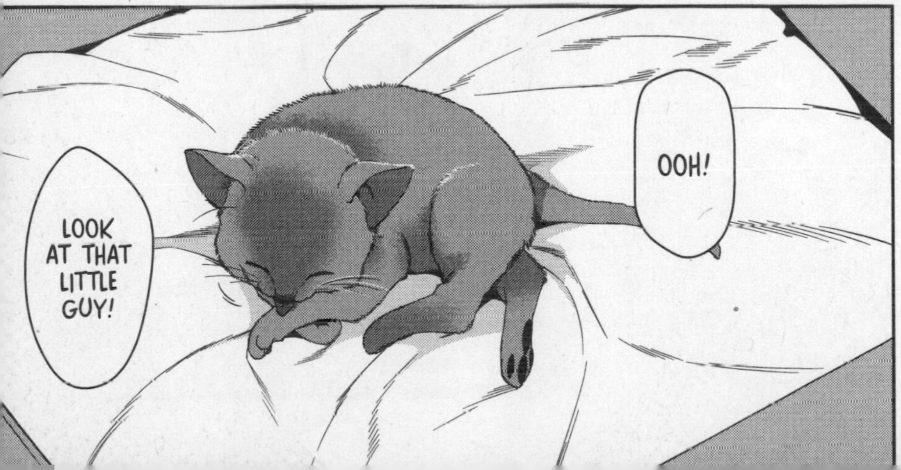
OOH!
LOOK AT THAT LITTLE GUY!

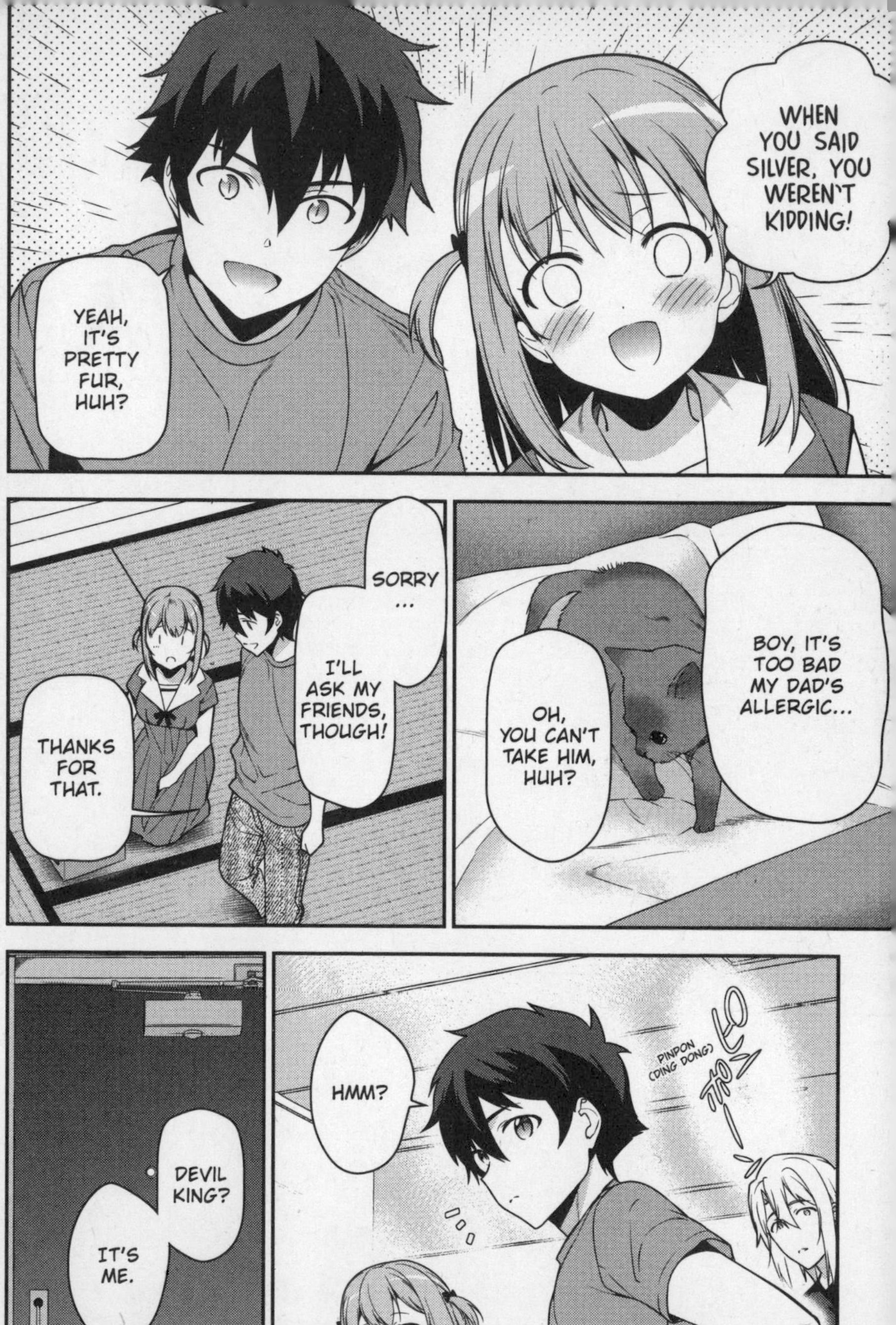
WHEN YOU SAID SILVER, YOU WEREN'T KIDDING!
YEAH, IT'S PRETTY FUR, HUH?
BOY, IT'S TOO BAD MY DAD'S ALLERGIC...
OH, YOU CAN'T TAKE HIM, HUH?
SORRY...
I'LL ASK MY FRIENDS, THOUGH!
THANKS FOR THAT.
PINPON (DING DONG)
HMM?
DEVIL KING?
IT'S ME.

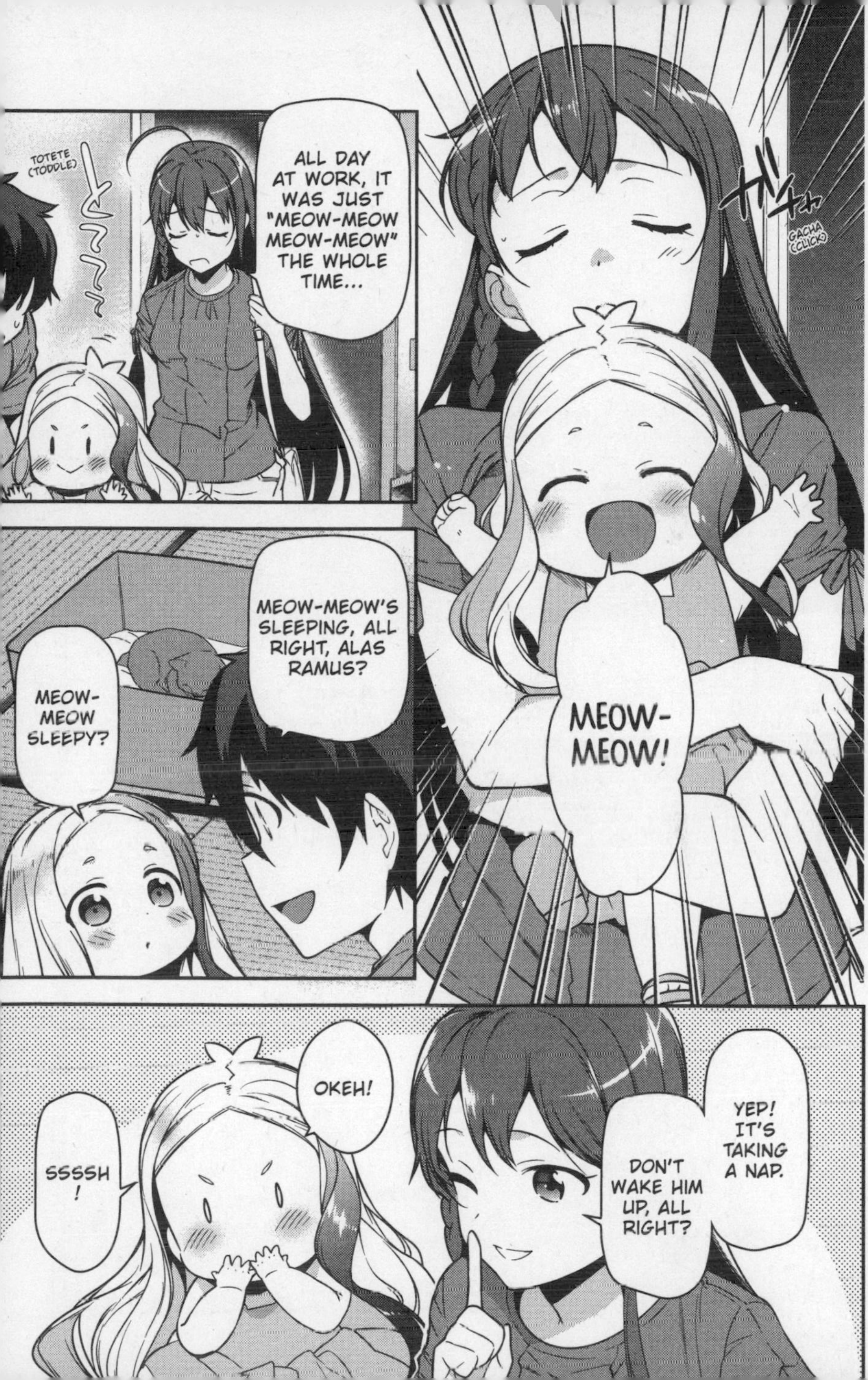
GACHA (CLICK)
MEOW-MEOW!
ALL DAY AT WORK, IT WAS JUST "MEOW-MEOW MEOW-MEOW" THE WHOLE TIME...
TOTETE (TODDLE)
MEOW-MEOW'S SLEEPING, ALL RIGHT, ALAS RAMUS?
MEOW-MEOW SLEEPY?
YEP! IT'S TAKING A NAP.
DON'T WAKE HIM UP, ALL RIGHT?
OKEH!
SSSSH!

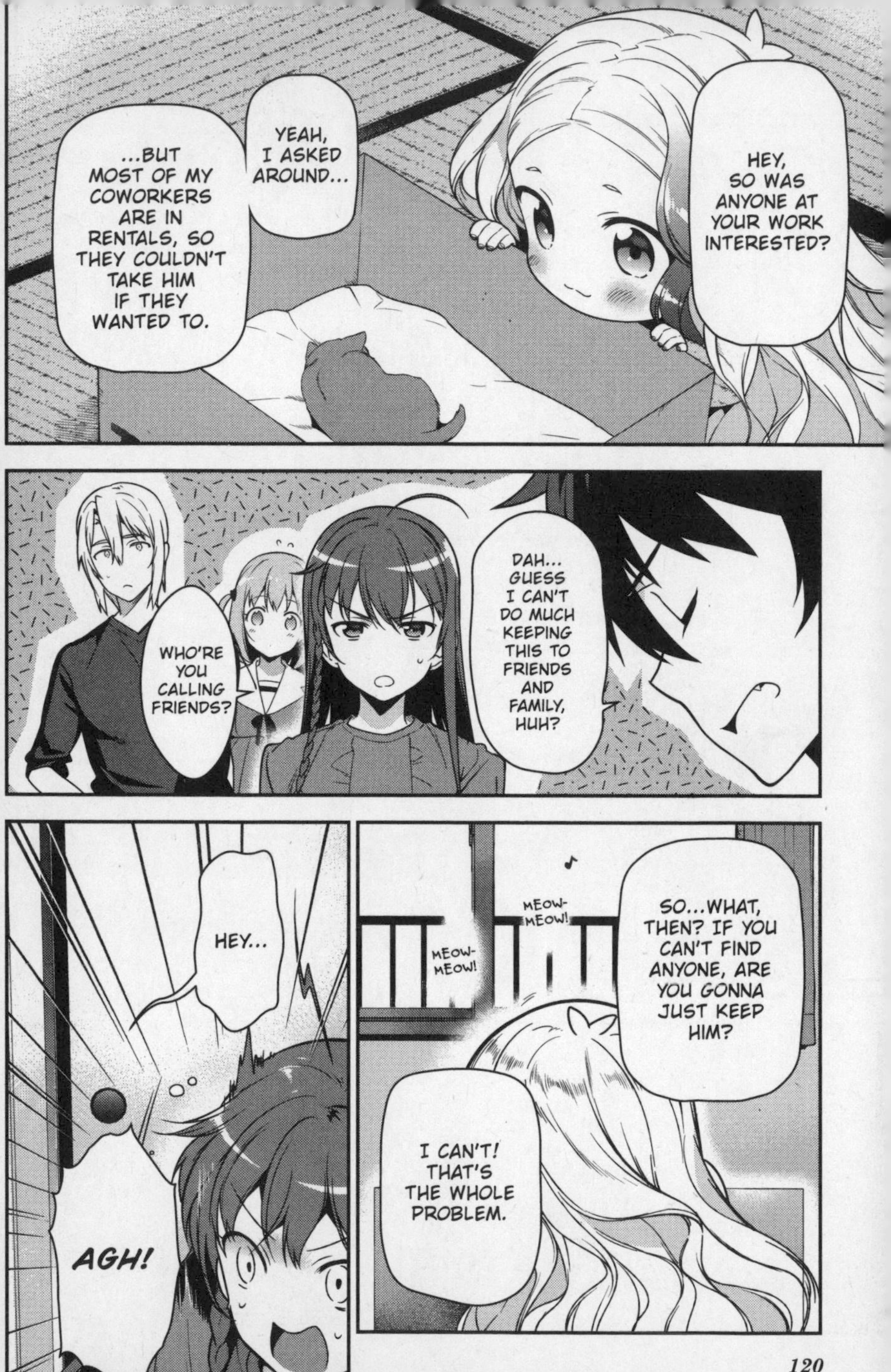
HEY, SO WAS ANYONE AT YOUR WORK INTERESTED?
YEAH, I ASKED AROUND...
...BUT MOST OF MY COWORKERS ARE IN RENTALS, SO THEY COULDN'T TAKE HIM IF THEY WANTED TO.
DAH... GUESS I CAN'T DO MUCH KEEPING THIS TO FRIENDS AND FAMILY, HUH?
WHO'RE YOU CALLING FRIENDS?
SO...WHAT, THEN? IF YOU CAN'T FIND ANYONE, ARE YOU GONNA JUST KEEP HIM?
MEOW-MEOW!
MEOW-MEOW!
I CAN'T! THAT'S THE WHOLE PROBLEM.
HEY...
AGH!

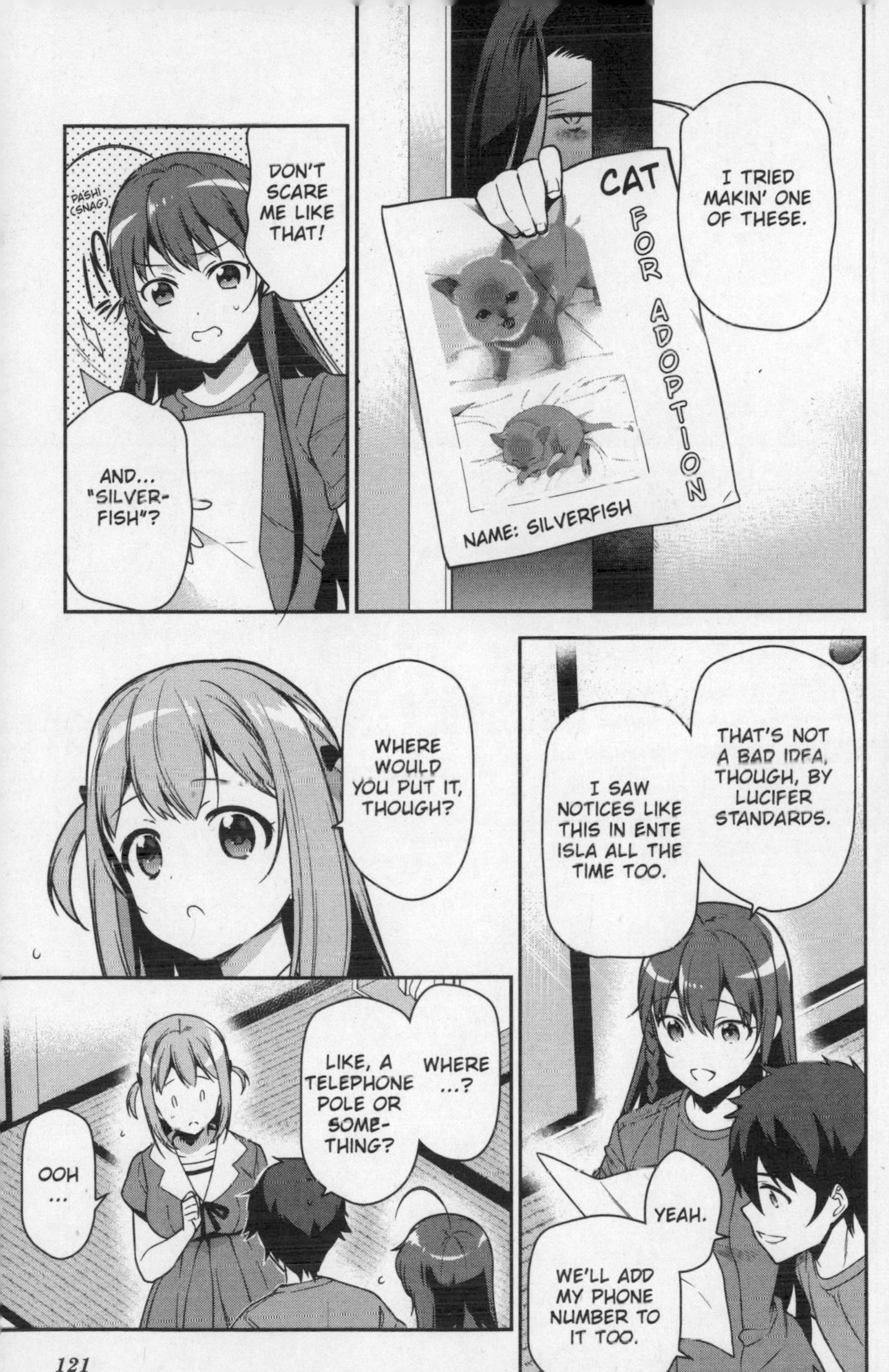
I TRIED MAKIN' ONE OF THESE.
CAT FOR ADOPTION
NAME: SILVERFISH
PASHI (SNAG)
DON'T SCARE ME LIKE THAT!
AND... "SILVER-FISH"?
THAT'S NOT A BAD IDEA, THOUGH, BY LUCIFER STANDARDS.
I SAW NOTICES LIKE THIS IN ENTE ISLA ALL THE TIME TOO.
YEAH.
WE'LL ADD MY PHONE NUMBER TO IT TOO.
WHERE WOULD YOU PUT IT, THOUGH?
WHERE ...?
LIKE, A TELEPHONE POLE OR SOME-THING?
OOH ...

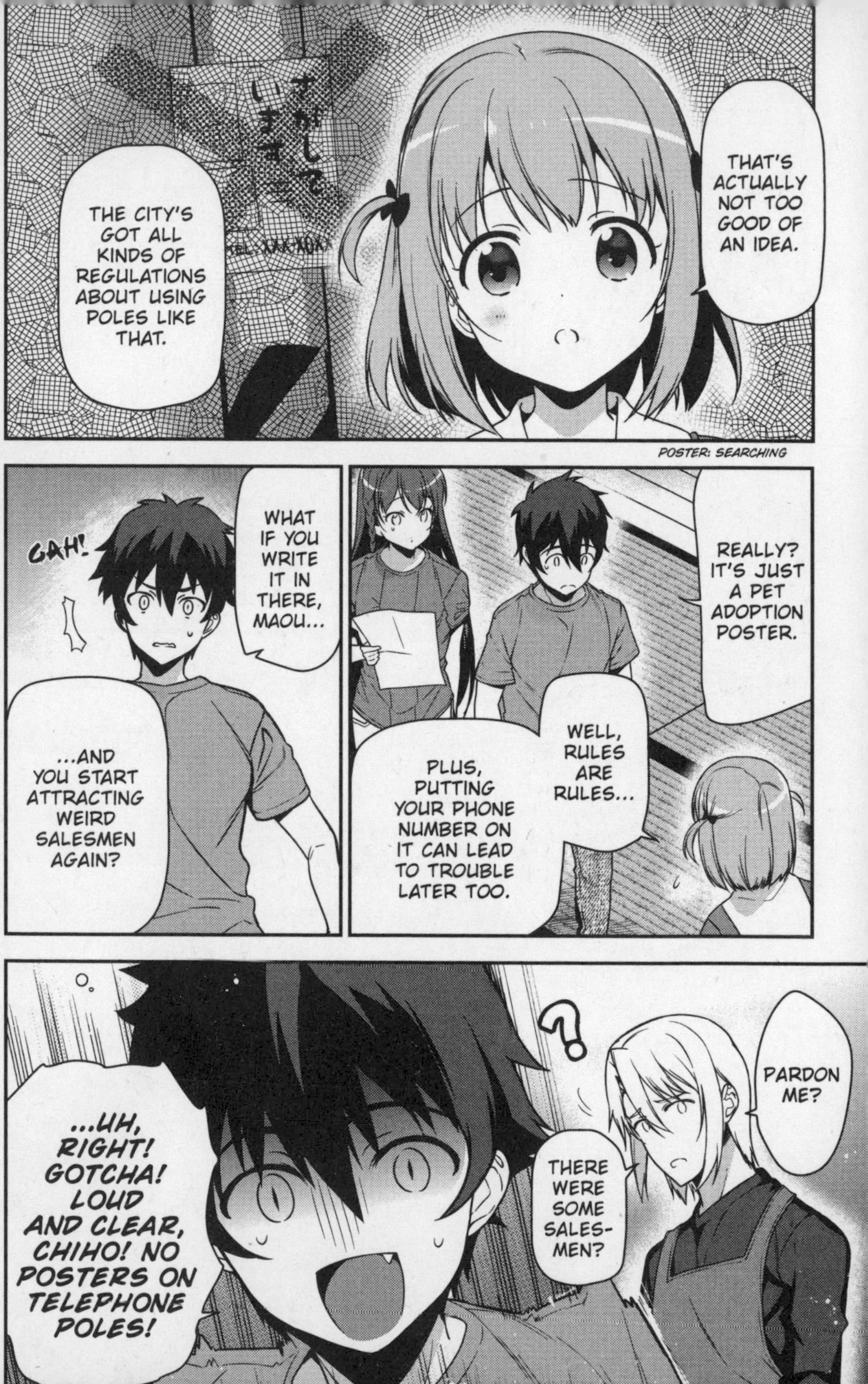
THAT'S ACTUALLY NOT TOO GOOD OF AN IDEA.
さがしています
THE CITY'S GOT ALL KINDS OF REGULATIONS ABOUT USING POLES LIKE THAT.
REALLY? IT'S JUST A PET ADOPTION POSTER.
WELL, RULES ARE RULES...
PLUS, PUTTING YOUR PHONE NUMBER ON IT CAN LEAD TO TROUBLE LATER TOO.
WHAT IF YOU WRITE IT IN THERE, MAOU...
GAH!
...AND YOU START ATTRACTING WEIRD SALESMEN AGAIN?
PARDON ME?
THERE WERE SOME SALES-MEN?
...UH, RIGHT! GOTCHA! LOUD AND CLEAR, CHIHO! NO POSTERS ON TELEPHONE POLES!
POSTER: SEARCHING

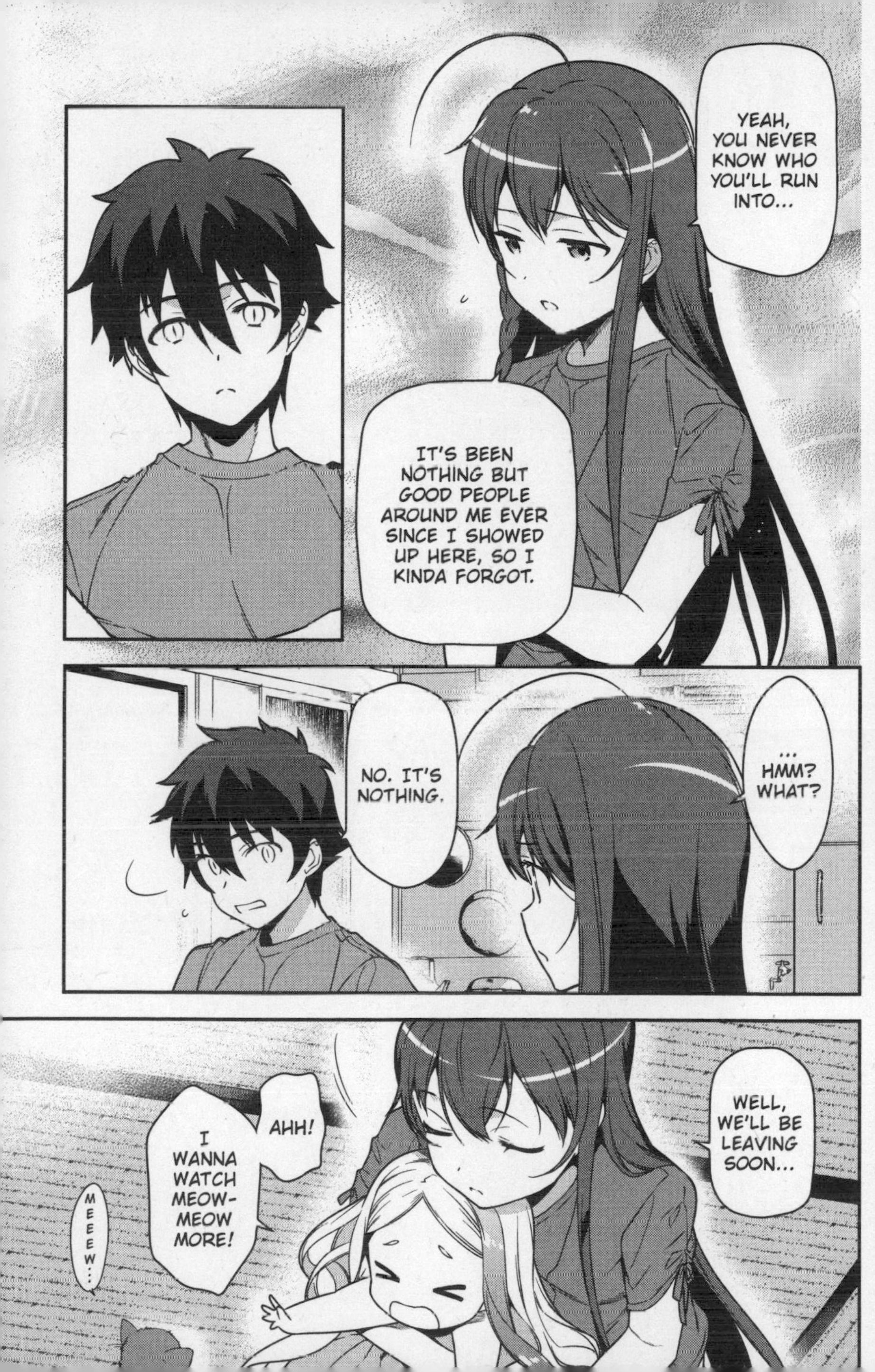
YEAH, YOU NEVER KNOW WHO YOU'LL RUN INTO...
IT'S BEEN NOTHING BUT GOOD PEOPLE AROUND ME EVER SINCE I SHOWED UP HERE, SO I KINDA FORGOT.
... HMM? WHAT?
NO. IT'S NOTHING.
WELL, WE'LL BE LEAVING SOON...
AHH!
I WANNA WATCH MEOW-MEOW MORE!
MEEEEW...

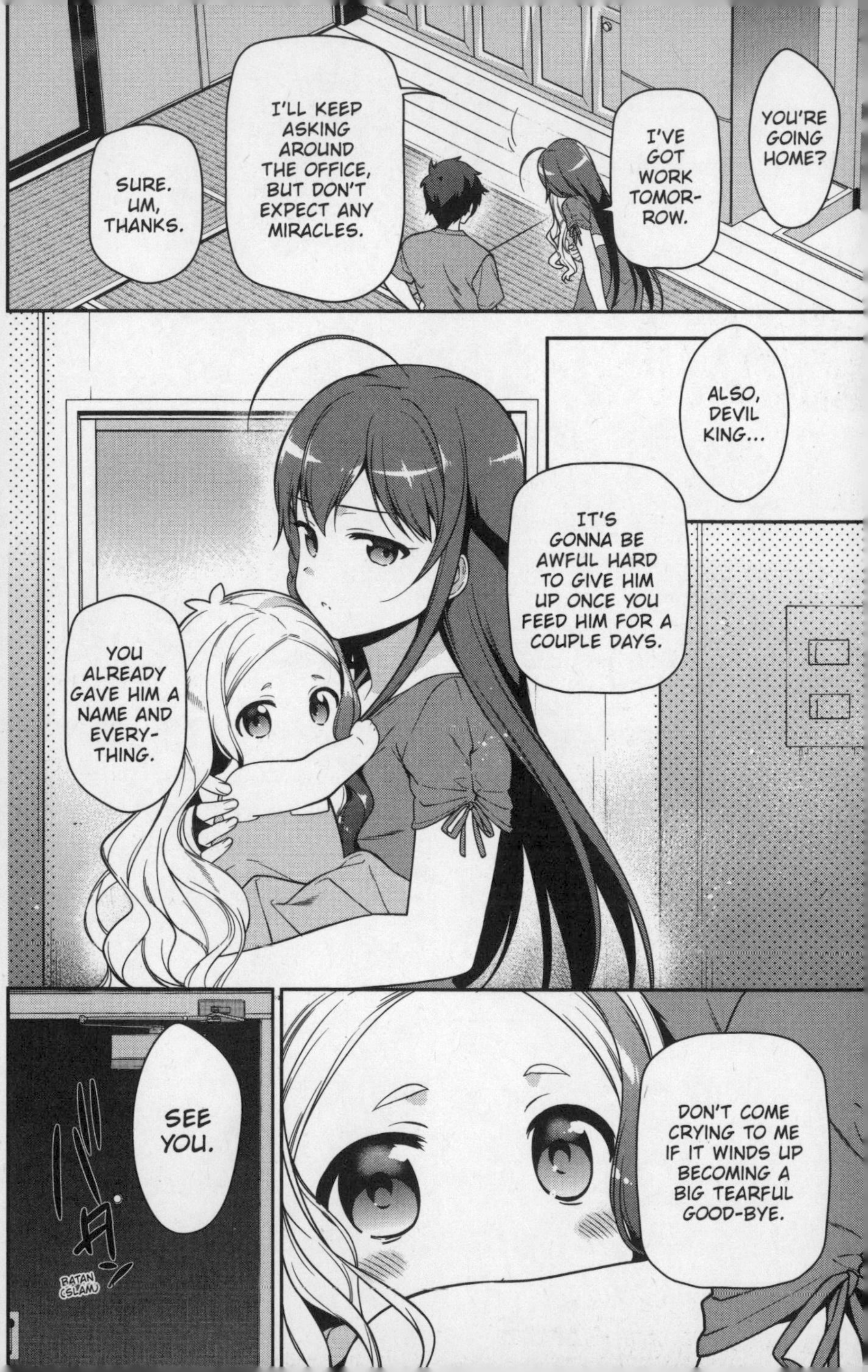
YOU'RE GOING HOME?
I'VE GOT WORK TOMOR-ROW.
I'LL KEEP ASKING AROUND THE OFFICE, BUT DON'T EXPECT ANY MIRACLES.
SURE. UM, THANKS.
ALSO, DEVIL KING...
IT'S GONNA BE AWFUL HARD TO GIVE HIM UP ONCE YOU FEED HIM FOR A COUPLE DAYS.
YOU ALREADY GAVE HIM A NAME AND EVERY-THING.
DON'T COME CRYING TO ME IF IT WINDS UP BECOMING A BIG TEARFUL GOOD-BYE.
SEE YOU.
BATAN (SLAM)

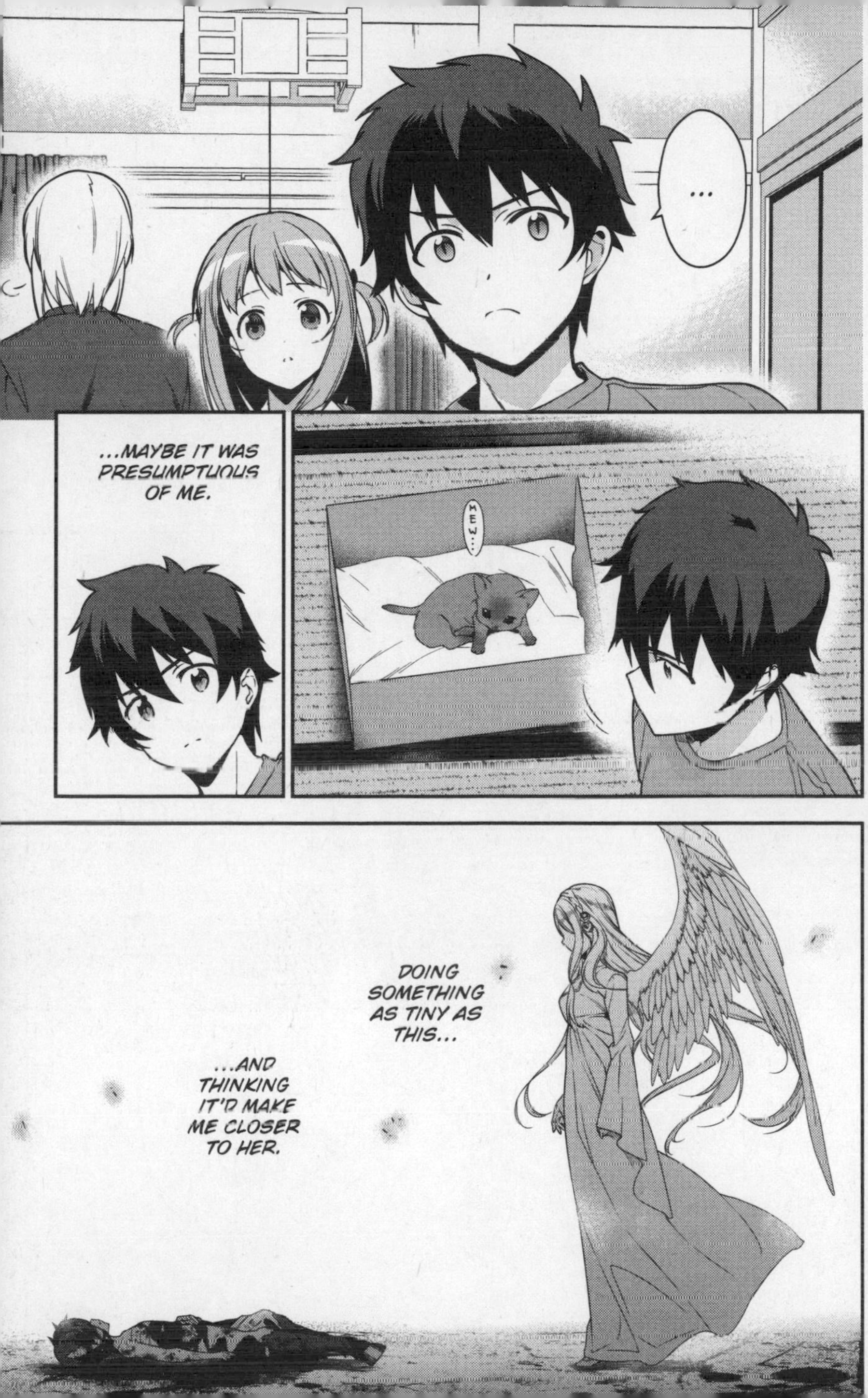
...
MEW...
...MAYBE IT WAS PRESUMPTUOUS OF ME.
DOING SOMETHING AS TINY AS THIS...
...AND THINKING IT'D MAKE ME CLOSER TO HER.

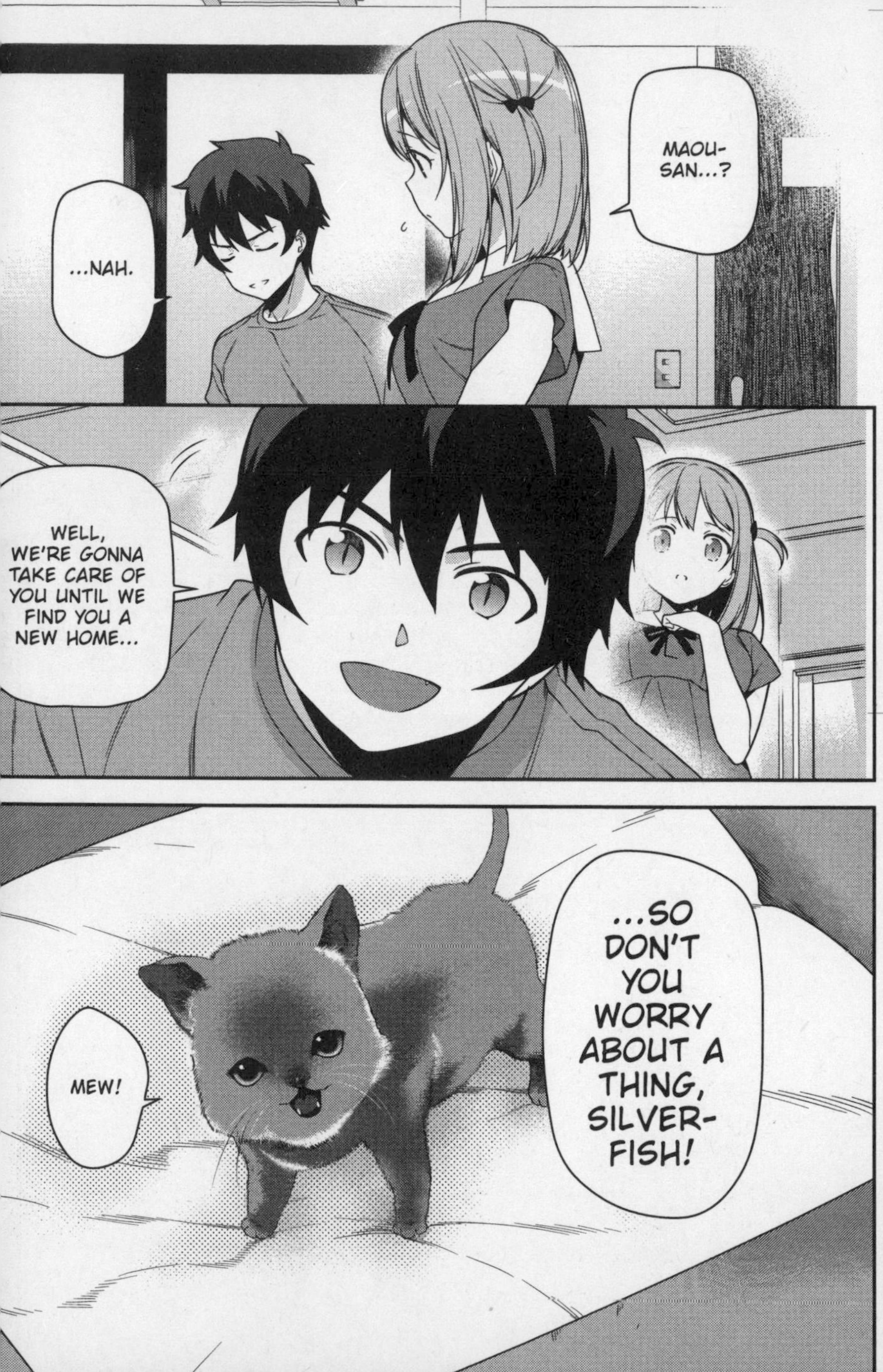
MAOU-SAN...?
...NAH.
WELL, WE'RE GONNA TAKE CARE OF YOU UNTIL WE FIND YOU A NEW HOME...
...SO DON'T YOU WORRY ABOUT A THING, SILVER-FISH!
MEW!

Hanzou
Urushihara

THE DEVIL IS A PART-TIMER!

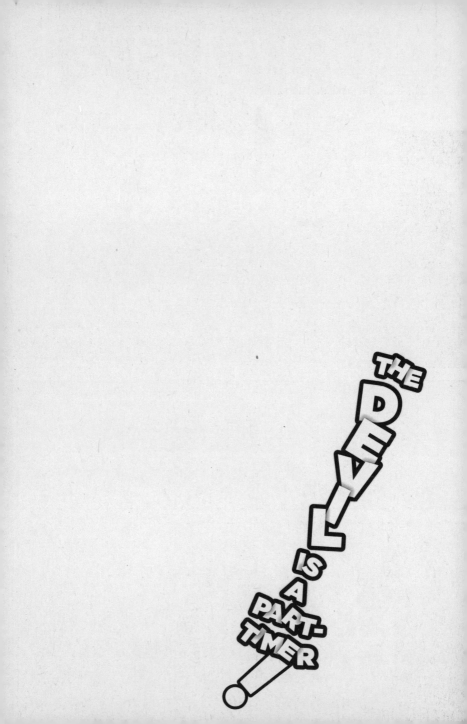

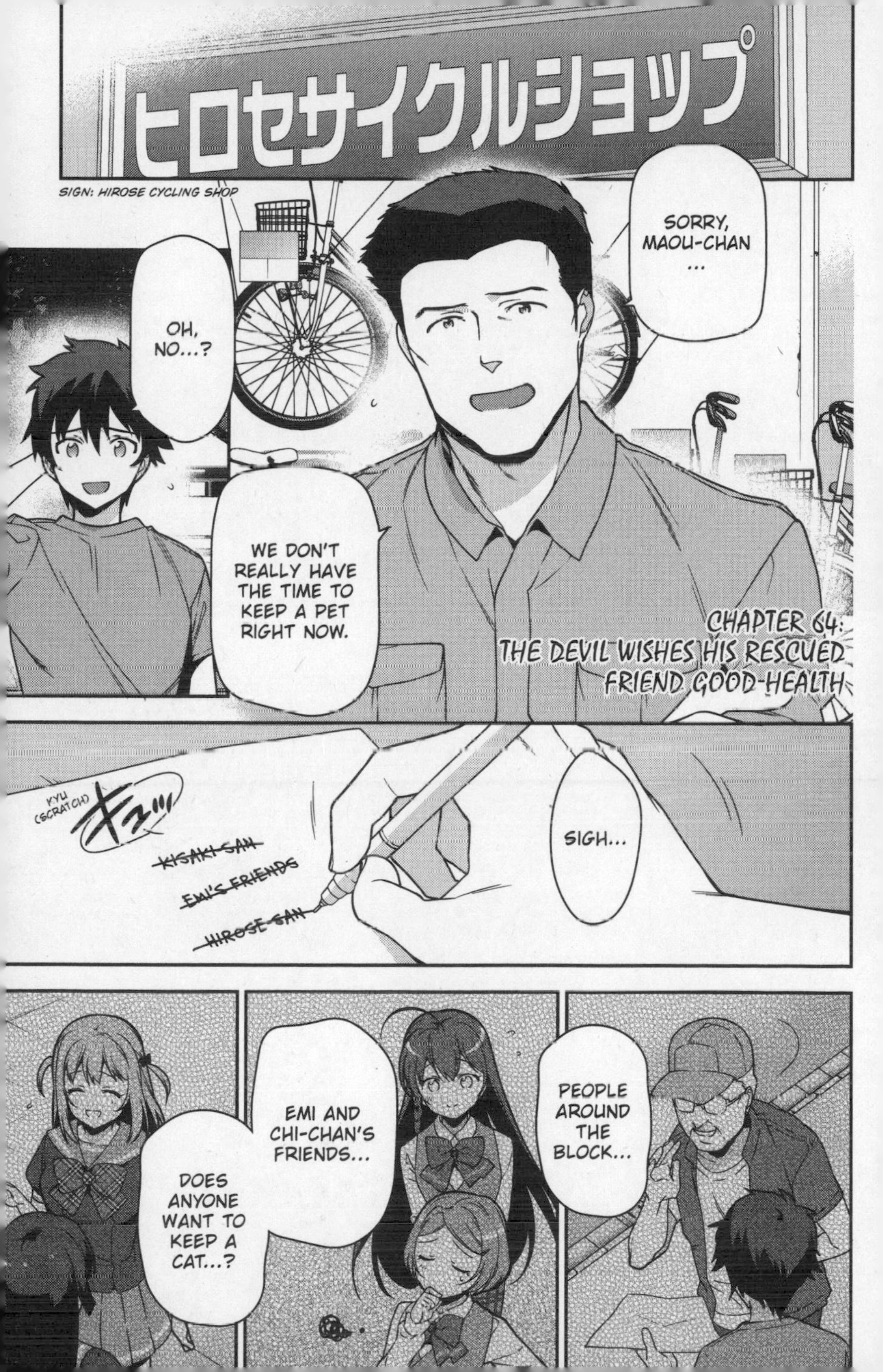ヒロセサイクルショップ
SIGN: HIROSE CYCLING SHOP
SORRY, MAOU-CHAN …
WE DON'T REALLY HAVE THE TIME TO KEEP A PET RIGHT NOW.
OH, NO…?
CHAPTER 64: THE DEVIL WISHES HIS RESCUED FRIEND GOOD HEALTH
KYU (SCRATCH)
KISAKI-SAN
EMI'S FRIENDS
HIROSE-SAN
SIGH…
PEOPLE AROUND THE BLOCK…
EMI AND CHI-CHAN'S FRIENDS…
DOES ANYONE WANT TO KEEP A CAT…?

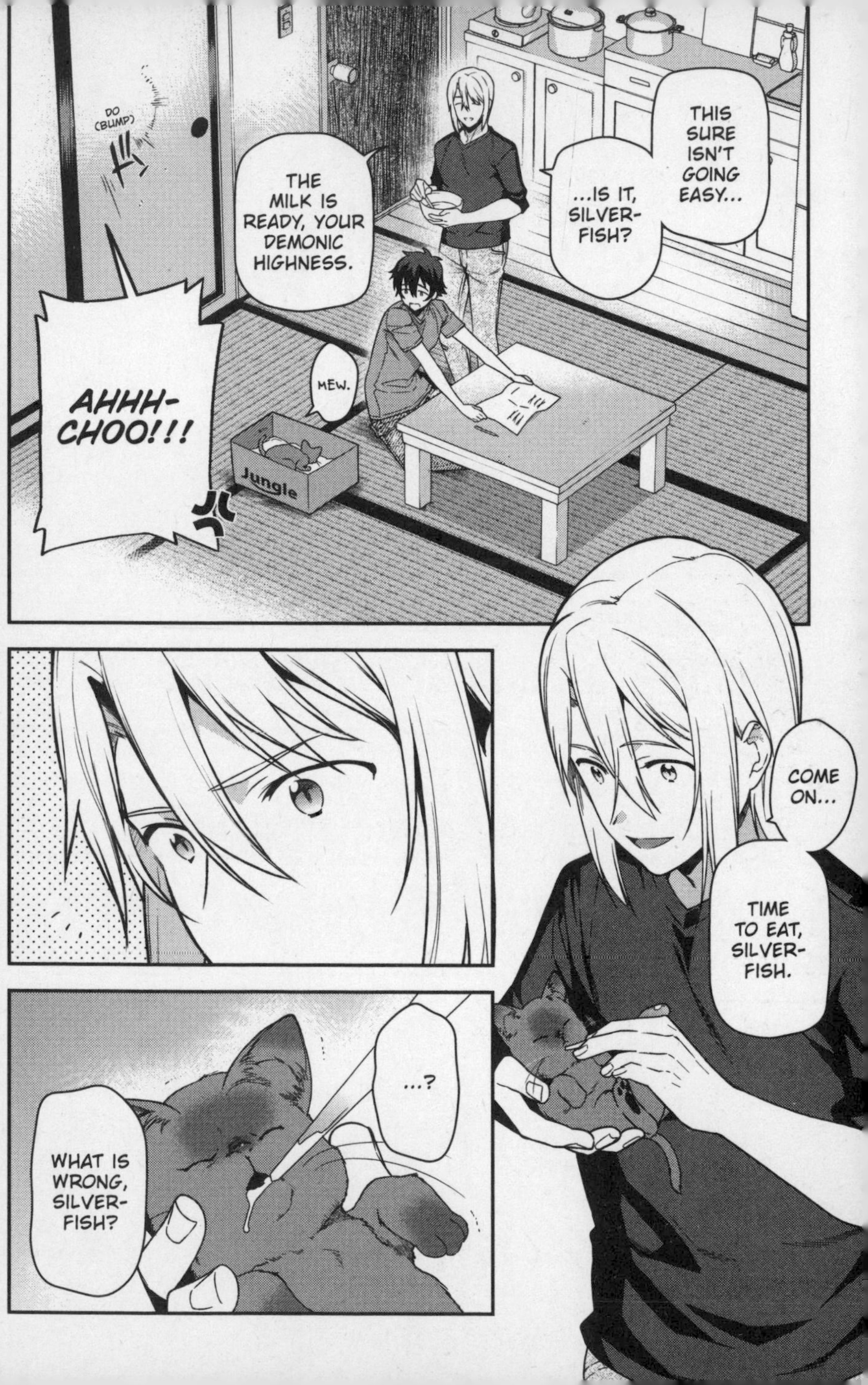
THIS SURE ISN'T GOING EASY...
...IS IT, SILVER-FISH?
THE MILK IS READY, YOUR DEMONIC HIGHNESS.
DO (BUMP)
MEW.
AHHH-CHOO!!!
COME ON...
TIME TO EAT, SILVER-FISH.
...?
WHAT IS WRONG, SILVER-FISH?

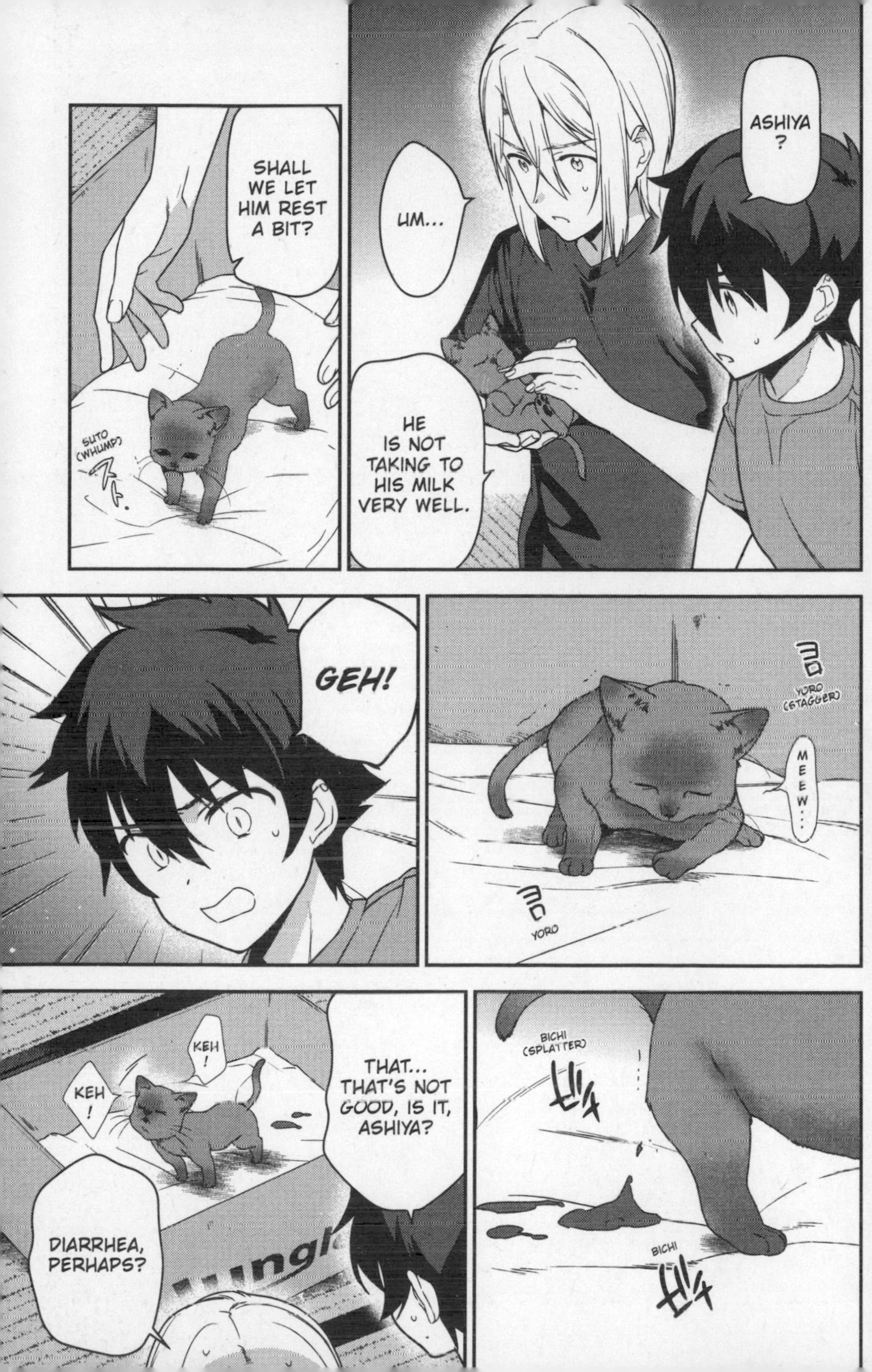
ASHIYA ?
UM...
HE IS NOT TAKING TO HIS MILK VERY WELL.
SHALL WE LET HIM REST A BIT?
SUTO (WHUMP)
YORO (STAGGER)
MEEW...
YORO
GEH!
BICHI (SPLATTER)
BICHI
THAT... THAT'S NOT GOOD, IS IT, ASHIYA?
KEH!
KEH!
DIARRHEA, PERHAPS?

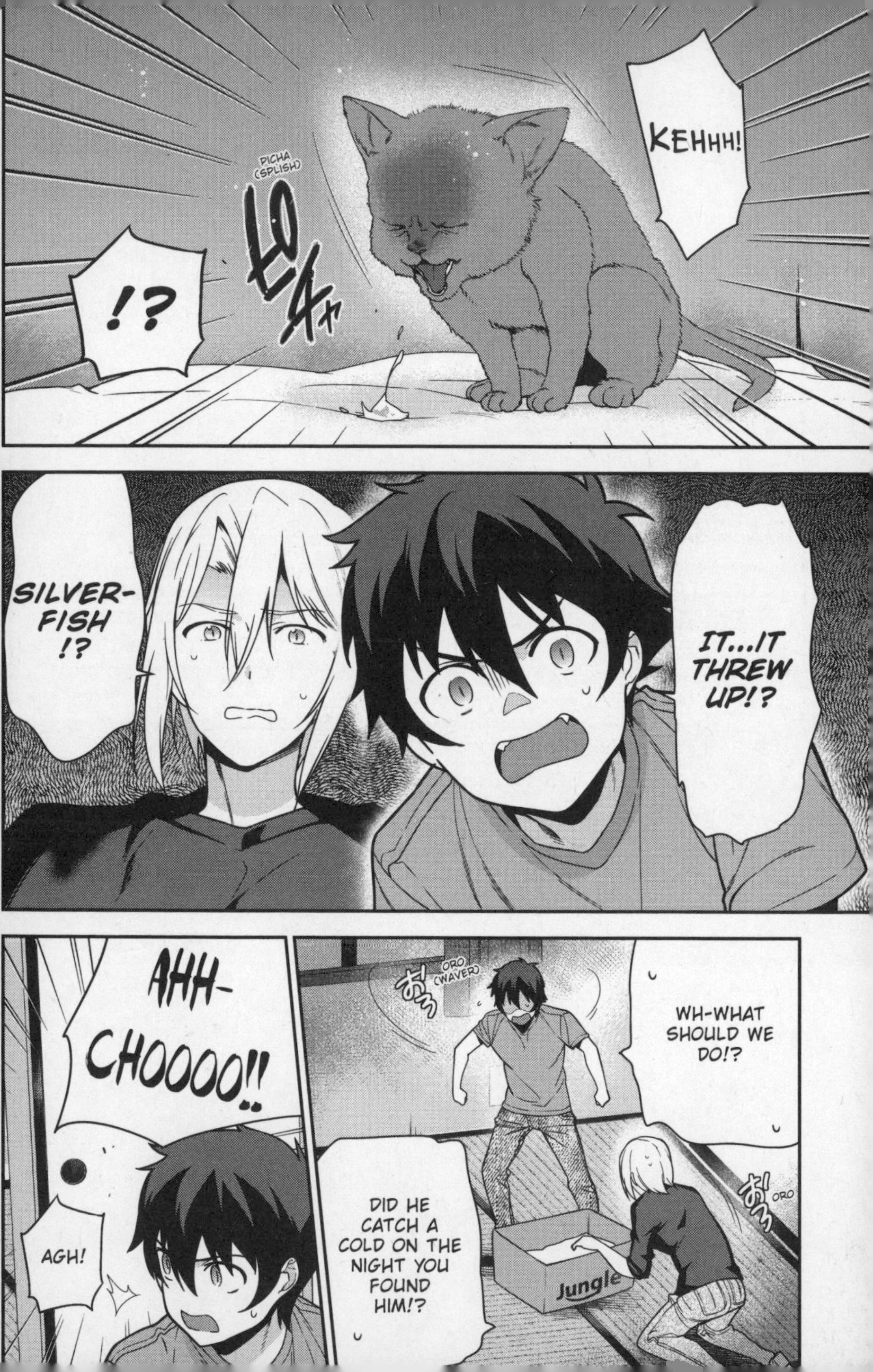
KEHHH!
PICHA (SPLISH)
!?
IT...IT THREW UP!?
SILVER-FISH!?
WH-WHAT SHOULD WE DO!?
ORO (WAVER)
ORO
DID HE CATCH A COLD ON THE NIGHT YOU FOUND HIM!?
Jungle
AHH-CHOOOO!!
AGH!

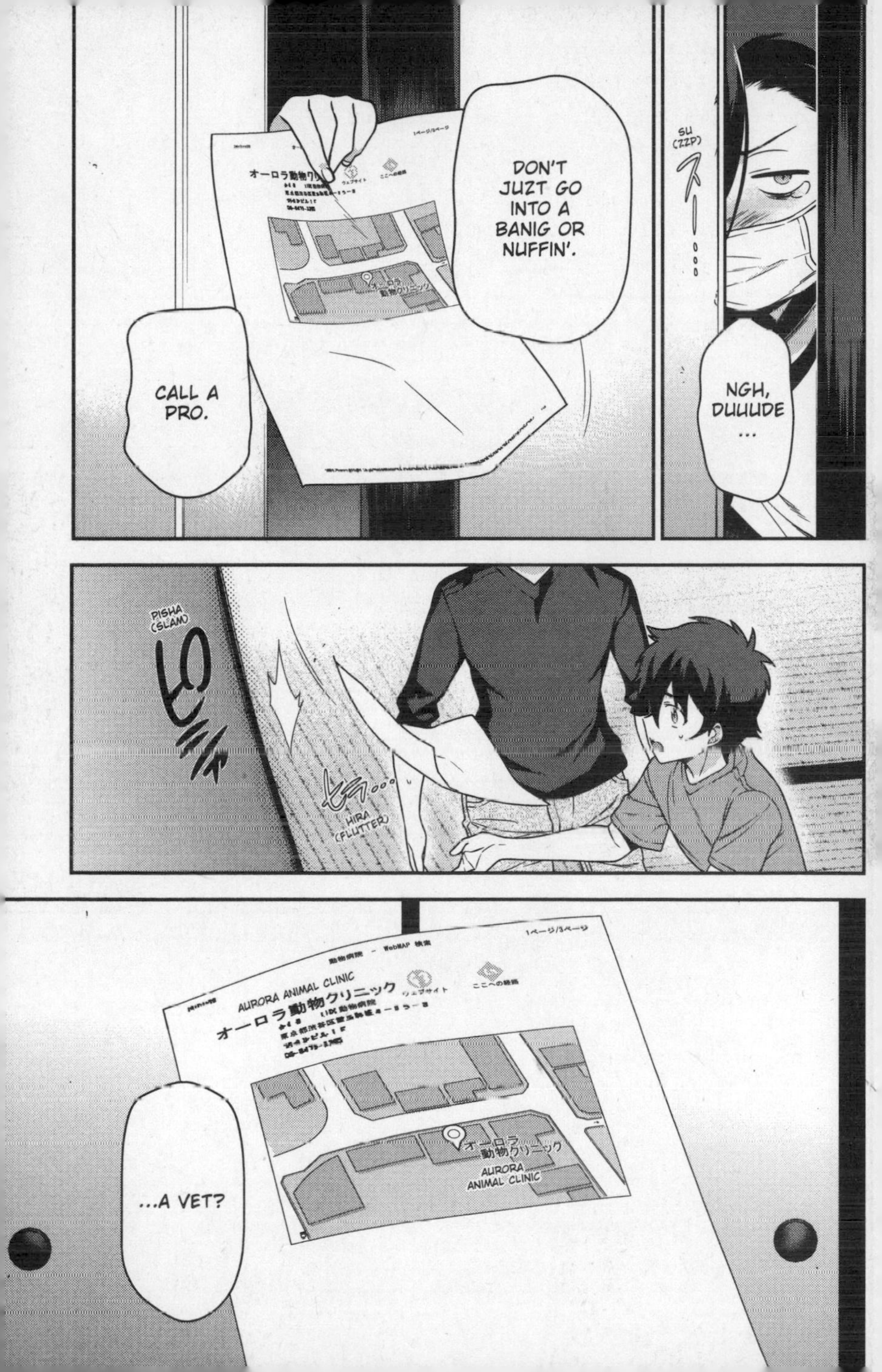
SU (ZZP)
NGH, DUUUDE ...
DON'T JUZT GO INTO A BANIG OR NUFFIN'.
CALL A PRO.
PISHA (SLAM)
HIRA (FLUTTER)
1ページ/3ページ
動物病院 – WebMAP 検索
AURORA ANIMAL CLINIC
オーロラ動物クリニック
ウェブサイト
ここへの経路
オーロラ動物クリニック
AURORA ANIMAL CLINIC
...A VET?

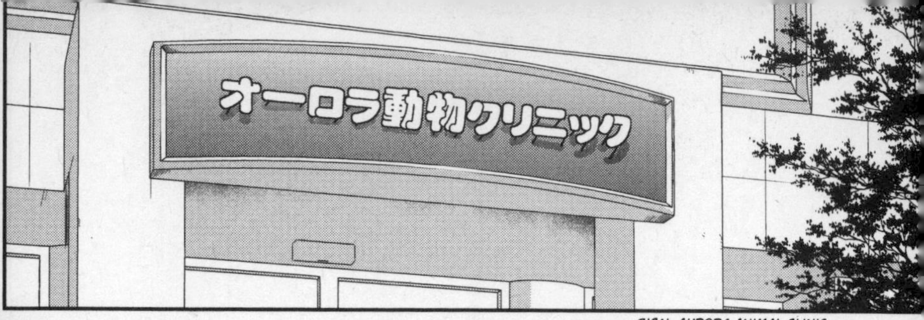
オーロラ動物クリニック

SIGN: AURORA ANIMAL CLINIC

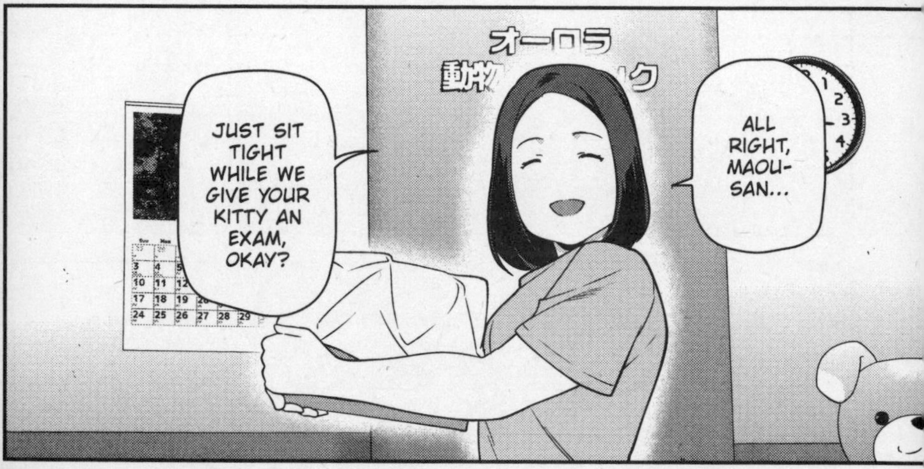
ALL RIGHT, MAOU-SAN...
JUST SIT TIGHT WHILE WE GIVE YOUR KITTY AN EXAM, OKAY?

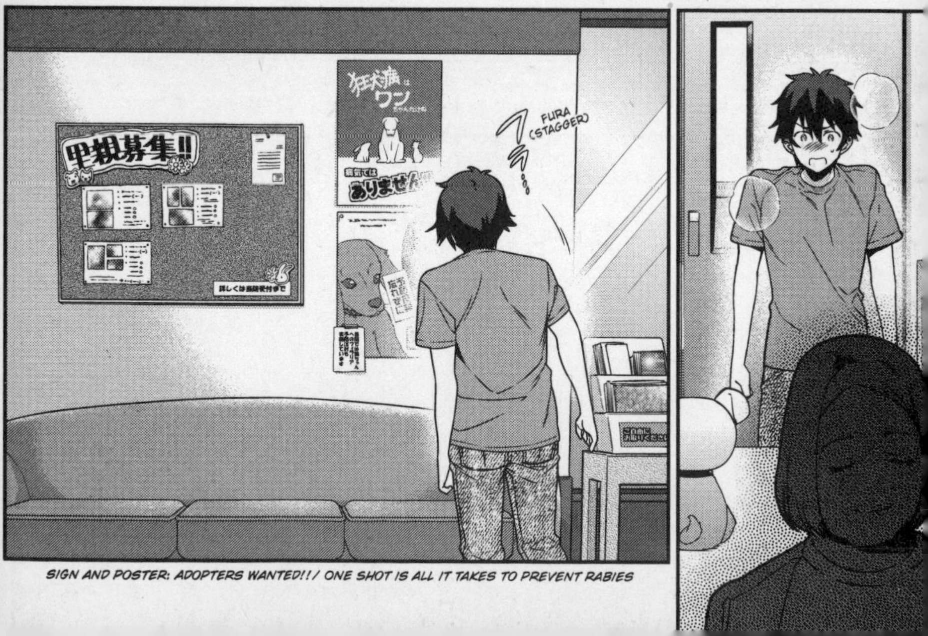
FURA (STAGGER)
里親募集!!
ありません

SIGN AND POSTER: ADOPTERS WANTED!! / ONE SHOT IS ALL IT TAKES TO PREVENT RABIES

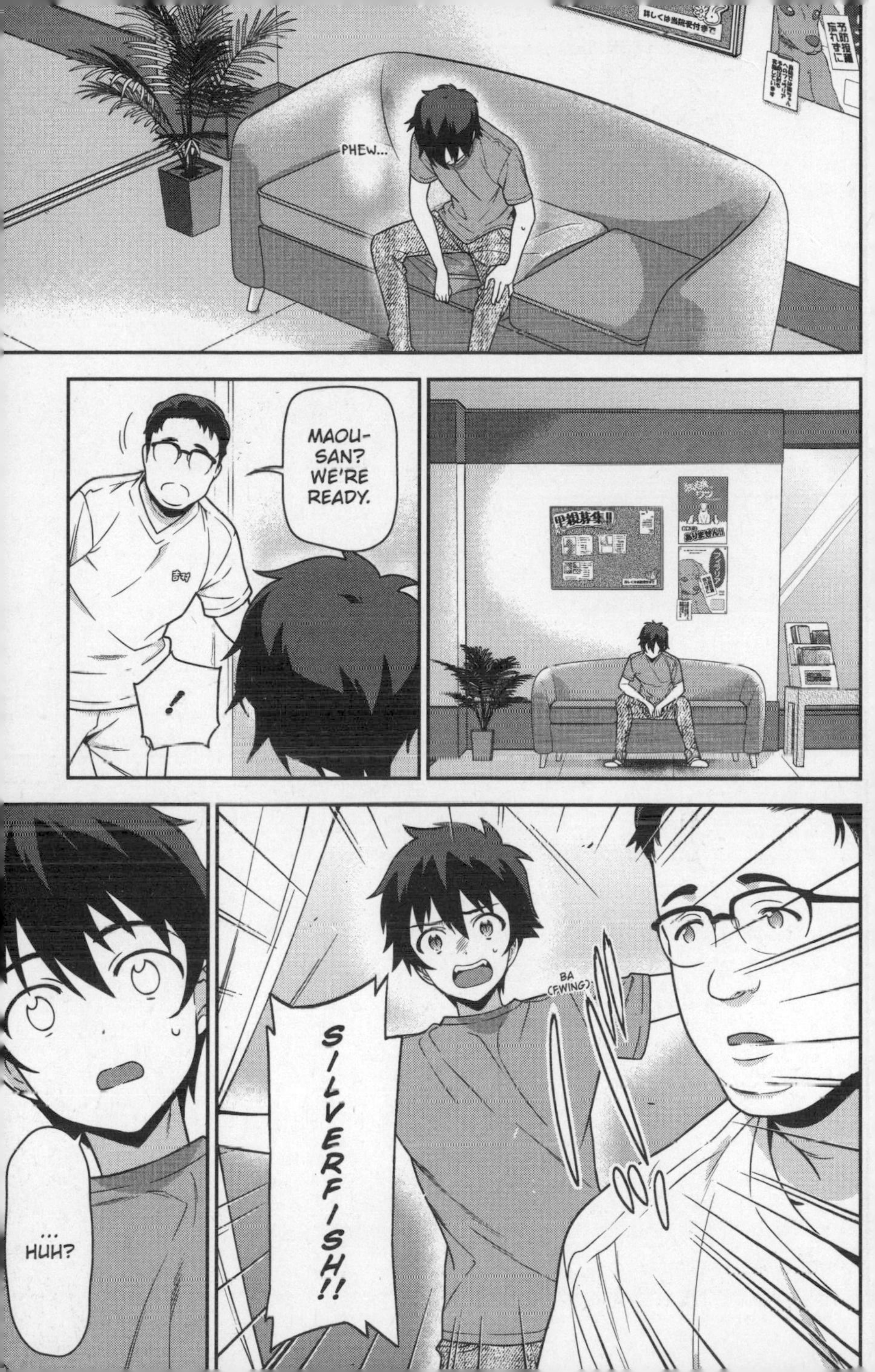
PHEW...
MAOU-SAN? WE'RE READY.
!
BA (FWING)
SILVERFISH!!
...HUH?

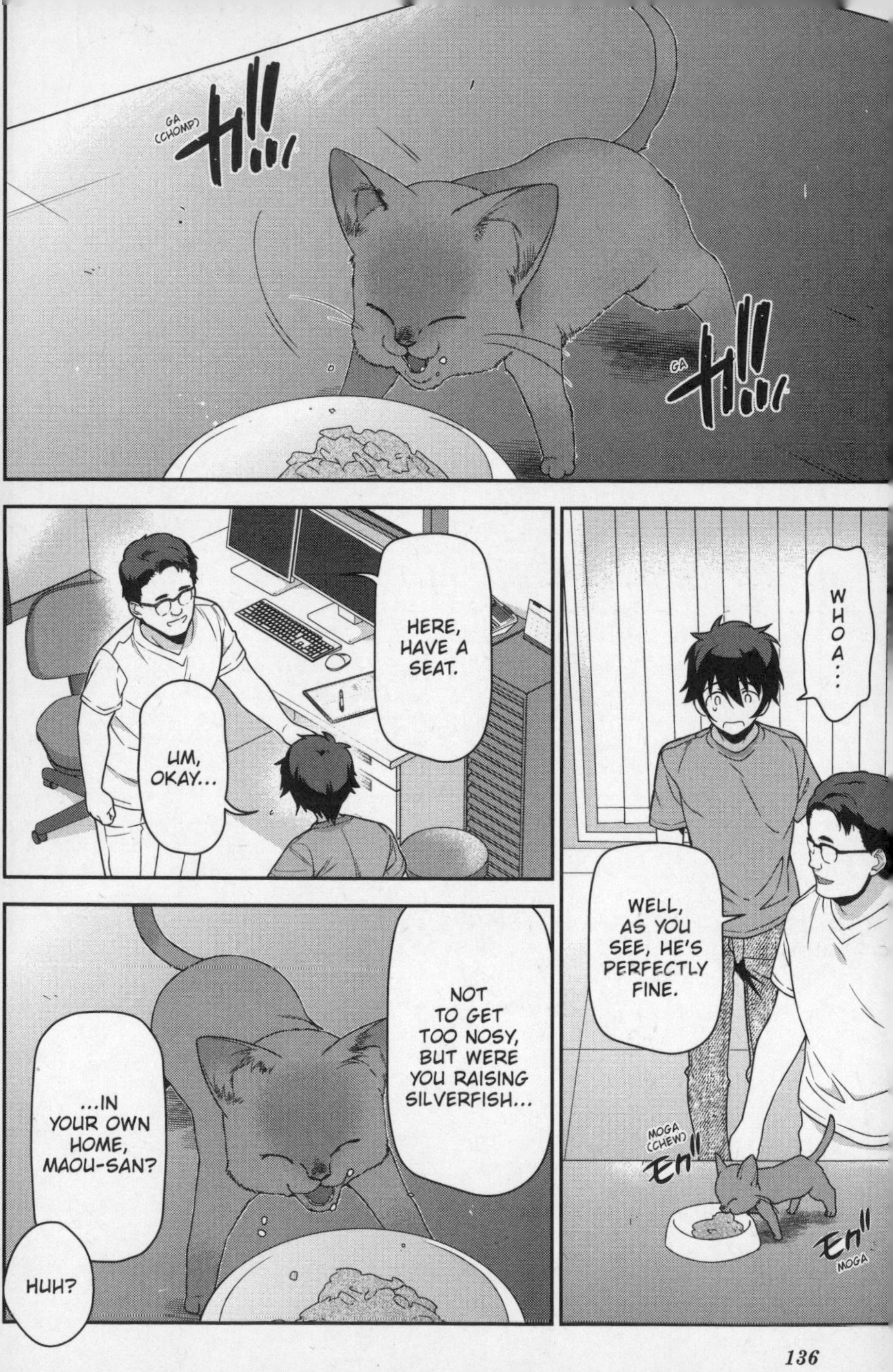
GA (CHOMP)
GA
WHOA...
WELL, AS YOU SEE, HE'S PERFECTLY FINE.
MOGA (CHEW)
MOGA
HERE, HAVE A SEAT.
UM, OKAY...
NOT TO GET TOO NOSY, BUT WERE YOU RAISING SILVERFISH...
...IN YOUR OWN HOME, MAOU-SAN?
HUH?

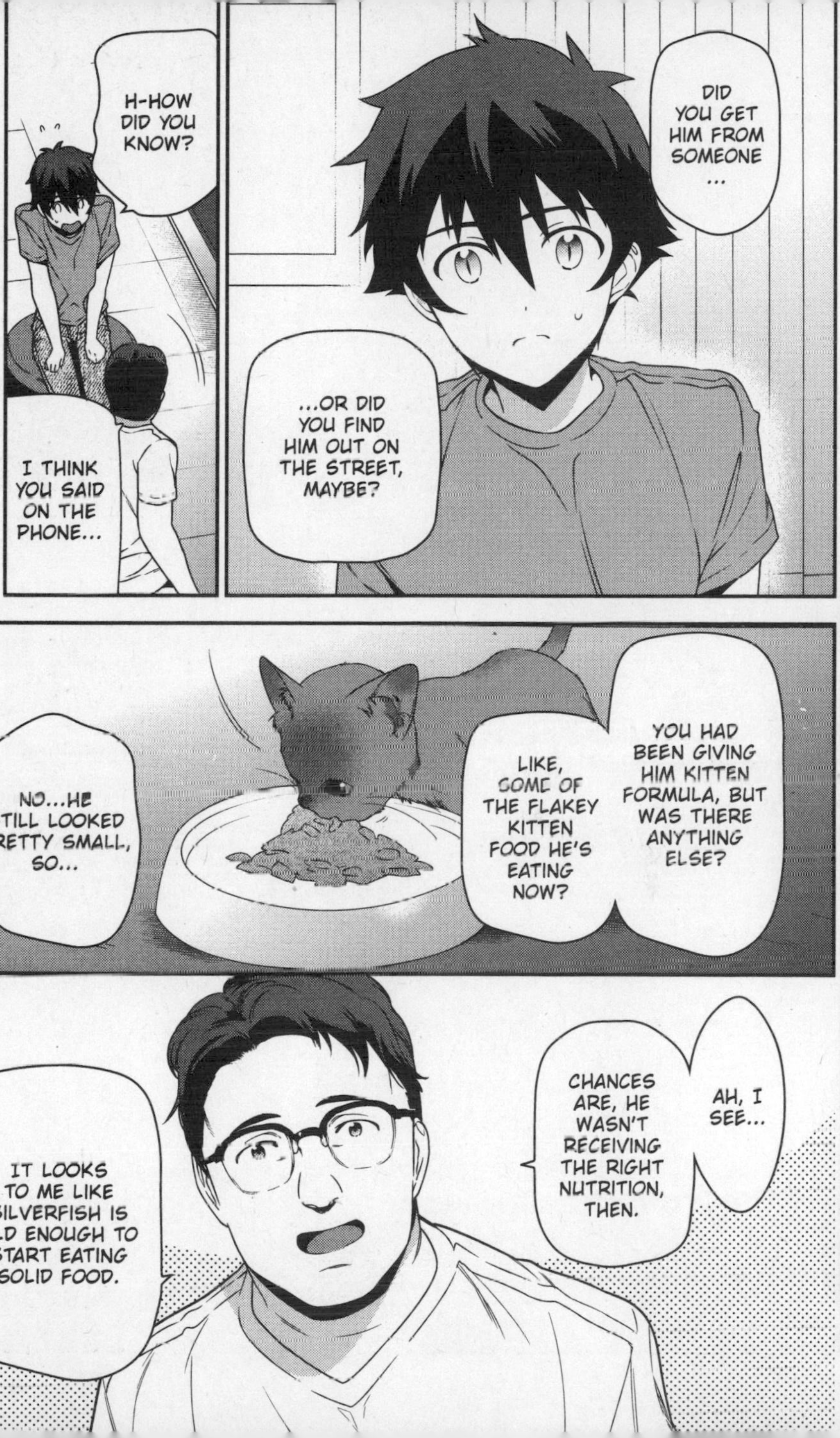
DID YOU GET HIM FROM SOMEONE...
...OR DID YOU FIND HIM OUT ON THE STREET, MAYBE?
H-HOW DID YOU KNOW?
I THINK YOU SAID ON THE PHONE...
YOU HAD BEEN GIVING HIM KITTEN FORMULA, BUT WAS THERE ANYTHING ELSE?
LIKE, SOME OF THE FLAKEY KITTEN FOOD HE'S EATING NOW?
NO...HE STILL LOOKED PRETTY SMALL, SO...
AH, I SEE...
CHANCES ARE, HE WASN'T RECEIVING THE RIGHT NUTRITION, THEN.
IT LOOKS TO ME LIKE SILVERFISH IS OLD ENOUGH TO START EATING SOLID FOOD.

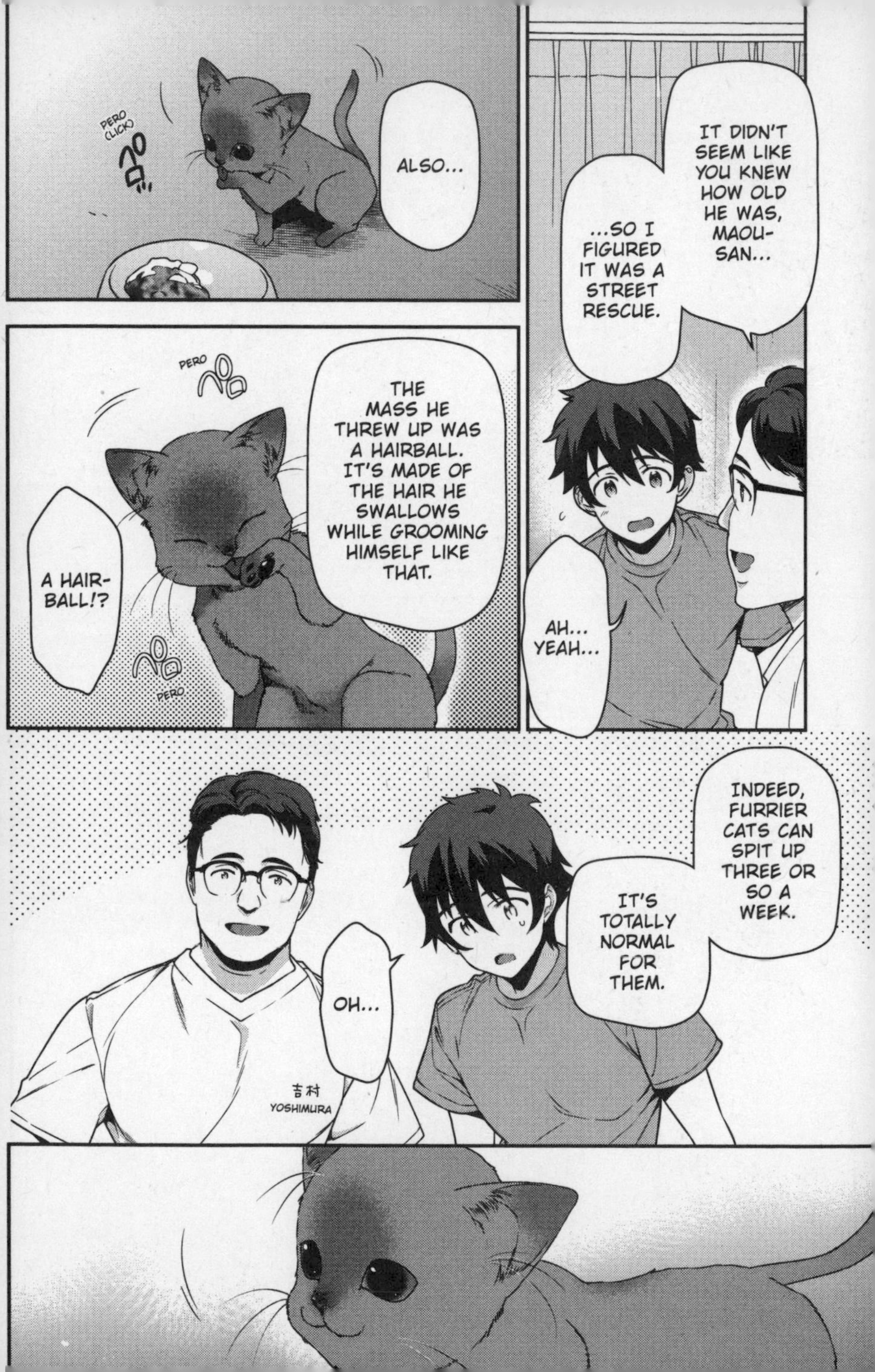
IT DIDN'T SEEM LIKE YOU KNEW HOW OLD HE WAS, MAOU-SAN...
...SO I FIGURED IT WAS A STREET RESCUE.
AH... YEAH...
PERO (CLICK)
ALSO...
PERO
THE MASS HE THREW UP WAS A HAIRBALL. IT'S MADE OF THE HAIR HE SWALLOWS WHILE GROOMING HIMSELF LIKE THAT.
A HAIR-BALL!?
PERO
INDEED, FURRIER CATS CAN SPIT UP THREE OR SO A WEEK.
IT'S TOTALLY NORMAL FOR THEM.
OH...
吉村
YOSHIMURA

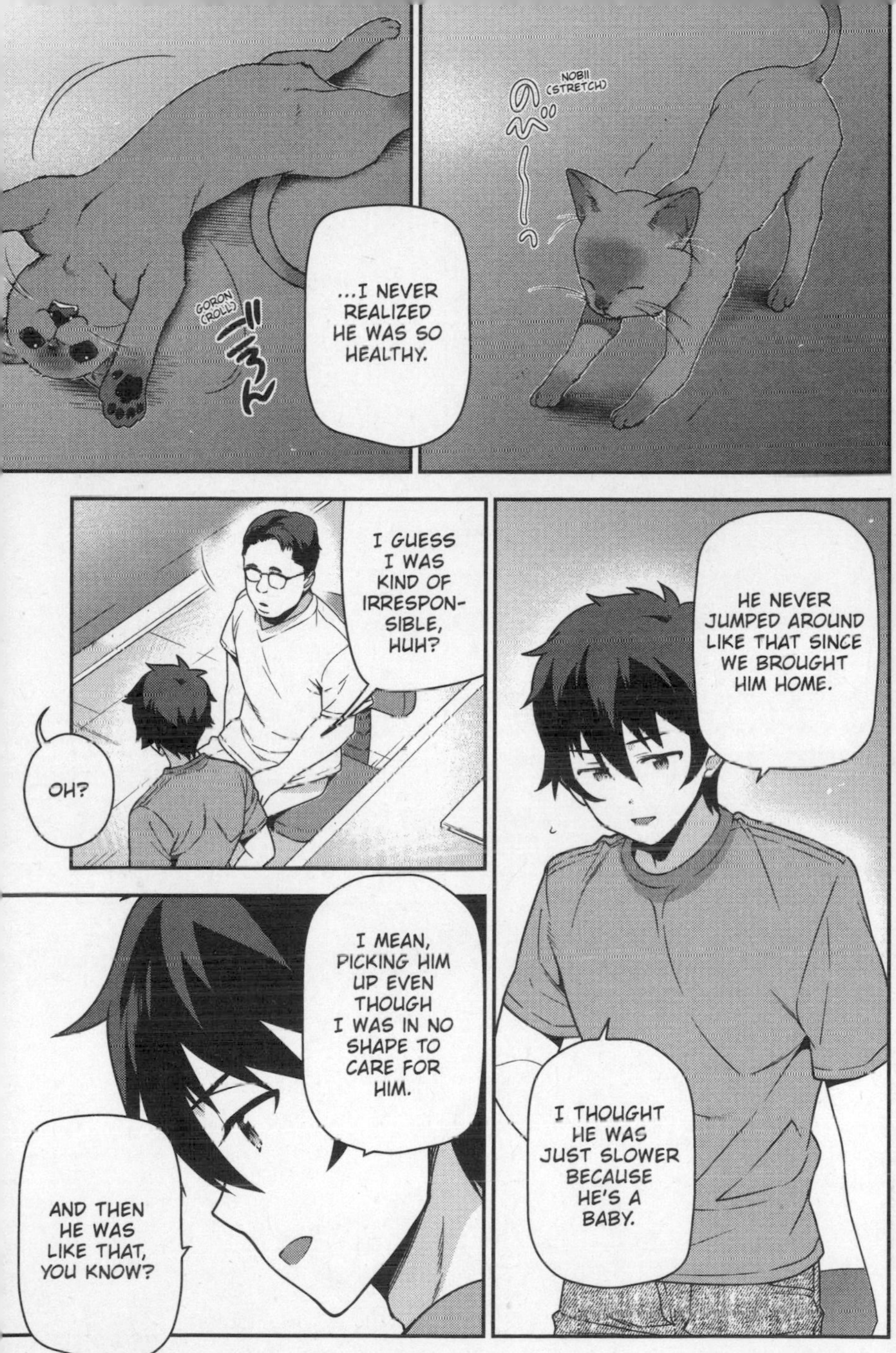
NOBII (STRETCH)
GORON (ROLL)
...I NEVER REALIZED HE WAS SO HEALTHY.
HE NEVER JUMPED AROUND LIKE THAT SINCE WE BROUGHT HIM HOME.
I THOUGHT HE WAS JUST SLOWER BECAUSE HE'S A BABY.
I GUESS I WAS KIND OF IRRESPON-SIBLE, HUH?
OH?
I MEAN, PICKING HIM UP EVEN THOUGH I WAS IN NO SHAPE TO CARE FOR HIM.
AND THEN HE WAS LIKE THAT, YOU KNOW?

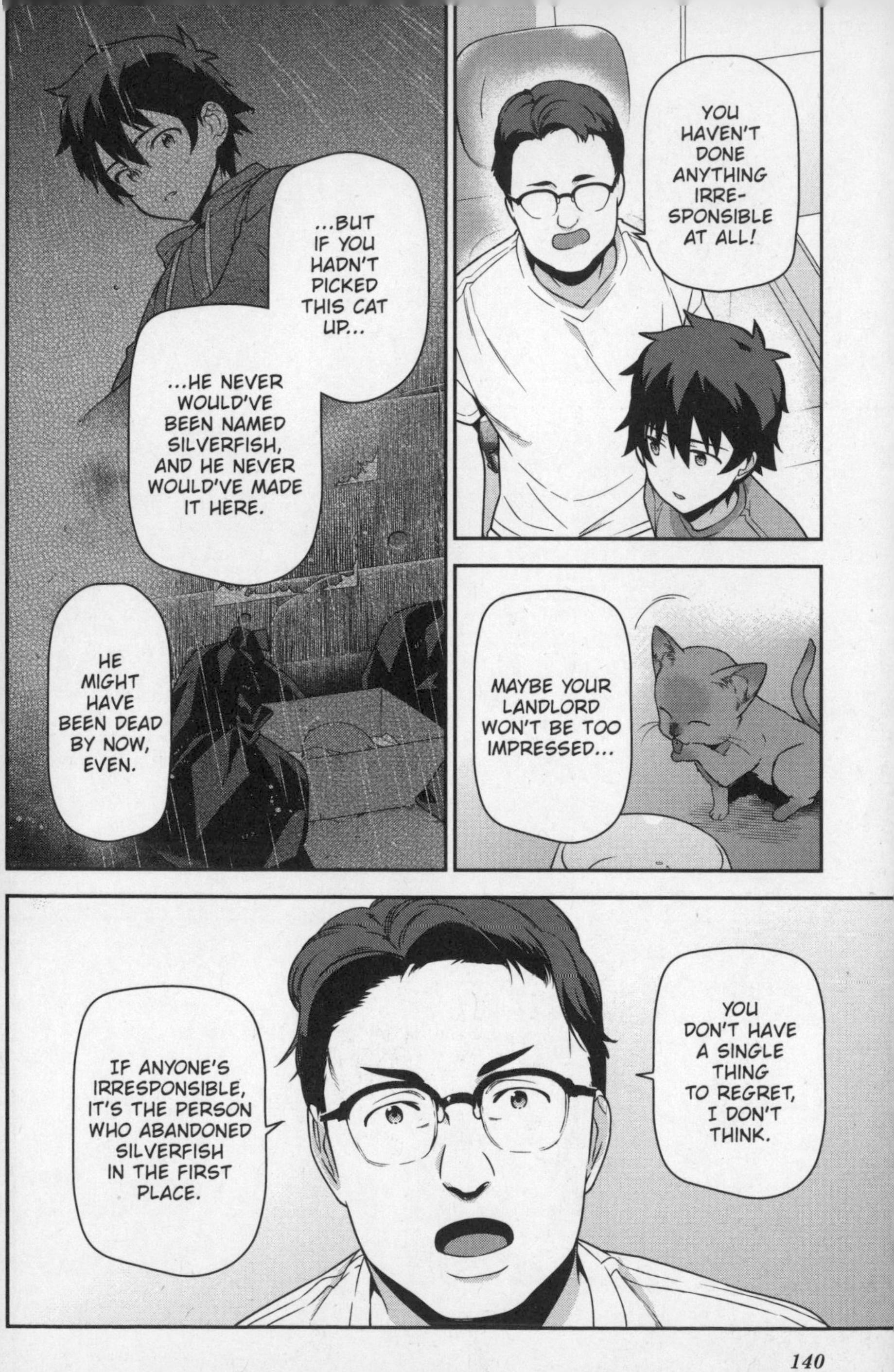
YOU HAVEN'T DONE ANYTHING IRRE-SPONSIBLE AT ALL!
MAYBE YOUR LANDLORD WON'T BE TOO IMPRESSED...
...BUT IF YOU HADN'T PICKED THIS CAT UP...
...HE NEVER WOULD'VE BEEN NAMED SILVERFISH, AND HE NEVER WOULD'VE MADE IT HERE.
HE MIGHT HAVE BEEN DEAD BY NOW, EVEN.
YOU DON'T HAVE A SINGLE THING TO REGRET, I DON'T THINK.
IF ANYONE'S IRRESPONSIBLE, IT'S THE PERSON WHO ABANDONED SILVERFISH IN THE FIRST PLACE.

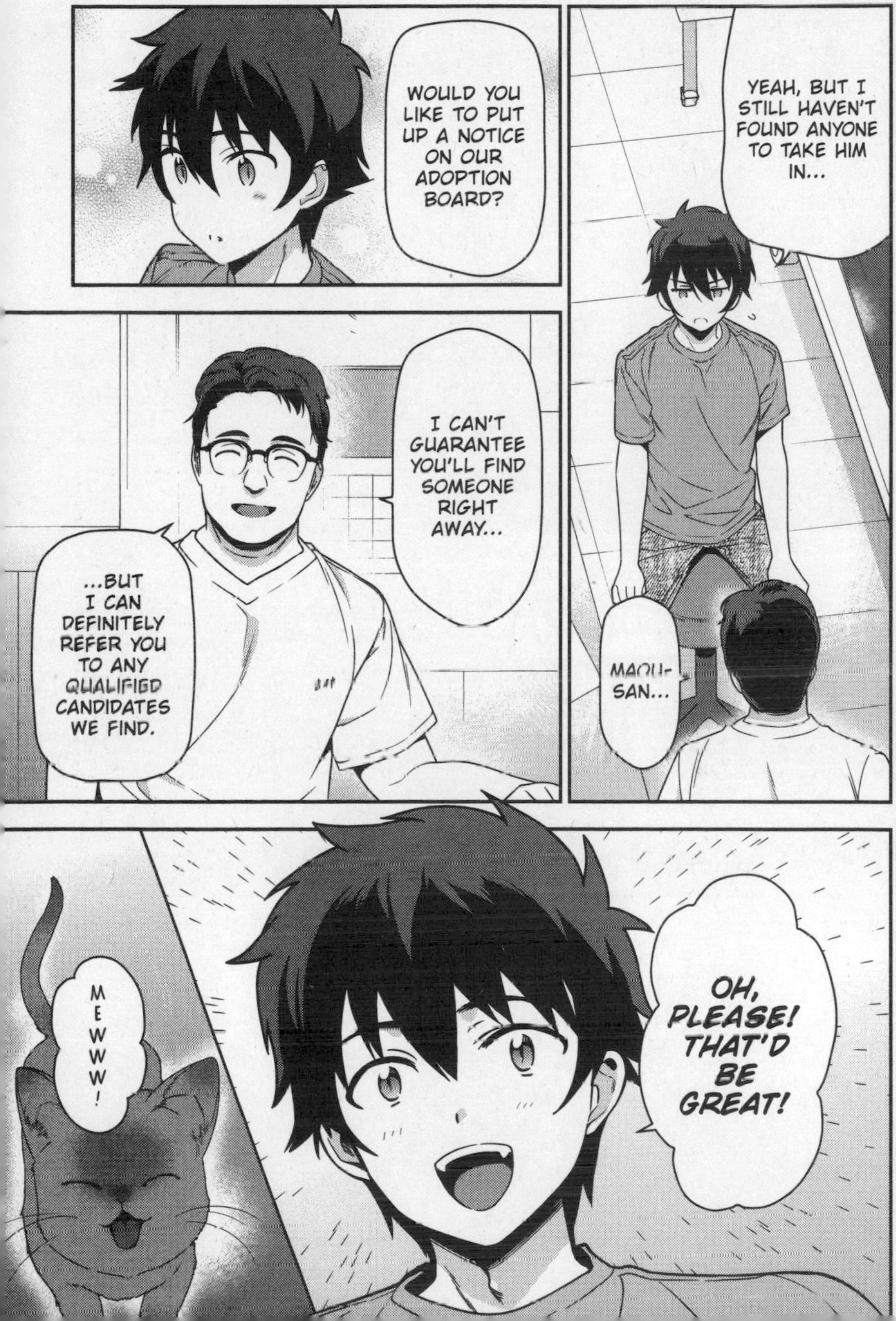
YEAH, BUT I STILL HAVEN'T FOUND ANYONE TO TAKE HIM IN...
MAOU-SAN...
WOULD YOU LIKE TO PUT UP A NOTICE ON OUR ADOPTION BOARD?
I CAN'T GUARANTEE YOU'LL FIND SOMEONE RIGHT AWAY...
...BUT I CAN DEFINITELY REFER YOU TO ANY QUALIFIED CANDIDATES WE FIND.
OH, PLEASE! THAT'D BE GREAT!
MEWWW!

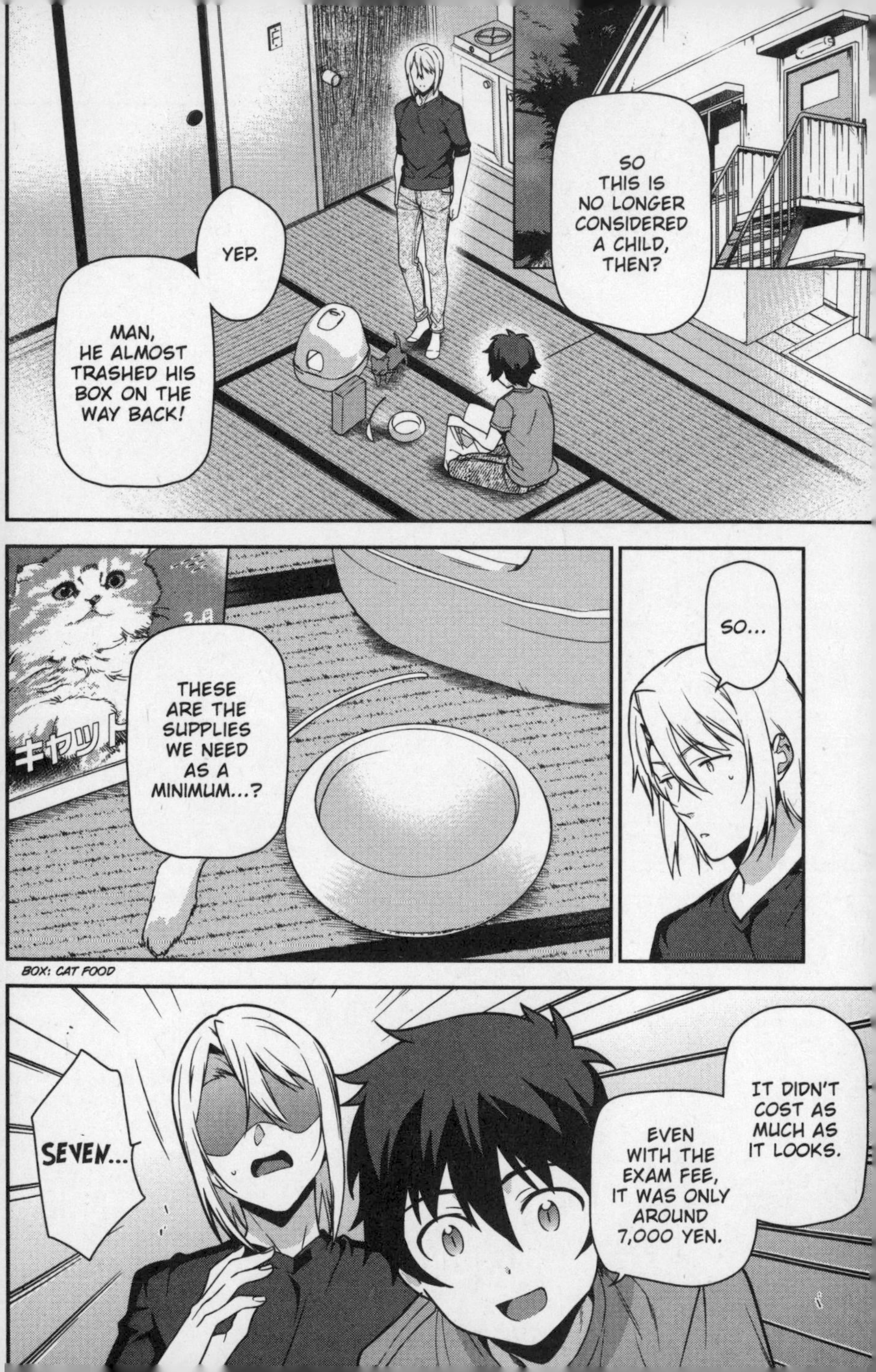
SO THIS IS NO LONGER CONSIDERED A CHILD, THEN?
YEP.
MAN, HE ALMOST TRASHED HIS BOX ON THE WAY BACK!
SO...
THESE ARE THE SUPPLIES WE NEED AS A MINIMUM...?
キャット
BOX: CAT FOOD
IT DIDN'T COST AS MUCH AS IT LOOKS.
EVEN WITH THE EXAM FEE, IT WAS ONLY AROUND 7,000 YEN.
SEVEN...

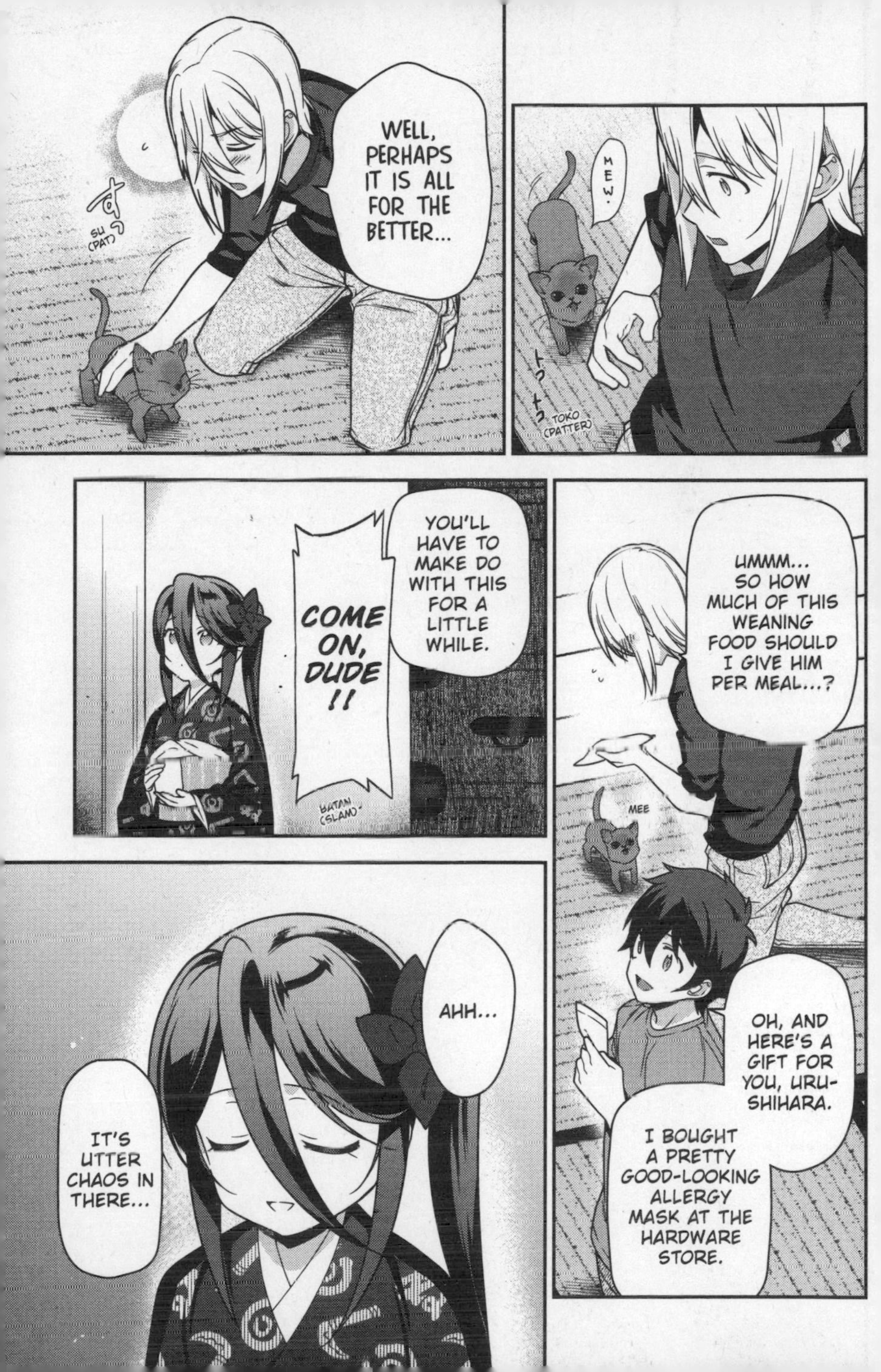
MEW.
TOKO (PATTER)
WELL, PERHAPS IT IS ALL FOR THE BETTER...
す
SU (PAT)
UMMM... SO HOW MUCH OF THIS WEANING FOOD SHOULD I GIVE HIM PER MEAL...?
MEE
OH, AND HERE'S A GIFT FOR YOU, URU-SHIHARA.
I BOUGHT A PRETTY GOOD-LOOKING ALLERGY MASK AT THE HARDWARE STORE.
YOU'LL HAVE TO MAKE DO WITH THIS FOR A LITTLE WHILE.
COME ON, DUDE!!
BATAN (SLAM)
AHH...
IT'S UTTER CHAOS IN THERE...

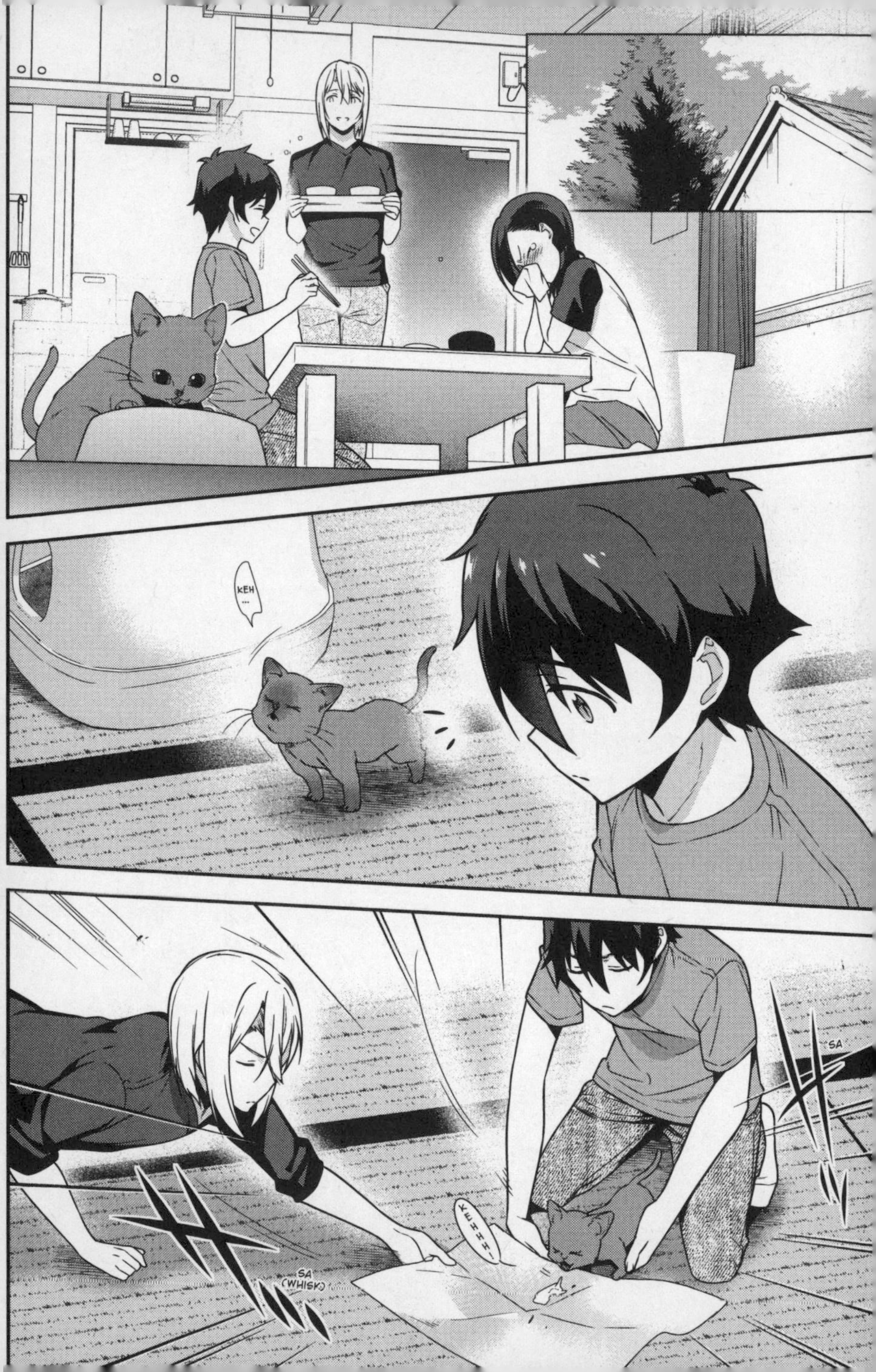
KEH...
SA
KEHHH!
SA (WHISK)

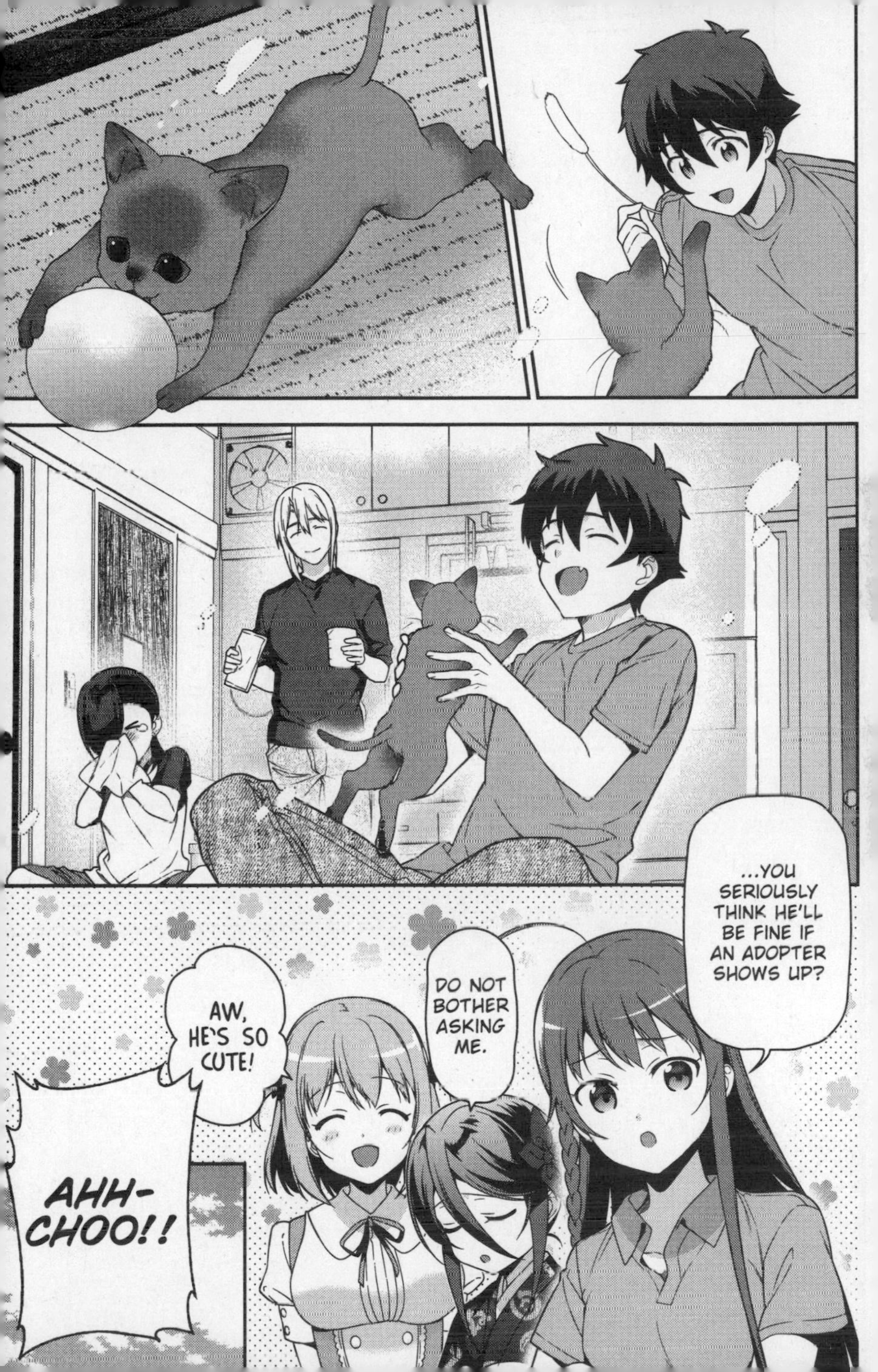
...YOU SERIOUSLY THINK HE'LL BE FINE IF AN ADOPTER SHOWS UP?
DO NOT BOTHER ASKING ME.
AW, HE'S SO CUTE!
AHH-CHOO!!

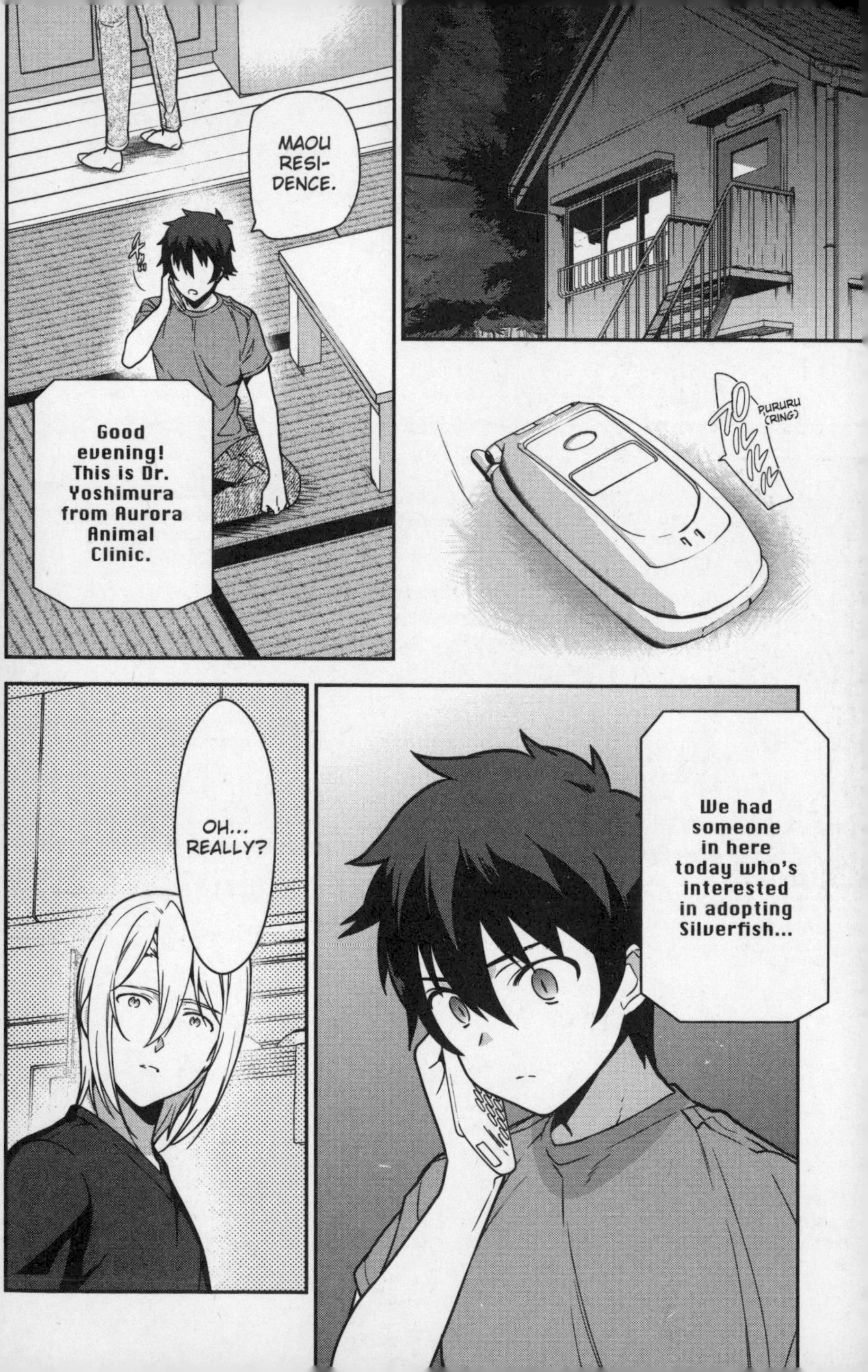
PURURU (RING)
MAOU RESIDENCE.
Good evening! This is Dr. Yoshimura from Aurora Animal Clinic.
We had someone in here today who's interested in adopting Silverfish...
OH... REALLY?

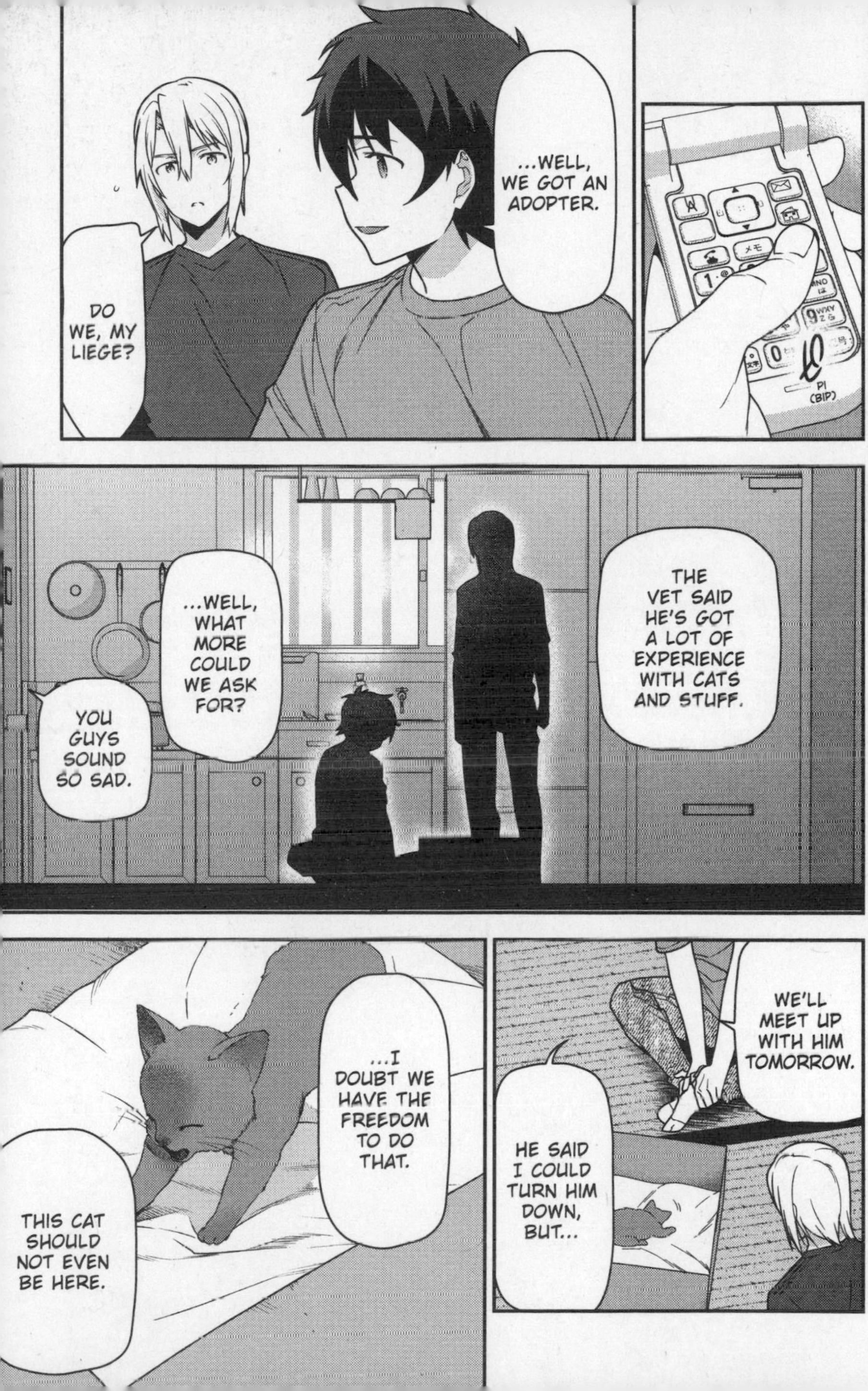
PI
(BIP)
...WELL, WE GOT AN ADOPTER.
DO WE, MY LIEGE?
THE VET SAID HE'S GOT A LOT OF EXPERIENCE WITH CATS AND STUFF.
...WELL, WHAT MORE COULD WE ASK FOR?
YOU GUYS SOUND SO SAD.
WE'LL MEET UP WITH HIM TOMORROW.
HE SAID I COULD TURN HIM DOWN, BUT...
...I DOUBT WE HAVE THE FREEDOM TO DO THAT.
THIS CAT SHOULD NOT EVEN BE HERE.

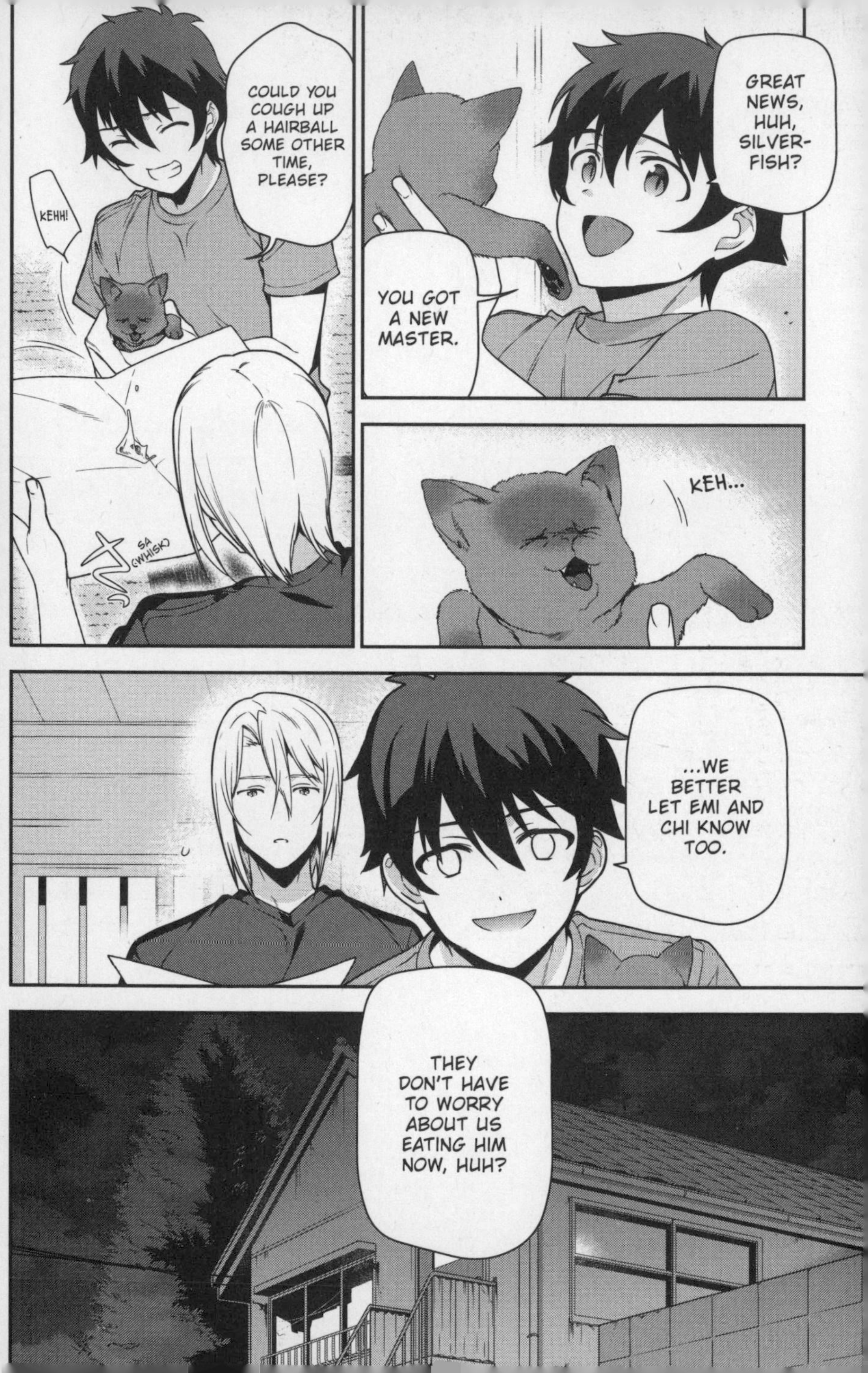
GREAT NEWS, HUH, SILVER-FISH?
YOU GOT A NEW MASTER.
KEH...
COULD YOU COUGH UP A HAIRBALL SOME OTHER TIME, PLEASE?
KEHH!
SA (WHISK)
...WE BETTER LET EMI AND CHI KNOW TOO.
THEY DON'T HAVE TO WORRY ABOUT US EATING HIM NOW, HUH?

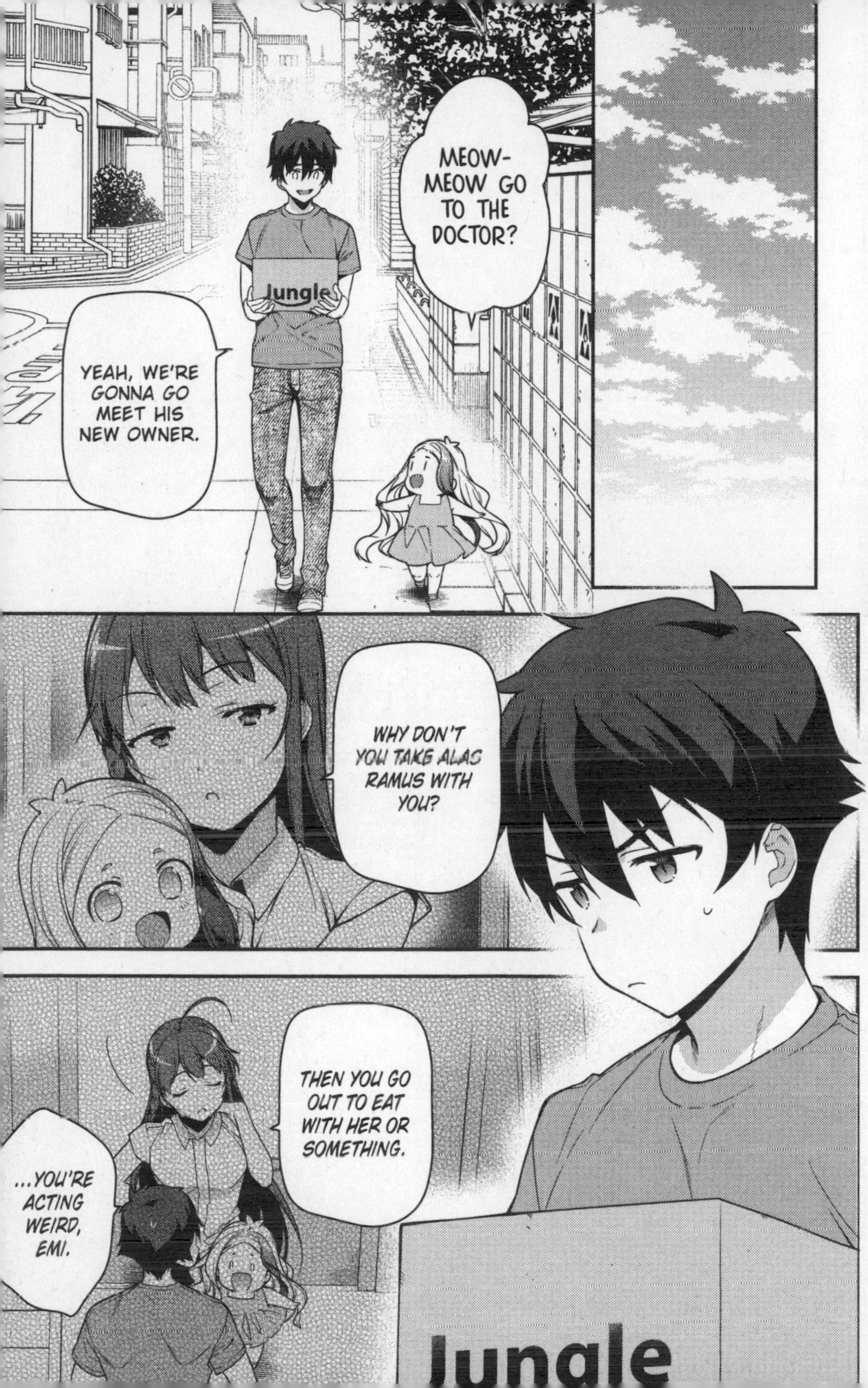
MEOW-MEOW GO TO THE DOCTOR?
Jungle
YEAH, WE'RE GONNA GO MEET HIS NEW OWNER.
WHY DON'T YOU TAKE ALAS RAMUS WITH YOU?
THEN YOU GO OUT TO EAT WITH HER OR SOMETHING.
...YOU'RE ACTING WEIRD, EMI.
Jungle

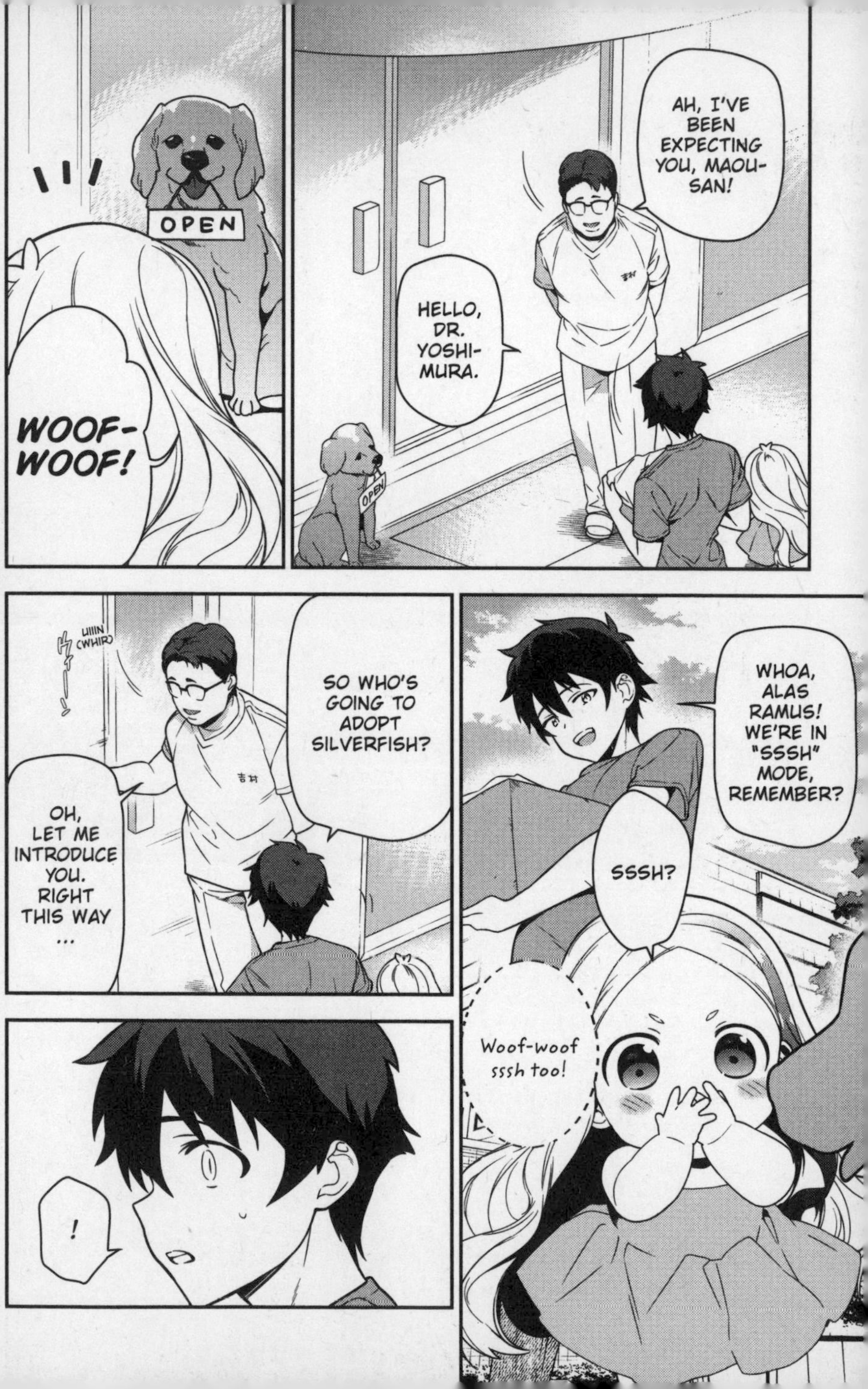
AH, I'VE BEEN EXPECTING YOU, MAOU-SAN!
HELLO, DR. YOSHIMURA.
OPEN
WOOF-WOOF!
WHOA, ALAS RAMUS! WE'RE IN "SSSH" MODE, REMEMBER?
SSSH?
Woof-woof sssh too!
UIIIN (WHIR)
SO WHO'S GOING TO ADOPT SILVERFISH?
OH, LET ME INTRODUCE YOU. RIGHT THIS WAY ...
!

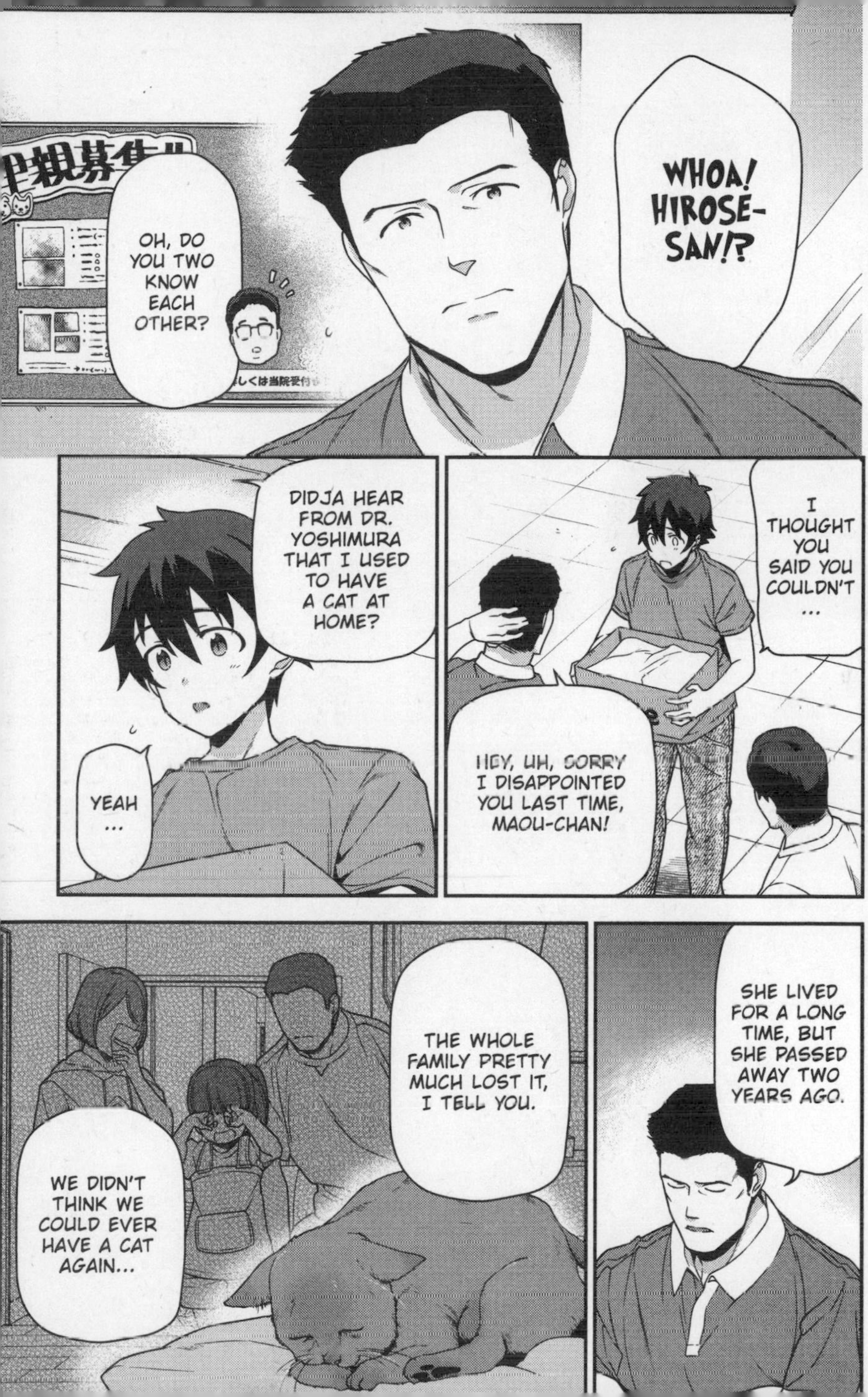
WHOA! HIROSE-SAN!?
OH, DO YOU TWO KNOW EACH OTHER?
I THOUGHT YOU SAID YOU COULDN'T ...
HEY, UH, SORRY I DISAPPOINTED YOU LAST TIME, MAOU-CHAN!
DIDJA HEAR FROM DR. YOSHIMURA THAT I USED TO HAVE A CAT AT HOME?
YEAH ...
SHE LIVED FOR A LONG TIME, BUT SHE PASSED AWAY TWO YEARS AGO.
THE WHOLE FAMILY PRETTY MUCH LOST IT, I TELL YOU.
WE DIDN'T THINK WE COULD EVER HAVE A CAT AGAIN...

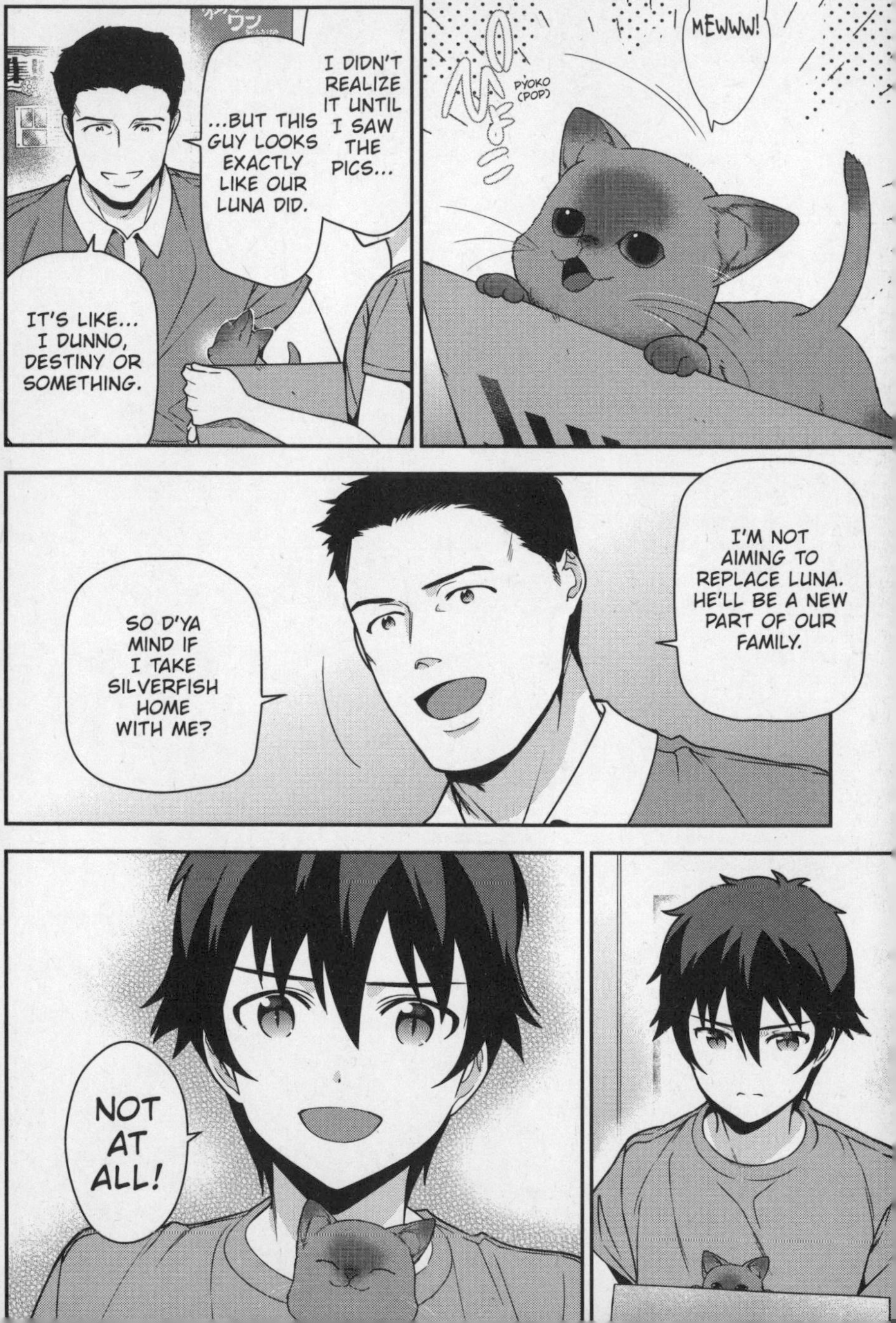
MEWWW!
PYOKO (POP)
I DIDN'T REALIZE IT UNTIL I SAW THE PICS...
...BUT THIS GUY LOOKS EXACTLY LIKE OUR LUNA DID.
IT'S LIKE... I DUNNO, DESTINY OR SOMETHING.
I'M NOT AIMING TO REPLACE LUNA. HE'LL BE A NEW PART OF OUR FAMILY.
SO D'YA MIND IF I TAKE SILVERFISH HOME WITH ME?
NOT AT ALL!

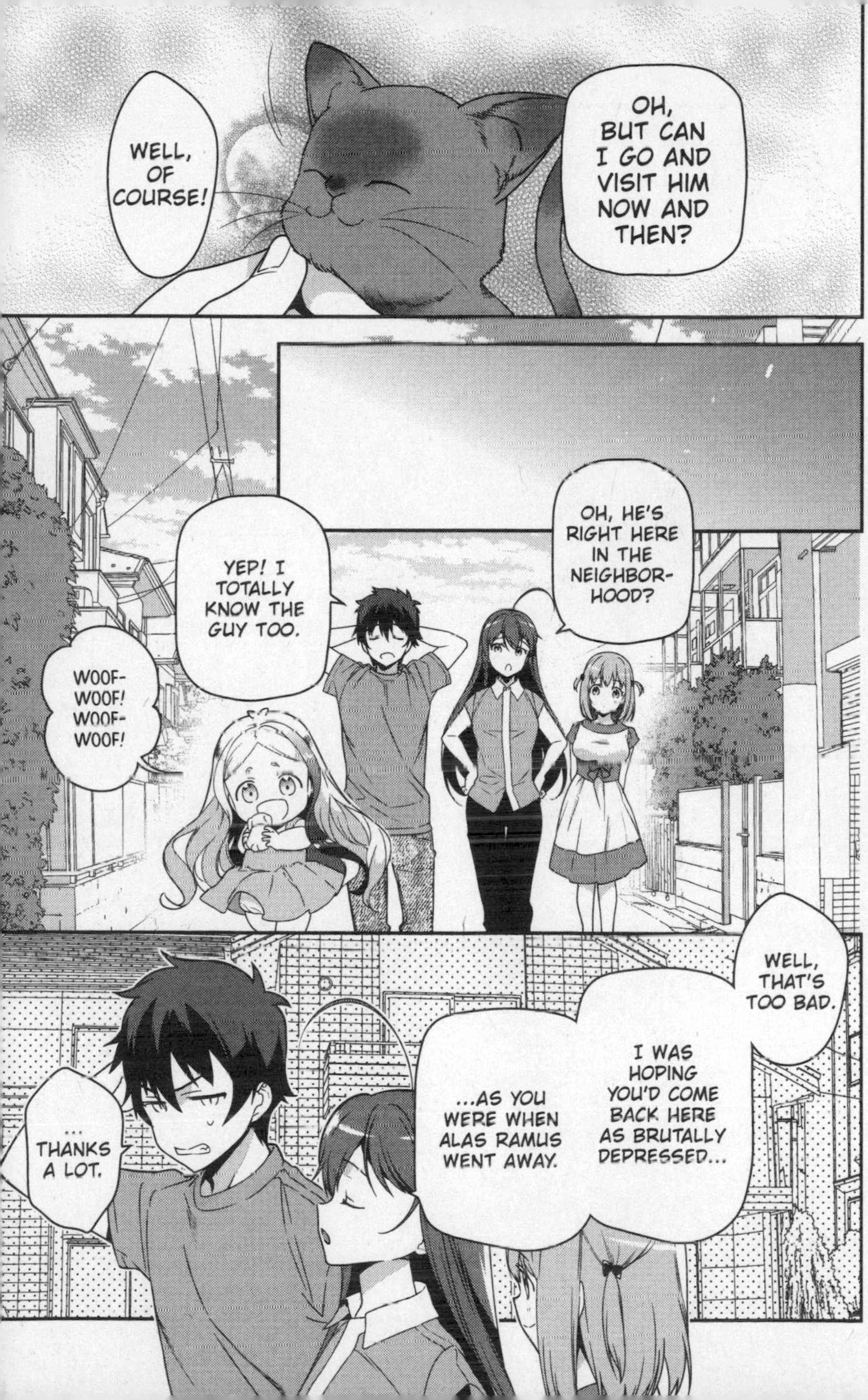
OH, BUT CAN I GO AND VISIT HIM NOW AND THEN?
WELL, OF COURSE!
OH, HE'S RIGHT HERE IN THE NEIGHBOR-HOOD?
YEP! I TOTALLY KNOW THE GUY TOO.
WOOF-WOOF! WOOF-WOOF!
WELL, THAT'S TOO BAD.
I WAS HOPING YOU'D COME BACK HERE AS BRUTALLY DEPRESSED...
...AS YOU WERE WHEN ALAS RAMUS WENT AWAY.
... THANKS A LOT.

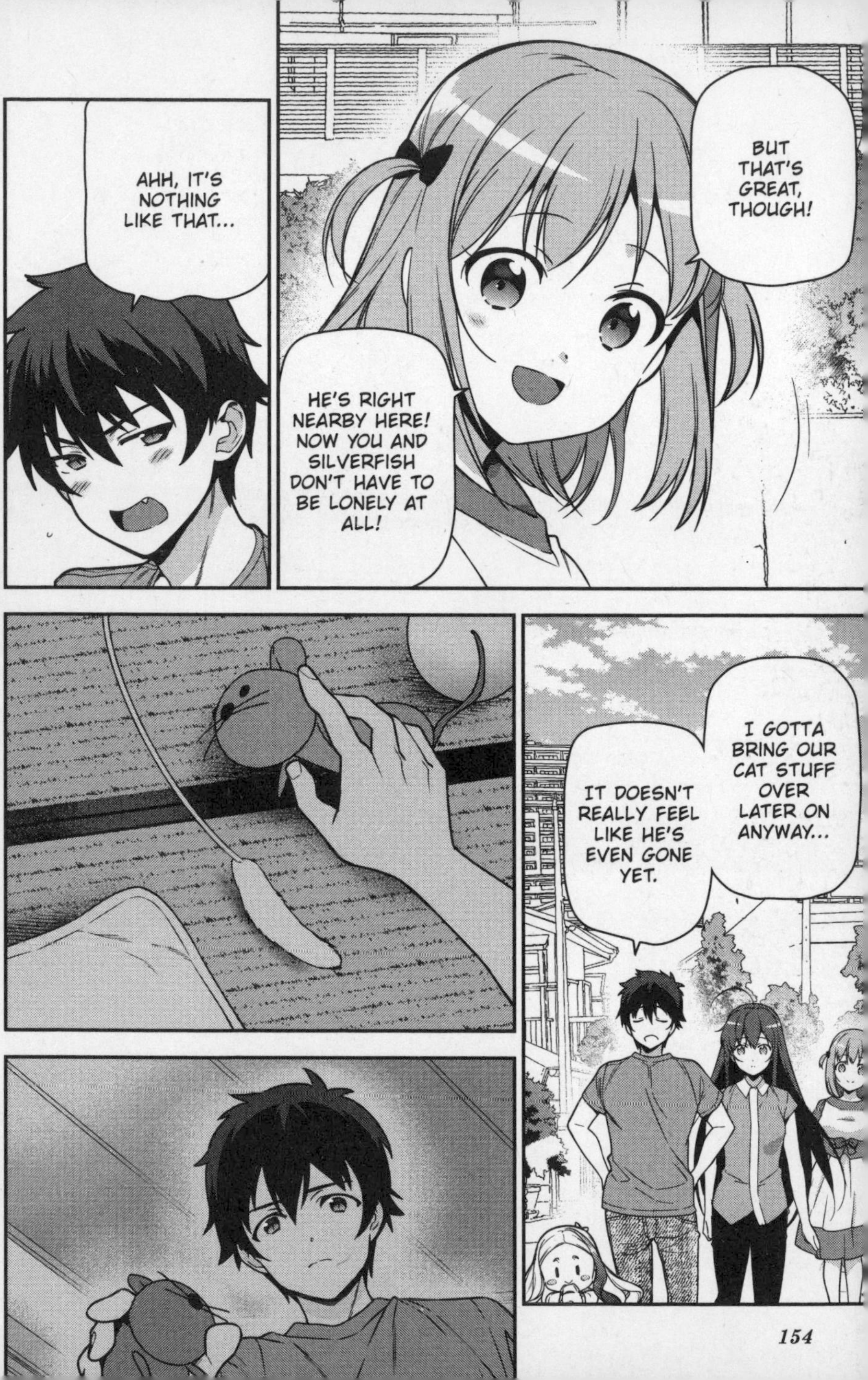
BUT THAT'S GREAT, THOUGH!
HE'S RIGHT NEARBY HERE! NOW YOU AND SILVERFISH DON'T HAVE TO BE LONELY AT ALL!
AHH, IT'S NOTHING LIKE THAT...
I GOTTA BRING OUR CAT STUFF OVER LATER ON ANYWAY...
IT DOESN'T REALLY FEEL LIKE HE'S EVEN GONE YET.

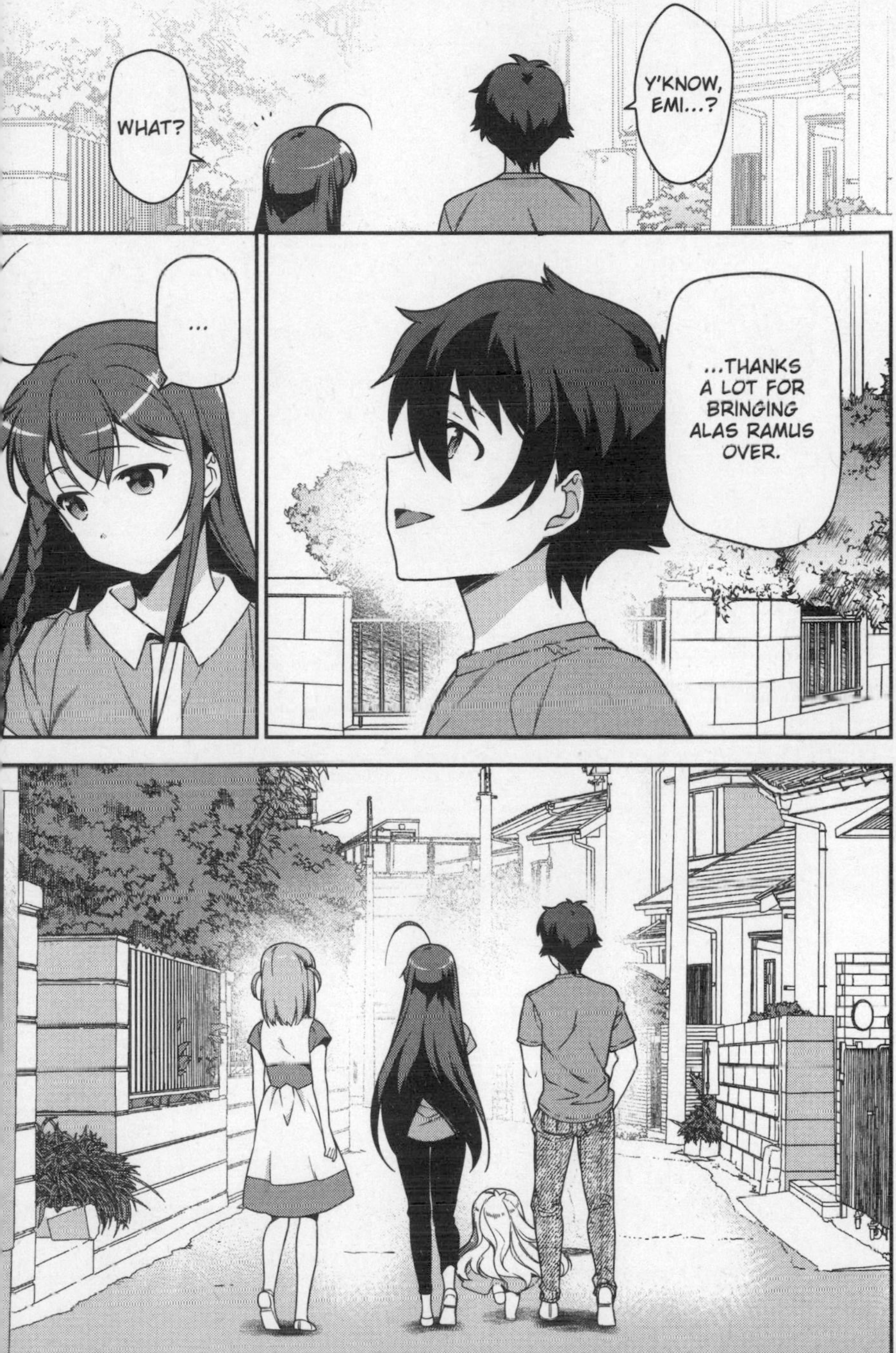
Y'KNOW, EMI...?
WHAT?
...THANKS A LOT FOR BRINGING ALAS RAMUS OVER.
...

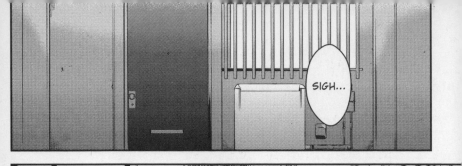

SIGH...

IT FEELS LIKE THE ENERGY HAS BEEN SUCKED OUT OF THE ROOM, MY LIEGE.

CAN YOU COME OUT OF THERE ALREADY, URUSHIHARA?

SILVER-FISH'S GONE, MAN.

SU (ZIP)

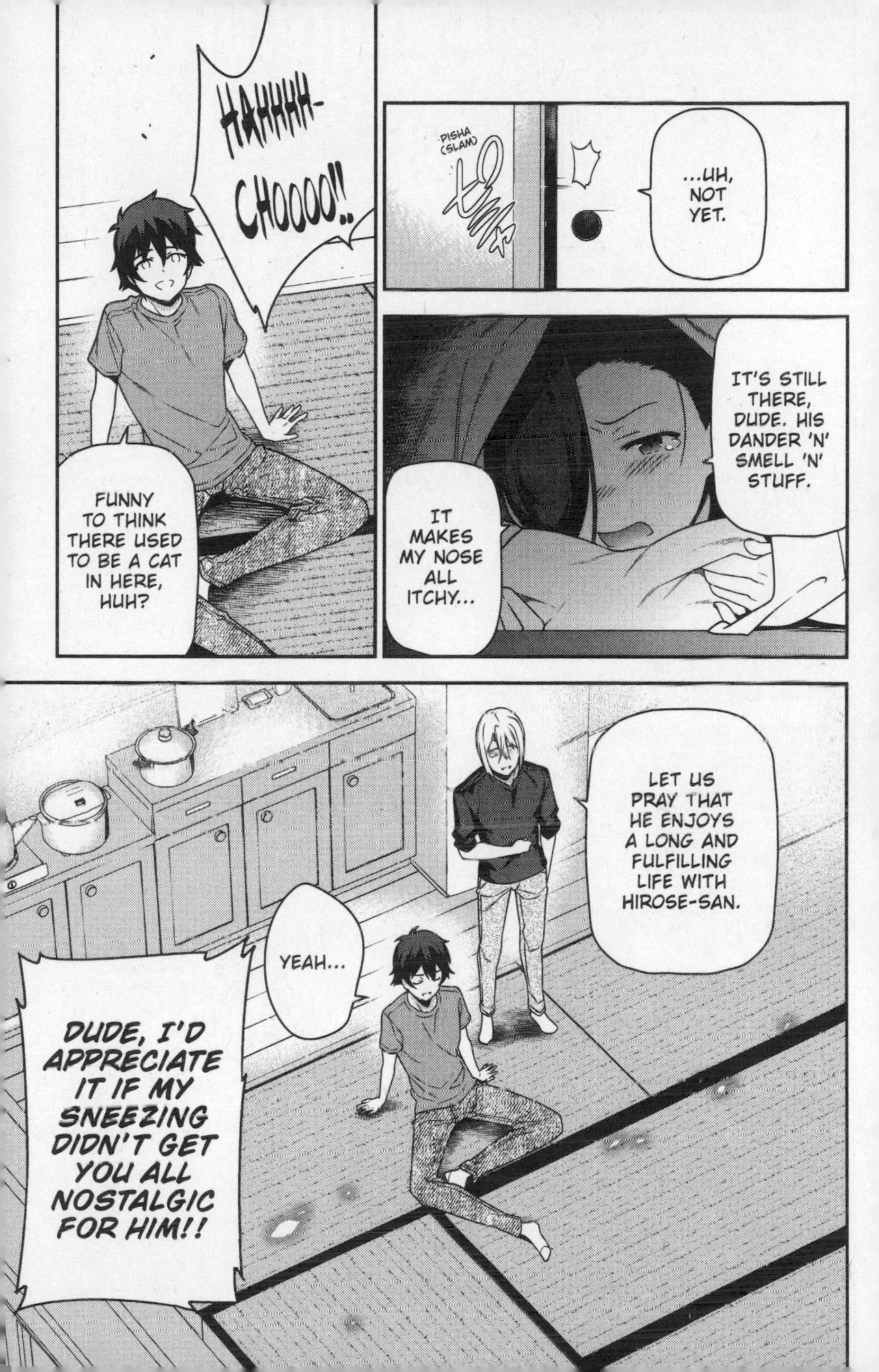
PISHA (SLAM)
...UH, NOT YET.
IT'S STILL THERE, DUDE. HIS DANDER 'N' SMELL 'N' STUFF.
IT MAKES MY NOSE ALL ITCHY...
HAHHHH-CHOOOO!!
FUNNY TO THINK THERE USED TO BE A CAT IN HERE, HUH?
LET US PRAY THAT HE ENJOYS A LONG AND FULFILLING LIFE WITH HIROSE-SAN.
YEAH...
DUDE, I'D APPRECIATE IT IF MY SNEEZING DIDN'T GET YOU ALL NOSTALGIC FOR HIM!!

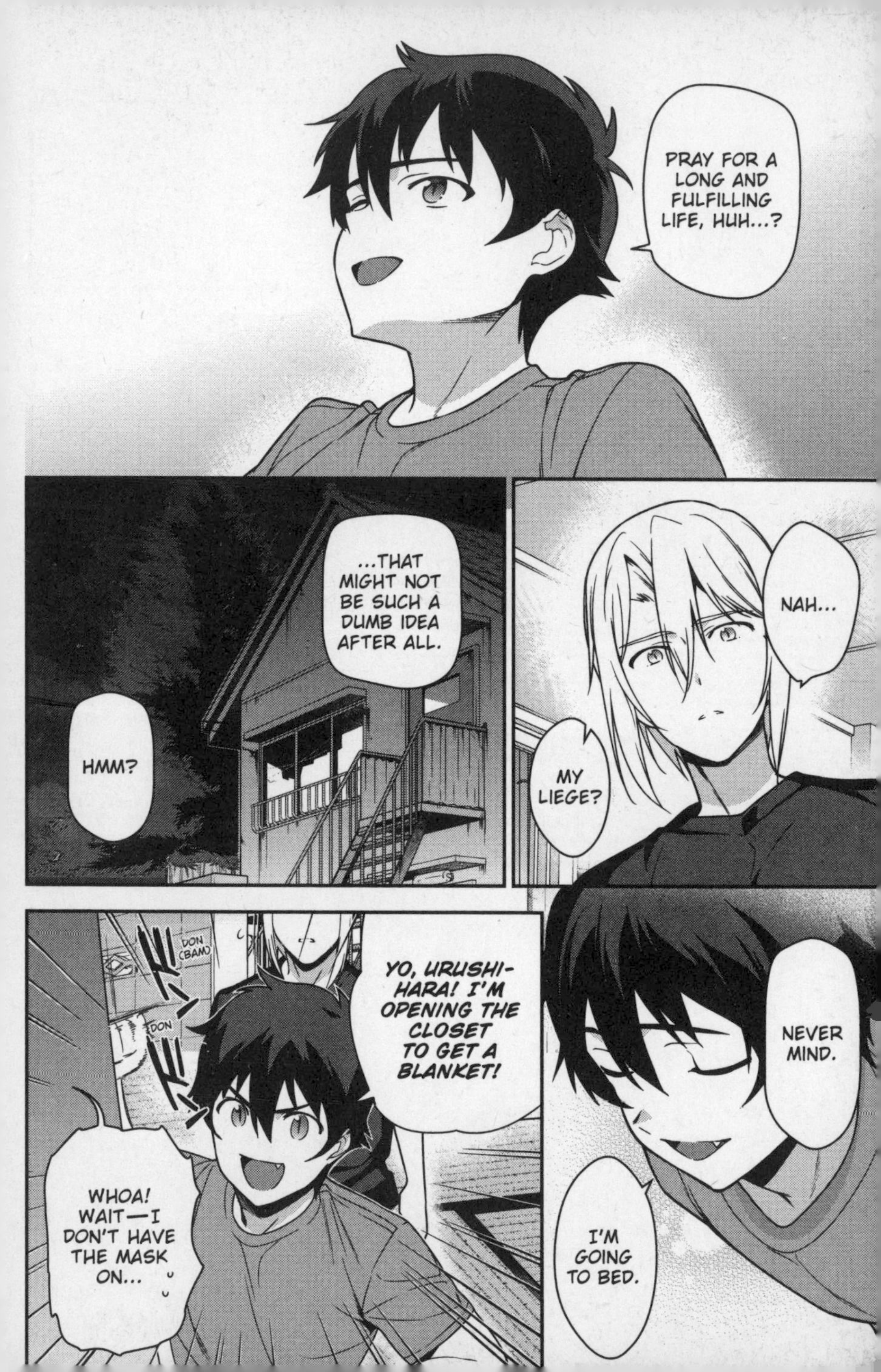
PRAY FOR A LONG AND FULFILLING LIFE, HUH...?
NAH...
MY LIEGE?
...THAT MIGHT NOT BE SUCH A DUMB IDEA AFTER ALL.
HMM?
NEVER MIND.
I'M GOING TO BED.
DON (BAM)
DON
YO, URUSHI-HARA! I'M OPENING THE CLOSET TO GET A BLANKET!
WHOA! WAIT—I DON'T HAVE THE MASK ON...

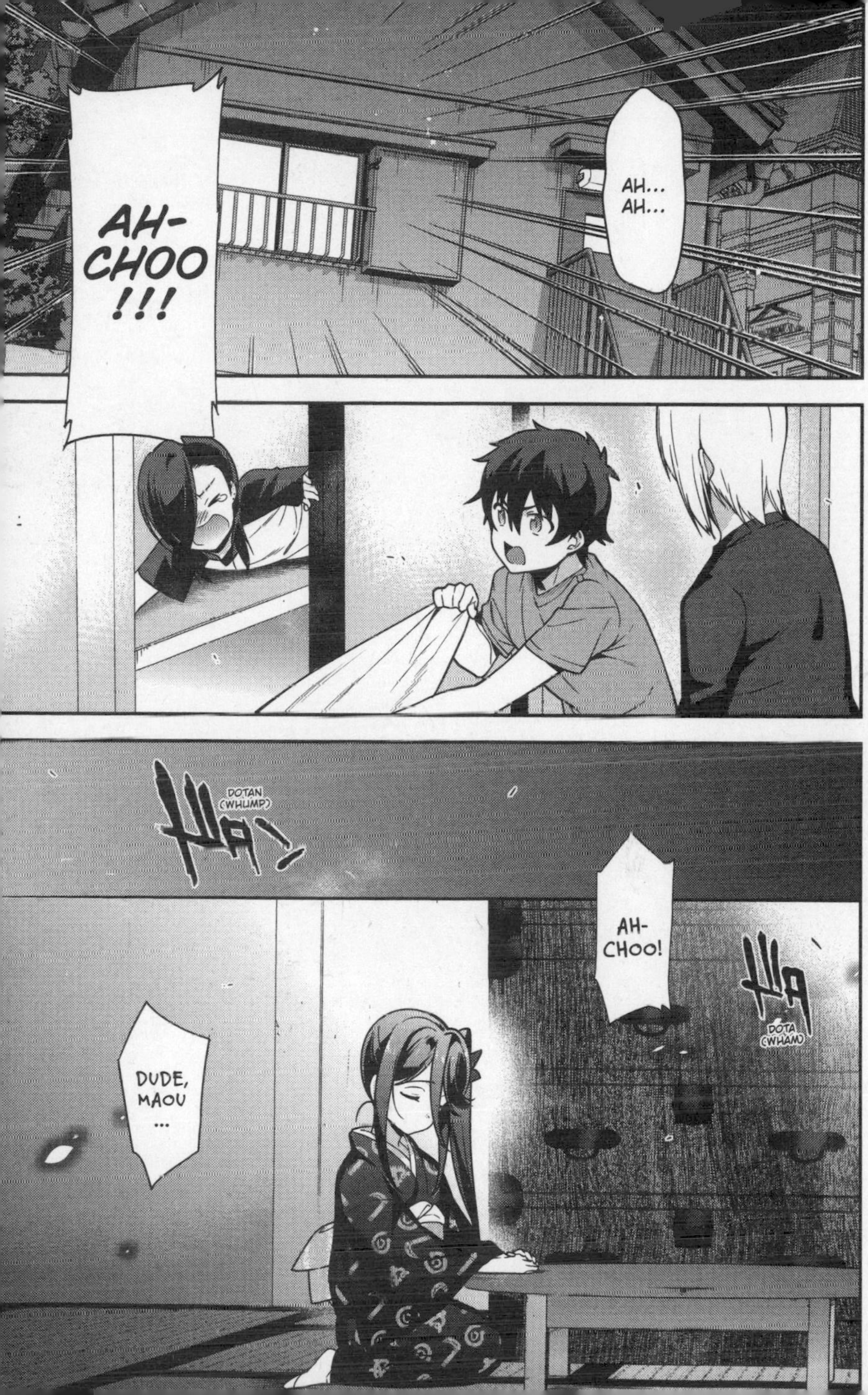
AH... AH...
AH-CHOO!!!
DOTAN (WHUMP)
AH-CHOO!
DOTA (WHAM)
DUDE, MAOU...

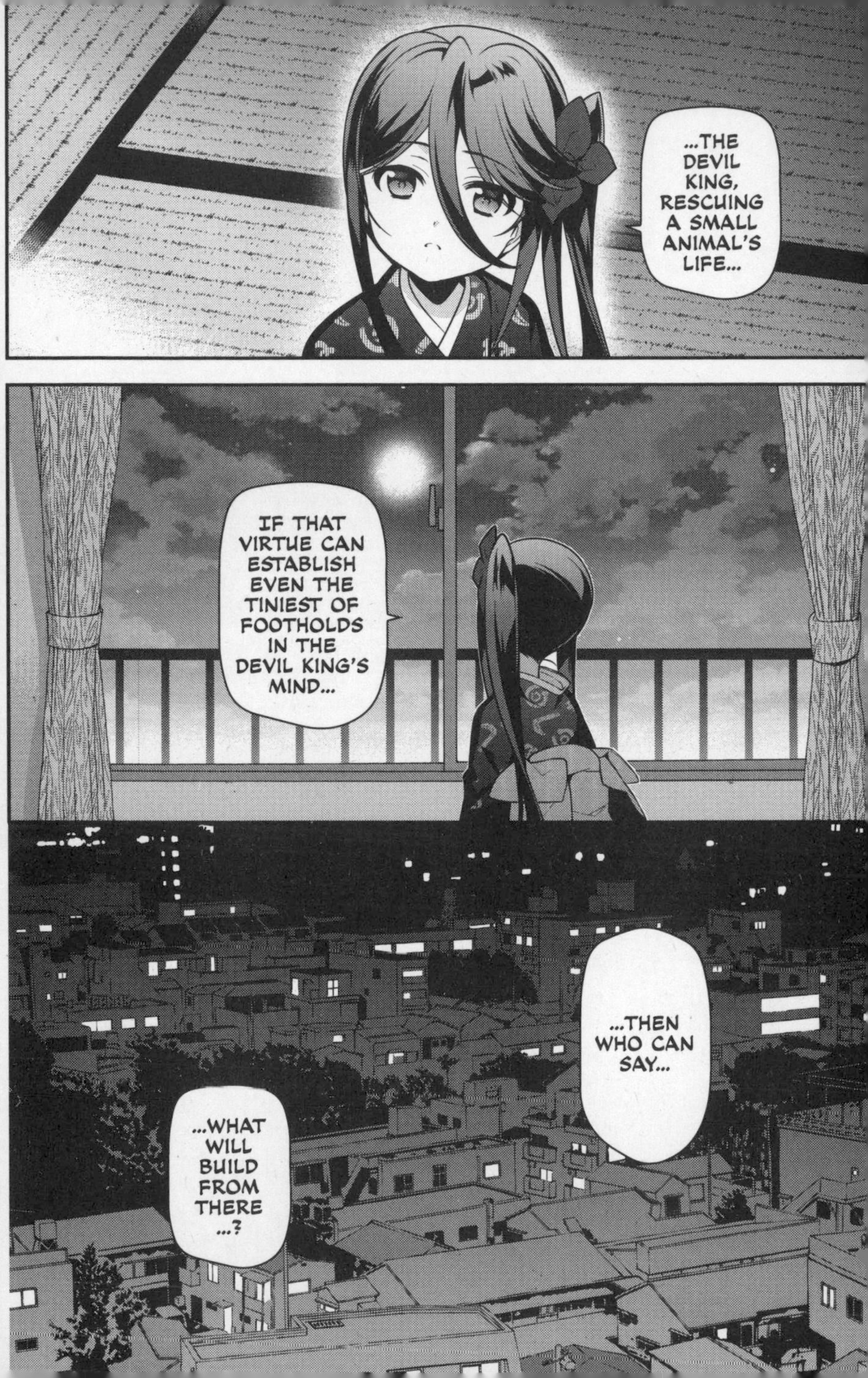
...THE DEVIL KING, RESCUING A SMALL ANIMAL'S LIFE...
IF THAT VIRTUE CAN ESTABLISH EVEN THE TINIEST OF FOOTHOLDS IN THE DEVIL KING'S MIND...
...THEN WHO CAN SAY...
...WHAT WILL BUILD FROM THERE ...?

Silverfish

THE DEVIL IS A PART-TIMER!

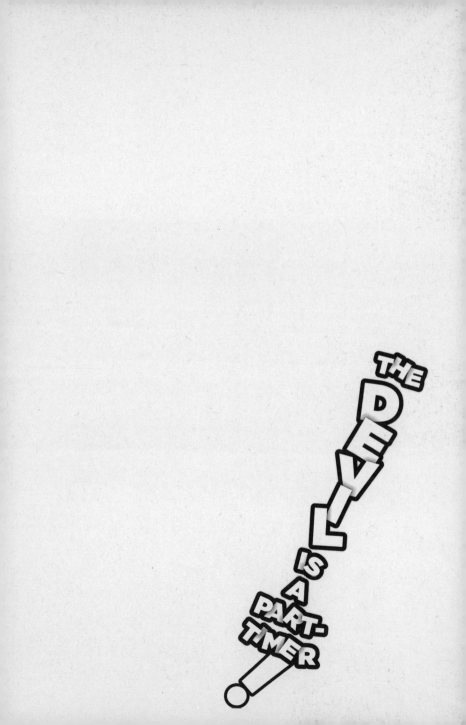

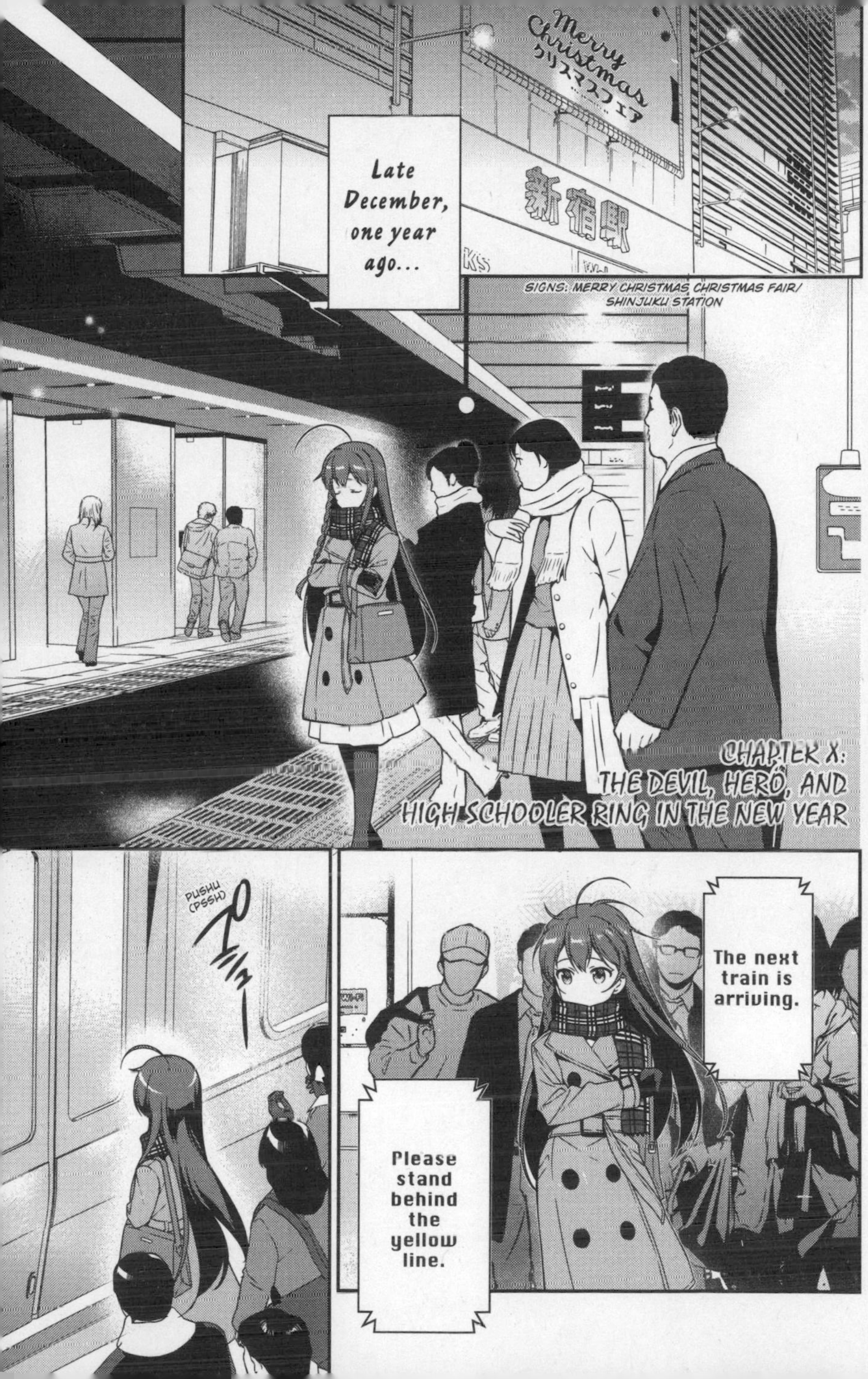
Merry Christmas
クリスマスフェア
新宿駅
Late December, one year ago...
SIGNS: MERRY CHRISTMAS CHRISTMAS FAIR/ SHINJUKU STATION
CHAPTER X: THE DEVIL, HERO, AND HIGH SCHOOLER RING IN THE NEW YEAR
The next train is arriving.
Please stand behind the yellow line.
PUSHU (PSSH)

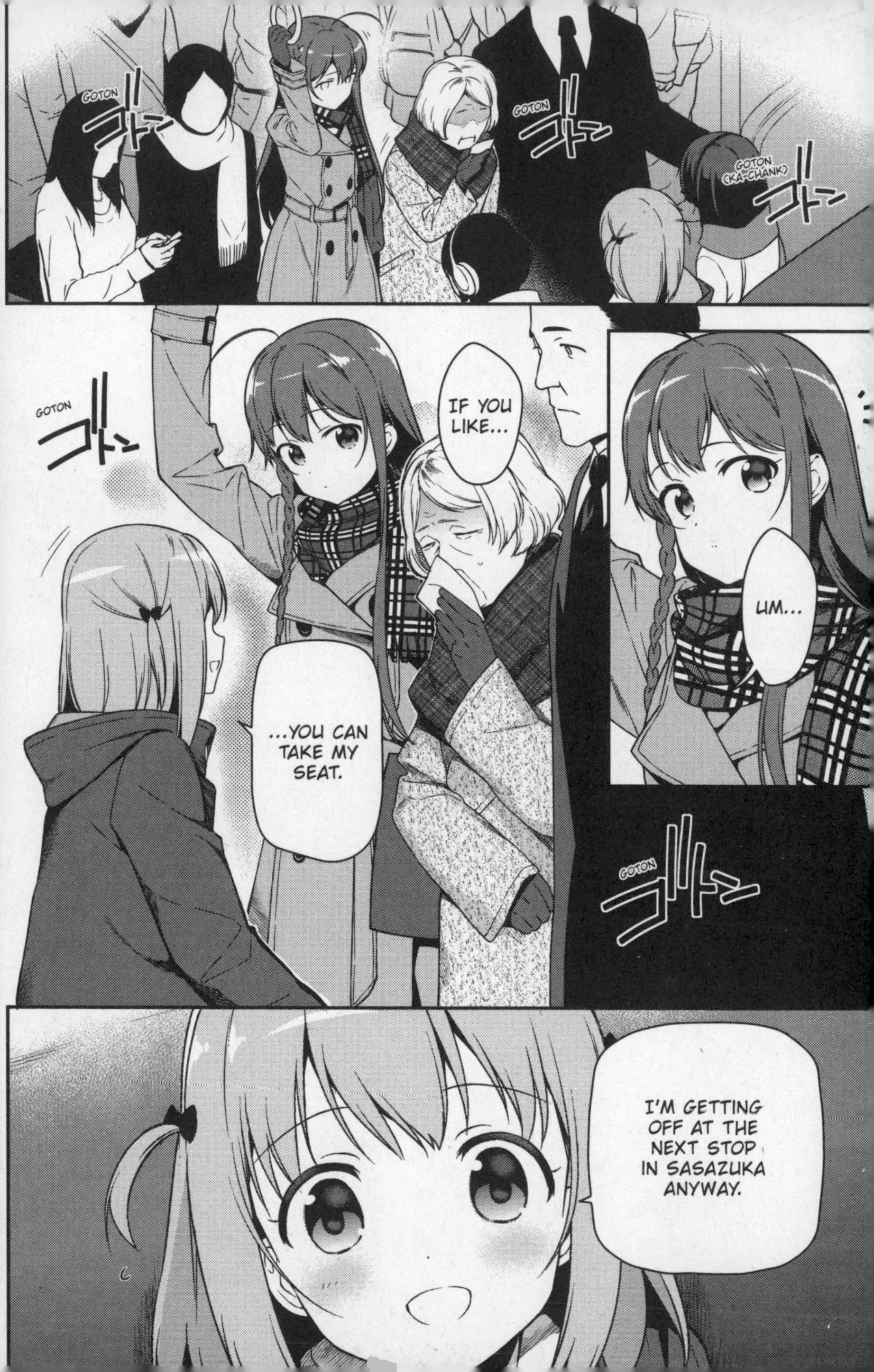
GOTON (KA-CHANK)
ゴトン
GOTON
ゴトン
GOTON
ゴトン
UM...
GOTON
ゴトン
GOTON
ゴトン
IF YOU LIKE...
...YOU CAN TAKE MY SEAT.
I'M GETTING OFF AT THE NEXT STOP IN SASAZUKA ANYWAY.

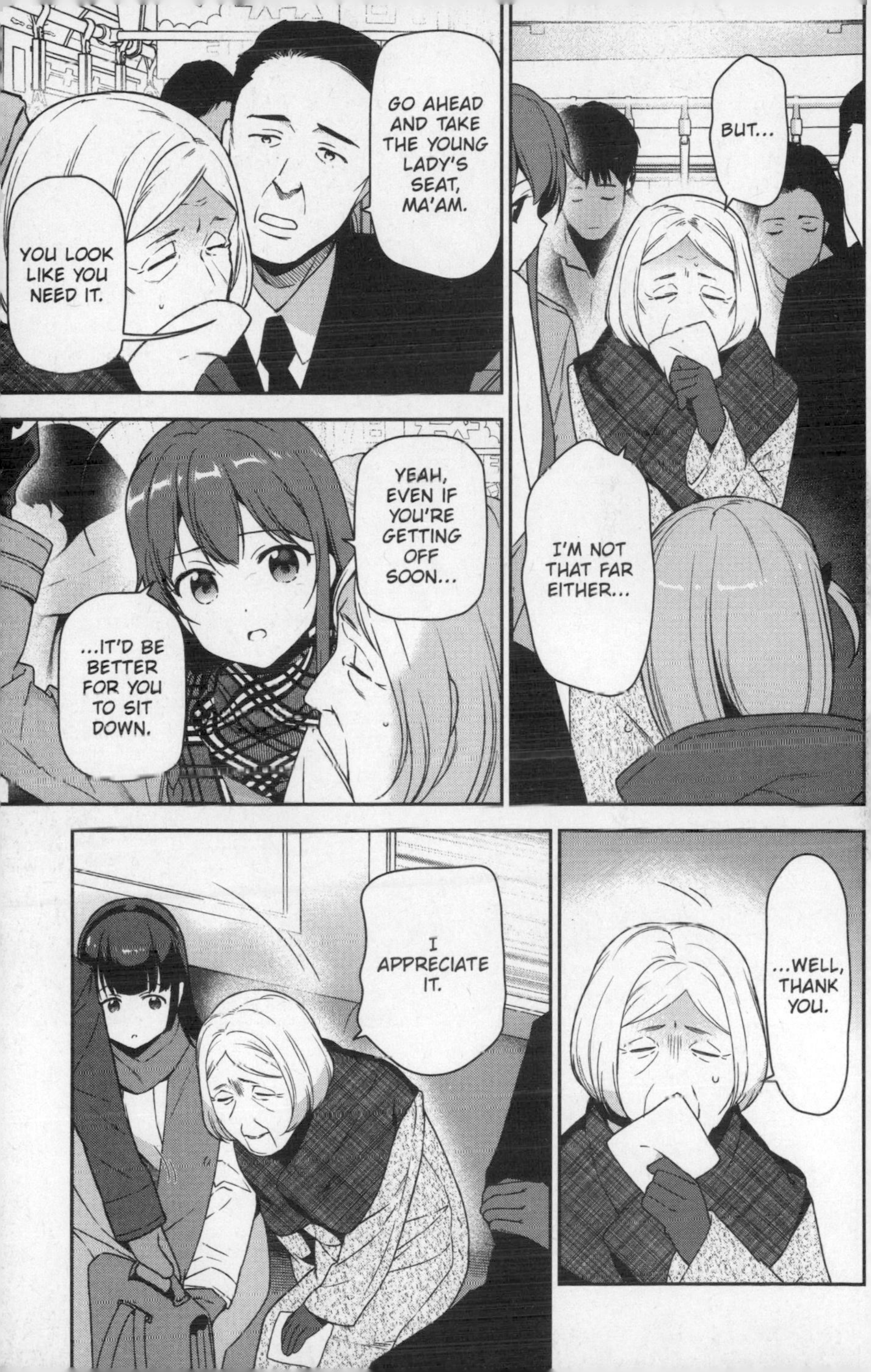
BUT...
I'M NOT THAT FAR EITHER...
GO AHEAD AND TAKE THE YOUNG LADY'S SEAT, MA'AM.
YOU LOOK LIKE YOU NEED IT.
YEAH, EVEN IF YOU'RE GETTING OFF SOON...
...IT'D BE BETTER FOR YOU TO SIT DOWN.
...WELL, THANK YOU.
I APPRECIATE IT.

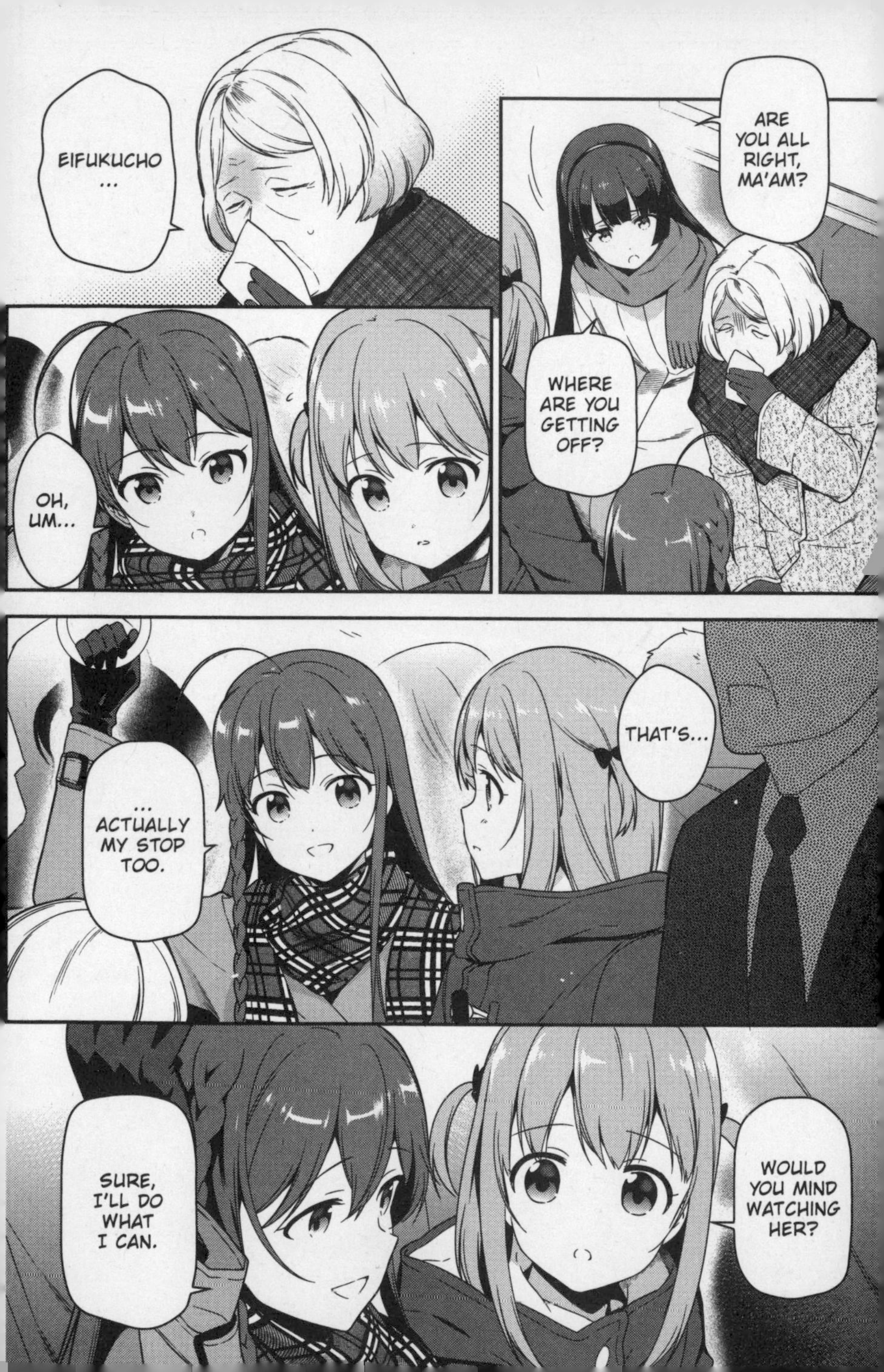
ARE YOU ALL RIGHT, MA'AM?
WHERE ARE YOU GETTING OFF?
EIFUKUCHO ...
OH, UM...
THAT'S...
... ACTUALLY MY STOP TOO.
WOULD YOU MIND WATCHING HER?
SURE, I'LL DO WHAT I CAN.

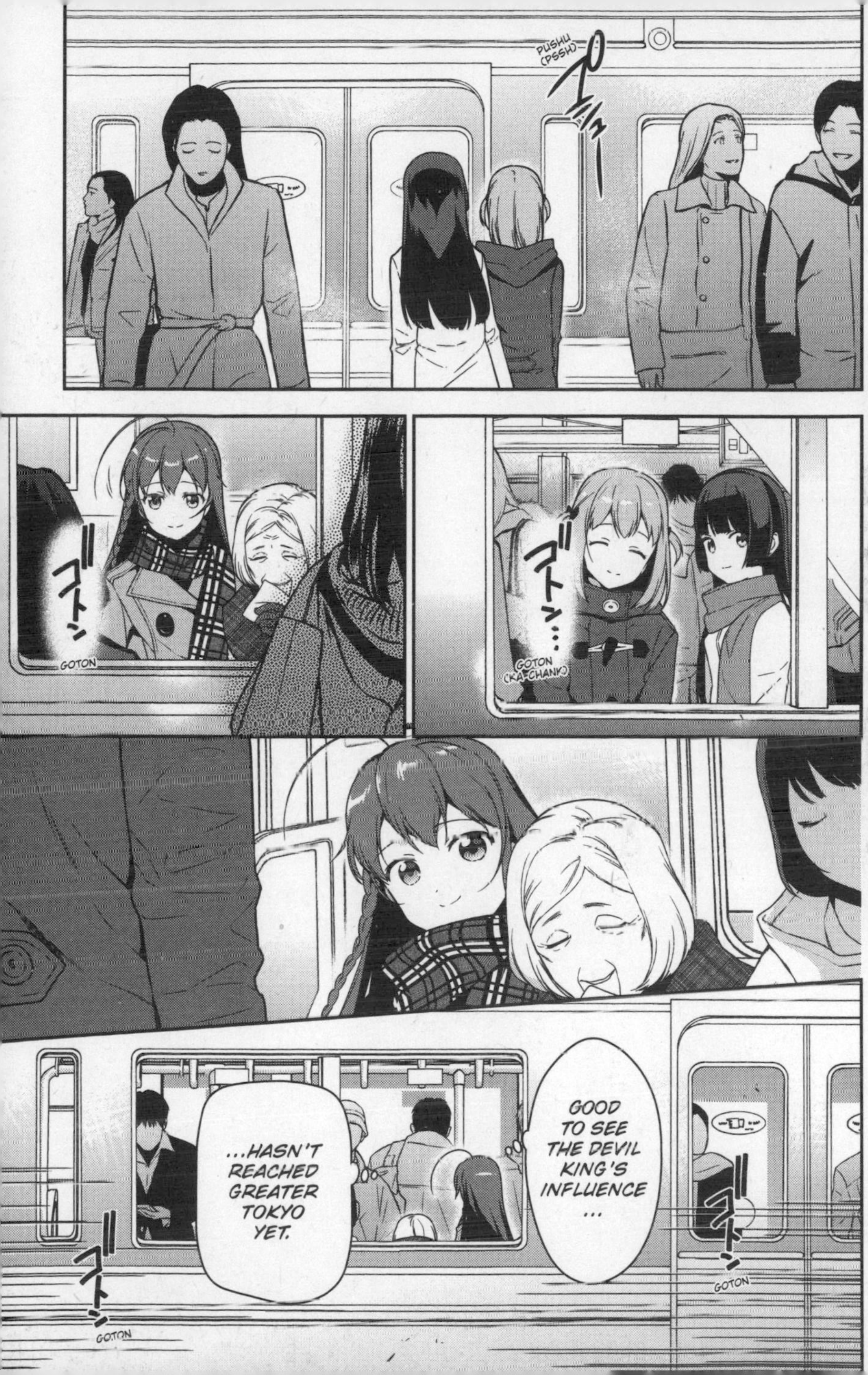

PUSHU (PSSH)
ゴトン…
GOTON (KA-CHANK)
ゴトン
GOTON
ゴトン
GOTON
GOOD TO SEE THE DEVIL KING'S INFLUENCE ...
...HASN'T REACHED GREATER TOKYO YET.
ゴトン
GOTON

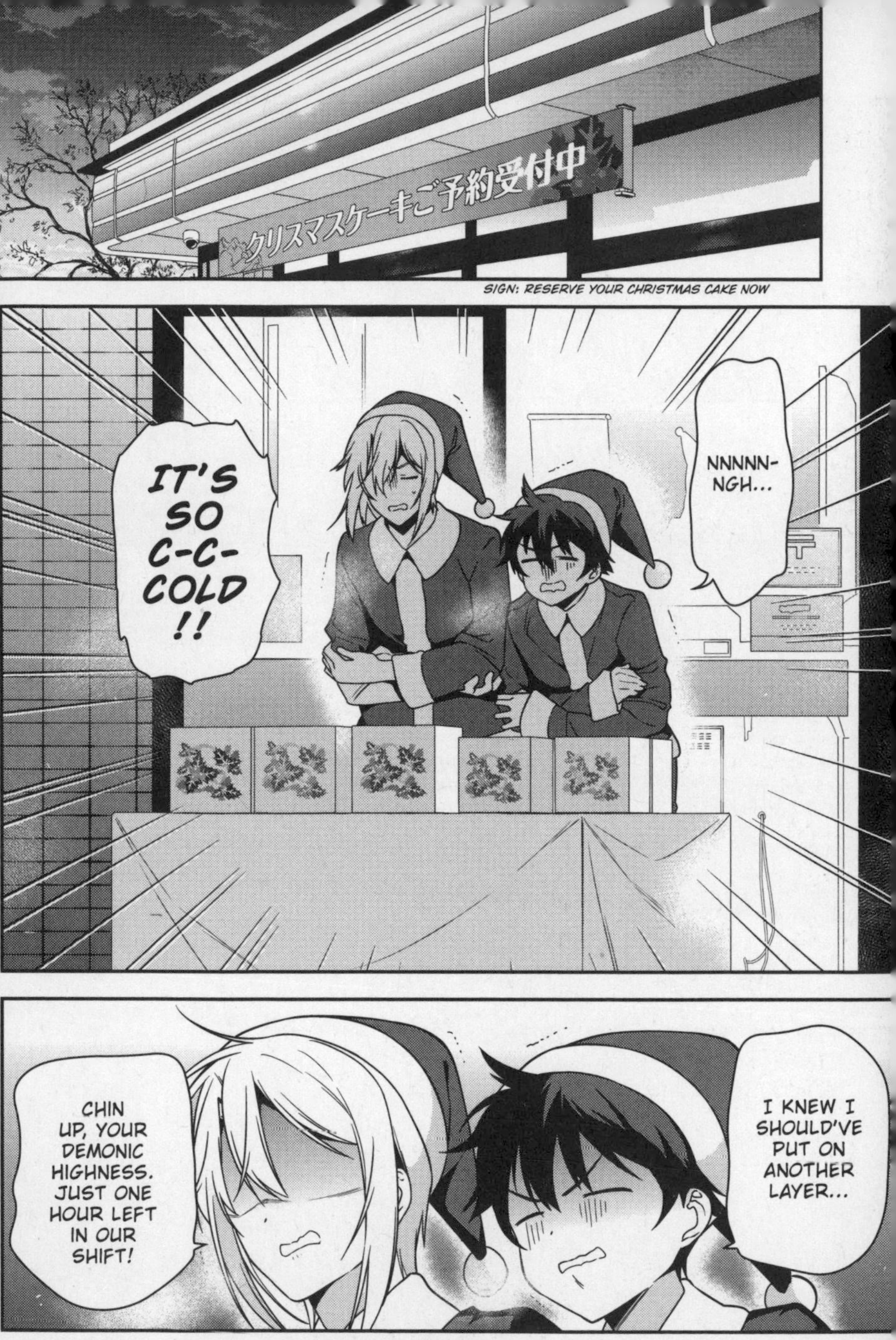
クリスマスケーキご予約受付中
SIGN: RESERVE YOUR CHRISTMAS CAKE NOW
NNNNN-NGH...
IT'S SO C-C-COLD!!
I KNEW I SHOULD'VE PUT ON ANOTHER LAYER...
CHIN UP, YOUR DEMONIC HIGHNESS. JUST ONE HOUR LEFT IN OUR SHIFT!

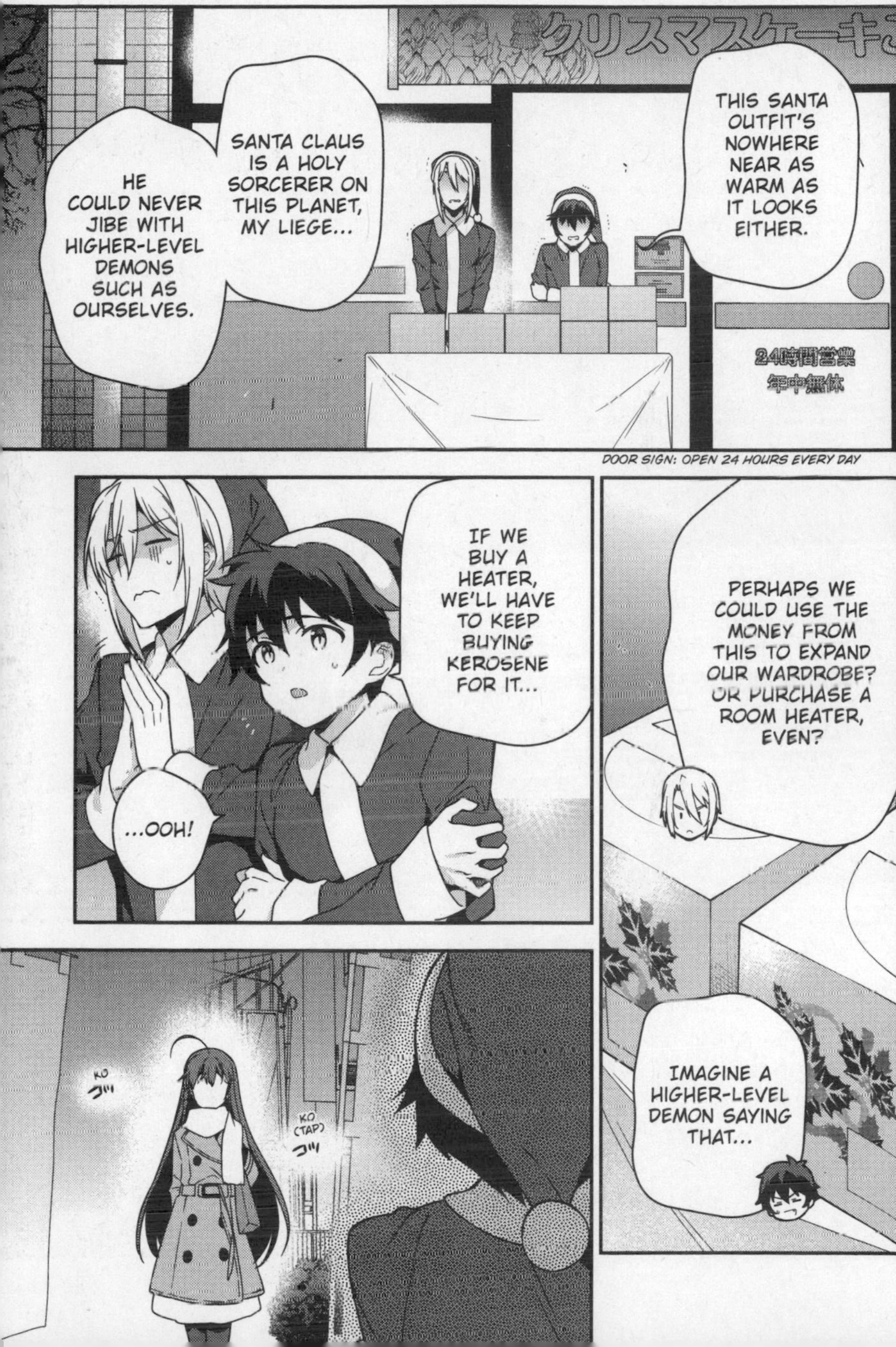
クリスマスケーキご
THIS SANTA OUTFIT'S NOWHERE NEAR AS WARM AS IT LOOKS EITHER.
SANTA CLAUS IS A HOLY SORCERER ON THIS PLANET, MY LIEGE...
HE COULD NEVER JIBE WITH HIGHER-LEVEL DEMONS SUCH AS OURSELVES.
24時間営業
年中無休
DOOR SIGN: OPEN 24 HOURS EVERY DAY
PERHAPS WE COULD USE THE MONEY FROM THIS TO EXPAND OUR WARDROBE? OR PURCHASE A ROOM HEATER, EVEN?
IMAGINE A HIGHER-LEVEL DEMON SAYING THAT...
IF WE BUY A HEATER, WE'LL HAVE TO KEEP BUYING KEROSENE FOR IT...
...OOH!
KO
ゴツ
KO (TAP)
ゴツ

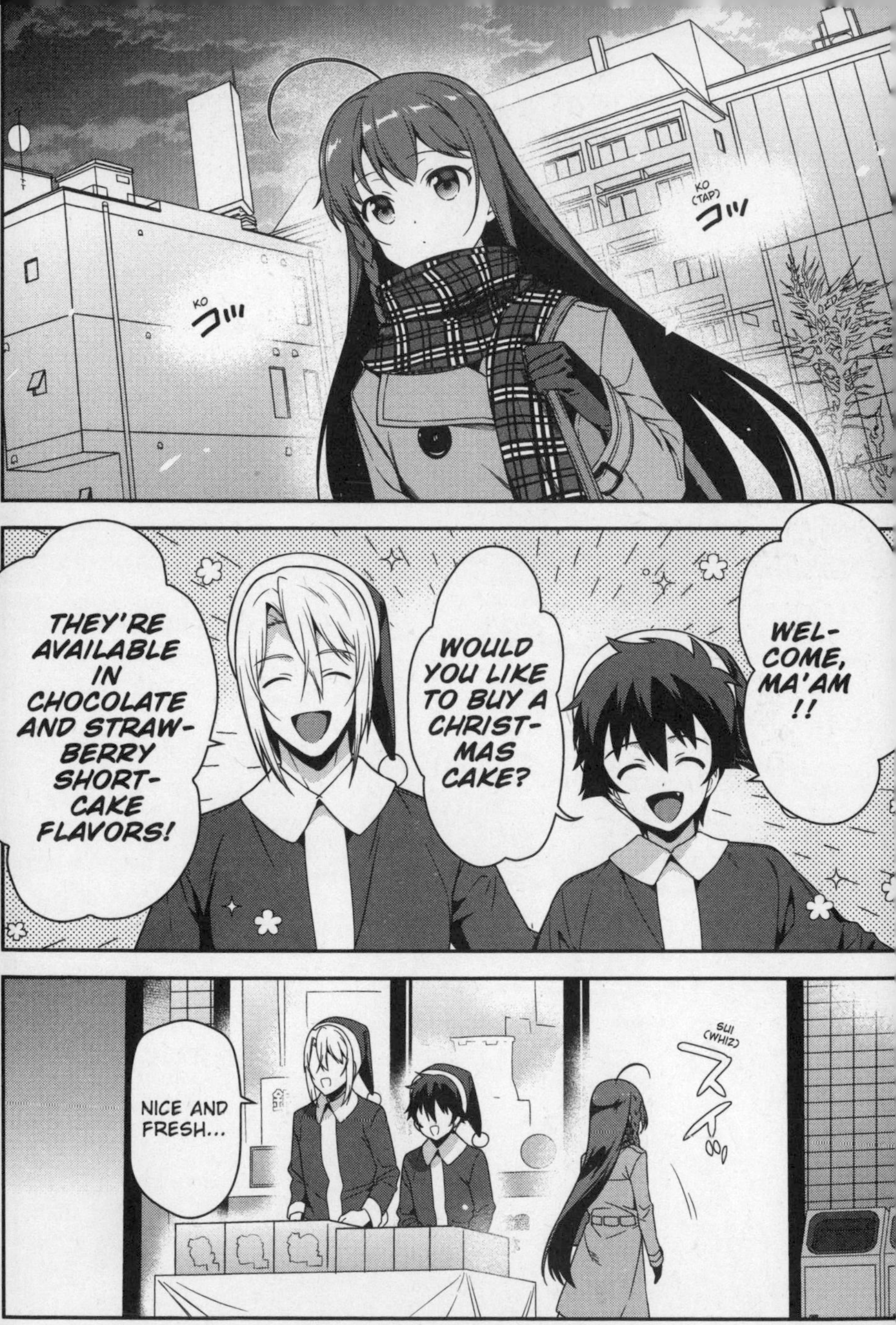
KO (TAP) コッ
KO コッ
WEL-COME, MA'AM!!
WOULD YOU LIKE TO BUY A CHRIST-MAS CAKE?
THEY'RE AVAILABLE IN CHOCOLATE AND STRAW-BERRY SHORT-CAKE FLAVORS!
SUI (WHIZ) ス
NICE AND FRESH...

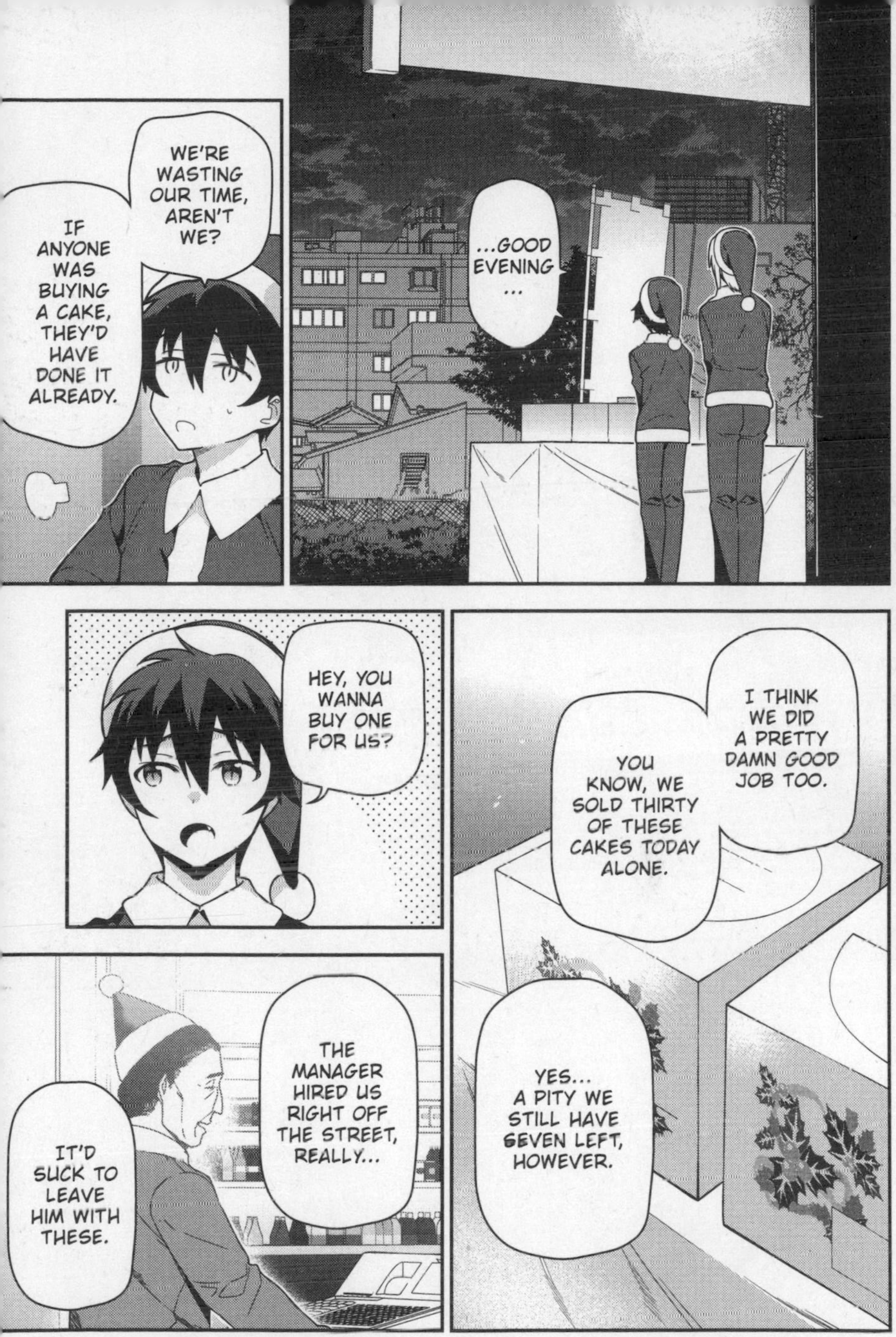
...GOOD EVENING ...
WE'RE WASTING OUR TIME, AREN'T WE?
IF ANYONE WAS BUYING A CAKE, THEY'D HAVE DONE IT ALREADY.
I THINK WE DID A PRETTY DAMN GOOD JOB TOO.
YOU KNOW, WE SOLD THIRTY OF THESE CAKES TODAY ALONE.
YES... A PITY WE STILL HAVE SEVEN LEFT, HOWEVER.
HEY, YOU WANNA BUY ONE FOR US?
THE MANAGER HIRED US RIGHT OFF THE STREET, REALLY...
IT'D SUCK TO LEAVE HIM WITH THESE.

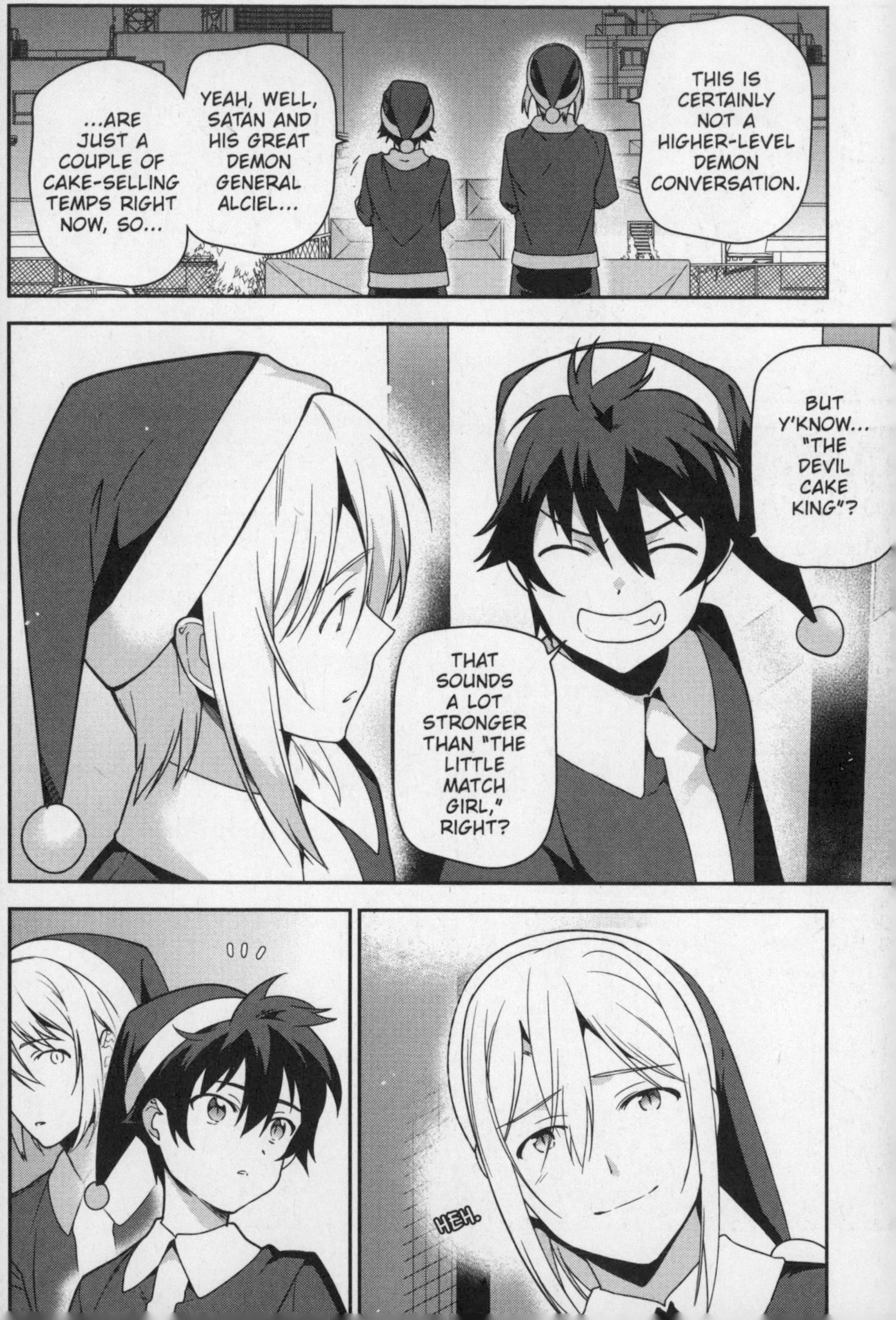
THIS IS CERTAINLY NOT A HIGHER-LEVEL DEMON CONVERSATION.
YEAH, WELL, SATAN AND HIS GREAT DEMON GENERAL ALCIEL...
...ARE JUST A COUPLE OF CAKE-SELLING TEMPS RIGHT NOW, SO...
BUT Y'KNOW... "THE DEVIL CAKE KING"?
THAT SOUNDS A LOT STRONGER THAN "THE LITTLE MATCH GIRL," RIGHT?
HEH.

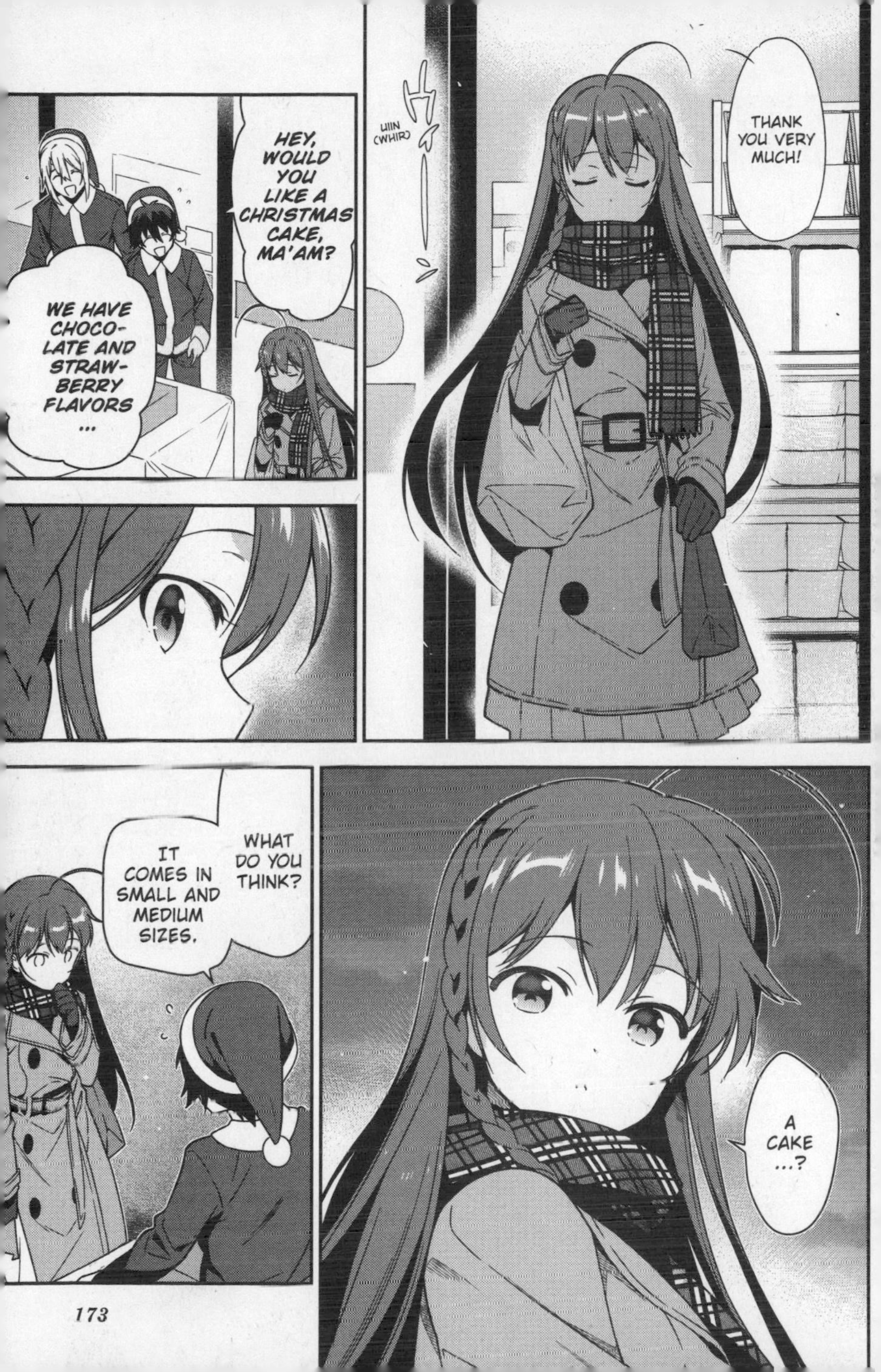
THANK YOU VERY MUCH!
UIIN (WHIR)
HEY, WOULD YOU LIKE A CHRISTMAS CAKE, MA'AM?
WE HAVE CHOCOLATE AND STRAWBERRY FLAVORS ...
A CAKE ...?
WHAT DO YOU THINK?
IT COMES IN SMALL AND MEDIUM SIZES.

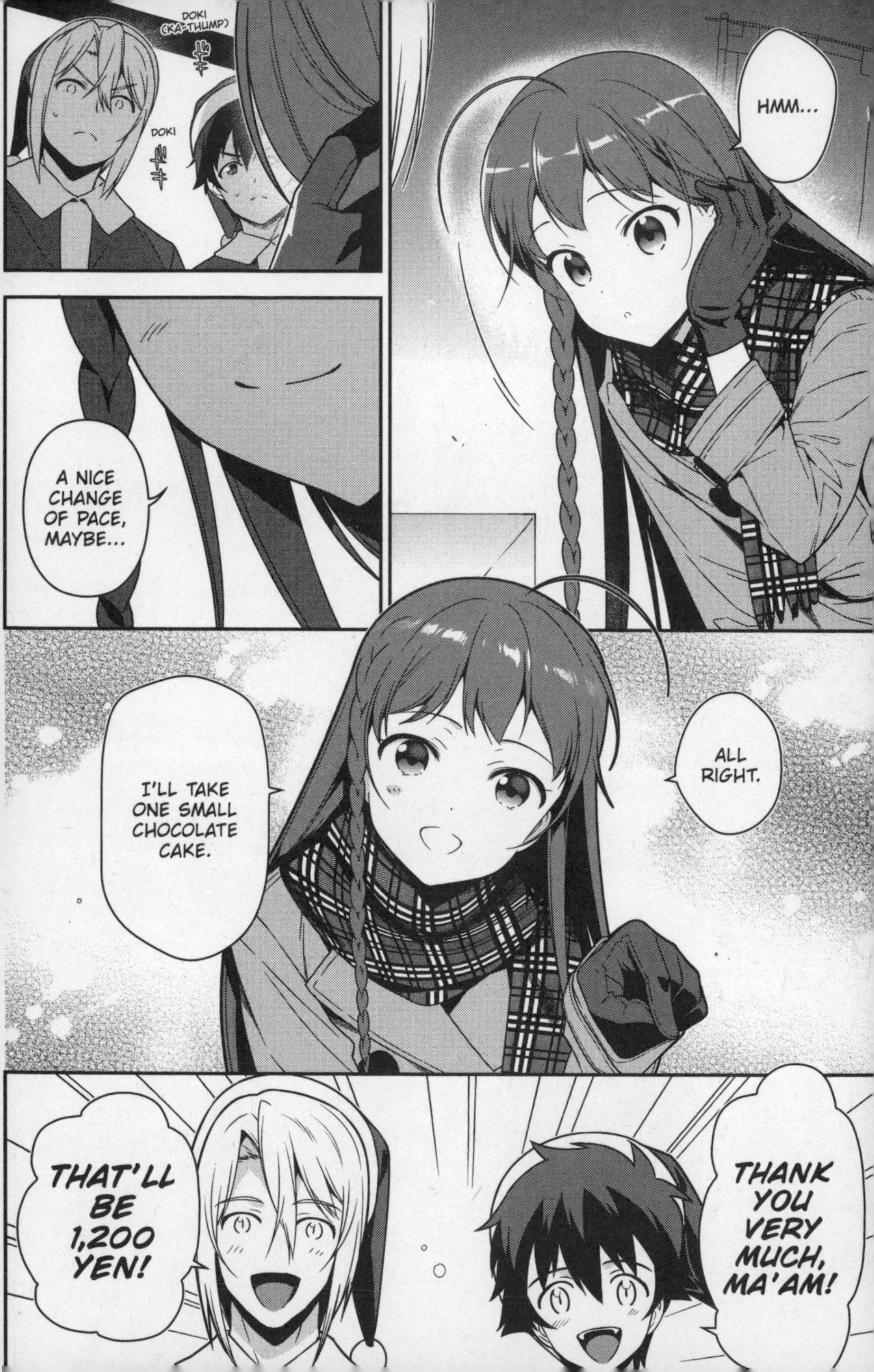
HMM...
DOKI (KA-THUMP)
DOKI
A NICE CHANGE OF PACE, MAYBE...
ALL RIGHT.
I'LL TAKE ONE SMALL CHOCOLATE CAKE.
THANK YOU VERY MUCH, MA'AM!
THAT'LL BE 1,200 YEN!

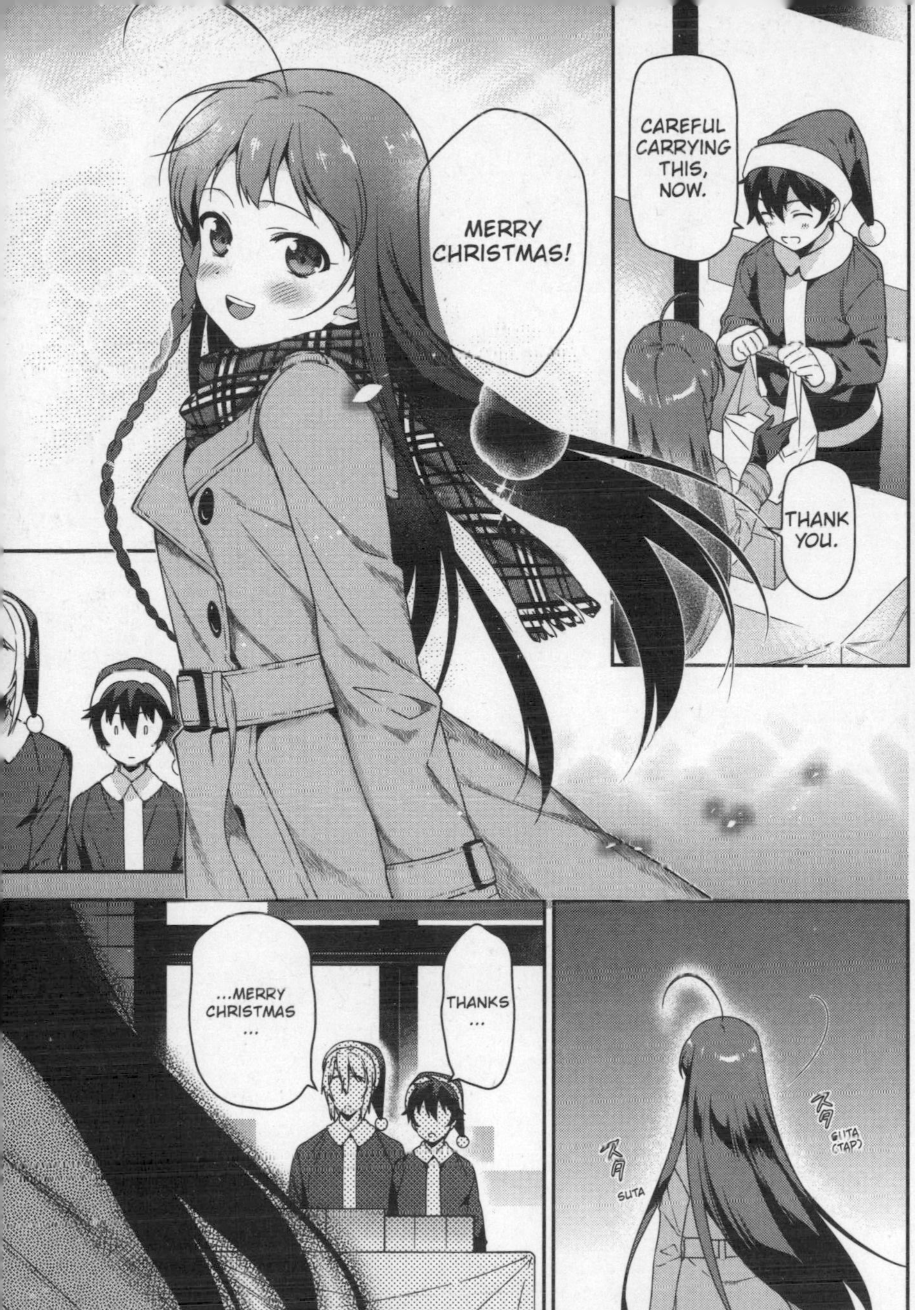
CAREFUL CARRYING THIS, NOW.
THANK YOU.
MERRY CHRISTMAS!
スタ
SUTA (TAP)
スタ
SUTA
THANKS ...
...MERRY CHRISTMAS ...

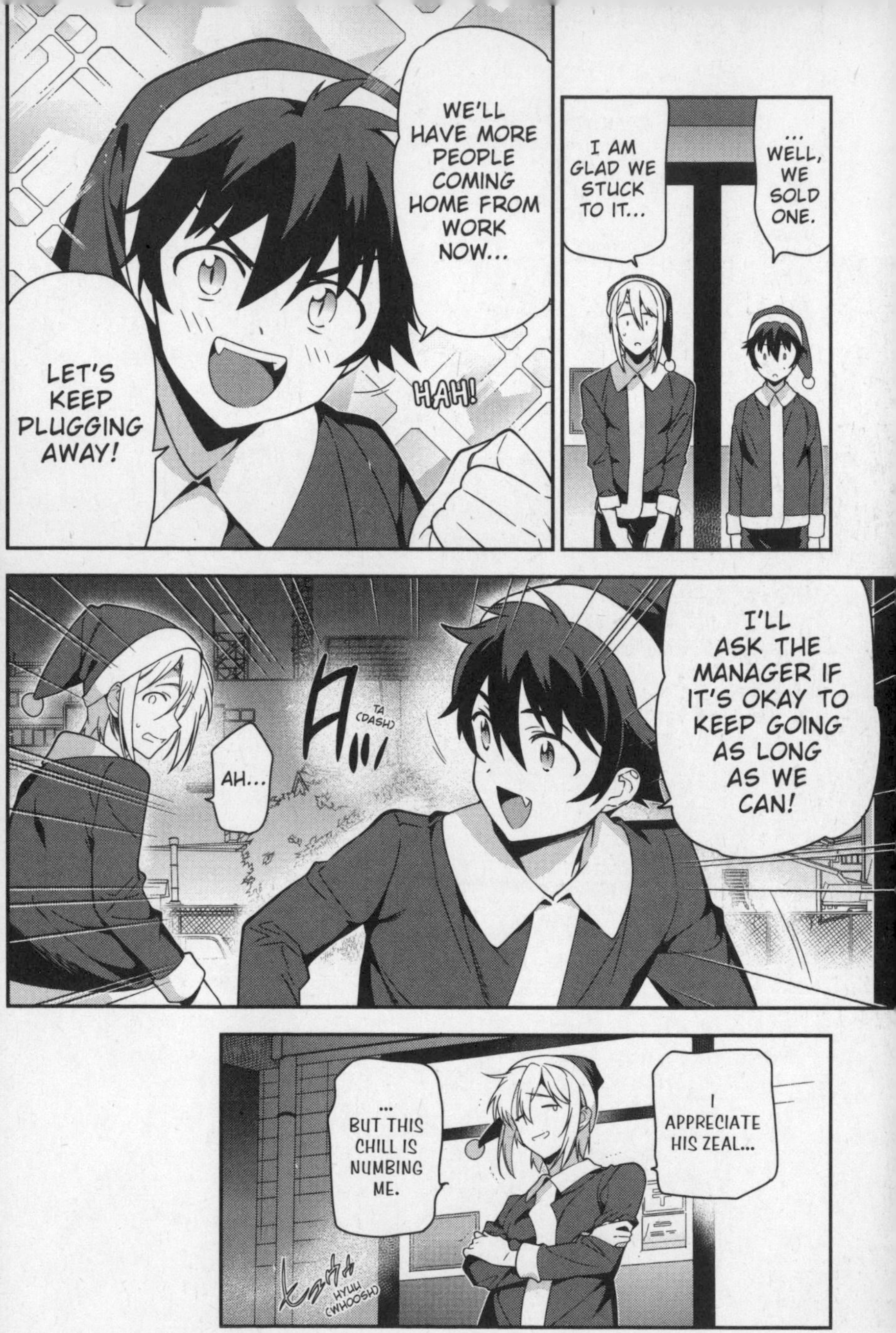
...WELL, WE SOLD ONE.
I AM GLAD WE STUCK TO IT...
WE'LL HAVE MORE PEOPLE COMING HOME FROM WORK NOW...
HAH!
LET'S KEEP PLUGGING AWAY!
I'LL ASK THE MANAGER IF IT'S OKAY TO KEEP GOING AS LONG AS WE CAN!
TA (DASH)
AH...
I APPRECIATE HIS ZEAL...
... BUT THIS CHILL IS NUMBING ME.
HYUU (WHOOSH)

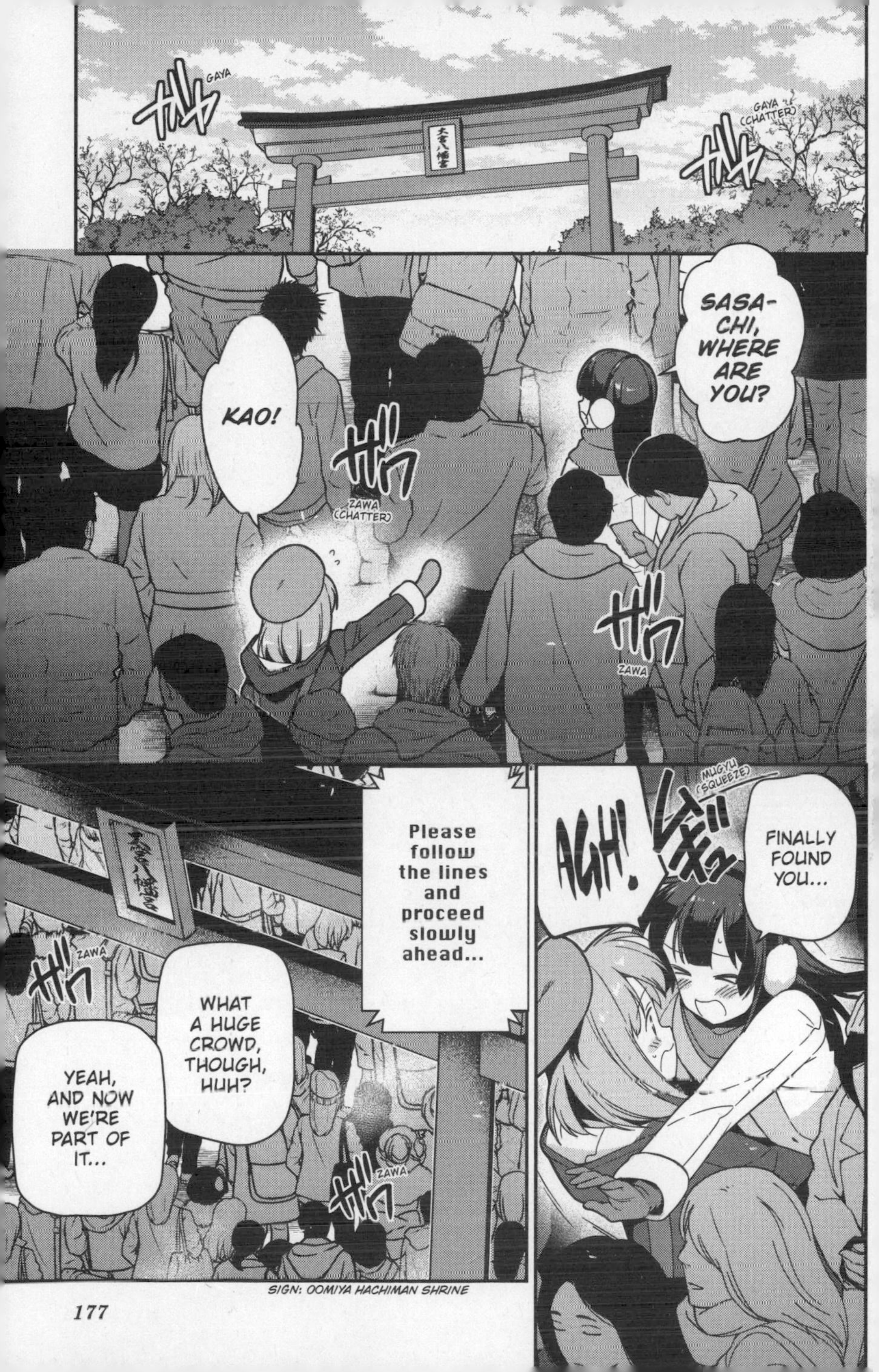
GAYA (CHATTER)
GAYA
SASA-CHI, WHERE ARE YOU?
ZAWA
ZAWA (CHATTER)
KAO!
FINALLY FOUND YOU...
MUGYU (SQUEEZE)
AGH!
Please follow the lines and proceed slowly ahead...
WHAT A HUGE CROWD, THOUGH, HUH?
YEAH, AND NOW WE'RE PART OF IT...
ZAWA
ZAWA
SIGN: OOMIYA HACHIMAN SHRINE

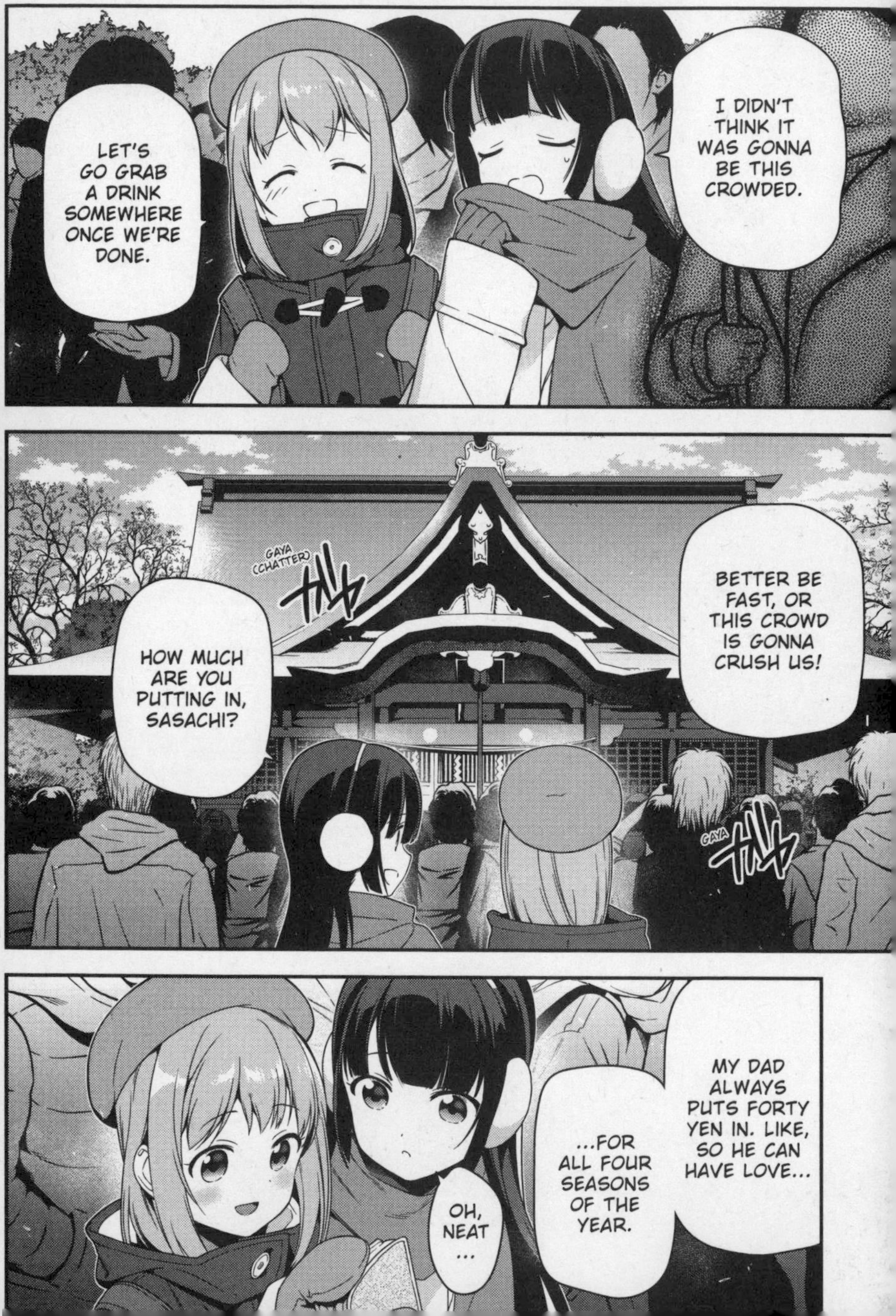
I DIDN'T THINK IT WAS GONNA BE THIS CROWDED.
LET'S GO GRAB A DRINK SOMEWHERE ONCE WE'RE DONE.
BETTER BE FAST, OR THIS CROWD IS GONNA CRUSH US!
GAYA (CHATTER)
HOW MUCH ARE YOU PUTTING IN, SASACHI?
GAYA
MY DAD ALWAYS PUTS FORTY YEN IN. LIKE, SO HE CAN HAVE LOVE...
...FOR ALL FOUR SEASONS OF THE YEAR.
OH, NEAT ...

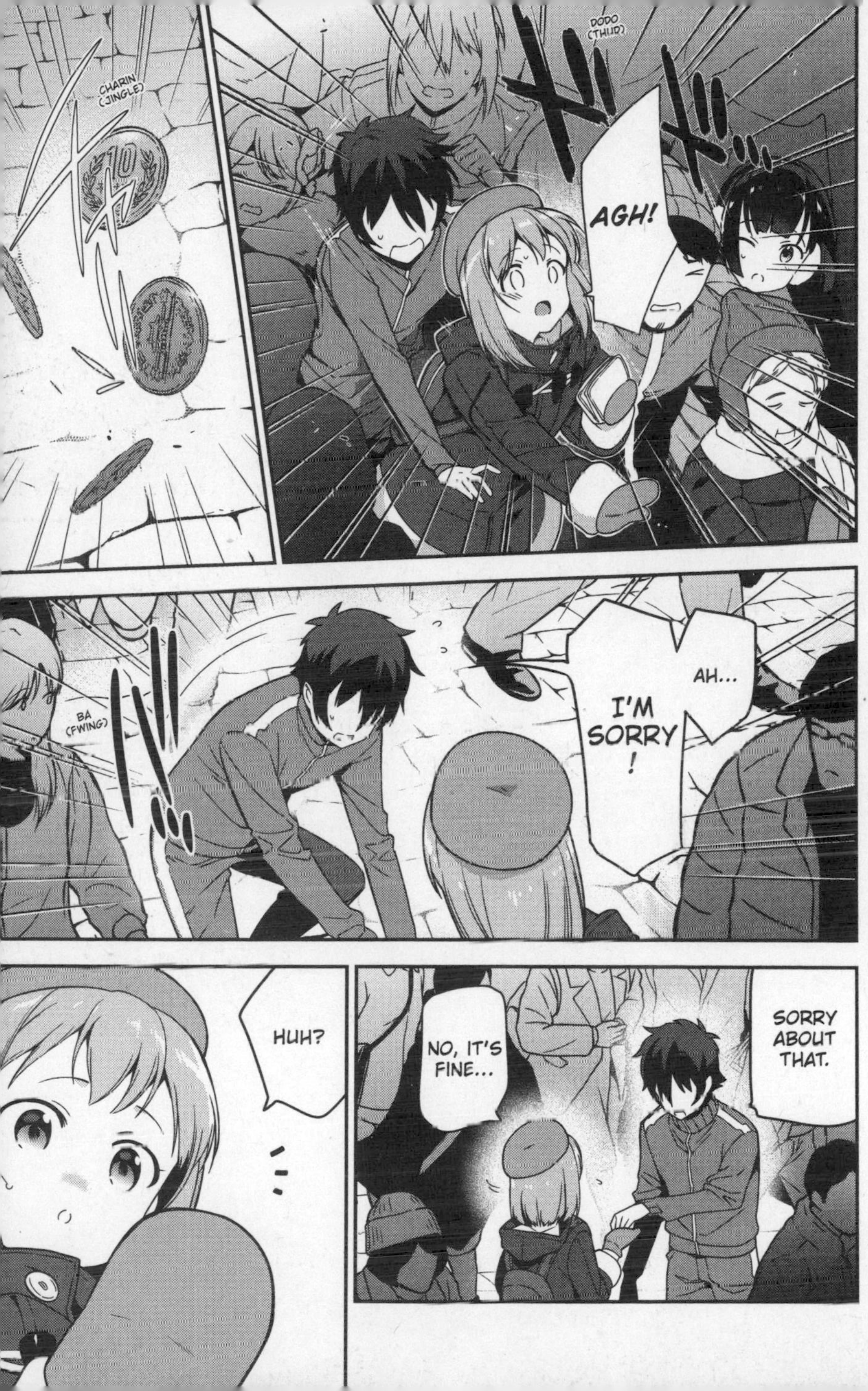
DODO (THUD)
AGH!
CHARIN (JINGLE)
AH... I'M SORRY!
BA (FWING)
SORRY ABOUT THAT.
NO, IT'S FINE...
HUH?

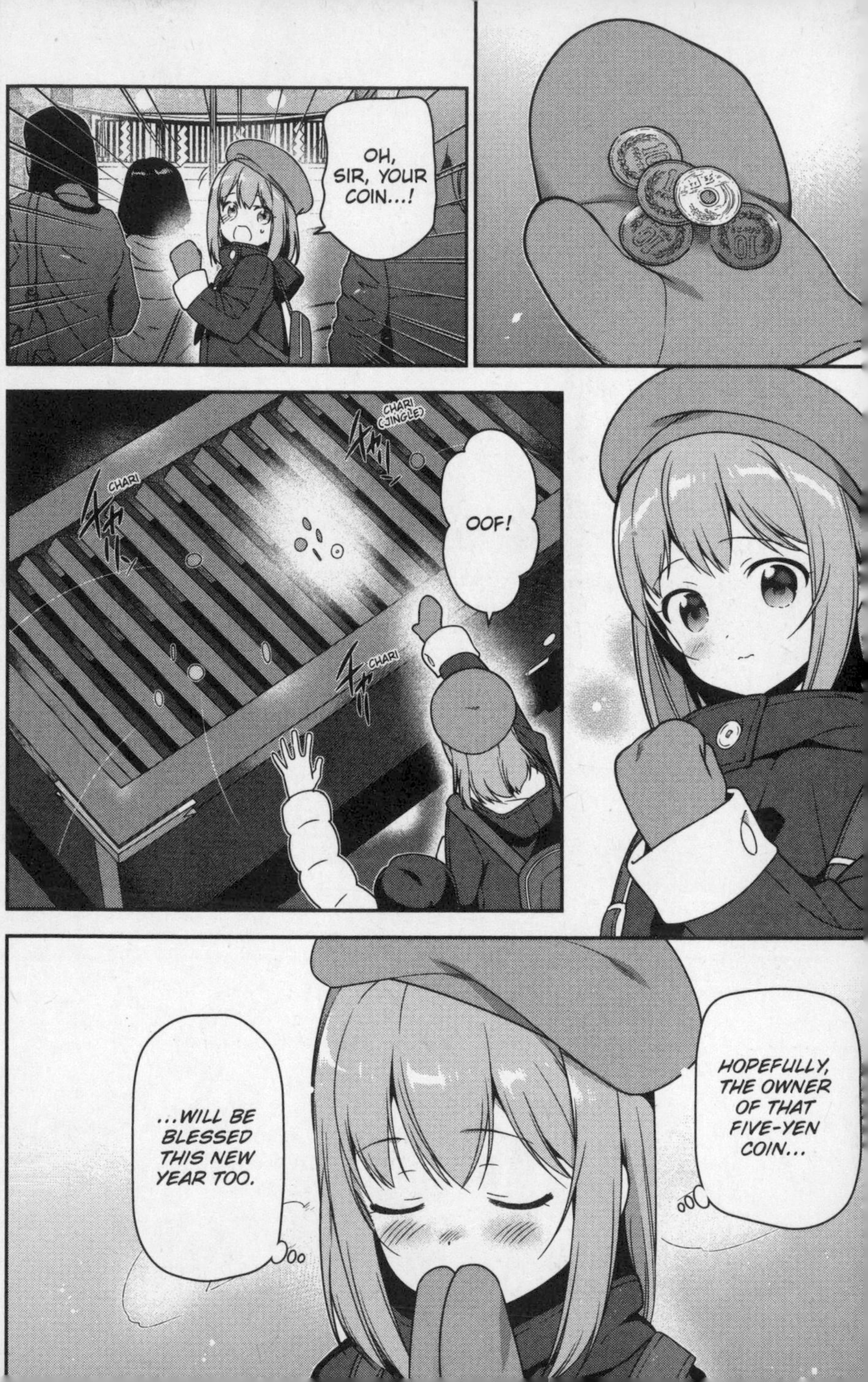
OH, SIR, YOUR COIN...!
CHARI (JINGLE)
OOF!
CHARI
CHARI
HOPEFULLY, THE OWNER OF THAT FIVE-YEN COIN...
...WILL BE BLESSED THIS NEW YEAR TOO.

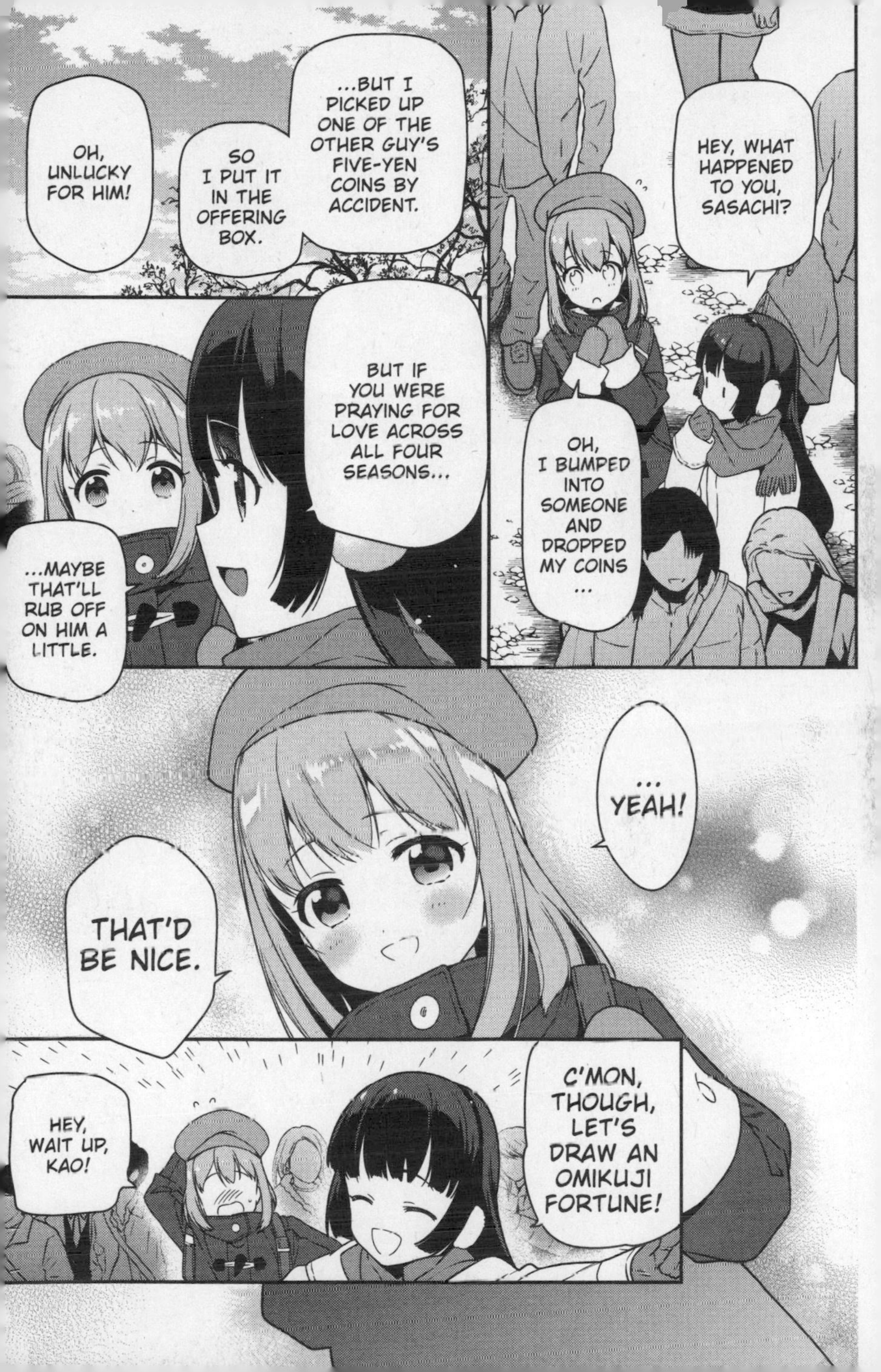
HEY, WHAT HAPPENED TO YOU, SASACHI?
OH, I BUMPED INTO SOMEONE AND DROPPED MY COINS...
...BUT I PICKED UP ONE OF THE OTHER GUY'S FIVE-YEN COINS BY ACCIDENT.
SO I PUT IT IN THE OFFERING BOX.
OH, UNLUCKY FOR HIM!
BUT IF YOU WERE PRAYING FOR LOVE ACROSS ALL FOUR SEASONS...
...MAYBE THAT'LL RUB OFF ON HIM A LITTLE.
...YEAH!
THAT'D BE NICE.
C'MON, THOUGH, LET'S DRAW AN OMIKUJI FORTUNE!
HEY, WAIT UP, KAO!

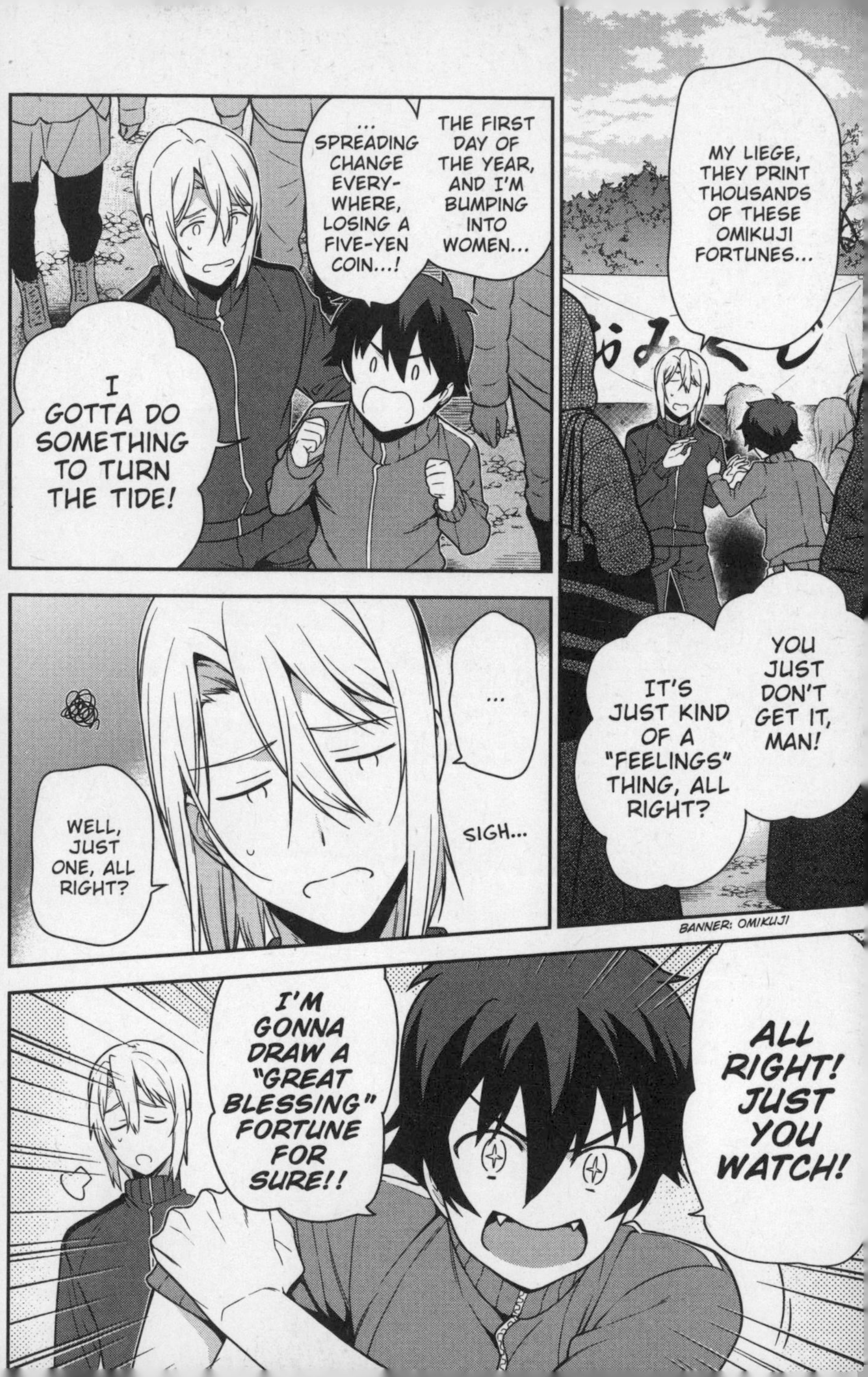
MY LIEGE, THEY PRINT THOUSANDS OF THESE OMIKUJI FORTUNES...
YOU JUST DON'T GET IT, MAN!
IT'S JUST KIND OF A "FEELINGS" THING, ALL RIGHT?
BANNER: OMIKUJI
THE FIRST DAY OF THE YEAR, AND I'M BUMPING INTO WOMEN...
... SPREADING CHANGE EVERY-WHERE, LOSING A FIVE-YEN COIN...!
I GOTTA DO SOMETHING TO TURN THE TIDE!
...
SIGH...
WELL, JUST ONE, ALL RIGHT?
ALL RIGHT! JUST YOU WATCH!
I'M GONNA DRAW A "GREAT BLESSING" FORTUNE FOR SURE!!

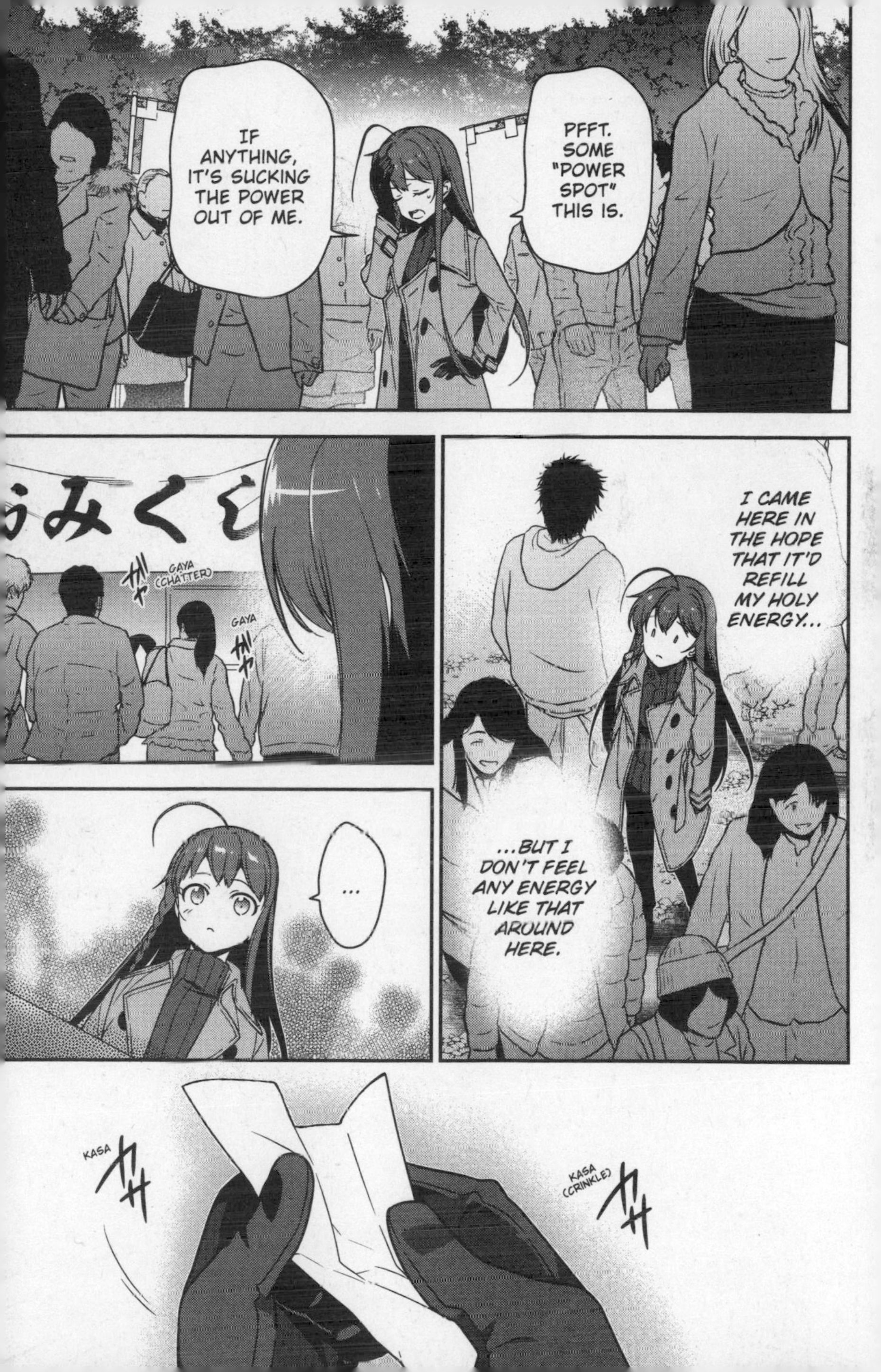
PFFT. SOME "POWER SPOT" THIS IS.
IF ANYTHING, IT'S SUCKING THE POWER OUT OF ME.
I CAME HERE IN THE HOPE THAT IT'D REFILL MY HOLY ENERGY...
...BUT I DON'T FEEL ANY ENERGY LIKE THAT AROUND HERE.
GAYA (CHATTER)
GAYA
...
KASA (CRINKLE)
KASA

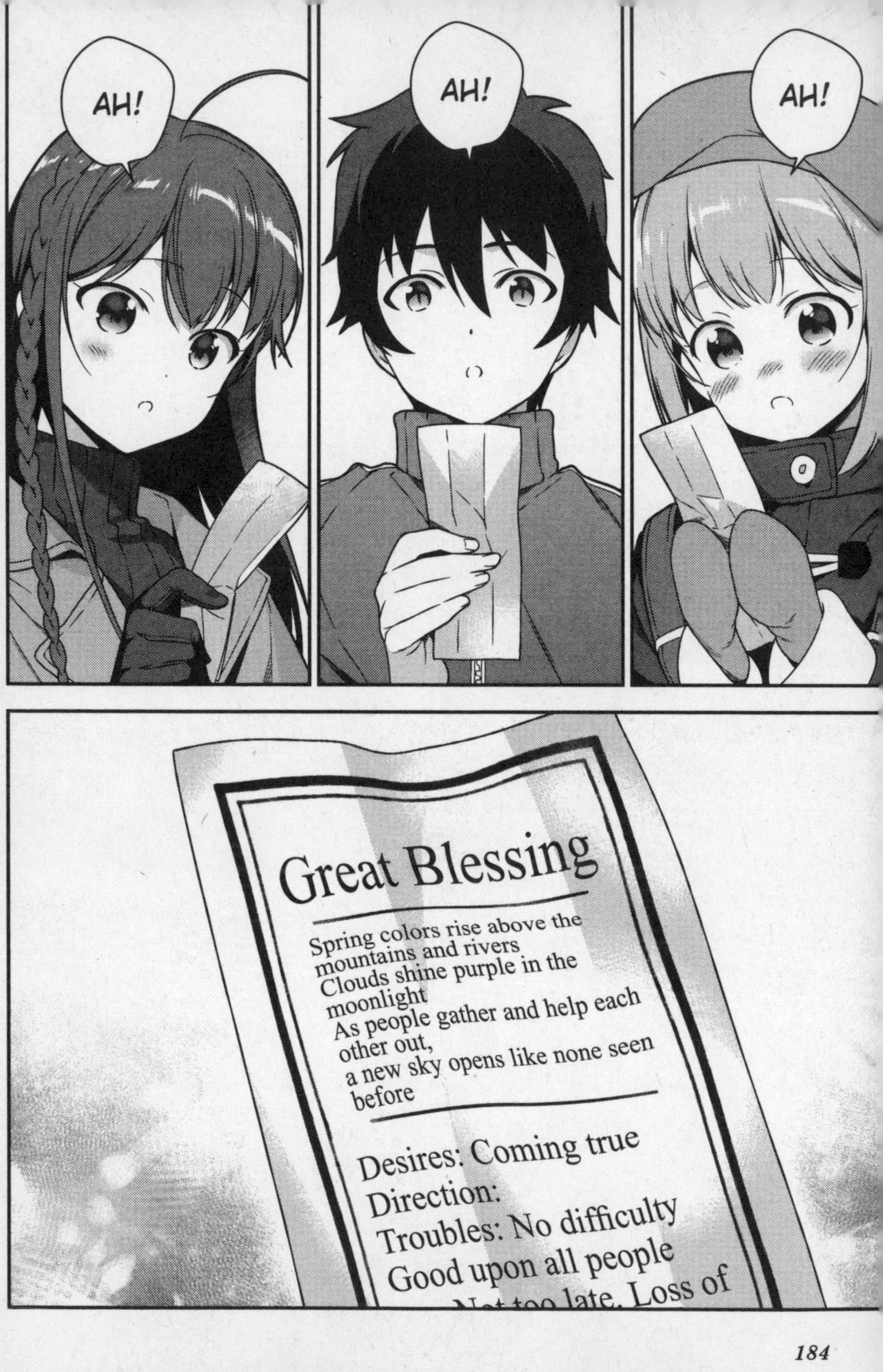
AH!
AH!
AH!
Great Blessing
Spring colors rise above the mountains and rivers
Clouds shine purple in the moonlight
As people gather and help each other out,
a new sky opens like none seen before
Desires: Coming true
Direction:
Troubles: No difficulty
Good upon all people
late. Loss of

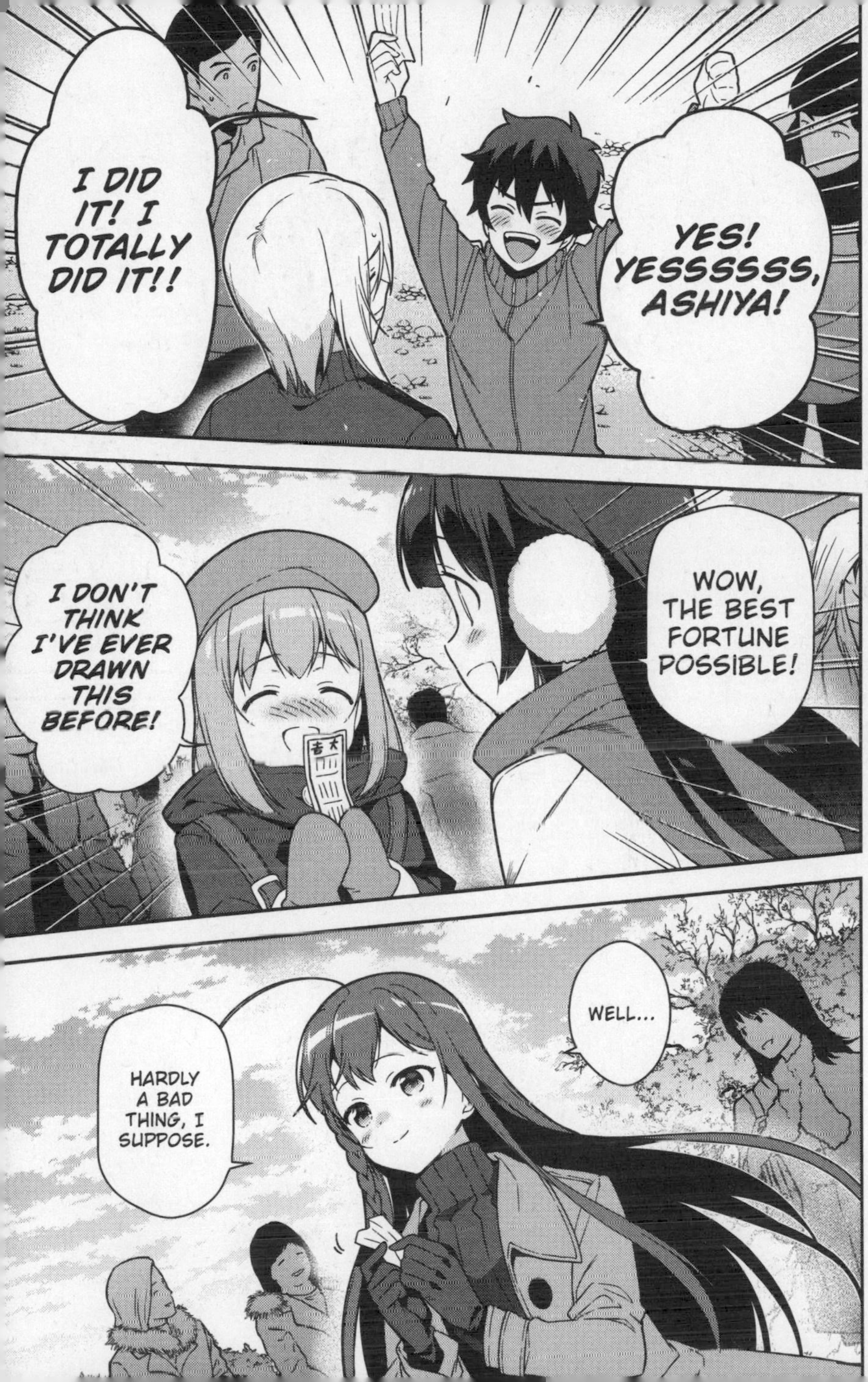
YES! YESSSSSS, ASHIYA!
I DID IT! I TOTALLY DID IT!!
WOW, THE BEST FORTUNE POSSIBLE!
I DON'T THINK I'VE EVER DRAWN THIS BEFORE!
WELL...
HARDLY A BAD THING, I SUPPOSE.

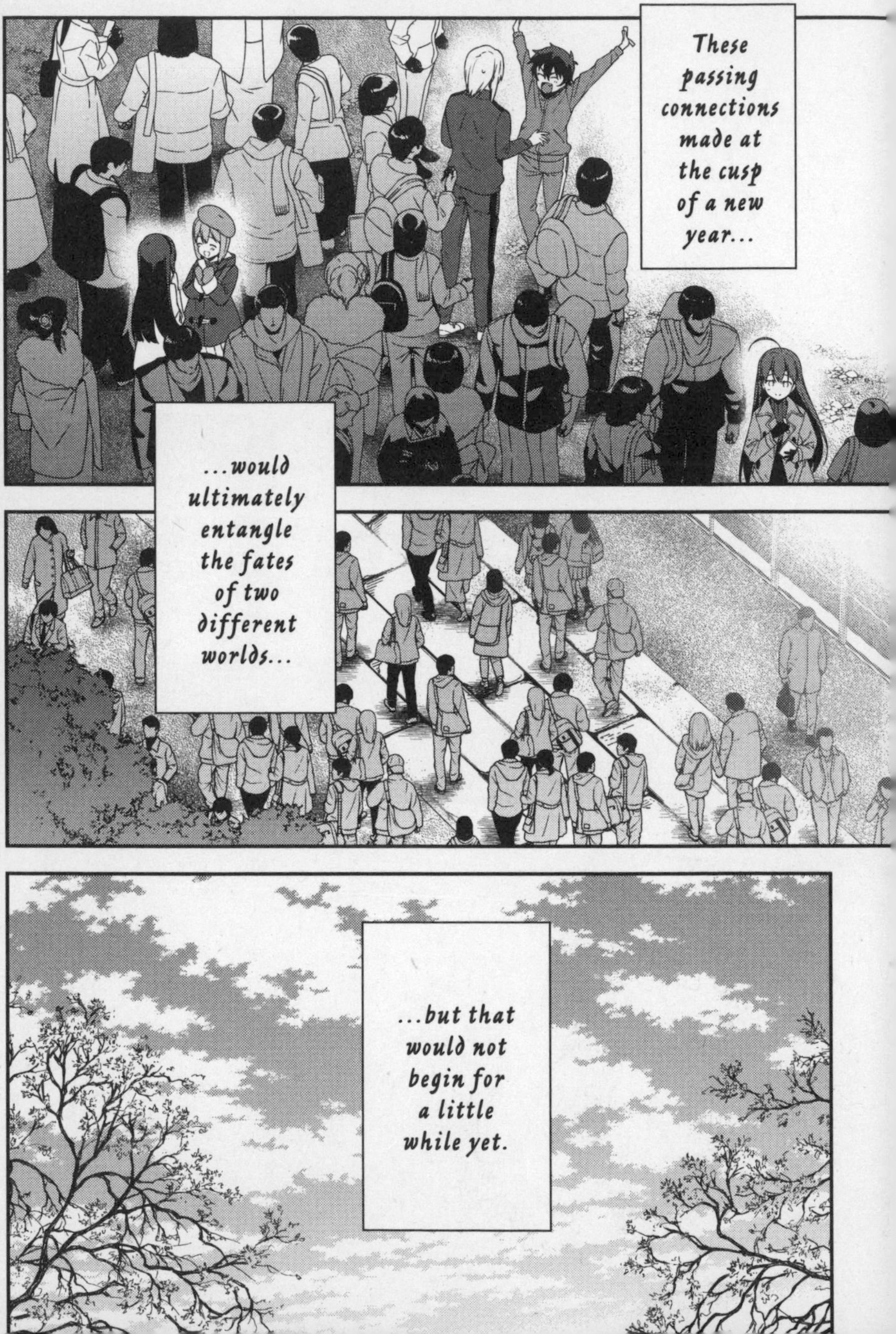
These passing connections made at the cusp of a new year...
...would ultimately entangle the fates of two different worlds...
...but that would not begin for a little while yet.

Kaori
Shoji

THE DEVIL IS A PART-TIMER!

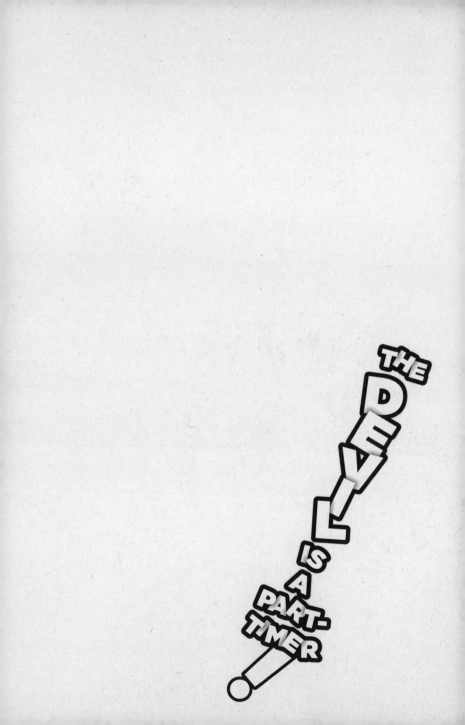

Between the vast natural beauty of Nagano, the old houses, the fields, and the RV, my assistants really worked hard to produce this story arc. Picking weeds in the field looks like pretty tough work, though...

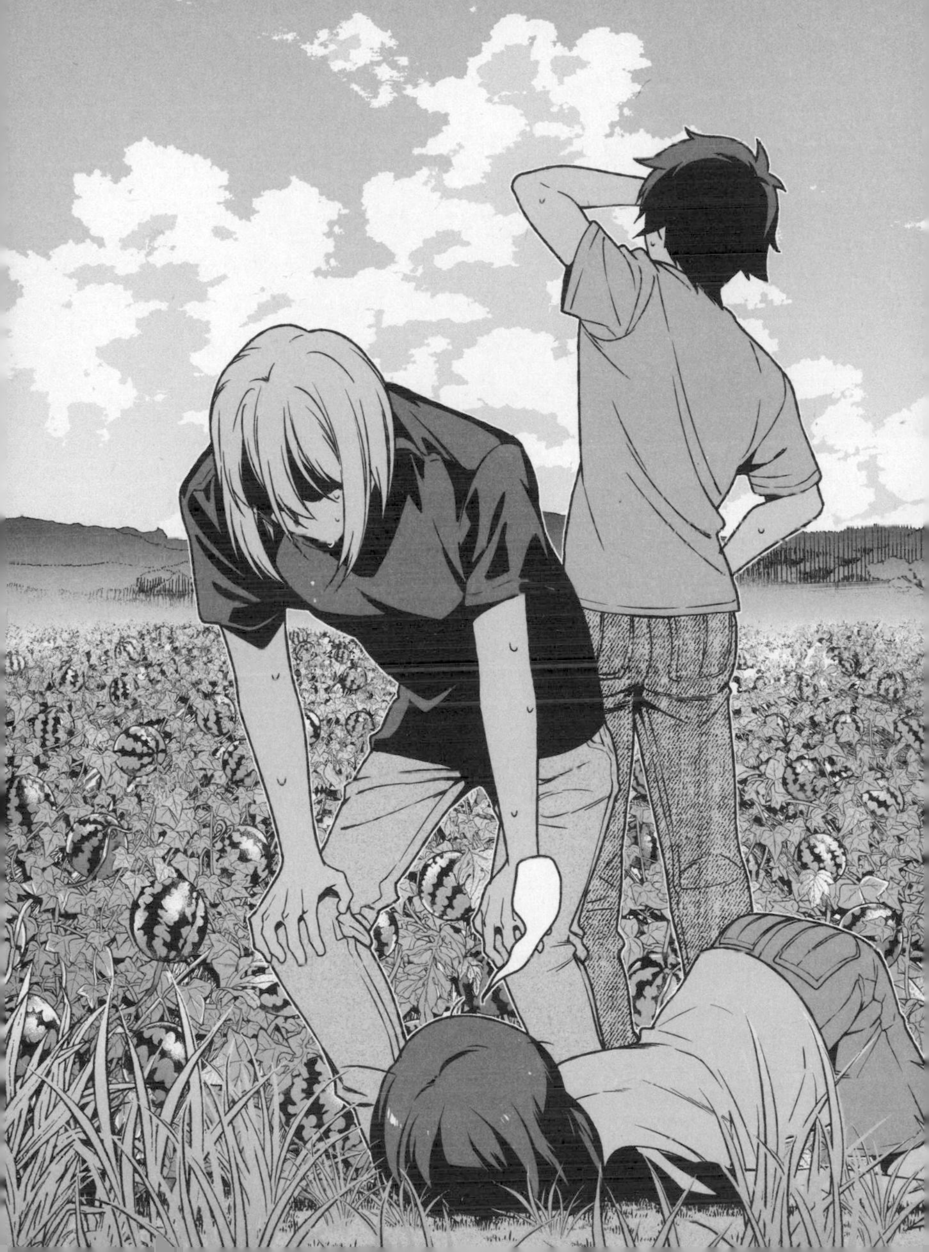

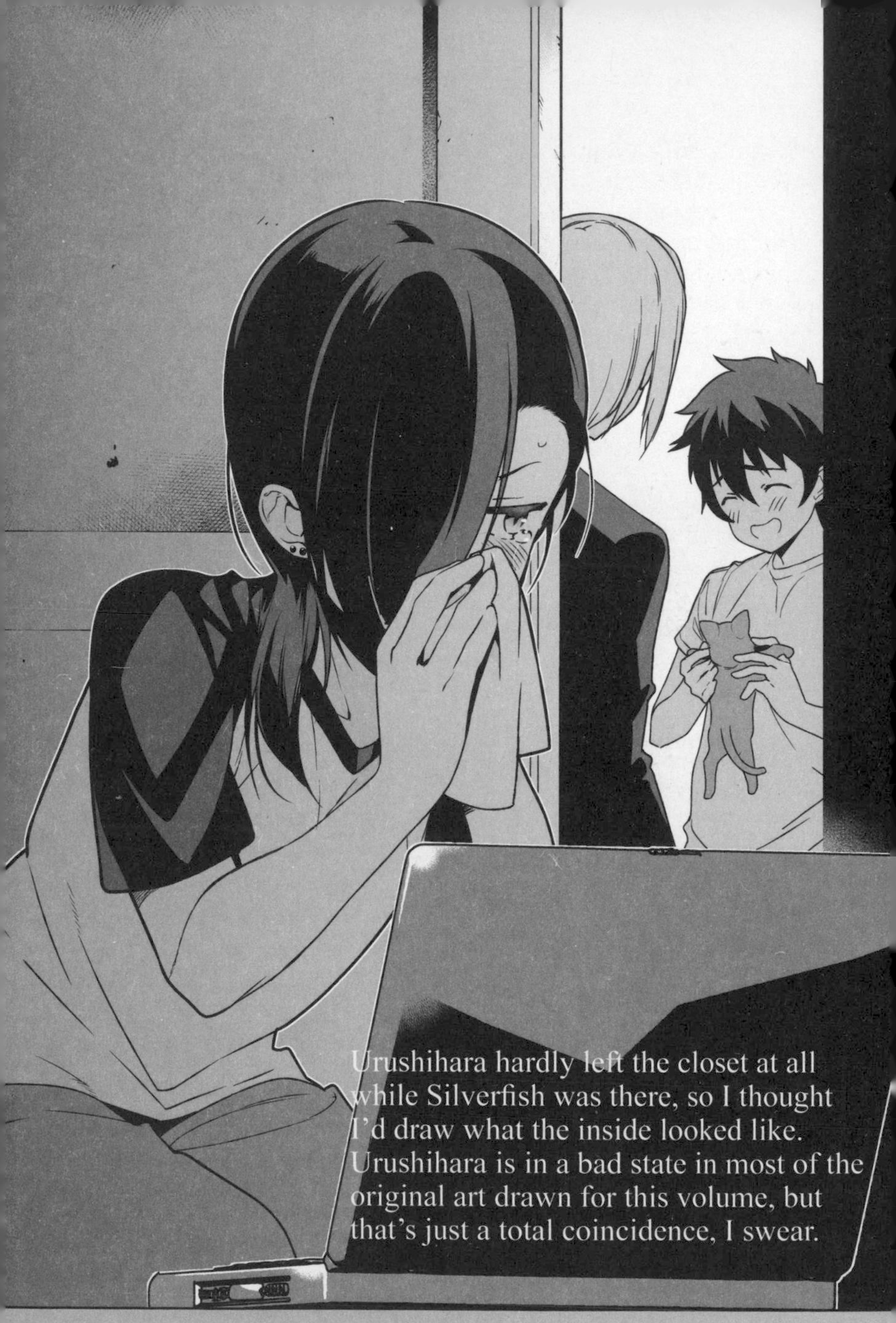
Urushihara hardly left the closet at all while Silverfish was there, so I thought I'd draw what the inside looked like. Urushihara is in a bad state in most of the original art drawn for this volume, but that's just a total coincidence, I swear.

It was fun drawing a female character apart from the main cast for the first time in a while. I drew Kaori with a scarf but didn't get around to tucking her hair under it the way I wanted to, so I saved that for this page.

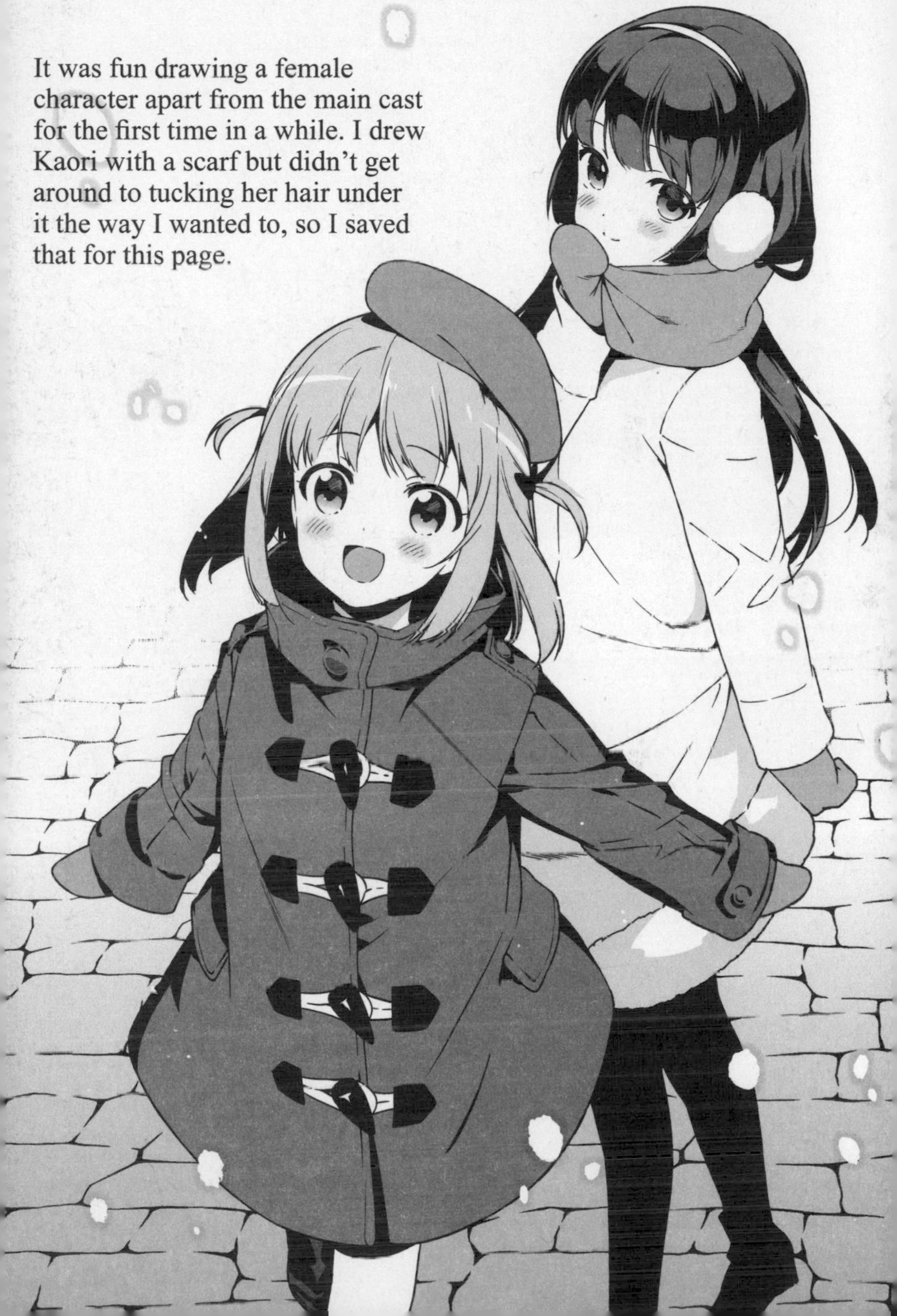

THIS VOLUME WRAPS UP THE NAGANO FARM STORY ARC AS WELL AS "THE DEVIL PLUCKS A CAT OFF THE STREET" FROM VOLUME 7 OF THE NOVELS AND "THE DEVIL, THE HERO, AND THE HIGH SCHOOLER" (ORIGINALLY RELEASED AS A DRAMA CD), MAKING FOR A PRETTY DIVERSE LINE OF CONTENT. I WAS HOPING TO DRAW ALL OF THOSE EPISODES IN MANGA FORM, SO THAT MAKES IT ALL THE MORE EXCITING FOR ME. I'VE BEEN GIVEN ALL THIS FREEDOM WITH THE MANGA THANKS IN NO SMALL PART TO WAGAHARA-SENSEI, 029-SENSEI, EVERYONE INVOLVED WITH DEVIL, AND (MORE THAN ANYTHING) OUR READERS. THANK YOU ALL VERY MUCH.

STARTING WITH VOLUME 14 OF THE MANGA, WE'LL BE PLUNGING INTO VOLUME 6 OF THE ORIGINAL NOVELS.
NEW DEVELOPMENTS, NEW CHARACTERS, AND MAOU AND HIS GANG EXPRESSING THEMSELVES IN BRAND-NEW WAYS. THAT—AND THE FIRST REAL (?) BATHHOUSE SCENE IN THE HISTORY OF THE MANGA. IT'S ALL SO EXCITING FOR ME TO DRAW! I'LL DO MY BEST TO MAKE THE MANGA VERSION AS ENTICING AS POSSIBLE FOR YOU ALL.

THANKS FOR YOUR CONTINUED SUPPORT!

SPECIAL THANKS:
AKIRA HISAGI / SHIBA / RUSUKE
AND YOU!

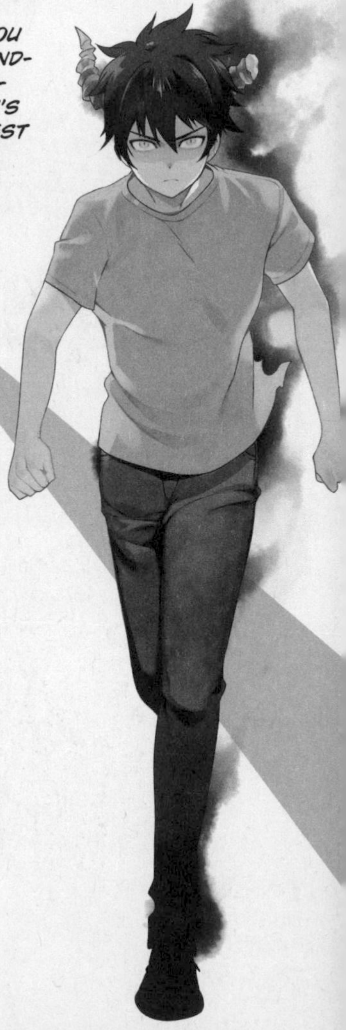

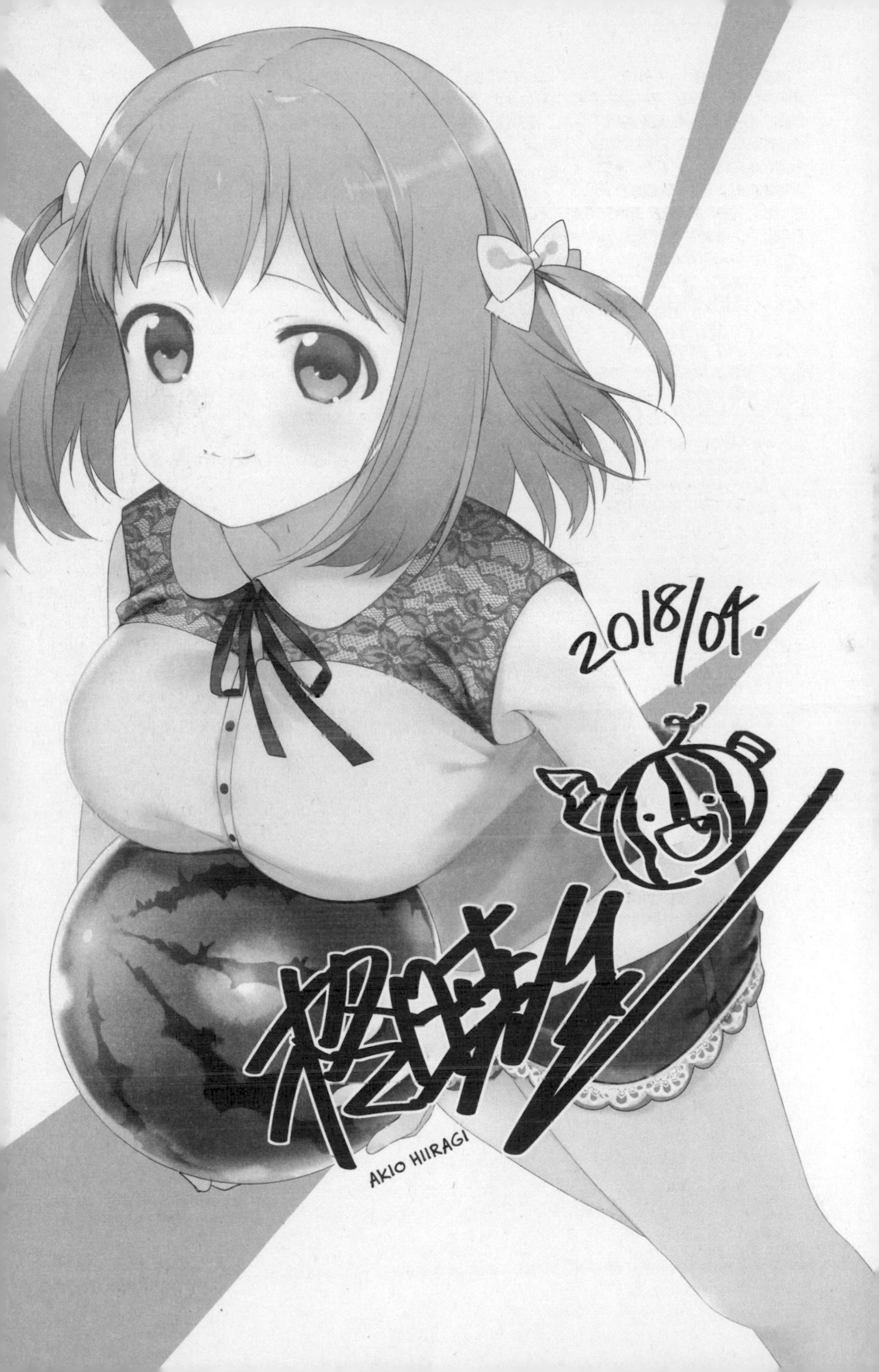
2018/04.
AKIO HIIRAGI

THE DEVIL IS A PART-TIMER! ⑬

ART: Akio Hiiragi
Original Story: Satoshi Wagahara
Character Design: 029 (Oniku)

Translation: Kevin Gifford

Lettering: Liz Kolkman

HATARAKU MAOUSAMA! Vol. 13
© SATOSHI WAGAHARA / AKIO HIIRAGI 2018
First published in Japan in 2018 by KADOKAWA CORPORATION, Tokyo.
English translation rights arranged with KADOKAWA CORPORATION, Tokyo,
through Tuttle-Mori Agency, Inc., Tokyo.

English translation © 2019 by Yen Press, LLC

Yen Press
1290 Avenue of the Americas
New York, NY 10104

Visit us at yenpress.com
facebook.com/yenpress
twitter.com/yenpress
yenpress.tumblr.com
instagram.com/yenpress

First Yen Press Edition: March 2019

Yen Press is an imprint of Yen Press, LLC.
The Yen Press name and logo are trademarks of Yen Press, LLC.

Library of Congress Control Number: 2014504637

ISBNs: 978-1-9753-0377-8 (paperback)
       978-1-9753-0467-6 (ebook)

10 9 8 7 6 5 4 3 2 1

WOR

Printed in the United States of America